only what we could carry

A PROJECT OF THE CALIFORNIA CIVIL LIBERTIES PUBLIC EDUCATION PROGRAM

The editor of this book and the publisher and staff of Heyday Books extend our gratitude to the California Civil Liberties Public Education Program (CCLPEP) for making available the funds to complete *Only What We Could Carry*.

The California Civil Liberties Public Education Program was created through legislation known as the California Civil Liberties Public Education Act, or AB 1915 (Chapter 570 Statutes of 1998). The legislation was introduced in the California State Assembly in 1998 by Assemblymember Mike Honda of San Jose.

In one of the most public and far-reaching of the reparation activities, the CCLPEP provides grants for the development of public educational materials and activities to ensure that the forced removal and incarceration of U.S. citizens and permanent resident aliens of Japanese ancestry will be remembered. CCLPEP is administered by the California State Library under the leadership of State Librarian Dr. Kevin Starr.

With this program, California has taken the initiative in recognizing the need for further education and materials on this important chapter in our nation's history. Besides being home to more Japanese Americans than any other state prior to this tragic incident, California was also the site of two incarceration camps and thirteen temporary detention centers.

For more information on the CCLPEP, contact Diane M. Matsuda, Program Director, California Civil Liberties Public Education Program, 916.653.9404, dmatsuda@library.ca.gov.

For additional resources on the Japanese American internment experience, please visit the Heyday Books' website at www.heydaybooks.com/books/owc.html.

only what we could carry

The Japanese American Internment Experience

Edited with an Introduction
by Lawson Fusao Inada

Preface by Patricia Wakida

Afterword by William Hohri

Heyday Books ∗ Berkeley, California
California Historical Society ∗ San Francisco, California

Library of Congress Cataloging-in-Publication Data

Only what we could carry : the Japanese internment experience / edited with introduction by Lawson Fusao Inada ; preface by Patricia Wakida ; afterword by William Hohri.

p. cm.

Includes bibliographical references.

ISBN 1-890771-30-9

1. Japanese Americans—Evacuation and relocation, 1942–1945. I. Inada, Lawson Fusao.

D769.8.A6 O55 2000

940.53'089956073—dc21

00-009182

Cover Photos: "Old Man" by Dorothea Lange, courtesy of the Bancroft Library (#1967.014); "Horse stalls at Tanforan," photographer unknown, courtesy of the National Japanese American Historical Society.

Cover/Interior Design: Dave Bullen Design

Typesetting: Rebecca LeGates

Printing and Binding: Publishers Press, Salt Lake City, UT

Published in conjunction with the California Historical Society. Since 1871, the California Historical Society has dedicated itself to collecting, preserving, and presenting accounts of California's remarkable, multicultural heritage. Through its historical library full of original manuscripts, first editions, and rare books; archives of over one-half million historic photographs; art collection; lectures, tours, and symposia; and quarterly publications, the Society makes the legacy of California's past available to all Californians. For more information, contact:

California Historical Society

678 Mission Street, San Francisco, CA 94105

Telephone: 415.357.1848, Fax: 415.357.1850

e-mail: info@calhist.org

For orders, inquiries, and correspondence, contact:

Heyday Books, P. O. Box 9145, Berkeley, CA 94709

510.549.3564, Fax 510.549.1889

www.heydaybooks.com

Printed in the United States of America

10 9 8 7 6 5 4 3 2

Dedicated to Michi Nishiura Weglyn

"... I hope this uniquely American story will serve as a reminder to all those who cherish their liberties of the very fragility of their rights against the exploding passions of their more numerous fellow citizens, and as a warning that they who say that it can never happen again are probably wrong."

from YEARS OF INFAMY

Table of Contents

Acknowledgments

In Japan, it is taught that we are born with a host of debts to the people who have built the road before us. This book was also brought into the world indebted to an enormous network that stretches across California and beyond. Our greatest thanks to the California Civil Liberties Public Education Program (CCLPEP), which funded this anthology, and the California State Library, which administered the funds. Our gratitude goes to the advisory board of the CCLPEP; State Librarian Dr. Kevin Starr, and Program Director Diane Matsuda.

This book is rooted in the thoughts and ideas shared by an advisory board assembled especially for this project. Members gave freely of their time, support, knowledge, and contacts. We wish to thank Karin Higa, Chizu Iiyama, David Mas Masumoto, Jim Houston, and Jeanne Wakatsuki Houston for the paths they cleared along the way.

Thanks to the staff of Heyday Books: Carolyn West for her keen eye and extraordinarily giving heart, Rebecca LeGates and David Bullen Design for their gorgeous design and crafting of the book, Rina Margolin for her excellent proofreading, Kathy Meengs, Julie Miller, and Victoria Shoemaker for their help with permissions and publicity, and Janice Woo, Apollonia Morrill, and David Ramonda, for a year's worth of patience, support, and never-exhausted faith and affection. And finally, our thanks to Malcolm Margolin, publisher of Heyday Books, for his unbending faith and inspiration, not to mention his belief that we need to tell this history and that we are privileged to do so.

The following archives, libraries, and special collections opened their doors and minds to our research and ideas: California Historical Society (Patricia Keats); California State Library Archives; California State University Fullerton, Oral History Project (Art Hansen); California State University Sacramento, Special Collections and Archives (Georgiana White); Eastern California Museum (Beth Porter and Bill Michael); Florin, California, Japanese American Citizens League; Fresno County Main Library (Yoshino Hasegawa); Japanese American National Museum (Cameron Trowbridge, Karin Higa, and Krissy Kim); Japanese American Resource Center/Museum of San Jose (Jimi Yamaichi and Joe Yasutake); Manzanar National Historic Site (Kari Coughlin); National Japanese American Historical Society (Ros Tonai and Meredith Oda); San

Francisco State University Labor Archives; Topaz Museum (Jane Beckwith); University of California, Berkeley, Bancroft Library (Susan Snyder); and the University of California, Los Angeles, Asian American Reading Room and Special Collections.

Numerous interviews and visits with writers, researchers, community activists, and academics were conducted with their graceful consent. Our warmest thanks to Frank Abe; Gordon Chang at Stanford University; Bessie Chin; Lok Chua; Violet de Cristoforo; Brian Komei Dempster; Gladys Dodds; Joy Harjo; Shim Hiraoka; Fred Hirasuna; Mamoru Inouye; Joanne and Frank Iritani; Tom Izu of the California History Center; Joanne Kagiwada; Elisa Kamimoto; Hiroshi Kashiwagi; Gary Kawaguchi; Stephanie Miyashiro of the Tule Lake Committee; Kenny Murase; Kerry Yo Nakagawa of the Nisei Baseball Research Project; Brian Niiya; Frank Nishio; Rick Noguchi; Seizo Oka of the Japanese American Historical Archives; Ruth Okimoto; Richard Oyama; Daisy Satoda; Eric Saul of the Holocaust Oral History Project; Rose Schrenini and Larry DiStasi of Una Storia Segreta; Grace Shimizu of the Japanese Peruvian Oral History Project; Karen Su; Toyo Suyemoto; Rita Takahashi and Amy Iwasaki Mass of the San Francisco State University Ethnic Studies Department; Wendy Tokuda; Marvin Uratsu of the Northern California Military Intelligence Service; Rich Wada; Doug Yamamoto; and Karen Tei Yamashita.

Research assistants extraordinaire Laura Benedict, Saikat Chatterjee, Lynn Itagaki, and Joshua Paddison are warmly commended for their hard work and sensitivity to the project's subject. Many pieces came from their uncovering of remarkable people and the stories they had to tell. Graphic associates Kimi Kodani Hill and Amy Hunter helped make final selections and procure reproductions and permissions for the many varied art works and photographs included in this book.

Project director Patricia Wakida especially wants to thank the Wakida and Kebo families for their support and collaboration on the project and Ahmed for love and truth.

Preface

During World War II, the United States government suspended due process, rounded up more than 110,000 Japanese resident aliens and American citizens of Japanese descent, and banished them to prison camps in desert wastelands. They were not charged with any crime, except, of course, being Japanese.

Although rooted in decades of anti-Japanese and anti-Asian prejudice, the internment of Japanese Americans was triggered by Pearl Harbor. At dawn on December 7, 1941, Japan launched a surprise attack on the U.S. fleet at Pearl Harbor, Hawaii, killing or wounding nearly 3,500 Americans. One hundred forty-nine airplanes and two battleships were destroyed, four other battleships sunk or run aground.

The devastation at Pearl Harbor inflamed an already pronounced resentment toward Japanese immigrant communities. Initiatives and legislation throughout the first four decades of the twentieth century had restricted or prohibited Japanese immigration, land ownership, and U.S. naturalization. Despite such initiatives, sizable communities of Japanese and their American offspring were scattered throughout the United States. In 1941, 127,000 Japanese Americans were living in the United States, of which 50 percent were engaged in agricultural businesses with notable success; 93,000 of them lived in California, mostly in rural farming communities, and an additional 19,000 lived in Washington and Oregon.

Within hours of the attack on Pearl Harbor, FBI agents swept through Japanese communities in California, Oregon, Washington, and Hawaii, arresting community leaders: teachers of the Japanese language, its culture, or its martial arts; Buddhist reverends and Christian ministers; businessmen; those with prominent political beliefs—indeed anyone who might be suspected of having sympathetic ties to Japan. Hundreds were rounded up, questioned, and shipped off under Justice Department orders to detention camps in Santa Fe, New Mexico; Bismarck, North Dakota; Crystal City, Texas; and Missoula, Montana. Some disappeared for months or years. Meanwhile, with United States entry into World War II, anti-Japanese reactions intensified, fueled by a storm of propaganda, hysterical stories of sabotage, and reports of American battlefield casualties. All Japanese branch banks were closed, and the U.S. Treasury froze all bank accounts belonging to anyone born in Japan. Ostensibly to protect people of Japanese descent from suspicion and arrest, a mandatory curfew was imposed, first on Japanese aliens and then on Japanese American citizens as well, while all were required to carry identification. Under Army pressure, the FBI and the Department of Justice conducted unannounced searches and seizure of "contraband" items in "enemy alien" homes, with special attention to cameras, weapons, and radio transmitters that might be used to signal Japanese ships offshore.

On February 19, 1942, nearly ten weeks after the outbreak of war, President Franklin Roosevelt signed Executive Order 9066. This order authorized the exclusion of all persons of Japanese descent—citizens and aliens alike—from designated areas of Washington, Oregon, California, and Arizona, with an emphasis on zones around airports, dams, power plants, railroads, shipyards, and military installations, in order to prevent any possible acts of sabotage and espionage. Although E.O. 9066 applied to German and Italian nationals and eventually to Aleutians in Alaska as well, it was clearly aimed at those of Japanese ancestry.

Within weeks of the signing of E.O. 9066, all Japanese Americans within the hastily defined exclusion zone were instructed to secure or sell their houses and possessions and report to designated civil control stations. Here they were first registered and labeled, then herded into buses and trains and taken to "assembly centers" until more permanent camps could be built. These assembly centers were, in fact, just off-season racetracks, unused fairgrounds, and abandoned stockyards. After an average of about three months, internees were moved into isolated prison camps surrounded by barbed wire, where they were kept under armed guard for most of the duration of the war. In all, there were sixteen assembly centers, all but three of them in California, and ten internment camps, scattered throughout the more remote areas of the United States: Utah, Arizona, Colorado, Wyoming, California, Idaho, and Arkansas. The last internment camp did not close until March, 1946.

These, at least, are the bare facts. But bare facts tell only part of the story. We created this wide-ranging anthology to further explore the complex thoughts, emotions, and personal histories of those affected by the internment—largely Japanese and Japanese Americans, but also the American population at large. All of us who worked on this book have realized that the tragedy of the internment should be part of every American's knowledge as part of our collective history, and we have strived to create a book capacious and varied enough to reflect that understanding.

Putting this book together involved an arduous process of gathering material up and down the valleys and coastal communities of California.

Stories sometimes came from unlikely places. We began research starting with an extended community of friends, acquaintances, and advisors. As we asked people about their experiences in the camps, they gladly gave us their stories. They pulled typed diaries from dark closets and dusty boxes tucked under beds; they slipped carefully preserved letters and memoirs into the mail; they let their stories unfold during long telephone conversations.

We also dug deeply into material that had already been gathered by libraries and historical societies. Institutions that had preserved vital pieces of history opened their files to us. One astonishing voice after another emerged, some in typed and bound volumes of collected oral histories, some written longhand in spiral-bound notebooks, their pages bent from wear. In contrast, other selections in this anthology had already had a distinguished history as literature. We selected from published novels, short stories, poems, and memoirs that had long served as powerful testimony to wartime experience.

While we became aware of the wealth of material available to us, we also became aware that much was already beyond our reach. Much writing from the internment period has been lost over the decades. Some writers hastily fed their poems to fire in the rising panic following Pearl Harbor. Others lost their personal records because with each relocation, only the most necessary belongings could be taken, and at such times, who would have given priority to short stories and private journals? Another dimension of literature—work written by the Issei in Japanese—has remained untranslated and thus is all but lost to younger generations. In making our selections, therefore, we tried to include the spirit of these voices, if not their actual words.

For many Californians—including most of us who worked on this project—the attitudes and events of World War II and the internment are distant history. Words and emotions that prevailed in the daily culture of 1940s America are lost on us today: Fifth column? The coming Gestapo? How many Americans under the age of fifty know the real meaning of these words, let alone feel their fear and threat? It's hard to picture receiving letters cut so full of holes that they resemble nets—and accepting the censor's damage as military necessity. The very thought of picking up a morning newspaper covered front to back with maps of the European theater, complete with military strategies in bold arrows and star patterns, strikes those of us from younger generations as in the realm of fantasy.

Despite the yawning gap between pre-war generations and those born after the war, there is nevertheless an unnerving familiarity to many of the dark themes running through this book. The neighbor who watches from a safe distance, the church employee who tries to make the best of a horrible situation, the racist politician whose vitriol fires others up with hatred, the anguished apologist who accepts egregious injustice as "necessity," the victim who blames himself—such voices are all still heard today. The story of the internment, while in most ways unique to its time, is disturbingly relevant. The targets have changed, but the themes have remained constant. Recent immigrant groups, gays and lesbians, those belonging to minority racial, ethnic, or religious groups still experience prejudice, hatred, and contempt. A larger purpose of this anthology, then, is not just to explore history, but to use that exploration to understand more deeply the consequences of racial prejudice, to confront more fully the harm that it does and the strengths that it calls forth, and by increasing intellectual and emotional awareness, to help ensure that such events cannot occur again.

As we worked on this book, we also came to realize how important it is to listen to the stories of those who came before us. As we move further and further away from the war years, the opportunity to gather firsthand accounts from a generation of people who experienced or witnessed the internment is rapidly diminishing. Fifty years has, of course, altered people's remembrance of the past and rubbed the edge off many memories. But as memories fade, so fades an entire period of culture and history. The writers of these pieces must have known, whether they wrote their thoughts down at the time, or with a different determination years later, that their words were a part of history in the making. With this in mind, we have compiled a collection of stories and pictures created by those who were there. They saw and they wrote down what they saw, so that one day their words could carry their burdens for them.

Patricia Wakida
May 2000

A Note to the Reader

It has been said that the value of a map lies as much in what is left out as in what is included. The same might be said for an anthology. The goal is to guide travelers—readers—through a set of identifiable landmarks, but to allow them to set their own paths, reach their own destinations. As we put this book together, we recognized that, almost paradoxically, our best chance at presenting the vastly different experiences of internment in both time and scope would come from setting limits. We decided to focus on the war years: from the bombing of Pearl Harbor on December 7, 1941 to the liberation of Dachau by Japanese American soldiers in 1945. Although we could have presented compelling material from much earlier and much later, the tight focus meant we would be able to explore the extremities of the unnatural situation of American internment camps all the better. We wanted to make the experience come alive again: the fear, the confusion, the anger, the interminable boredom, even the effort to rise above the insult and prove one's patriotism.

We chose to let the voices of those who wrote these pieces shine through. Thus our editorial hand was light. In these pages, an Issei father writes to his daughters in his new language of English, and it would diminish us all to have his grammar corrected. Likewise, the rough-and-tumble language of a soldier is left raw so the reader can better imagine the experience he endured. We did, in general, make spelling and punctuation uniform, but otherwise corrected sentences only when necessary for understanding. We noted it whenever we shortened pieces. The original notes that appeared with some of the previously published pieces were included as endnotes. There are many Japanese words and phrases, as might be expected. These are defined in a glossary at the back of the book rather than in notes that would likely distract the reader from the stories being told. The important thing was that these voices be clearly heard again.

Our main focus has been on literature that explores the human experience of the camps. We did not set out to provide a comprehensive history. However, we did provide resources throughout the book to help orient the reader. At the beginning of each selection, we provided a short essay with information not only about the piece, but also about its historical context. A series of appendices supplement the text with some of the historical documents that set the stage for the internment camps. The reader will also find in the appendix the text of apologies that constituted official redress.

As with any complex human experience, there are a number of words that are used to refer to the imprisonment of Japanese Americans. The camps themselves were called "relocation camps," "internment camps," "prison camps," even "concentration camps" by President Roosevelt himself. Word choice can be a political statement. Yet again, we chose to let the words of the authors stand. The careful reader will notice the differences. In our introductory paragraphs, we deferred to the most commonly used terminology in the collected pieces: "internment camps," "internee," "evacuation," "relocation," "resettlement."

Throughout the book, we refer to the generations of Japanese Americans by Japanese terms. Issei is the Japanese word for "first generation." It refers to the generation of Japanese people who immigrated to the United States, largely in the earliest decades of the twentieth century. Nisei, or "second generation," refers to their children, whose birth on American soil makes them United States citizens. The Kibei are Japanese Americans born in the U.S. but educated to varying degrees in Japan. Most of the first-person accounts in this book are from these three groups. The majority of Sansei, or "third generation," were born during or after the war. The Yonsei are "fourth-generation" Japanese Americans, many reaching adulthood as we enter the twenty-first century.

Introduction

"Only what we could carry"
was the rule; so we carried
Strength, Dignity, and Soul

Papa

i

Ah, a May morning in California. Slightly overcast with coastal fog, clearing by afternoon. That's the way it is around here, on the south shore of the San Francisco Bay.

Yes, it's going to be another great day: sunny and mild over rolling hills, the fragrance of spring. And last evening, another glorious sunset.

Papa watched it from his porch.

ii

Certain things can be assumed about the unidentified man in the photo: He was "Papa" in his household, he was born in Japan to a farming family, and he came to America around the turn of the century. Times were tough in those days, with little or no mobility in the homeland, so he set his sights on a better future, toiling to earn passage to America, the "land of opportunity."

It was tough to get here, and it was tough when he arrived.

He brought only what he could carry.

iii

But he persevered, survived, like many other newcomers from Europe and Asia. He was determined, resourceful; he had plans. He had a keen mind, a strong back, a good heart, and skillful hands—hands that could dig, plant, pick, fix, improvise; hands that could build a living from scratch; hands that could construct a home, raise and support a family.

Today, though, those hands are holding something in his lap, something that must be of value to him. What could it be?

With his hands, he holds a piece of memory.

iv

There's more to this photo than meets the eye. Holding the camera is Dorothea Lange, on assignment from the War Relocation Authority. This is a big day for the agency, the culmination of months of work and planning, involving offices from the West Coast to the White House, a joint effort of civilians and the military. Countless hours have been consumed with countless details, devising and discarding strategies, making decisions, mapping movements, coordinating communications, issuing orders, securing locations, and marking calendars, for to have troops and transportation at the ready to move tens of thousand of humans was as complicated as staging an invasion.

Everything had to go off without a hitch; and after all the practice drills, today was the real day in this region, the day to get all this cargo and humanity across the bay to a strategic site south of San Francisco. Fingers were crossed, and a hired photographer was on hand for accountability and documentation.

Papa watched her from his chair.

v

His heart went out to her—this small woman lugging a big camera, scurrying about with a severe limp. Perhaps she was a victim of polio, like the president himself. And she was obviously tired.

So when she approached and pointed to her camera, he smiled and nodded yes. Then he stood to introduce himself and they shook hands. He would also have introduced Mama, but she was preoccupied. And though it didn't surprise Dorothea that he could speak some English, she was a bit taken aback when he said, "Dorothea, such a pretty name. My granddaughter there is named Ginger."

That got to her. But whistles were blowing, vehicles were roaring, voices were shouting, everything was moving, fast, so she simply asked him to be seated, please, for a moment.

And she didn't say "Smile!"

vi

Foremost in Papa's mind, of course, was Family. It had been wrenching to part from loved ones in Japan, but marriage in America had brought him his own: Family. Children, grandchildren making their way in this land. What more to ask?

And to hear their voices echoing in the house last night, bodies spread out on the floor.

He could hear them now.

vii

Tuesday. I should be working.
Tuesday. In my Sunday shoes.
Tuesday. They should be in school.

Grandson

i

My dog would bark when I rang my tricycle bell. That was funny. I was going to be four years old and have a party.

But instead I was taken away with my family. Was I kicking and screaming? Was I stoic and mute? I don't remember. My mind could not contain the chaos, would not retain the memory.

However, I certainly do remember, and can still feel, the two events that were to happen shortly.

How could I forget?

ii

I got lost. With our dog, Jimmy, I was accustomed to visiting friends, young and old, in our familiar neighborhood. Everybody knew us, welcomed us in. So, naturally, even without Jimmy (left with a friend who informed us: "Jimmy starved himself to death"), when my protective parents were occupied with unpacking, I simply went out into the "neighborhood," visiting.

And immediately got lost in the rush and crush of crowds, the rows and rows of similar buildings. Papa Ikeda found me bawling and took me "home." And although I knew where I was, generally, from having been to the fair in familiar Fresno, since I could not comprehend why I was there, I remained "lost" for the duration of all the camp years.

I got shocked. Bored, at a loss, stuck in our quarters without toys, as my parents busied themselves covering the window, my idle fingers found a nail that needed something to do. The next thing I knew, I was flying across the room, landing by a cot, bleeding from the nose.

That wouldn't have happened at home. And that stunning, numbing current that had raged through my brain, my body, must have had a lingering effect on my system, for I evolved from a robust child to a frequenter of infirmaries in the swampland of Arkansas, the windswept plain of Colorado, beset by infections, diseases, nightmares.

The pattern was set.

iii

Children being children, they adapted to conditions. They observed, they absorbed, they got what was given.

Children being children, they grasped the situation. They said their prayers, they sang their carols, they pledged to serve their nation.

Children being children, they grew to accept their station. They knew what they deserved.

They belonged in camp.

iv

When I began school in Arkansas, a young teen was attending school in Georgia. He had an inquiring mind, continually posing questions to his teachers. For one so young, he was remarkably persistent, and wouldn't settle for the conventional answers. Finally, his teachers would have to say:

"Martin, just do your lessons."

v

When we came back from camp, "it" stayed on my mind. For one thing, when our contingent left, "it" was still occupied, flying the flag, and we slipped out quietly. For another, though my grandfather regained our family home, some of my playmates were sheltered in basements, garages, churches, and were still living like camp. One parent even threatened to send a playmate back to camp for leaving food on the plate. So "it" assumed a life of its own.

In school, however, like Rudolfo, I was "from Colorado," which was the truth, requiring no explanation—which I couldn't provide anyway. And with so many of us newly arrived from the South, Southwest, Mexico, even China, the focus was naturally on the rough-and-tumble present, and fitting in as prescribed.

So, like everyone else, I put my name, grade, and room on my notebook. But one day, after doing the lesson, I inscribed, in small print, under my current location, two words: "EHCAMA" and "EMOREJ."

Places where "NOSWAL" had lived.

vi

On the last day of school, Ollie Mae and I were strolling home. We were a pair—the best spellers in second grade, and from the same street. She had arrived in the middle of the year, and immediately established a radiant presence. And her older sister even watched out for us at recess.

We were chatting along in the heat, and as we passed Bobby's house, she exclaimed, "Oh, look—we used to have a big garden like that in Arkansas!" And I replied, "We used to live there too. But in a camp." And she looked at me and said,"Is that what that was?"

She stared into my eyes. I glanced at the ground. We resumed walking, and never mentioned Arkansas again. Ollie Mae was to die that summer, from rheumatic fever.

Yes, Ollie Mae. That's what that was.

vii

The infant in the photo reminds me of my infant grandson, Samuel Dorje Inada.

Here, child—this is our family number: 19228.

Dorothea, Papa

i

Click. Done. Then, in a flurry of activity, Papa and Family were gone. Just like that. Swallowed by history. Workers were packing boxes, folding tables, loading trucks, gathering trash. So far, so good; everything had gone according to plan, orderly, with proper teamwork. But today's work, in this one region, was just one small part of the total effort throughout California, Oregon, and Washington; and the work was just beginning. There were reports to be made, records to be kept on over 110,000 people, and in a matter of months, if everything went well, these same people would be moved again, from slapdash quarters to actual camps engineered and created in remote locations, for whatever duration. If anything, that removal would be even more arduous to implement. But this was war, and the WRA had to be up to the challenge.

Dorothea stood there. It looked like some festivities had ended, a parade had passed. Such effort expended. A crumpled ID tag lay at her feet like a discarded ticket.

And, of all things, standing in place over there was the chair. Forgotten, abandoned? She thought to photograph it, but didn't have the heart. Then she considered taking it to the man tomorrow, seeking him out somehow, but she couldn't imagine facing him.

Still, it was a good chair, strong and practical, purchased as part of a set, probably, to go with a card table, the kind of chair children sat on for

Thanksgiving dinner. She couldn't just leave it there, so she dragged it to the back seat of her car.

There had to be some use for it.

ii

It would be a long drive home. She had been in this area before, scouting out the possibilities of Mission San Jose. It wasn't much to see, photograph, and it struck her as an agency of destruction. In all her years in the state, she had never knowingly met one California Indian. She had also scouted the Hetch Hetchy Aqueduct which went through here, and which carried water for San Francisco from Yosemite, but it wasn't much to see, either. Still, as a New Yorker, she was impressed by California ingenuity.

Little towns went by, farmland. She remembered the man's hand, the sinews and texture. He must have been a farmer. She could see his clean-shaven face.

Would they take his razor?

iii

It was dark when she got to Berkeley. The town felt somehow deserted. There was that nursery. Closed. She had bought their plants, relied on their advice, chatted with the family. She knew many of these people, from fellow photographers to her pharmacist. With their thriving communities, active churches, prominent businesses —including this nursery and that restaurant across the street—closed. Closed.

She parked and stood before the fence. Emptied of plants, the enclosed property resembled a miniature prison now. She pulled out the chair, unfolded it, and left it standing at the gate.

It was anyone's property now.

iv

Dorothea got home gritty with dust and sweat. She ran a hot bath and soaked. Then, over a snack of apple pie and hot coffee, she broke into sobs. Her husband came in to console her: "Honey, you were just doing your job."

She headed to the darkroom.

v

In the meantime, Papa and Family were experiencing the darkness of incarceration. The place of captivity felt like a human zoo. Sunset had come and gone, unnoticed.

A cough resounded. Papa was startled awake, startled to find he had fallen asleep on his feet, standing at the door like a sentry. Good. They are all asleep. We must survive, endure. We'll be moving to a better place. We won't be here too long. After all, this racetrack is a place of business, and someone could be losing money on us.

While someone could be making money on us.

vi

On the long journey aboard ship, a jovial Japanese crewman with much experience had instructed him about dollars and cents, along with the rudiments of language, both Spanish and English. "San" was easy to say, like Japanese, but "Francisco" took practice. "America" fell into place, but "seagull" was a tongue-twister, along with "California."

Then along came other places with exotic names: "Livermore," "Watsonville," "San Leandro," and finally, "Centerville," the farm. Such a vast, grand country. Mountains, valleys, rivers, ocean. Mysterious "coyotes," and trees called "eucalyptus." He had proudly planted one himself for shade outside the house on land he had cleared of rocks and brush. It was a farm now, with a shaded house.

And with an old car came picnics in "Niles Canyon," fishing along "the Bay" and "Alameda Creek;" and, of course, graduations and weddings in a "Berkeley," a "Sacramento." What more to ask?

He recalled studying the same books as the children who grew up fluent in English. After a while though, he could conduct his own business, hold his own at the bank, even tell a joke. But when he first arrived he had to watch his tongue, search his mind: "Howdy. Adios. Two-bits. Cup coffee. Piece pie."

He even had to learn how to say "Japan."

vii

The scent of manure, urine.

A young man raises his eyes to the sky. Sunset. Sweat on the brow.

With his hands, he guides a horse-drawn plow.

Lawson Fusao Inada
April 2000

I

Arrest

The time has come
For my arrest
This rainy night.
I calm myself and listen
To the sound of shoes.

Sojin Takei

The Day We Left

Ben Iijima

Soon after its entry into World War II, the U.S. government issued orders to forcibly remove over 110,000 American citizens and resident aliens from their homes and communities. Those evacuated were instructed to meet at civil control stations that had been quickly set up throughout the West Coast. From there they were taken to hastily constructed assembly centers where they were temporarily detained—often for months—until the more long-term internment camps could be built.

Ben Iijima was a nineteen-year-old student at UC Berkeley when war broke out. "The Day We Left" is an essay written in 1942 at Tanforan Assembly Center in San Bruno, the racetrack home that would temporarily house evacuees from the San Francisco Bay Area. Iijima wrote an extensive diary of his incarceration experience, which is now housed in the Japanese American Evacuation and Resettlement Records at the Bancroft Library. In most cases evacuees had only a few weeks to discard all possessions, sell or lease businesses, secure their property or homes, pack, and register. They had no idea what awaited them, how long they would be gone, or where they were headed.

One of the things in all this evacuation process which I believe will remain indelible to my personal memories is the day we left for Tanforan.

The evening before I left home, I had just come back from the WCCA [Wartime Civil Control Administration] offices in San Mateo after conferring with the people there. I brought there a list of items concerning the furniture, our personal belongings and all such matters, and had them checked. We went to sleep on the floor, as we had all our mattresses packed and made ready for the storage man who was to come the next day. The front room was littered with our baggage, a huge trunk, the beds which had been taken apart, the rolled up carpet, and small cardboard boxes filled with things we had repacked over and over again. "Let's leave these things here; no let's take them." How very confusing, how utterly hesitant we were.

We had been doing our daily shopping each day, someone going to town on the bus to buy odds and ends. I remember spending a whole day in Palo Alto picking up clothing in one store after another; and they weren't luxury wears either, in fact, they consisted of basic clothing, shirts for dad and myself, jeans, sweaters, and jackets. I went to the Montgomery Ward to buy some trunks, good lord we had seven trunks of varied sizes, besides our small hand grips and luggage bags. I recall how insistent Mother was about getting boots for when the rains come, the ground will be soggy with black molasses. Warm things—woolen underwear, heavy stockings. We need everything like that she said. Both our radios had been checked in at the police department, but sis wanted to get something to listen to so I went down to Poly to get a radio with the required frequency, and also a small tool chest in a drug store. Most of the wooden items, such as ironing boards and old attic furniture I broke with an iron pipe and burned them to a crisp. All the garden tools and heavy equipment—such as an old oil drum used as an incinerator, our garbage can, the mail box, the garden hose—went to our neighbors.

I remember I had to stand on the curb and pass it to our neighbors, for technically we were not to leave our residence after [8:00] in the evening. "Someday when you folks come back we'll return all these things," they said. A few days before we left, we received a letter from one of the earlier evacuees to Tanforan that it was advisable to come stocked with a plenitude of canned goods. So I rode down to the grocery store and purchased some $10.00 worth of fruit juices, canned soups, crackers, canned sardines, canned tobacco for father. Mother assembled a whole baggage grip full of medicine including iodine, bandages, aspirin, Murine, corn healers, Cuticula, plaster, Ungentine. Besides this were facial and washing soap, toothpastes and face towels.

I had an old bike in the back shed which I was going to sell, but I decided instead to bring it through the government warehouses and have it sent when we were relocated to the permanent centers. In order to create the box a friend came over and together we cut a box, banged boards over it, and had it ready before the leaving day.

Mother heard that the easiest luggage holder was a sailor's pack, and so going to Montgomery Ward's, purchased a very strong material, somewhat like corduroy, and made five such sacks, one for each member of the family, plus a miscellaneous bag.

Before we left the house, we all spent a day cleaning it. With heavy soap and water, I washed the kitchen, repainted the heater and sink, and cut the front hedges. Mother and sis cleaned the parlor and dining room, while dad went mopping and washing windows. I spaded the front garden and cut as much of the weeds in the back as I could.

We called the junk man over and had him appraise the furniture which he rated at such ridiculous prices we refused the first time, but at the end finally agreed. Despite our anticipation that our packing would be through before 5:00 in the evening of the evacuation eve, we actually stayed up until 12:00. We spread the blankets on the floor, put the alarm on for 4:00 in the morning and slept but three hours. As soon as the alarm rang we rolled up the blankets into the jeans material cover, and bound them firmly with the clothesline. Then, latching each grip I took them out to the front, checking to see that each was labeled with our family number and identification. The neighbors drove Mother and sis to the New Ranch where all the people from Redwood were to leave, while Dad and I waited for the moving man to come.

Not having a car or truck available, we wondered how we could arrange to have the baggage taken to our leaving point in San Mateo. There were two alternatives: The evening before a neighbor came and said that he was hoping to arrange for one of the moving vans to get all the material from a central point in New Ranch, hence all the individual baggage would have to be brought there by small trucks; the second, was to phone for a van directly and have our baggage brought to San Mateo. We choose the latter because, if we brought our baggage to the central point they would have to be left there overnight in a shed, and while a bolt would be put on the door, there was no absolute assurance that things would not disappear. So sis phoned up the van man, and the next day when I went, there were two men waiting for the mover. He was away from the office for lunch so we waited, and I learned they were representatives of the group who desired to have their baggage taken from one central point, namely New Ranch. Finally, the owner returned and he told us all that they were exceptionally busy tomorrow and pondering through his schedule replied laconically, "Just can't do it." I insisted that my sis had called up the evening before and received assurance from him that a reservation had been made and accepted. On second thought, he asked my name, and then added, "Oh, yes." He assured me he would have the small truck at the house tomorrow morning at 7:00, since we had to be in San Mateo by 9:00. He asked me how many baggages I had and while actually there were some twenty-five I put the estimate very conservatively and said fifteen. The two men who were seeking one of the giant vans to accommodate the majority of the baggages from this town were finally able to obtain a van for 7:00 as well.

As dad and I waited for the moving truck to appear, we saw three cars pass by—one after another in fifteen minute intervals, laden with trunks, baggage, and families. One had a trailer attached to the truck, and turning laboriously around the curve by the bridge, headed slowly towards New Ranch.

When the truck came I don't exactly remember, but I found out soon enough as he blew the horn and backed into our driveway. The truck—a small panel type—looked diminutive beside our baggage piled on the sidewalk. The driver jumped off and his first ejaculation was, "Holy Christ, Whatta pile." Somehow he managed to pile everything at the head of the

Military orders showed four separate and distinct groups divided by the railroad tracks and Florin Road. Each group had a different destination. New fears were suddenly thrust into our hearts. Was it by design that families and friends faced never seeing one another again—an elaborate scheme to keep us separate? Or was it the first of what were to be many decisions from high authorities that were irrational, illogical, or lacking of common sense?

MARY TSUKAMOTO

Salinas, California, March 31, 1942. Photograph by Clem Albers.

loading space, contiguous to the cab and as the wheels sagged he exclaimed, "I still have to go to New Ranch to pick up some more!" We got on, the door slammed, the truck puttered and we started down the road. When we turned into the road leading into New Ranch, the people, attired in suits and neat apparel, were waiting for the Greyhound bus which had been especially chartered to drive the people to San Mateo. As we passed the crowd, we saw a huge van—one of those giant busses—lumbering up the road obviously packed as tightly as a can of sardines. The driver waved at us, and our driver returned the salutation, as he was owner of this moving company and one of his "boys" was driving the "big baby" today.

When the baggage from the shed had been loaded, our truck looked like an overloaded wagon, but the driver—knowing his trade—managed to utilize every bit of space without drastically upsetting the balance.

When we began to pick up speed along Woodside Road and began to swing into stride along El Camino, I thought how for the last time I was looking at my home town. Redwood wasn't a big city; but I thought it was big in the sense that people were liberal and not rabble-rousers despite the feverish clamor of the papers—the residents had not a feeling of hatred toward me. The town was still inactive early in the morning, and it wasn't long before we passed the town line and descended down the long bend approaching San Carlos.

The driver was, I learned, a former Stanford graduate, and he began to talk of the big things they used to do at the big games, how they upset street cars, had really big bonfires, and we didn't talk a bit of evacuation or the war.

Soon the green hedges and eucalyptus trees, sign posts of San Mateo along the El Camino appeared and then the truck suddenly wheeled into a main thoroughfare of the city, and in fifteen minutes I saw the Masonic Temple—our depot for Tanforan bustling with vans, Greyhounds, soldiers, cars, spectators, and bewildered evacuees.

Headquarters
Western Defense Command
and Fourth Army

Presidio of San Francisco, California
May 17, 1942

Civilian Exclusion Order No. 82

1. Pursuant to the provisions of Public Proclamations Nos. 1 and 2, this Headquarters, dated March 2, 1942, and March 16, 1942, respectively, it is hereby ordered that from and after 12 o'clock noon, P.W.T., of Saturday, May 23, 1942, all persons of Japanese ancestry, both alien and non-alien, be excluded from that portion of Military Area No. 1 described as follows:

All the Counties of Del Norte, Humboldt, Trinity, Mendocino, and Lake, State of California.

2. A responsible member of each family, and each individual living alone, in the above described area will report between the hours of 8:00 A. M. and 5:00 P. M., Tuesday, May 19, 1942, to the Civil Control Station located at:

Palace Hotel Building,
181 Smith Street,
Corner, Main and Smith Streets,
Ukiah, California.

3. Any person subject to this order who fails to comply with any of its provisions or with the provisions of published instructions pertaining hereto or who is found in the above area after 12 o'clock noon, P.W.T., of Saturday, May 23, 1942, will be liable to the criminal penalties provided by Public Law No. 503, 77th Congress, approved March 21, 1942, entitled "An Act to Provide a Penalty for Violation of Restrictions or Orders with Respect to Persons Entering, Remaining in, Leaving or Committing any Act in Military Areas or Zones," and alien Japanese will be subject to immediate apprehension and internment.

4. All persons within the bounds of an established Assembly Center pursuant to instructions from this Headquarters are excepted from the provisions of this order while those persons are in such Assembly Center.

J. L. DeWitt
Lieutenant General, U. S. Army
Commanding

Evacuation procedures, Ukiah, California. Wartime Civil Control Administration, May 17, 1942.

THE FOLLOWING INSTRUCTIONS MUST BE OBSERVED:

1. A responsible member of each family, preferably the head of the family, or the person in whose name most of the property is held, and each individual living alone, will report to the Civil Control Station to receive further instructions. This must be done between 8:00 A. M. and 5:00 P. M. on Tuesday, May 19, 1942. Should such individual reside over 30 miles from the Civil Control Station and be unable to provide transportation to such Civil Control Station, he will telegraph or telephone on Monday, May 18, 1942, to the Manager of the Civil Control Station for instructions.

2. Evacuees must carry with them on departure for the Assembly Center, the following property:

(a) Bedding and linens (no mattress) for each member of the family;

(b) Toilet articles for each member of the family;

(c) Extra clothing for each member of the family;

(d) Essential personal effects for each member of the family.

All items carried will be securely packaged, tied and plainly marked with the name of the owner and numbered in accordance with instructions obtained at the Civil Control Station. The size and number of packages is limited to that which can be carried by the individual or family group.

3. No pets of any kind will be permitted.

4. No personal items and no household goods will be shipped to the Assembly Center.

5. The United States Government through its agencies will provide for the storage, at the sole risk of the owner, of the more substantial household items, such as iceboxes, washing machines, pianos and other heavy furniture. Cooking utensils and other small items will be accepted for storage if crated, packed and plainly marked with the name and address of the owner. Only one name and address will be used by a given family.

6. Each family, and individual living alone, will be furnished transportation to the Assembly Center. Private means of transportation will not be utilized. All instructions pertaining to the movement will be obtained at the Civil Control Station.

Go to the Civil Control Station between the hours of 8:00 A. M. and 5:00 P. M., Tuesday, May 19, 1942, to receive further instructions.

J. L. DeWitt
Lieutenant General, U. S. Army
Commanding

May 17, 1942

See Civilian Exclusion Order No. 82.

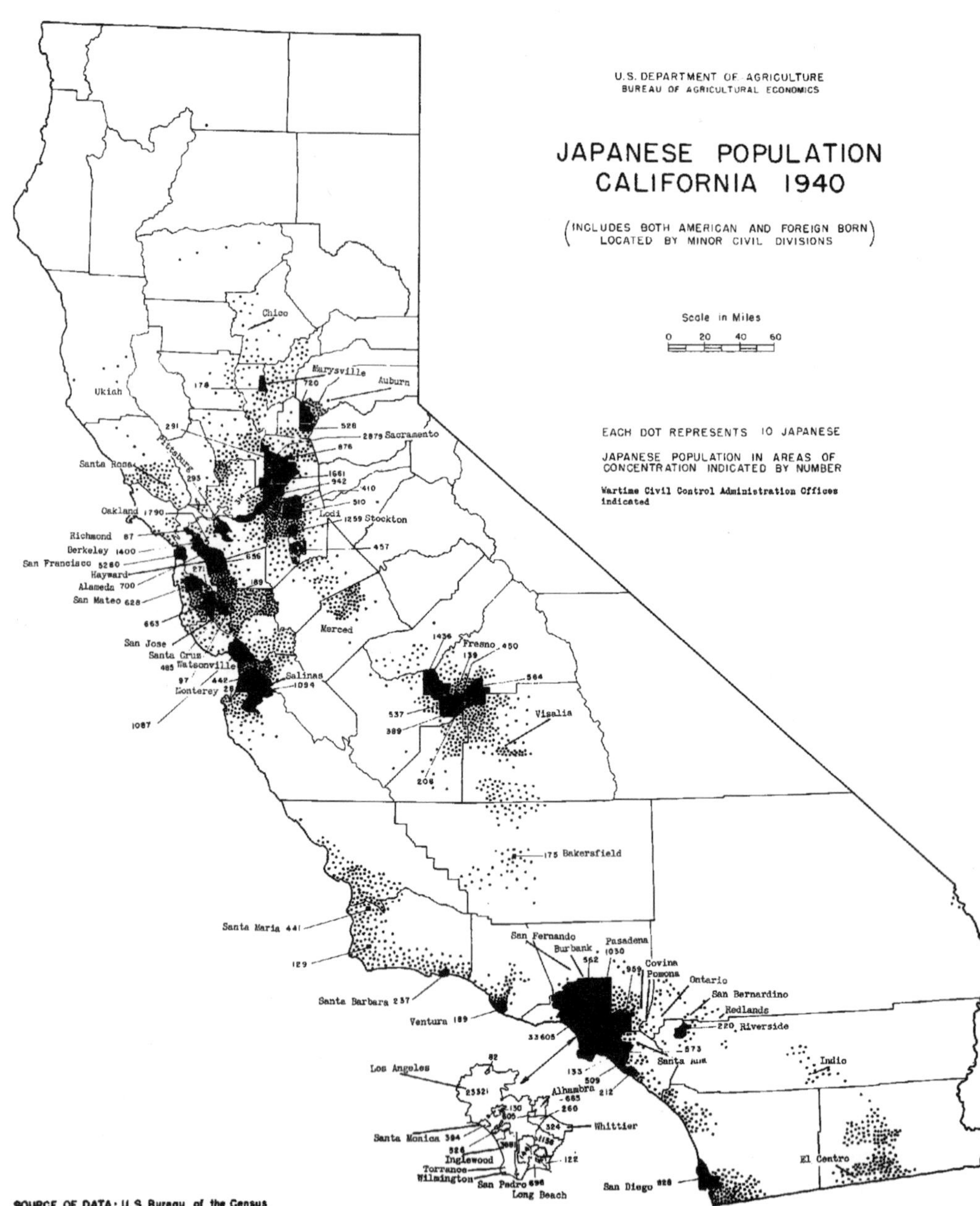

"Japanese Population in California," 1940. Wartime Civil Control Administration/U.S. Department of Agriculture.

Editorials in the Wake of Pearl Harbor

While the attack of Pearl Harbor by the Japanese on December 7th, 1941, was a surprise, the lash of public opinion and violent anti-Japanese outrage was not. Fear and humiliation in the face of the losses suffered at Pearl Harbor, along with reports of American battlefield deaths throughout the months of January and February 1942, fueled inflammatory newspaper accounts and editorials throughout California.

People's World *was the West Coast newspaper of the Communist Party, read by liberals, intellectuals, and labor unionists. Its editorials generally advised a more levelheaded approach to the dilemma the Japanese Americans faced. On the other extreme, on the whole, were two prominent California newspapers that still exist today: the* Sacramento Bee, *headed by an openly anti-Japanese editor, V. S. McClatchy; and the* San Francisco Chronicle, *then the most influential newspaper on the Pacific Coast, whose stand against Japanese immigration dated to the early 1900s. In all three examples of mainstream newspaper editorials, there is a marked change of attitude that can be traced over the weeks between December 1941 and March 1942, when stories urging the evacuation of the Japanese filled the press and airwaves.*

In 1942, the Japanese comprised only 1.6 percent of the population of California, and were most heavily concentrated in and around Los Angeles. The Rafu Shimpo, *a Los Angeles newspaper, was established in 1903 to serve that readership. In the case of the Japanese American press, there were few editors and publishers who were brave enough or even legally capable of printing their voices during such a volatile time. Indeed, the* Rafu Shimpo *was closed the day after Pearl Harbor was bombed, but on Tuesday, December 9, it resumed publication, releasing two pages in English only. The two inside pages of the newspaper, which would have contained the articles in Japanese, were ominously blank, having been censored by the government. The* Rafu Shimpo *ceased publication for the duration of the war on*

April 4, 1942, with a parting editorial entitled "Itsuka mata omemoji no hi made" ("Until we meet again") and signed "Before long, we will be your Rafu Shimpo *again."*

*

Rafu Shimpo
December 10, 1941

All-out Victory

The treacherous infamy of Japan's attack upon the United States has united the minds of all Americans, regardless of race, color, or creed. The American people are determined that victory is the supreme objective. The grim determination of a united people has set in motion a tremendous force that will not stop until the Japanese empire is defeated.

To that main objective, the resident Japanese, both citizens and permanent resident aliens, join to preserve their freedom and security in a free world.

The bombing of innocent women and children in a surprise attack without even a hint of declaring war can never be forgotten. The defeat of Japan is a certainty. By her cowardly and dishonorable stab in the back while extending, on the other hand, peaceful gestures by her diplomatic representatives in this country, she has sealed her doom. The anger of the American people have been aroused to the maximum and nothing short of victory will satisfy us now.

Words alone, we are aware, will not win this struggle against Japan. We realize the real meaning of this gigantic struggle against Nazi and fascist regimes. We are ready to sacrifice our lives to bring a clear-cut victory to the United States.

These are indeed dark days, and we feel somewhat lonely that our efforts are not entirely appreciated by all Americans. Suspicion is frequently aroused because of our similarity in facial characteristics to the enemies. But blood ties mean nothing now. We do not hesitate to repudiate and condemn our ancestral country.

We have lived long enough in America to appreciate liberty and justice. We cannot tolerate the attempt of a few to dominate the world. We have faith in free institutions, of individual freedom, and we have the courage of our convictions to back up our words with deeds of loyalty to the United States government!

Heretofore the American people have argued the rights and wrongs of committing the United States to the whole world struggle. Some arguments were justified then, to be sure. We were to give practical assistance by furnishing military supplies. When American blood was shed, when Japan deliberately attacked us, however, the long withheld patience of the United States was finally exhausted of Japanese villainy.

Japan began this war and it is now up to the United States to end the war by crushing the Japanese empire and her ruthless, barbaric leaders. We have a just cause, a common cause, to fulfill a mission that freedom shall not perish from this earth.

Fellow Americans, give us a chance to do our share to make this world a better place to live in!

Rafu Shimpo
December 20, 1941

Give Us a Chance

An American war correspondent who, after watching the valiance of the British fliers in combat with the numerically superior enemy air force, wrote:

"These are times when only those ready to die can hope to survive!"

We Americans, even the most humblest of us, must keep in our minds the potence of those words.

In order to live, we must be ready to die for our country.

Americans of Japanese ancestry, it has been assumed by our Caucasian countrymen, are willing to die for the United States. Yet many Americans are not too sure whether to trust us; they still have their doubts.

We haven't had the opportunity to prove our loyalty to the country of birth, the United States. Hence Americans doubt our patriotic motives. Some Americans of European descent think the Nisei are led by conclusive reasoning and fear to stimulate loyalty rather than through actual love for this country.

Most positively, Americans of Japanese ancestry must prove their loyalty to America does not emanate from verbal expressions alone. Willingness to prove their love for this country by performing patriotic deeds has greater significance to the American people.

Therefore, we were highly elated to read in the official report by Secretary of Navy Frank Knox in his investigation of the damages wrought to Pearl Harbor by Japan's initial attack on Hawaii that Americans of

Japanese ancestry had distinguished themselves by their heroic efforts to defend American soil.

Mr. Knox told of the Nisei deserting their benches in the Navy yard to help the Marine defense battalion man machine gun nests. Two of them, with hands badly blistered from holding hot gun barrels, required emergency treatments.

What more can be said of the loyalty of Americans of Japanese ancestry? The story of heroism of the Nisei at Pearl Harbor speaks for itself. Can the Nisei be trusted? If not, why? We have confidence in our fellow citizens that they will not let America down in this hour of grave national crisis.

We Americans must win this war. Only a conclusive victory will satisfy us. We are ready to die for America so others that will follow us can live in perpetual peace. We have faith in humanity and sincerely believe that right will triumph over sheer force and tyranny.

In our willingness to sacrifice our lives, we ask fellow Americans to give us the opportunity to serve our cause at the front ranks, not in the back lines, relatively unimportant places, but where the danger is most conspicuous.

These are times when the American people and their democratic virtues of fair play and tolerance must be manifested to bring unity within the nation and give every American, regardless of race, color, or creed, the equal opportunity to serve his country.

The *Sacramento Bee*
January 5, 1942

President Warns Against Persecution of Aliens

In a statement issued from the White House last Friday, President Roosevelt made a strong appeal for fair treatment of noncitizens of this country.

He confessed grave concern over reports which had come to him of the discharge of good and industrious workers simply because they happen to be aliens and in some instances foreign-born American citizens.

And he added:

> This is a very serious matter. It is one thing to safeguard American industry, and particularly defense industry, against sabotage, but it is very much another to throw out of work honest and loyal people who are sincerely patriotic.
>
> Such a policy is stupid and unjust.

It is hoped this statement of the president will have a deterrent effect on the trend which he deplores.

A majority of the foreign born in America, whether citizens or noncitizens, come from nations which are the allies of America in this war—Britain, Canada, Mexico, Poland, Norway, Australia, Holland, Belgium, Russia, etc. There can be no question as to what their feelings are.

Even those whose ancestors came from the Axis nations are, in the vast majority of cases, antifascist and anti-Nazi. They are eager to do their share in America's war effort.

As for the other kind, the agents of the FBI will take care of them.

The persecution mania—the race hatred theme—is a jarring note of discord in the American war symphony.

It is, as President Roosevelt says, the direct antithesis of liberty, justice, and decency.

Racial hatred belongs in the arsenal of Nazi weapons and is used to inflict deep and bitter wounds in the nations which Hitler would conquer.

Race against race, religion against religion, prejudice against prejudice—that is the Nazi gospel. The wise and sensible American will avoid any of them as he would a deadly poison or a fatal pestilence.

The president has pointed out what is the traditional and time honored American policy—fairness to all who love the Flag, no matter where the accident of parentage may have located their birthplace.

The casualty list at Pearl Harbor, as will the casualty list in the Philippines, contains names which show the diversity of our origins.

Let us remember that and conduct ourselves accordingly.

The *San Francisco Chronicle*
January 7, 1942

Japanazis or Japaryans

Our Chinese friends dislike to hear the Japanese referred to as "yellow," even when that adjective is followed by terms like "devils," "bandits," "snakes," or "bedbugs." They think of the word in its racial significance and remember that the yellow or Mongolian race includes many other peoples than the Japanese; the Koreans, for example, who hate the Japanese, and the Chinese themselves. So the Chinese, probably the Koreans, too, shiver at hearing a racial term that includes them used as one of opprobrium.

The point is well taken. And we do the Japanese too much honor by using for them a term which has been made honorable by the Chinese. Call them Japanazis if you please, or better still, Japaryans. That puts them where they belong, in Hitler's pocket, but call them nothing that puts them in association with the honorable peoples of the yellow race.

People's World
January 9, 1942

Counterfeit Patriotism

Shortly after the Japanese attack on Pearl Harbor, a certain David P. Bailey gained momentary notoriety in San Francisco by printing posters reading "Jap Hunting License, Good for Duration of Hunting Season, Open Season Now. No Limit."

Some people may have thought that these signs were the products of patriotic fervor. However, Mr. Bailey's patriotism was suspect from the outset because he was operating a scab printing shop.

Now it turns out that Bailey and some associates have been jailed by the FBI and indicted for operating a huge counterfeit ring. Mr. Bailey, at the very same time that he was printing the lynch-inciting jingo signs, was also printing phony money orders, it appears.

Whenever you see people engaging in chauvinistic lynch incitement against the Japanese here, you may conclude that in nine cases out of ten, their patriotism is as counterfeit as Mr. Bailey's money orders seem to have been, and in the tenth case, the person is just the dupe of some counterfeit patriots.

People's World
February 2, 1942

On Treatment of Aliens

Mayor Bowron of Los Angeles sounded a proper note when he warned against any hysteria in the handling of Japanese and other "enemy aliens" or their children.

Mayor Bowron urged that "all residents of Los Angeles continue to treat both aliens and native-born Japanese with courtesy and respect and that no advantage of any kind be taken of the Japanese people."

World War II propaganda poster. U.S. and State Forest Services, c. 1942.

Unfortunately, not all public officials are as levelheaded as Mr. Bowron, or possessed of the good sense he has shown in this instance.

Of course, action must be taken to eliminate danger from actual or potential fifth column elements among Japanese, Italian, and German residents in California. (It should be added that action also should be taken to guard against native fifth column elements as well.)

But to fan hysteria in dealing with the problem will only defeat the legitimate end of strengthening and safeguarding our defense. Hysteria can only let loose those passions which sow dissension and division among our people and tend to demoralize them in fulfillment of their duties to the nation.

Certainly, this should not be the occasion when some cheap politicians, seeking publicity and glory, are permitted to make political capital of the situation by indiscriminate and ill-advised action against foreign born persons in our midst.

Certainly, this is not an occasion for permitting sinister and unscrupulous men to enrich themselves at the expense of these poor people by taking their lands and other properties from them.

And just as certain is the fact that there are cheap politicians and profit-hungry capitalists who will attempt to do exactly those things.

It is just as incumbent upon responsible authorities to curb these politicians and profit-grabbers as it is to guard us against fifth column elements. Each in his own way contributes to defeat of the war effort.

It is also incumbent upon the proper authorities, in instances where evacuations of aliens are deemed necessary, to carry through these evacuations in a humane manner and provide economic assistance to the evacuees.

Only a few of the thousands of Japanese residents in California are fifth columnists. To isolate these few, it may be necessary to move many. But it would be wrong to impose terrible economic hardship upon these many innocent persons.

The *San Francisco Chronicle*
February 6, 1942

Alien Hysteria Mostly Imaginary

Reports from the "grass roots" indicate that the supposed "hysteria" over enemy aliens and their citizen descendants scarcely exists among the people themselves. Perhaps there is even too little of it, because there are real dangers involved, against which the Government is taking real steps. But the excitement is visible almost entirely in political and journalistic quarters, which presumably are not themselves excited at all. They are seeking to capitalize on the supposed excitement of others, which is mostly a figment of their own imaginations.

On the real dangers, the Government is taking very vigorous steps. But it is the Government, facing facts, not politics, reflecting popular hysteria.

This lack of popular hysteria, in the presence of what may well be real danger, is in interesting contrast with the situation in the last war, when the witch-hunting seemed to emanate from the people themselves—though it did reach, finally, some departments of the Government, which were among the worst offenders.

We do not want to be caught off our guard in some sudden emergency.

But, also, we do not want to do to Hitler's "racial" compatriots what he, in like case, would do to ours.

The *San Francisco Chronicle*
February 9, 1942

These Decisions Were After the War

It is reported that Justice Department officials in Washington are weighing the possibility of asking Congress for legislation that would permit the "protective custody" arrest of any citizen for the duration of the war. The purpose, apparently, is the arbitrary detention of native-born citizens of Japanese ancestry, without the necessity of either making or proving any charges against them.

Being members of the Justice Department, these officials of course have law books accessible and know how to read them. They know, therefore, the sole conditions under which the Constitution authorizes the suspension of the privilege of the writ of habeas corpus. They know also the famous case of ex parte Milligan in which the Supreme Court defined the meaning of this provision. And they will find very great difficulty in bringing any such proposal within either of these authorities.

The privilege of the writ cannot be suspended except when, in case of invasion or rebellion, the public safety may require it. There is no "rebellion" now, and no "invasion," at least yet. When, during the Civil War, there was "rebellion," Congress authorized President Lincoln to suspend the writ, which, as to certain cases, he did. After the war the Supreme Court, in an opinion by Justice David Davis, Lincoln's appointee and friend, decided that it was only the "privilege," not the writ itself, that could be suspended. The writ could not be suspended in any districts where there were courts open to issue it. The privilege of it might be suspended as to persons properly involved in the war, but even as to them the writ should issue and the person under custody must be brought before the court, for it to decide whether he was one of the persons to whom the suspension applied.

This was in time of domestic war, with hostilities actually going on, on American soil, with persons in civil life aiding and abetting them. Even they were entitled to a hearing and to have the evidence against them presented.

The Constitution is still the supreme law of the land; it still provides that all persons born or naturalized in the United States are citizens thereof; that there shall be no discriminations by reason of race, and that all persons shall have the equal protection of the laws.

In peacetime or in wartime, we can do no less.

Rafu Shimpo
February 15, 1942

There's Work to Do for Every Loyal Nisei

We want this straight for the record.

We feel we represent majority Nisei sentiment when we say that whatever we do, we do in absolute loyalty to the United States.

These are not so much words.

We see our objective clearly—Defeat Japan!

That can be done. It will be done.

We know with confidence that we can be of service to the cause of American victory.

We are fighting an enemy whose mental processes we undoubtedly are qualified in measure to analyze.

We are equipped with the background to be of peculiar value to the United States.

If there are disloyal ones among us, and this is proving to be the case, put them out of harm's way.

But in all this excitement and hysteria about every Japanese face on the street, let's not forget that the loyal Americans of Japanese ancestry have a definite part to play in the war effort to defeat Japan.

We have the training, the mental equipment, the background, and the spirit to do the job.

Let's not minimize the useful value of Americans of Japanese ancestry truly loyal to the United States.

There's a job for every Nisei to do NOW.

Your Congressmen in Washington, D.C. are undoubtedly being influenced by the flood of talk now current that every one of us is to be distrusted as a potential enemy.

The least you can do is to let them know something about you.

Let's quit being unknown quantities and question marks.

Write, wire, communicate with Washington, D.C. You've got a story to tell. TELL IT!

HOW TO SPOT A JAP

HERE ARE TWO MEN JUST PICKED UP BY A PATROL... THE FIRST THING TO CONSIDER IS APPEARANCE.... THE CHINESE IS "C"...THE JAP IS "J" NOTICE THAT C IS ABOUT THE SIZE OF AN AVERAGE AMERICAN: J IS SHORTER —AND LOOKS AS IF HIS LEGS ARE JOINED DIRECTLY TO HIS CHEST!..

C IS DULL BRONZE IN COLOR—WHILE J IS LIGHTER—MORE ON THE LEMON-YELLOW SIDE. C'S EYES ARE SET LIKE ANY EUROPEAN'S OR AMERICAN'S—BUT HAVE A MARKED SQUINT.... J HAS EYES SLANTED TOWARD HIS NOSE...

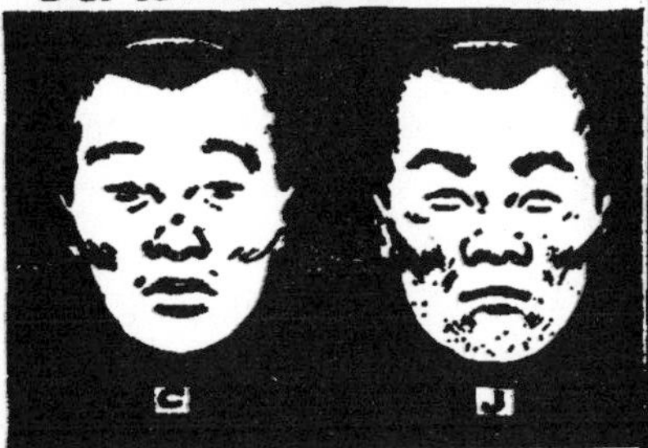

THE CHINESE HAS A SMOOTH FACE...THE JAP RUNS TO HAIR.....LOOK AT THEIR PROFILES AND TEETH...C USUALLY HAS EVENLY SET CHOPPERS—J HAS BUCK TEETH...THE CHINESE SMILES EASILY—THE JAP USUALLY EXPECTS TO BE SHOT... AND IS VERY UNHAPPY ABOUT THE WHOLE THING...ESPECIALLY IF HE IS AN OFFICER!

YOU MAY FIND JAPS AMONG ANY ORIENTAL CIVILIAN GROUP... THAT IS A FAVORITE INFILTRATION TRICK...MAKE YOUR MAN WALK...THE CHINESE STRIDES...THE JAP SHUFFLES (BUT HE MAY BE CLEVER ENOUGH TO FAKE THE STRIDE)...MAKE HIM REMOVE HIS SOCKS AND SHOES, IF ANY...

THE CHINESE AND OTHER ASIATICS HAVE FAIRLY NORMAL FEET...THE JAP WORE A WOODEN SANDAL ("GETA") BEFORE HE WAS ISSUED ARMY SHOES... HE WILL USUALLY HAVE A WIDE SPACE BETWEEN THE FIRST AND SECOND TOES... OFTEN CALLOUSED FROM THE LEATHER STRAP THAT HELD THE "GETA" TO HIS FOOT...

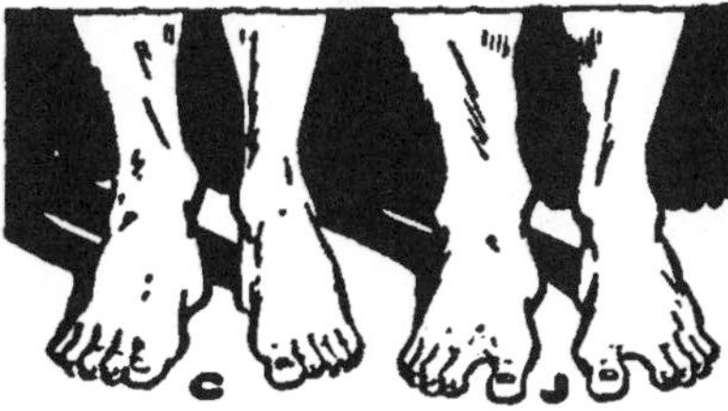

TO SUM IT UP, SPOTTING A JAP DEPENDS UPON THREE THINGS: ① APPEARANCE ② FEET ③ PRONUNCIATION

HE CAN'T PRONOUNCE OUR LIQUID "L"... HISSES ON ANY "S" SOUND

SHORT, SQUAT, FAIRLY HEAVY BEARD...LEMON-YELLOW SKIN SLANTED EYES

G-STRING

ALMOST NO WAIST-LINE

WIDE SPACE BETWEEN FIRST AND SECOND TOES...CALLOUS ON THE WEB

STOCKY BUILD

"How to Spot a Jap," by Milton Caniff, 1943.

The *San Francisco Chronicle*
February 21, 1942

Facts Force America to Stop Pussyfooting

The President's order, which is just one step short of full martial law in such strategic areas as the Army may designate, means the removal of Japanese from coastal and other military contacts.

The order specifies that persons removed by the Army as unwanted, may be excluded regardless of whether they be aliens or citizens. Attorney General Biddle makes it clear that the immediate effect will be upon Japanese.

This brings to a focus a painful necessity that has been crystallizing as the details of the Pearl Harbor affair have been reluctantly accepted as facts.

We know that thousands of Japanese in Hawaii were ready and went into action with clockwork precision the instant the attack was started. Swarms of wheezing jalopies, ancient light trucks, poured from cane fields and truck gardens into the roads. Traffic was choked. Navy officers and men, Army officers and men, on leave in the outskirts, had to fight their way through not against armed forces, but through a tangle of blocked traffic, broken down cars, flat tires, while the bombs were crashing on their ships and stations.

Among all the thousands of Japanese who knew the plot there was not one, no matter where born, who came forward to warn the United States. This is not to say that there was not a person of Japanese blood in the Islands who was loyal to the United States. It is a fact that code advertisements that to any Japanese eye must have created suspicion even though their full significance might not have been known, were not brought to American attention as something at least requiring special vigilance.

From these circumstances, the conclusion has been forced that whatever the personal exceptions, and there must be many, Japanese loyalty is primarily to Japan. We do not regard this as a reason to hate Japanese persons, foreign born or of immigrant extraction, who are among us. We would consider it nothing reprehensible if Americans born in Japan and who spent their lives there, and there are many such, remained at heart faithful to the United States in a war to the death.

The situation reluctantly accepted is a blow to personal sentiment in many cases, and a delicate one in view of our principles of civil rights. Mr. Biddle says specifically that the Presidential military order does not suspend the habeas corpus, but he says he doubts whether Federal courts will issue any writs in the cases of persons, citizens or otherwise, against the expressed policy of the Army. Cases somewhat analogous that arose in the Civil War were finally adjudicated, but after the close of [that war].

A great many American citizens, every American citizen in fact, [is often called] upon to submit to some infringement upon rights whose infringement in any particular we would, under usual circumstances, resent and resist. This is being done with the reservation that the surrender is voluntary, to keep a means of recapturing full rights as Americans, suspended only to preserve the American right to those rights. It is a principle that persons of Japanese blood who are loyal to the United States and its ideals can show that loyalty by recognizing necessity. This is a fight for survival. In this fight we cannot pussyfoot. We have to be tough, even if civil rights do take a beating for a time.

People's World
February 23, 1942

Hysteria Is Going to Help the Axis

We think that when Governor Olson on February 7 cautioned against hysteria in dealing with the problem of Japanese on this coast, he said something that should have received more attention than it has.

That military necessity and security should take first place is right. But hysteria, and falling in with the race war campaign being incited by Hearst, Martin Dies, and others is quite another matter. That's right down Hitler's alley.

More to the point, hysteria is very helpful to Japan's campaign to convince the colored peoples of the Far East that white Americans are just as barbarously racial-bigoted as the Nazis, and why should they fight for America and "white superiority" that hates brown people of any race. Now that the Army is authorized to take any step it thinks needed, let us hope that its actions will not only eliminate the hysteria, but make clear that race war is not its policy.

Martin Dies, the same fascist as always, is issuing a "yellow paper" of 1,000 pages against the Japanese in America, labeling them all, American born as well as alien, as dangerous and demanding they be straightway at least sent 500 miles to the interior and there interned. Whether the Army or the Administration thinks this is required for security is nothing to Martin Dies. He is plainly crawling in under his self-raised umbrella of anti-Japanese hysteria to help Hearst and Hitler start a race war.

And he's getting plenty of help from other Congressmen. One, Rankin of Mississippi, actually stood up in Congress and howled that he would intern all Japanese, he wouldn't take any of their race's proof of loyalty, because he said "once a Jap, always a Jap." And all the old gang of leather-lunged appeasers, the Hiram Johnsons and the rest, are sputtering racial idiocies and crying out that nothing's being done. These incitations to hysteria bear vile fruit down below. A columnist of the *L.A. Times* thus spouts:

> You can't walk down the street without bumping into Japs. They take the parking space. They get before you in line at the stamp window in the post office. They occupy their share of the space in streetcars. ...This is crazy. We must have done with the alien Jap and everyone with Jap blood in their veins.

This is nothing less than pre-historic tribalism. And it is a wave of filthy race hysteria on which ride the even more dangerous fifth columnists of German and Italian origin, and, more important, the native American fifth columnists that seek to tear national unity to shreds on any and every issue. This is duck soup for them, as witness Hearst, who one day attacks Britain for denying freedom to India, and the next howls that the colored races of the Far East menace "occidental civilization."

That action to safeguard our security from spies and saboteurs is necessary is unquestioned. Prompt and effective action. But from ALL spies, Japanese of course, but others, too. The FBI has nabbed some very dangerous men of recent days, of German origin. Where's the howl by the race maniacs to hang, draw, and quarter every German and everyone of German blood? This discrimination in the anti-Japanese hysteria really protects all other spies and saboteurs.

The *Sacramento Bee*
February 23, 1942

Army Is Given Free Hand to Curb Aliens, Citizens

President Roosevelt has issued a sweeping order giving the United States Army control of all persons—aliens and citizens alike—in areas which it considers strategic to the defense of the United States.

The commander in chief thus has authorized the military arm to determine what persons may be excluded from restricted areas and also to decide the right of any person to enter, leave, or remain in such districts.

This is not technically described as a declaration of martial law, but in essence it is just that thing.

The president's timely order puts the decision as to what is to be done with and about enemy aliens and even their descendants squarely where it belongs—in the hands of the Army high command entrusted with the duty of protecting the Pacific Coast from foes within as well as from without.

It knows what must be done to safeguard California, in particular, against the kind of treachery which the Roberts report all too clearly disclosed had preceded the Japanese attack on Pearl Harbor.

Our people realize complacency and the "it can't happen here" type of thinking already have been the cause of too many irreparable disasters to America's cause to permit the taking of any chances on the Pacific Coast.

To be forewarned is to be forearmed!

So whatever measures the Army determines on must and will be supported loyally and thoroughly enforced, for this is war. And in this war Americans are dealing with an enemy whose most effective weapons are stealth, chicanery, and deceit.

In the enforcement of the decree of the President of the United States, many who are innocent of any intent of wrong doing or who even may be loyal to the United States will be compelled to face hardship and sacrifice.

But if such persons are truly loyal, they will accept such hardship as part of their obligation to their adopted country, and remember that at the worst their situation will be blessed compared to the Japanese-created hell which the American airmen and American sailors and soldiers are facing in Java, the Philippines, and other points in the South Pacific today.

This is a war for national survival.

And in such a fight there are many civilities of more serener days which must go overboard for the duration.

The necessity for action has been growing for the last ten weeks as the possibility of a Japanese attack on the coast has loomed ever larger.

The roundup of known subversive agents has been carried on continuously by agents of the FBI. They have done a good job.

But it has become increasingly apparent that it is not enough.

Californians never can feel reasonably secure until all enemy aliens—and fifth column citizens, too—are put in a place and surrounded with conditions which will make it utterly impossible for them to serve their superiors in any totalitarian capital whose deadly purpose is to destroy the United States of America.

The *San Francisco Chronicle*
March 7, 1942

Not Civil Liberties but Military Necessity

The American Civil Liberties Union urges modification of the order evacuating Japanese. It says the order is "far too sweeping to meet any proved need." That is proved to the satisfaction of the ACLU.

This is typical of conflict between the intellectual abstract and practical necessity. The ACLU is not, as it assumes, talking about civil liberties, about which it knows a great deal, but about military necessity, about which it knows nothing.

If there were no war, the position of the ACLU would be correct beyond reproach. There being a war, the position is untenable.

The ACLU would not tell the Navy where not to send the fleet, or the Army what kind of guns not to use. But when action touches its particular interest, the ACLU sets up as judge not only of civil liberties but also of military necessity, of which it knows no more than of ships or guns. It would seem also that it does not know there is a war.

Eyewitness to Pearl Harbor

Clay H. Musick

Throughout the 1930s, Japan aggressively expanded into the Pacific, actions that conflicted with U.S. interests, which opposed Japan's attempts to establish military and economic control of Asia. At dawn on December 7, 1941, Japan launched a surprise attack on the U.S. fleet at Pearl Harbor, Hawaii. Two battleships were destroyed, four others sunk or run aground, and one hundred forty-nine airplanes were reduced to burning wrecks. Clay H. Musick was a U.S. Navy Seaman assigned to the USS Arizona *when Japan attacked. More than 80 percent of the USS* Arizona *crew of over 1,500 men were killed. Musick's battle station was ammunition hoistman at the port antiaircraft magazine located just below the* Arizona's *main deck. His eyewitness account of December 7 was published in* Remembering Pearl Harbor: Eyewitness Accounts by U.S. Military Men and Women.

*

We heard a loud blast of noise. I looked up, and right over there, why, that's the first Jap plane I saw. The first bomb hit Ford Island. He, the Japanese aviator, had his canopy pushed back and had his hand alongside the plane. He was so close that you could have knocked him down with a hand grenade. He had his goggles up, but I really didn't even look at his face. I saw that rising-sun emblem on his plane. The first thing I thought of was, "How did those damned Japs get over here?"

There were two other motor launches out there, and the officer of the deck of the USS *Arizona* was telling those guys to come in there so that they wouldn't get machine-gunned. So we got off of the motorboat onto the quays and from the quays to the pilings and from the pilings to the blister[1] top of the USS *Arizona,* and then we ran down the blister top to a ladder.

I went directly to the third deck and met two or three others on the way down, and we rigged the hoist and the conveyor before we went down to the magazine. I'd say there were at least six of us in the magazine. The first round of ammunition was handed to me, and I pushed it onto the conveyor to take it up to the third deck. At about the same time, we took our first hit.

I went forward first, then I went backwards, and then forward again, and then I fell and got up. The lights went out except for the battle lights, so that stopped the motor from taking the ammunition up. I reached up to get the crank to start cranking the ammunition up, but I no more than got that crank in my hand, and that's when the second one hit. The second blast was a little bit greater. It seemed like it didn't shove me forward, but it shoved me backwards and then back again and then to the floor.

They claim that the *Arizona* was hit by torpedoes, but I really don't know. I'd rather think that it was bombs. I got up, and I was trying to find the crank. There was just one battle light still on. I got the crank, and I started to put it in the socket, and that's when a bomb went down the chimney....

Then we went up. We started climbing this ladder up the wall. It was so hot you could hardly touch the rungs. I got to the third deck, but I couldn't find this opening. It was hot down there. Anyhow, I got up there, and the gunner's mate got me out, and he says, "Musick, can you go the rest of the way?" I said, "Yes." The minute he turned me loose I passed out. I went up two ten-foot ladders unconscious. The only thing I can remember was that that man asked me if I could go the rest of the way myself. He had hold of my arm, and he turned me loose. I remember starting up that ladder, but I don't remember another thing until I started to step out on topside.

There were fires all on the forecastle. Anyhow, I started to step out on topside, and there were people underneath the turret. Some were from the magazines, and some from other parts of the ship. They said, "Musick, go back down, go back down! They're machine-gunning the deck!" Well, you know, being half stunned, I just walked on out. I said, "Well, I'd better go up on the boat deck and see what I can do up there!" So I started wandering all around up there, and everything was silent. I couldn't see any movement. All I could see was flames and fire.

So I walked to the port side of the quarterdeck. Then I walked around on the starboard side, and when I got around there, there was a marine coming out of the *Arizona.* I think he had a pair of khaki shorts on and a skivvy shirt. But his hair had been scorched and burnt like these Indians that just had this row of hair down their head. That's the way he looked to me. Mooring lines were cracking and popping and cracking and popping. There were men on fire rolling all over the deck trying to put the fire out. We both stood there for a while and kind of looked around. He was dazed and I was dazed. He said, "I guess we'd better get off of this thing." A gangway was rigged from the ship to this mooring quay. He was in front. The mooring lines were still popping and cracking, but I got off. I just stepped off onto the quay, and the gangway fell in the water. That's how fast the ship was listing.

By that time sailors off the USS *Solace,* a hospital ship, were coming aboard to help all the wounded that they possibly could. I kind of turned around and saw a second marine in the water. He was hollering for help, so I got down off of this quay and on the pilings, and there was a piece of line there. I threw that piece of line to him, and I pulled him over. I hollered at one of the corpsmen, and they said that they'd be right there. I told him to just hold onto that line, that they would be there. The only thing that I can remember that that man had on was his side arm. Now whether he had shoes on, I don't know. Whether his clothes were blowed off him or burned off him, I don't know. But that's all I could see—his sidearm. He had been standing guard on the bridge.

Then I came back over to where the first marine was—the marine sergeant. There was a boat landing on the other side of this quay. He said, "We'd better get down here because if those things, the mooring lines, bust or break, they'll cut you in half!" Well, we no more got down there and this big tugboat—seagoing tug—came up trying to put the flames out. But they couldn't get any waterpower. So they was backed up, and they started taking on survivors. The marine and myself were the first two. The marine just kind of hopped on, but I held my hand out, and a sailor pulled me on. When he pulled me on, I found out then that I couldn't walk. I was just laying on my back. So they backed out, and they got in the channel. I think they picked up maybe one or two more men. I can't recall—maybe one more man. Anyhow, this tug was picking up survivors, and as they're going across the channel, I was laying on my back, and I could see three horizontal bombers.

They got me aboard there and on the shore now, and they had me in one of these wire baskets. I kind of looked over, and I said, "Well, the *Arizona* has already capsized." The corpsman said, "No, that's the *Oklahoma* that's capsized." He said, "The *Arizona* is just all in flame!" He said, "Man, that is really burning!"

Then they took me to the hospital. They had little houses out here. They started with "A," but it seems like they had me in Letter "H" hut. It had bunks, and they put you in a bunk and asked you where you hurt and all of that kind of business, you know, how you felt, if you wanted a drink of water. That was the corpsman. Pretty soon a nurse came by, and she started giving everybody a hypo, a morphine shot. Pretty soon the hut got full.

A doctor came in about that time, and he said, "How's it going?" She said, "Well, everything's all right." He said, "Who have you given a hypo to and who haven't you?" She started over and put a red cross on their head. So everybody got another hypo. That's two.

They started shoving these beds together so they could put more beds in there. I was right at a window, a little window. A bomb must have hit pretty close to this hut because it shattered glass all over me. So they got me out of the bunk and changed the sheets real quick and everything, and put me back. Then they took a sheet and nailed it over that window so that the wind wouldn't come through.

There were so many that was hurt worse than I. I can't remember, but I believe it was Wednesday before they saw me because I wasn't bleeding anyplace. I had a couple of bad burns here on my legs, and I had a busted hip. It seems like it was Wednesday morning when they took me to X-ray my hip. They took about three different poses of this hip—flat, on your side, and I think they even took one from the back side. Then after they took me out of the X-ray, they took me back to this hut. Later on in the day, they moved me into the main building of the hospital at Pearl Harbor in a ward.

*

The next night, President Roosevelt expressed the nation's shock and rage in an address that proclaimed December 7 as "a day of infamy." The United States' declaration of war on Japan passed with one dissenting vote.

ENDNOTE

1. In naval terminology, a blister is a bulge built into a warship to protect the vessel against torpedoes and mines.

World War II propaganda poster, c. 1942.

Pearl Harbor Remembered

Kay Uno

For several years before Pearl Harbor, the Japanese community had been under watch by the FBI, which conducted extensive intelligence studies both in Hawaii and on the West Coast. In October 1941, President Roosevelt commissioned Curtis B. Munson to investigate the Japanese in the United States According to Munson's report, "There is no Japanese problem." Yet within hours of the attack at Pearl Harbor, FBI agents arrested anyone suspected of having sympathetic ties to Japan. Hundreds of Japanese were rounded up, questioned, and shipped off to Justice Department internment camps. Despite the FBI's efforts to uproot traitors and segregate potentially dangerous Japanese in these high-security camps, not one instance of sabotage was ever found.

Kay Uno grew up in Los Angeles, the youngest of ten children. Published in a collection of memories entitled, A Fence Away from Freedom, *Kay Uno's firsthand account illustrates the conflict faced by an Americanized Nisei generation because of their Issei parents' impossible position as aliens.*

I was nine at the time of Pearl Harbor, and I was in third grade. That Sunday we were on our way home from church and we had the radio on in the car. Everybody was excited. We said, "Oh, those Japs, what are they doing that for?" We didn't think of ourselves as Japs.

When the war happened, my parents were really torn. Japan was their country. They were Japanese, and they couldn't have citizenship here. Buddy, my oldest brother, was in Japan, and my relatives were all there. But all of us kids were Americans. In a lot of ways, my parents were very American. They flew the flag for every national holiday. My father was born on the Fourth of July, and he celebrated the Fourth in a big way.

We lived six blocks from where I went to school, and I always walked. All the merchants and everybody knew me. "Hi. How are you?" Monday, they turned their backs on me. "There goes that little Jap!"

I'm looking around. Who's a Jap? Who's a Jap? Then it dawned on me, I'm the Jap.

After Pearl Harbor, the kids began to shun me. My friends. One person started it, and then pretty soon it went throughout the school. My classmates were the last ones to leave me. My teacher and the music teacher were both very supportive all through the time. When I had to leave, one of them gave me a gift, a gold leaf pin. It was the first real piece of jewelry I ever had. I still have it.

There was the curfew at eight. You had to be off the streets and in the house. It didn't bother me, but it was hard for my sisters and brothers. People couldn't travel more than a certain number of miles. We had a friend, Chris. Going to work was outside his range, so he moved in with us. When the evacuation came, he evacuated as part of our household.

There was a lot of tension in the house with the FBI coming. My family would shoo me off upstairs or into the kitchen or the back yard. But I knew something serious was happening. Big ears, I listened.

The boys all made model planes bought in Woolworth's. My father had sent a model to my oldest brother, Buddy, who was in Japan. The boys had them hanging in the bedroom window and on the table where they were working. They had the model plans tacked on the wall. The FBI took all of that away. They said my father was a spy, sending airplane plans to Japan.

When Father was taken, we knew it was because of Buddy. A few years later my dad told me they were accusing him of poisoning the American food chain because he was working for an insecticide company. They also said he was directing [Japanese] farmers how to plant signals, and he was spying on crop-duster airports that were strategic airfields. Some of the airports became training fields, but not until after he was gone!

One of these days somebody's got to write a comedy about these FBI men making up all these stories and trying to find out who this man, my father, is. A friend said it's too serious and too sad. I said, "I know, but at a certain point you have to laugh."

*

Ten weeks after Pearl Harbor, on February 19, 1942, President Franklin D. Roosevelt signed Executive Order 9066, authorizing the exclusion of any persons from designated areas in order to secure national defense against sabotage and espionage. Evacuaction of all persons of Japanese ancestry off the West Coast was now imminent.

The Total Community

Ron Dellums

On September 17, 1987, California Congressman Ronald Dellums gave the following testimony to the 100th Congress, First Session, in support of Japanese American redress, a U.S. government bill that would eventually issue apologies and reparations of $20,000 to each surviving internee. Dellums represented California's 8th Congressional District from 1970 to 1999 and served as chair of the Congressional Black Caucus. Throughout his Congressional career, Dellums championed efforts to reverse military spending and improve social values in the political arena. Dellums, who was born and raised in Oakland, California, reveals the powerful emotional impact the evacuation had on the non-Japanese living in California.

*

One of my distinguished colleagues on the other side of the aisle stated that he was born in 1942 and has no recollection of the war. This gentleman was born in 1935, so I do recall the war and felt the war through the body of a child and saw it through the eyes of a child.

My home was in the middle of the block on Wood Street in West Oakland. On the corner was a small grocery store owned by Japanese people. My best friend was Roland, a young Japanese child, the same age. I would never forget, Mr. Chairman, never forget, because the moment is burned indelibly upon this child's memory, six years of age, the day the six-by trucks came to pick up my friend. I would never forget the vision of fear in the eyes of Roland, my friend, and the pain of leaving home.

My mother, bright as she was, try as she may, could not explain to me why my friend was being taken away, as he screamed not to go, and this six-year-old black American child screamed back, "Don't take my friend."

No one could help me understand that, no one, Mr. Chairman.

So it was not just Japanese Americans who felt the emotion, because they lived in the total context of the community and I was one of the people who lived in the community.

So I would say to my colleagues, this is not just compensation for being interned. How do you compensate Roland, six years of age, who felt the fear that he was leaving his home, his community, his friend, Ron, the black American, who later became a Member of Congress; Roland, the Japanese American, who later became a doctor, a great healer.

This meager $20,000 is also compensation for the pain and the agony that he felt and that his family felt. This meager $20,000—in 1942 terms $2,800—is also compensation for the thousands of dollars of personal belongings that were strewn in the streets, on 10th and Wood Streets in West Oakland in 1942, because in case you do not know it, they could only take what they could carry.

So the little football that we played with in the streets, the games that we played that took up hours of our time in the streets, the furniture that we walked on and wrestled upon as children in 1942 in the streets; so this $20,000 and this formula that if you were in for one day you get a few nickles, if you were in for three years you get the whole $20,000, as if we could play that game.

This is not about how long you were in prison. It is about how much pain was inflicted upon thousands of American people who happened to be yellow in terms of skin color; Japanese in terms of ancestry, but this black American cries as loudly as my Asian American brothers and sisters on this issue.

So this formula, while well intended, does not in any way address the reality of the misery, Mr. Chairman. It must be rejected out of hand because it does not address the misery.

Vote for this bill without this amendment and let Roland feel that you understood the pain in his eyes and the sorrow in his heart as he rode away screaming, not knowing when and if he would ever return.

War Comes to the Church Door

Eleanor Breed

Evacuation day was the final step in a series of discriminatory orders against Japanese—as well as German and Italian—enemy aliens that were enforced as "a military necessity." On the West Coast, a sweep of suspected spies or traitors was conducted, followed by a freeze of all Japanese banks and businesses. Contraband items such as shortwave radios, cameras, and guns were seized. Finally, a nighttime curfew and severe travel restrictions were imposed. To add to the confusion, a "voluntary" resettlement for the Japanese—both alien and citizen—was set in place; the Japanese were free to go where they chose beyond the prohibited Military Areas No. 1, which included the western half of Washington State, Oregon, California, and the southern half of Arizona. Between January 31 and February 7, 1942, Attorney General Francis Biddle proclaimed additional sites to be Military Areas No. 2. These included eighty-four specifically prohibited areas in California, seven in Washington, twenty-four in Oregon, and eighteen in Arizona. There were 135 zones around airports, dams, power plants, harbors and other military installations that forbade the presence of enemy aliens. Meanwhile, public pressure continued as the press and politicians overwhelmingly recommended removing all Japanese aliens from the state of California.

Despite the climate of intense racial hatred and wartime hysteria, there were sympathizers who risked public scorn and even physical danger to themselves to defend and support the Japanese Americans. Of those, many represented religious groups. Eleanor Breed worked as church secretary at the First Congregational Church of Berkeley, which served as a civil control station for evacuating Japanese. This excerpt is from Miss Breed's diary of the time, War Comes to the Church Door: Diary of a Church Secretary in Berkeley, California, April 20 to May 1, 1942, *now preserved in the UC Berkeley Bancroft Library collection on the Japanese American evacuation.*

*

Monday, April 20

This was a day I hoped to give almost completely to China Relief, but little jobs at the church kept me there 'till eleven, when I turned things over to a substitute and hurried away. A luncheon of the China Relief Committee, where everyone was pleased to know we have received in the first week $5,500 of Berkeley's $10,000 quota. Someone suggested we send out another 3,000 letters to a district not covered in our first 11,000 letters, so that devolved on me as secretary. Off I hustled to printer to order more copies of letter, pledge card, and return envelope; to the addressograph office to arrange for envelopes to be addressed; and back to my own office at the church to round up volunteers to handle the mailing job.

Army officers were looking over the parish house when I returned, making plans for use of the building as a control center for the registering and evacuating of Japanese from the Berkeley area. Dr. Loper, the minister, and I welcome the use of the church by the government, but wonder what some of the old-timers will say when the word gets around.

Tonight at 7:30 a special meeting of the Church Council was held for presentation of this project. The Board of Trustees had already given their consent, but the Council had to discuss mechanics of how to get along, with fifteen organizations or more scheduled to use the building over the weekend. There was consideration of where the choir would rehearse, how they would reach the choir loft without going through Pilgrim Hall, what the Boy Scouts could do, where the lively Winthrop Leaguers, high school age, could meet. And when these issues had been settled, Dr. Loper went on with another project: should the church extend hospitality in some form to the Japanese being evacuated? He outlined his thought that, through a committee of the Women's Association, arrangements could be made to have flowers in the various rooms, to open the church parlors and the kindergarten room, to have cots available for people to rest, to serve tea and fruit and sandwiches, and have hosts and hostesses on hand to give the evacuees friendliness. When he asked for discussion no dissenting opinion was evident, though I suspected that here and there the group enthusiasm was a bit thin. He suggested having a letter go out over his signature, expressing the church people's interest and sympathy toward the evacuees. Everything was approved, and as the meeting broke up into little groups Mrs. Fulmer remarked, "I wouldn't have missed this meeting for anything!" and Mrs. Brock said "I'm proud of my church for initiating this!" Home at 10:45. Long day.

Tuesday, April 21

Dr. Loper drew up a first draft of the letter to be given to the Japanese evacuees, and I phoned ministers of leading churches to be sure they would meet him at the Berkeley Fellowship luncheon this noon to discuss it. I tried to get a head start on my church calendar for the printer, but couldn't catch Dr. Loper long enough to get information from him for it. He had two funerals and a death today, poor man. I've suggested that he not preach next Sunday on "Has Science Outmoded Religion?" as announced—that when history, in the form of government evacuation of Berkeley citizens, comes to our doorstep he shouldn't ignore it. "Yes, yes," he says, on the fly, "but I can't think now. Maybe tomorrow I'll have a bright idea."

Mrs. Hadden phoned in to say that she had heard of the church's program for the Japanese and was so proud she wanted to weep, and Dr. Madden wanted to be called on for duty as host on Saturday, if he could be of service.

Dr. Loper came back from luncheon with the Berkeley ministers and said his draft of the letter to evacuees would have to be done over, that their feeling was that all churches should have a share, and not just the First Congregational do it all. So Dr. Loper retired into his study to labor over a new version, to go out over two signatures, his and that of the Berkeley Fellowship of Churches. After he labored over it a while he read it, over the phone, to Kim Obata, president of the Japanese American Association and son of Professor Obata of the University, and to Galen Fisher and Mrs. Kingman of the Fair Play Committee, to be sure everything is said in such a way no one can take offense. Then he brought it in to my desk and plunked it down. "Now you give it a final working-over and send it off to the printer. See if we can get it back tomorrow." The printer groaned. "Miss Breed! What kind of miracles do you expect of us?" [...]

The government officials [...] began getting the Large Assembly ready for use as the Civil Control Station. A switchboard was installed at the far end by the stage, with some eight telephones around the room. The dining tables, end to end, made a counter across part of the space. I couldn't get on with my church calendar and publicity—they kept calling me to ask where this turned on and whether we had thumbtacks. I put an assistant to work making signs, long arrows saying "Public Telephone," "Lounge," "Women's Rest Room," "Kindergarten," etc.

The *[Berkeley] Gazette* came out this evening with a long story on the evacuation order and the fact that the Civil Control Station is to be in Pilgrim Hall, with the registration to start Saturday and Sunday. Now everyone knows—and we don't have to be mum about our military secrets.

Wednesday, April 22

Fifteen people turned up to help on my China Relief letters, and went vigorously to work in the Small Assembly while I dashed in and out, answering questions for the government people preparing the Large Assembly for the Japanese evacuation. "Let not your right hand know," etc. We finished the whole 3,000 letters at noon, and Julean Arnold took the three big cartons full down to the Post Office. It was one of my days for commandeering all who dropped by. I caught Ruth Stage and put her to addressing envelopes, grabbed Dayton Axtell when he came to see Dr. Loper and put him to work helping Jean Hecox on the painting of signs, phoned Elsie Culver and put her to work on Dr. Loper's air warden file making a duplicate card system.

Still no calendar information from Dr. Loper, so I can't complete my copy for the printer. He is getting organization under way for the hospitality to evacuees, working out a system whereby the Congregational women are in charge the first day, the Episcopalians the second, and so on. Worked late. A thousand people came by to ask a thousand questions.

Thursday, April 23

Finally pinned Dr. Loper down long enough to get data for the calendar. He has changed his subject to "Paying the Fiddler"—not good, but better than the other. [...] I wrote a paragraph re the evacuees, and Dr. Loper was too busy to edit or change it, so in it went, and I phoned it all down to the printer.

Big Army man appeared in my door to inquire what room had been assigned for the soldiers; first I knew soldiers were to be quartered in the building. Dr. Loper let them take their choice, and came back to report that we now had five strapping privates bedded down in the Nursery for the week. [...]

At last I got my church ads and news stories off to the papers, and broadcast announcements off to the studio, and cleaned up my regular work, and the printer brought the completed copies of the letter to the evacuees.

I left at 5:00 for the International House [of UC Berkeley], to see the display of pictures by Professor Obata of the Art Department, who is being evacuated with the rest. He gave a demonstration of his brush work, and ended with a brief announcement that he hoped to come back from his absence from Berkeley with a series of paintings of the desert. The sale of his pictures ($3 to $15) brought in some $450, which will be used at the University as the Obata Scholarship, to be given to the student most in need because of war, regardless of race or creed....

[...] Marion Rosen [...] and I walked up the hill together. "It was such a lovely exhibit," she said in that gentle voice of hers with the merest hint of accent. "Everybody was so kind. I feel so sorry for the Japanese." And she would—a refugee from Hitler herself, her own family scattered over the world, parents in England, sister in Sweden, brothers in Switzerland, and now suddenly even here in America she has become an enemy alien who must be careful to be in her room every night at curfew time....

Friday, April 24

Ran about the building sticking up signs, labeling the North Room "Lounge" and the Parlor "Berkeley Church Hospitality Committee," etc. The government officials have a long afternoon conference on procedure, beginning tomorrow. They have their room divided off and their own signs up: "Federal Security," "Federal Reserve Bank," "Employment Service," and the like. Many Japanese come to my door, and I wave them on to the door that says "Civil Control Station." The letter to the evacuees is ready now for distribution. Miss Ruth Price, busy teacher at Berkeley High School, phoned in to ask if she could work at the church as hostess tomorrow. "So many of the Japanese young people have been my students, you know," she said, "and I want to do anything I can to help." Dr. Raoul Auernheimer, who is to speak Sunday evening, called [...]. Very appropriate to have a refugee from Naziism speaking at a time when our own refugees are lining up in queues for evacuation. He said he liked the title I'd given him, "Hitler—Today's Napoleon."

At the end of a long day of many interruptions, when I was in my late afternoon sag, came a telephone call: "Is this the Congregational Church? Well, will you answer one question for me? Why do we have to be so nice to the Japs, feed them lunch, give them tea and hospitality? They aren't treating our boys that way." I drew a long breath and rose to the challenge, hinting that of course we with our higher (we think) standards wouldn't want to imitate what Japan was doing anyway, reminded her that someone once had said "Love your enemy," went on to describe the hectic week this had been with government plans changing from day to day and ours having to change as fast to keep up, told of various good and gentle Japanese who were as sensitive and humiliated by this experience as *we* would be, etc. "I know," the voice went on. "There are good ones and bad ones, I guess. I get all mixed up." "So do I," I admitted, and she laughed and I laughed, and she thanked me very nicely and hung up. Never did tell me her name....

Saturday, April 25

Down to the church at 7:45 A.M., and it was something of a shock to find one soldier with gun stationed at the curb, and two at the door with another inside at the door to the Control Station office. A big crowd of stenographers and government officers were all at their desks. Mrs. Kingman of the Fair Play Committee was receptionist, directing people hither and yon. The soldiers and their lieutenant were very considerate of the Japanese, I noticed, treating them like human beings. Good old America!

Dr. Loper was streaking here and there, greeting Japanese ministers, seeing that all the church hosts and hostesses were on their jobs and yet were out from under governmental feet. I had to haul one of our dear old men—who considers his white hair a badge of special privilege—out of the Large

Sketches made on the day of departure from Berkeley, by Chiura Obata. Sumi on lined paper, 3½ x 6 in. April 30, 1942.

Assembly and explain that this was our church all right, except that we'd loaned it to Uncle Sam temporarily and right now he was making the rules.

A young Japanese came to my door with a question: "Could we leave the ashes of someone here in this church?" I turned him over to Dr. Loper who made arrangements, and the young man left, returning in half an hour with a square box wrapped in a white silk furoshiki. "These are the ashes of the children and my mother," he said to Dr. Loper as they went down the hall. The white box was deposited in the locked Trustees' Room in the Tower, and I think Dr. Loper made a little ceremony of it, for he came back looking rather upset.

"Bet you've got your sermon for tomorrow ready now," I ventured.

"Well, maybe, but do I dare to use it?" [...]

At noon friends dropped in to lure me out to lunch with them, but I couldn't leave. I showed them around the building with its many changes, and they [...] seemed [...] happy that their church was trying to ease the evacuation for the Japanese a little. They said that Sato, who usually does their gardening, came to them today to say politely that he was so sorry but he couldn't come today—he had to go to the First Congregational Church and register. "You know," he told them, "they are going to serve tea. It is the only church in the state of California that is serving tea to the Japanese." My friends hastened to claim membership in this wonderful church, and said they could see their stock rise in his estimation.

A telephone call: "Will there be church tomorrow? Oh, I thought maybe the Japanese were taking over."

The *Berkeley Gazette* this evening has a long, full, front-page story of the use of Pilgrim Hall for evacuation, telling of the Army being quartered in the Nursery and ending with a long quote from our much-labored-over letter to the evacuees. There is also a long article I sent them about the changes in the Sunday program for the various church groups. And there is a congratulatory editorial on the China Relief Drive, which reached its quota of $10,000 today. Good old Berkeley!

Sunday, April 26

Down to the church by 8:00, and Pilgrim Hall crowded, with people two-deep waiting in the Reception Room, and Mrs. Kingman standing at the doorway to the government office like the head waiter at a popular restaurant, giving out pink tickets with numbers on. Soldiers are still on guard at the doors, which must be startling to parents in the habit of unloading children there each Sunday morning. I stationed one of the men there to direct people around Pilgrim Hall and into the main church for services.

Dr. Loper's sermon on "Paying the Fiddler" was pretty good, considering that he hasn't had time all week to collect his thoughts. He hinted that I had nagged him into changing his subject at the last moment—but he would have anyway. He spoke on how this evacuation that was going on behind the doors of Pilgrim Hall was the result of a stream poisoned at its source, saying that you couldn't name patly what was the particular cause any more than you could tell who crucified Jesus. Was it the Jews? The money-changers? Pilate? He spoke of some of the problems we are trying to meet, mentioning that one was to find people to take the much-beloved pets of the children who were having to depart and who didn't want their cats and dogs to be killed. One of the deaconesses met me at the close of the service. "I'd be glad to take a Japanese cat," she said, "if it will get along all right with my American cat."

Home from church late—waited to see the wedding of a soldier and his bride, both new here from Minnesota.

Monday, April 27

Rainy and cold, and the soldiers at the door stand inside for shelter. "No Parking on This Street Today" signs along Durant and Channing, with exceptions for the Army jeep. Everything was very quiet today. All 1,100 Japanese were registered in the first two days, and this was the lull before the beginning of the actual evacuation. Today was assigned to the Quakers for hospitality, and they came very eager to be of help, and I had to tell them there were no Japanese today.

A miscellany of questions: "Are there any dogs left? I'll be glad to take one, only I don't want a good dog. I just want a mutt puppy."

"Do you have any Chinese members of this church? My Japanese servant has had to leave, and I thought maybe you could find a Chinese for me. I just don't know what I'm going to do."

"Got any more dogs? I'd like one. I live in a trailer and work at Richmond shipping yard. And by the way, do you know where my wife and I should go to adopt a baby?"

One of the soldiers on guard mentioned that he'd been over at Miss Chandler's for strawberry shortcake, that she'd sent out word that all the soldiers at the church were invited. Little Miss Chandler has an unconquerable spirit. The deaconesses have tried for years to get her to go to a rest home, but she won't give up her independence and her modest little apartment next door to Pilgrim Hall. Deaf, crippled so she can't sit—she can only lie down or hobble about on a crutch—she reads avidly, crochets bedspreads for an assortment of nieces, and occasionally shuffles into my office for a chat. Usually she catches me at a time when I'm too busy to shout into her ear phones, poor dear, and then she beams brightly and shuffles back out.

I decided Miss Chandler couldn't get the best of me, so I invited three of the soldiers up to dinner. Hurried to grocery and home to start things off, then got panicky about what would I do to entertain three young men all evening, so phoned Gertrude Jacobs at the International House, and up she came. Three friends dropped in during the evening, and we had a lively game of skittles and much fun. The soldiers were from North Dakota and Arkansas and Oregon—very nice lads.

I don't know whether it was this trio or some of the other soldiers, but a group of them went downtown with some of the Japanese boys the other night for dinner. That's a secret we aren't supposed to tell the Lieutenant.

Tuesday, April 28

The beginning of the evacuation. The pioneer group of evacuees was waiting at the church this morning, including lovely Ann Saito of the staff of the International House, who had a secretarial job at Tanforan waiting for her; so she went on the first bus. The Control Office has lists posted around its walls saying who is to go when, and many Japanese come to read. Among the first group was a pair of newlyweds, arm in arm, the bride with a collegiate bandanna around her head and a flower in her pompadour, and a big American flag in brilliants on her lapel. There were two babies in baskets, a three-week-old little girl, and a six-months-old boy. And everyone, young, middling, and old, wore a tag around his neck or hanging from his lapel, with name printed on and a number, for his family group. One pert little college girl in slacks had her name tag around her neck tied to a chain from which dangled her Phi Beta Kappa key. The preliminary group today is a small one. Their duffel bags were loaded into the big bus, and the evacuees went aboard, waiving merrily and cracking jokes with their friends who were to follow in the next few days. But as the bus pulled out Ann Saito was crying.

This is the Baptists' turn at hospitality, and they've sent over a nice group of women but also a retired minister who is just too godly. He bustles in everywhere and goes around shaking hands with the evacuees and saying a hearty, "God bless you!" I caught Ann and Michi looking at each other with a twinkle he missed. Dr. Loper is embarrassed. That sort of thing is just what he wanted to avoid—yet how to deal with a fellow minister?

Wednesday, April 29

When I arrived at the church at 8:00, I found a long line of baggage down the block from Channing to Durant, with duffel bags, suit cases, folding chairs, ironing boards, cartons, bundles, blankets, card tables, cribs. Noted one good-looking suitcase with stickers saying "Rome," "Paris," and one that caught me up short: "Hotel Metropole, Beyreuth." The street was blocked off, with policemen at each end permitting only Japanese unloading more bundles to go through. Pretty soon along came a big moving van and trailer, and the call went forth for young men to help. In a jiffy the Japanese lads had organized a sort of old-fashioned fire brigade and were swinging the bundles and duffel bags along a line and into the truck, joking and laughing as they did so, perhaps glad to have activity instead of the monotony of waiting. I note that they take pains not to speak Japanese.

Pilgrim Hall when I went in was already a-bustle—people reading the announcement boards, learning their assignments to Groups 1, 2, 3, 4, and 5, finding the location for their groups and settling down with admirable patience to wait. Dr. Loper was busy organizing hospitality, pulling tables into place, working out a system to speed up the serving, and soon tea and sandwiches were going the rounds. This is the Methodists' day, and they're going at it vigorously, feeding not only their multitude of Japanese but offering luncheon for the government workers and coffee and sandwiches for the soldiers and the bus drivers. They have even made so many sandwiches they have some left over, for the Presbyterians to inherit tomorrow.

I am continually on a trot—now out in front to see off a bus load of evacuees, now back to hunt up the janitor and get him to refill the t.p. and towels in the rest rooms, now upstairs to look for Dr. Loper, now back to my office because the switchboard is buzzing, then off again for the janitor to get him to turn off the heat. Lucky, I got my calendar off to the printer last night.

Dean Deutsch of the University, out of a clear sky, wrote us today:

> Allow me to express my own appreciation for the attitude which you and your church have taken with reference to the Japanese and the American Japanese who are being evacuated. Your action has been one that is proper and will impress these people with the fact that the ideals which we profess we try to put into practice. If any criticize you for it, my only thought would be that they are not truly Americans or Christians.
>
> People who fail to recall that these people who are being evacuated have had no charges against them individually; they are not guilty of misconduct. They are being removed because of fear, which is gripping the hearts of some people. Personally, I feel that our country will

someday feel ashamed of its conduct in this entire matter. In the meantime, however, it is good to know of actions such as you and the members of our church have taken.

Good old Deutsch. I'm including that first paragraph on the calendar—though so far if anyone in the church disapproves of this project I haven't been able to smoke him out.

Thursday, April 30

Down to the church by 8:00 again, and again the long high line of duffel bags and miscellany along Dana Street, with soldiers on guard. The first groups of evacuees were already in their places, and hordes of Presbyterian women were flying around in the kitchen and up and down the hall. I saw one sentimental old lady sympathizing so warmly with one family that the little girl, aged ten or so, was sobbing her heart out. I caught Mrs. Stanley Hunter, the Presbyterian minister's wife, pointed out the old lady, and told her to scold the daylights out of her.

A Japanese young man came to the office and said, "Would you mind if I left the church a small donation? We appreciate very much what you are doing."

"Goodness," I said, "what we are doing is only a small thing—we'd like to do lots more. But we'd be happier if you would save your donation for some play equipment for the children when you get to camp."

The man smiled and bowed. "We do appreciate what your church has done," he said again, adding as an afterthought, "I'm Buddhist."...

Our soldiers quartered in the church Nursery are bemoaning the fact that soon they will pull out of here. They've liked this job, they tell us, with its coffee and sandwiches in the afternoon and the Boy Scout room to lounge in, and people inviting them out to dinner. One of the soldiers who comes up from Tanforan with the buses played hide-and-seek around a tree this morning with a Japanese lad of five, and drew quite a gallery. A group of Japanese high school girls stood about chatting with one of the soldiers on guard, and I heard one of them say coyly, "We hope you'll be stationed at our camp so we'll see you some more."

Friday, May 1

Down to the office earlier than ever—7:30 A.M., as the first bus was to leave at 8:00. Ambulances were sent around to the homes to collect eight cases of mumps and ten measles, today, to be taken to the hospital in San Bruno until recovery. There were more of the lame and halt among the evacuees coming into Pilgrim Hall today, it seemed. One paralyzed old man was carried in on the back of his son; one old lady had to be lifted up the steps of the bus. Dislocation from their homes and familiar surroundings is going to be hard on people as frail as these.

Today's babies were particularly enchanting. One, wrapped in blue blankets, was a mite ten days old. I stopped by a basket holding a baby somewhat older, wrapped in pink. "What's his name?" I asked.

"Ronald," his mother said. "He's third-generation American, so of course he has an American name."

My pet was Patty Yoshida, aged eight months, dressed in a knitted pink jumper suit that set off her chubby red-apple cheeks. Her pretty young mother agreed readily to my wish to take snapshots of her, but alas, they will be in black-and-white, and Patty, to do her justice, should have color film.

Another of the International House staff, Marii Kyogoku, left today with her family, and many from the House came down to say good-bye, including Lo Jung-pang of Peking, graduate of Yenching University, who has been studying for his Ph.D. here. Marii was in Group 5, which was assigned the North Room upstairs for assembling, [...] but there didn't seem to be enough helpers to pass plates of sandwiches and tea, so Mr. Lo helped. Another picture to remember; the young Chinese serving the Japanese evacuees as they have to leave their American homes. Good old China!

And hooray—Julean Arnold called this afternoon to say that in the final mopping up of the United China Relief drive Berkeley had turned in $14,000, and he was going to wire the news to Madame Chiang Kai-shek.

Dr. Loper had me outline for Mrs. Kingman of the Fair Play Committee the steps of development in our work here with the evacuees, in the hope that other churches may want to do something along the same line. Mrs. Kingman feels that even the little we have done has been helpful in changing the attitude of some who were most bitter, citing one Japanese who was a veteran of the first World War and who now is removed from his successful shop in Chinatown and sent into camp as if he were a suspect. "The fact that he came here to an American church and was given friendly treatment," she says, "helped a lot to soften his hurt and disillusionment. 'I know now there are Americans who don't hate us,' he told me, 'and that makes a world of difference—just to have friends.'"

A Methodist minister who has been working in Montana among the Japanese in internment camps commented to Dr. Loper today, "Your church is doing a fine job—but if it were in some areas it would be burned to the ground." He cited horror tales of hysteria such as we have feared, but have not found, in our area. It came over me suddenly, and with shock, that

Dressed in a uniform marking service in the first World War, this veteran enters Santa Anita assembly center. Arcadia, California, April 5, 1942. Photograph by Clem Albers.

the soldiers who have been on guard have been here not to protect us from the Japanese so much as to protect the Japanese against us.

The last bus left at just noon, and it was a lovely sunny day. I'd hate to leave Berkeley when it looks so beautiful!

And then as the government workers dwindled away came the business of collecting signs again, replacing [...] posters, clearing up debris, shrinking back into the business of being a church again. The old office seems unearthly quiet, and I'm not sure I'm going to like it.

PAGE 2 TOPAZ TIMES JAN. 1, 1943

1

流水の旅

眞珠湾軍港へ爆弾一下してその瞬間我々の運命は大いなる意志によって決定された、然し誰かその運命の路順を知り得たものがあらうか、今となって我々は自分の歩いて来た路を回顧、そこにたまらない郷愁と共にある「運命のパノラマ」を見る—啜り泣く春雨に送られて宿命の兒らの旅が始まる（バクレー出發）

2

借り切り（?）のバスがひた走りに走る、何時の日にか再び見られよう懐しい桑港、鉄橋上から雨に煙るシスコの一角に向って皆が皆心のうちで「さようなら」を云ったに違ひない、大聲をあげて泣きたい様な愛着だ

3

「泥海」とはよく言った、飛んでもない泥濘だ、泥に足をとられ喘ぎ喘ぎやっと馬小屋へころがり込んで、果して泣かなかった者が幾人かあらう、そして我々のタンフォーランに於ける生活が始められた、

4

然し「えらい」ものだ、人間一萬が寄ってたかってノコを引き、ツチを振ひ、ノミを打てば、そこに遮二無二「生活」を打ち立てる、と同時に断ち切り難い愛着の絆を引く、それなのに、あゝ、それなのに、宿命の兒らの『流水の旅』はまだまだ済まなかったのだ、屹立するグランドスタンドにもやがて別れを告げねばならなかった、

Nagare no Tabi, by Chiura Obata. Mimeograph, 14 x 8½ in. January 1, 1943. Originally printed in the *Topaz Times* New Year's edition.

5

6

7

8

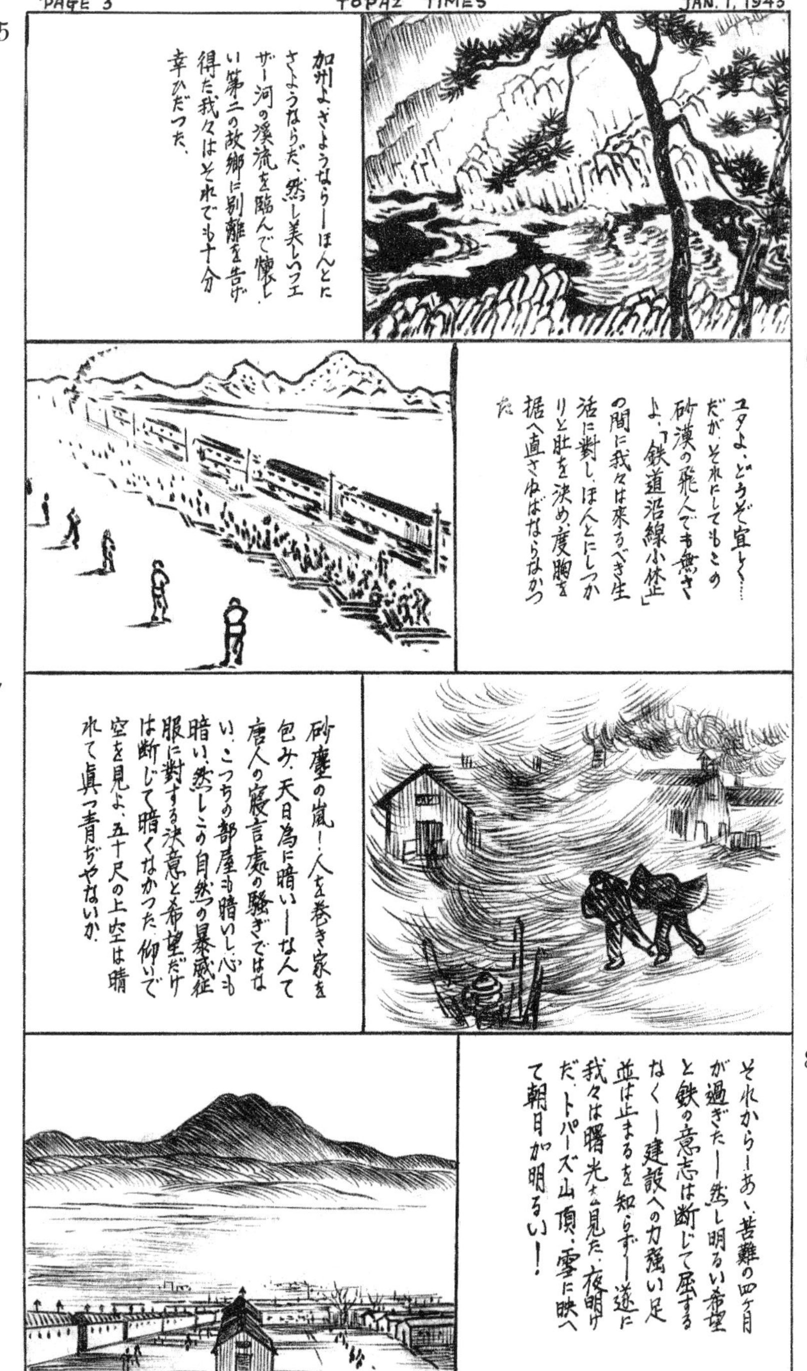
加州よ、さようなら—ほんとに
さようならだ、然し美しいフエ
ザー河の渓流を臨んで懐し
い第二の故郷に別離を告げ
得た我々はそれでも十分
幸ひだつた、
ユタよ、どうぞ宜しく……
だが、それにしてもこの
砂漠の飛人でも無さ
よ、「鉄道沿線小竝」
の間に我々は來るべき生
活に對し、ほんとにしつか
りと肚を決め、度胸を
据へ直さねばならなかつ
た
砂塵の嵐！人を巻き家を
包み、天日為に暗い——なんて
唐人の寝言處の騒ぎではな
い、こつちの部屋も暗いし、心も
暗い、然しこの自然の暴威征
服に對する決意と希望だけ
は断じて暗くなかつた、仰いで
空を見よ、五十尺の上空は晴
れて真つ青ぢやないか、
それから—あゝ、苦難の四ヶ月
が過ぎた—然し明るい希望
と鉄の意志は断じて屈する
なく—建設への力強い足
並は止まるを知らず—遂に
我々は曙光を見た、夜明け
だ、トパーズ山頂、雪に映へ
て朝日が明るい！

Translations for *Nagare no Tabi* *(a stream's journey)*

1. Under the spring sun, our fateful journey began from Berkeley, California. Our destiny after "Pearl Harbor" was to be determined by a Higher Power—who could foretell our fate? Now, looking back, we feel nostalgia as we see the panorama of the past eight months of our life.

2. While buses carried us across the great San Francisco Bay Bridge, we caught a glimpse of the San Francisco skyline silhouetted in the rain. We felt a tug in our hearts as we bid farewell to the familiar surroundings to which we had become so attached.

3. We waded in rain, through slush and mud up to our knees, only to stumble into empty horse stalls. Many an involuntary sob escaped our lips as we began our life at Tanforan.

4. The spirit of ten thousand people, however, could not be crushed for long. Presently, we made our own way of life among ourselves and found a bond of attachment with everything around us. But our journey was not yet over. We were soon to say farewell to the community we had helped to build and to the familiar grandstand which towered above.

5. Good-bye, California! Good-bye to our beloved mother state. Our last adieus were said as we sped past the beautiful Feather River.

6. Hello, Utah! But how dry and wild the desert country is! Resting beside the railroad, we girded our spirits and prepared ourselves for our coming life.

7. The desert dust storm! Barracks, rooms—everything, everywhere was sunk in darkness! But not so our hopes and determination to conquer nature's violence. We looked up, and there, as if in answer, not fifty feet above us we saw the pure blue of the skies.

8. Four months of hardship have passed. Our strong hopes and iron will to succeed have never wavered. At last, we see the beautiful dawn as reflected in the morning sun bright against snow-covered Mt. Topaz!

Can't Tell

Nellie Wong

The strain on relationships between the Japanese and other Asians was especially difficult during the approach and outbreak of America's involvement in World War II. Socialist feminist poet Nellie Wong was born and raised in Oakland, California, the first daughter of Chinese immigrants. She was eight years old when the war broke out. Her father owned a grocery store in Berkeley next to a Japanese American butcher shop.

*

When World War II was declared
on the morning radio,
we glued our ears, widened our eyes.
Our bodies shivered.

A voice said
Japan was the enemy,
Pearl Harbor a shambles
and in our grocery store
in Berkeley, we were suspended

next to the meat market
where voices hummed,
valises, pots and pans packed,
no more hot dogs, baloney,
pork kidneys.

We children huddled on wooden planks
and my parents whispered:
We are Chinese, we are Chinese.
Safety pins anchored,
our loins ached.

Shortly our Japanese neighbors vanished
and my parents continued to whisper:
We are Chinese, we are Chinese.

We wore black arm bands,
put up a sign
in bold letters.

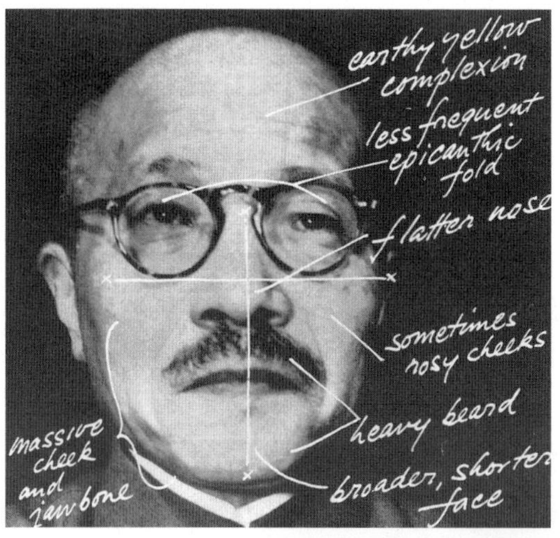

"How to tell Japs from the Chinese," December 22, 1941. *LIFE* magazine. The top photo is of Japanese Army General Hideki Tojo.

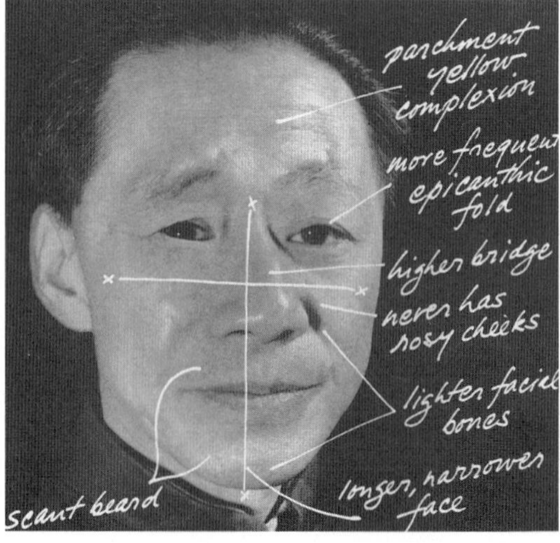

FROM *I Know Why the Caged Bird Sings*

Maya Angelou

Maya Angelou is an internationally acclaimed poet, historian, author, actress, playwright, civil-rights activist, producer, and director. She is the author of ten best-selling books, including the renowned autobiographical account of her youth, I Know Why the Caged Bird Sings. *In the following excerpt from that book, Angelou describes the San Francisco's Fillmore District as the Japanese were being evacuated and many Southern Blacks, enticed by a war economy, began moving in.*

In the early months of World War II, San Francisco's Fillmore district, or the Western Addition, experienced a visible revolution. On the surface it appeared to be totally peaceful and almost a refutation of the term "revolution." The Yakamoto Sea Food Market quietly became Sammy's Shoe Shine Parlor and Smoke Shop. Yashigira's Hardware metamorphosed into La Salon de Beauté owned by Miss Clorinda Jackson. The Japanese shops which sold products to Nisei customers were taken over by enterprising Negro businessmen, and in less than a year became permanent homes away from home for the newly arrived Southern Blacks. Where the odors of tempura, raw fish, and cha had dominated, the aroma of chitlings, greens, and ham hocks now prevailed.

The Asian population dwindled before my eyes. I was unable to tell the Japanese from the Chinese and as yet found no real difference in the national origin of such sounds as Ching and Chan or Moto and Kano.

As the Japanese disappeared, soundlessly and without protest, the Negroes entered with their loud jukeboxes, their just-released animosities, and the relief of escape from Southern bonds. The Japanese area became San Francisco's Harlem in a matter of months.

A person unaware of all the factors that make up oppression might have expected sympathy or even support from the Negro newcomers for the dislodged Japanese. Especially in view of the fact that they (the Blacks) had themselves undergone concentration camp living for centuries in slavery's plantations and later in sharecroppers' cabins. But the sensations of common relationship were missing.

The Black newcomer had been recruited on the desiccated farm lands of Georgia and Mississippi by war-plant labor scouts. The chance to live in two- or three-story apartment buildings (which became instant slums), and to earn two- and even three-figured weekly checks, was blinding. For the first time he could think of himself as a Boss, a Spender. He was able to pay other people to work for him, i.e. the dry cleaners, taxi drivers, waitresses, etc. The shipyards and ammunition plants brought to booming life by the war let him know that he was needed and even appreciated. A completely alien yet very pleasant position for him to experience. Who could expect this man to share his new and dizzying importance with concern for a race that he had never known to exist?

Another reason for his indifference to the Japanese removal was more subtle but was more profoundly felt. The Japanese were not whitefolks. Their eyes, language, and customs belied the white skin and proved to their dark successors that since they didn't have to be feared, neither did they have to be considered. All this was decided unconsciously.

No member of my family and none of the family friends ever mentioned the absent Japanese. It was as if they had never owned or lived in the houses we inhabited. On Post Street, where our house was, the hill skidded slowly down to Fillmore, the market heart of our district. In the two short blocks before it reached its destination, the street housed two day-and-night restaurants, two pool halls, four Chinese restaurants, two gambling houses, plus diners, shoe-shine shops, beauty salons, barber shops, and at least four churches. To fully grasp the never-ending activity in San Francisco's Negro neighborhood during the war, one need only know that the two blocks described were side streets that were duplicated many times over in the eight- to ten-square-block area.

The air of collective displacement, the impermanence of life in wartime and the gauche personalities of the more recent arrivals tended to dissipate my own sense of not belonging. In San Francisco, for the first time, I perceived myself as part of something. Not that I identified with the newcomers, nor with the rare Black descendants of native San Franciscans, nor with the whites or even the Asians, but rather with the times and the city. I understood the arrogance of the young sailors who marched the streets in marauding gangs, approaching every girl as if she were at best a prostitute and at worst an Axis agent bent on making the U.S.A. lose the war. The undertone of fear that San Francisco would be bombed which was abetted by weekly air raid warnings, and civil defense drills in school, heightened my sense of belonging. Hadn't I, always, but ever and ever, thought that life was just one great risk for the living?

Then the city acted in wartime like an intelligent woman under siege. She gave what she couldn't with safety withhold, and secured those things which lay in her reach. The city became for me the ideal of what I wanted to be as a grownup. Friendly but never gushing, cool but not frigid or distant, distinguished without the awful stiffness.

To San Franciscans "the City That Knows How" was the bay, the fog, Sir Francis Drake Hotel, Top o' the Mark, Chinatown, the Sunset District and so on and so forth and so white. To me, a thirteen-year-old Black girl, stalled by the South and Southern Black life style, the city was a state of beauty and a state of freedom. The fog wasn't simply the steamy vapors off the bay caught and penned in by hills, but a soft breath of anonymity and shrouded and cushioned the bashful traveler. I became dauntless and free of fears, intoxicated by the physical fact of San Francisco. Safe in my protecting arrogance, I was certain that no one loved her as impartially as I. I walked around the Mark Hopkins and gazed at the Top o' the Mark, but (maybe sour grapes) was more impressed by the view of Oakland from the hill than by the tiered building or its fur-draped visitors. For weeks, after the city and I came to terms about my belonging, I haunted the points of interest and found them empty and un-San Francisco. The naval officers with their well-dressed wives and clean white babies inhabited another time-space dimension than I. The well-kept old women in chauffeured cars and blond girls in buckskin shoes and cashmere sweaters might have been San Franciscans, but they were at most gilt on the frame of my portrait of the city.

Pride and Prejudice stalked in tandem the beautiful hills. Native San Franciscans, possessive of the city, had to cope with an influx, not of awed respectful tourists but of raucous unsophisticated provincials. They were also forced to live with skin-deep guilt brought on by the treatment of their former Nisei schoolmates.

Southern white illiterates brought their biases intact to the West from the hills of Arkansas and the swamps of Georgia. The Black ex-farmers had not left their distrust and fear of whites which history had taught them in distressful lessons. These two groups were obliged to work side by side in the war plants, and their animosities festered and opened like boils on the face of the city.

San Franciscans would have sworn on the Golden Gate Bridge that racism was missing from the heart of their air-conditioned city. But they would have been sadly mistaken.

A story went the rounds about a San Franciscan white matron who refused to sit beside a Negro civilian on the streetcar, even after he made room for her on the seat. Her explanation was that she would not sit beside a draft dodger who was a Negro as well. She added that the least he could do was fight for his country the way her son was fighting on Iwo Jima. The story said that the man pulled his body away from the window to show an armless sleeve. He said quietly and with great dignity, "Then ask your son to look around for my arm which I left over there."

Photo Essay:
An Uncertain Future

Overnight, the evacuation reduced individual and family names to numbers on tags. Instructions by the Army explicitly ordered the Japanese to assemble voluntarily for mass evacuation on a given date and time, with no more than what could be carried by hand. In the few days that the evacuees had to prepare for evacuation, bargain hunters descended onto the evicted, taking what they could for a pittance. In some instances, trustworthy neighbors stored and cared for the belongings, homes, and properties of the evicted Japanese, but the pilfering and vandalism often began before the evacuees had left their homes. With it, nearly a lifetime of perseverance and struggle disappeared overnight.

*

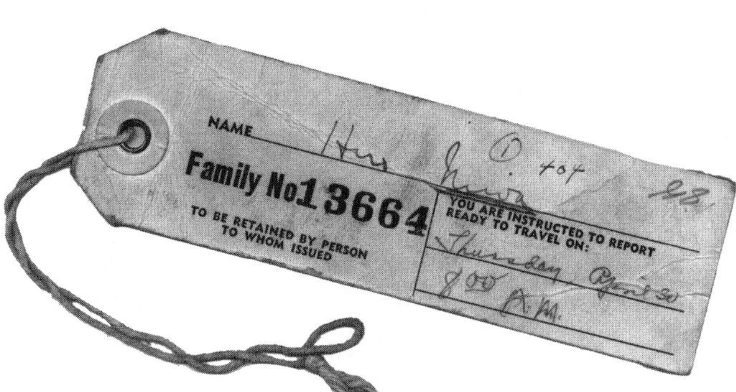

Hiro Niwa's evacuation tag #13664.

FBI agent searching personal belongings of a Japanese American family. December 1941. Photographer unknown.

They slit all the couches to see if anything was hidden.
MARION KANEMOTO

When internment came down, as I recall, it was a very terrifying experience, especially for a lot of Chicano-American people. And this I could speak on for my own family and the impact it had on them.

For example, one night after Pearl Harbor, as our family was asleep, in the middle of the night we heard a loud banging on the door and I remember my father getting up to answer it. Before he had a chance to approach the door, the door was broken down. It was the FBI or INS or what have you.... Then they proceeded to go down the street doing the same thing to all the houses.

What happened was...that they were after the Japanese. They took the neighbors that we did have, in the middle of the night.
GILBERT SANCHEZ

Issei and Nisei turning in radios, cameras and other articles considered "contraband" to the local police station. Little Tokyo, Los Angeles, California, 1942. Photographer unknown.

Someone was pulling a hoax. The news over the radio had the unreal quality of Orson Welles' Martian broadcast, of something out of the pulps.

On the subway going home, the gateman mistook me for a Chinese. "Now we are going to give them hell," he said. "I hope we do it quick," I replied. He opened the door and closed it again at a station. The train roared on its way. He leaned toward me. "The Mayor has ordered them all to stay home," he said, looking at me from the corner of his eye. "Yeah," I said.

I felt self-conscious; every eye was upon me, and I was glad to reach my apartment. A detective and two FBI men stopped me in the lobby but okayed me after looking at my Class 1B draft registration card. They went upstairs and apparently arrested someone from their list.

Tooru Kanazawa

Oakland, California, March 13, 1942. Photograph by Dorothea Lange.

> *I think the thing that we felt the most was that the people who stopped in at our store thought maybe we should close it up. For our safety. But my husband said, "No there's no need to do that. We're American citizens." But as things came out in the newspaper and on the radio as days went by, it really got worse. So then I felt too, that we had to stay inside, and then we had a curfew. We had to have our lights out at eight.... When April came along, we knew that we had to go. So my husband started selling things in the store.*
>
> Emi Somekawa

Oakland, California, February 27, 1942. Photograph by Dorothea Lange.

> *Herd 'em up, pack 'em off and give 'em the inside room in the badlands. Let 'em be pinched, hurt, hungry, and dead up against it [...]. Let us have no patience with the enemy or with anyone whose veins carry his blood [...]. Personally, I hate the Japanese.*
>
> HENRY MCLEMORE, THE *San Francisco Examiner*

This farm owner has just completed arrangements for leasing his acreage, buildings, and equipment for the duration of evacuation. San Jose, California, March 27, 1942. Photograph by Dorothea Lange.

You hurt. You give up everything that you worked for that far, and I think everybody was at the point of just having gotten out of the Depression and was just getting on his feet. And then all that happens! You have to throw everything away. You feel you were betrayed.

Yuri Tateishi

Bainbridge Island evacuees escorted to trains taking them to Manzanar. Seattle, Washington, March 26, 1942. Photographer unknown.

Right away, all of these junk dealers came into town, and oh, it was terrible. These poor women whose husbands were rounded up by the FBI; they were all fairly young and they had small children and no one to help them, and they had to somehow make ready to leave [Terminal] island in forty-eight hours. And here come these junk dealers, these opportunists. This was in December, so a lot of the families had already bought their Christmas presents, like new phonographs or radios, refrigerators—and they had no men around the house. These guys would come in and offer ten or fifteen dollars and because they had to leave, they'd sell.

FRED FUJIKAWA

Woodland, California, May 20, 1942. Photograph by Dorothea Lange.

This morning, the winding train,
Like a big black snake,

Takes us away as far as Wyoming.

The current of buddhist thought
always runs eastward.

This policy may support the
tenacity of the teaching.

Who knows?

Nyogen Senzaki, Zen Master

A seventy-acre fruit ranch, formerly operated by M. Miyamoto. This ranch, now not being worked, once yielded plums, peaches and pears. Penryn, California, November 10, 1942. Photograph by Francis Stewart.

Rhododendron blooms
about to leave this house
where my child was born
Yotenchi Agari

II

Rounded up
In the sweltering yard.
Unable to endure any longer
Standing in line
Some collapse.

Shizue Iwatsuki

FROM Desert Exile

Yoshiko Uchida

Evacuating the West Coast as quickly as possible meant moving the Japanese into temporary assembly centers until preparations were complete at the more permanent internment camps. Of the sixteen assembly centers that were established for the Japanese American internment, thirteen of them were in California. Most people stayed three to four months before they were ordered to pack again, this time destined for remote camps scattered in interior parts of the United States, where they faced either harsh desert or swampland climates at one of ten internment camps: Topaz, Utah; Poston, Arizona; Gila River, Arizona; Amache, Colorado; Heart Mountain, Wyoming; Jerome, Arkansas; Manzanar, California; Minidoka, Idaho; Rohwer, Arkansas; and Tule Lake, California. The train journey from the assembly centers to the internment camps usually lasted several stifling days, as the evacuated Japanese were instructed to keep the shades drawn to hide the evacuation from prying eyes.

Yoshiko Uchida, her older sister, and Issei mother were interned at the Tanforan Assembly Center, where they were forced to live in a horse stall before they were moved to cramped barracks at Topaz, Utah. Uchida's father, who had been arrested by the FBI, joined them after his release from the Justice Department camp in Missoula, Montana. Her mother often wrote haiku, both before the war and during the internment period, three of which are included at the end this selection. In her lifetime, Uchida published more than twenty-five books, both fiction and nonfiction. Desert Exile *is a vivid account of her incarceration written and published after the war.*

*

TANFORAN: A HORSE STALL FOR FOUR

As the bus pulled up to the grandstand, I could see hundreds of Japanese Americans jammed along the fence that lined the track. These people had arrived a few days earlier and were now watching for the arrival of friends or had come to while away the empty hours that had suddenly been thrust upon them.

As soon as we got off the bus, we were directed to an area beneath the grandstand where we registered and filled out a series of forms. Our baggage was inspected for contraband, a cursory medical check was made, and our living quarters assigned. We were to be housed in Barrack 16, Apartment 40. Fortunately, some friends who had arrived earlier found us and offered to help us locate our quarters.

It had rained the day before and the hundreds of people who had trampled on the track had turned it into a miserable mass of slippery mud. We made our way on it carefully, helping my mother who was dressed just as she would have been to go to church. She wore a hat, gloves, her good coat, and her Sunday shoes, because she would not have thought of venturing outside our house dressed in any other way.

Those stables just reeked. There was nothing you could do. The amount of lye they threw on it to clear the odor and stuff, it didn't help. It still reeked of urine and horse manure. It was so degrading for people to live in those conditions. It's almost as if you're not talking about the way Americans treated Americans.

Ernest Uno

Horse stalls at Tanforan racetrack in San Bruno converted to living quarters. San Bruno, California, 1942. Photographer unknown.

Everywhere there were black tar-papered barracks that had been hastily erected to house the 8,000 Japanese Americans of the area who had been uprooted from their homes. Barrack 16, however, was not among them, and we couldn't find it until we had traveled half the length of the track and gone beyond it to the northern rim of the race track compound.

Finally one of our friends called out, "There it is, beyond that row of eucalyptus trees." Barrack 16 was not a barrack at all, but a long stable raised a few feet off the ground with a broad ramp the horses had used to reach their stalls. Each stall was now numbered and ours was number 40. That the stalls should have been called "apartments" was a euphemism so ludicrous it was comical.

When we reached stall number 40, we pushed open the narrow door and looked uneasily into the vacant darkness. The stall was about ten by twenty feet and empty except for three folded Army cots lying on the floor. Dust, dirt, and wood shavings covered the linoleum that had been laid over manure-covered boards, the smell of horses hung in the air, and the whitened corpses of many insects still clung to the hastily white-washed walls.

High on either side of the entrance were two small windows which were our only source of daylight. The stall was divided into two sections by Dutch doors worn down by teeth marks, and each stall in the stable was separated from the adjoining one only by rough partitions that stopped a foot short of the sloping roof. That space, while perhaps a good source of ventilation for the horses, deprived us of all but visual privacy, and we couldn't even be sure of that because of the crevices and knotholes in the dividing walls.

Because our friends had already spent a day as residents of Tanforan, they had become adept at scrounging for necessities. One found a broom and swept the floor for us. Two of the boys went to the barracks where mattresses were being issued, stuffed the ticking with straw themselves, and came back with three for our cots.

Nothing in the camp was ready. Everything was only half-finished. I wondered how much the nation's security would have been threatened had the Army permitted us to remain in our homes a few more days until the camps were adequately prepared for occupancy by families.

By the time we had cleaned out the stall and set up the cots, it was time for supper. Somehow, in all the confusion, we had not had lunch, so I was eager to get to the main mess hall which was located beneath the grandstand.

The sun was going down as we started along the muddy track, and a cold piercing wind swept in from the bay. When we arrived, there were six long weaving lines of people waiting to get into the mess hall. We took our place at the end of one of them, each of us clutching a plate and silverware borrowed from friends who had already received their baggage.

Shivering in the cold, we pressed close together trying to shield Mama from the wind. As we stood in what seemed a breadline for the destitute, I felt degraded, humiliated, and overwhelmed with a longing for home. And I saw the unutterable sadness on my mother's face.

This was only the first of many lines we were to endure, and we soon discovered that waiting in line was as inevitable a part of Tanforan as the north wind that swept in from the bay stirring up all the dust and litter of the camp.

Once we got inside the gloomy cavernous mess hall, I saw hundreds of people eating at wooden picnic tables, while those who had already eaten were shuffling aimlessly over the wet cement floor. When I reached the serving table and held out my plate, a cook reached into a dishpan full of canned sausages and dropped two onto my plate with his fingers. Another man gave me a boiled potato and a piece of butterless bread.

With 5,000 people to be fed, there were few unoccupied tables, so we separated from our friends and shared a table with an elderly man and a young family with two crying babies. No one at the table spoke to us, and even Mama could seem to find no friendly word to offer as she normally would have done. We tried to eat, but the food wouldn't go down.

"Let's get out of here," my sister suggested.

We decided it would be better to go back to our barrack than to linger in the depressing confusion of the mess hall. It had grown dark by now and since Tanforan had no lights for nighttime occupancy, we had to pick our way carefully down the slippery track.

Once back in our stall, we found it no less depressing, for there was only a single electric light bulb dangling from the ceiling, and a one-inch crevice at the top of the north wall admitted a steady draft of the cold night air. We sat huddled on our cots, bundled in our coats, too cold and miserable even to talk. My sister and I worried about Mama, for she wasn't strong and had recently been troubled with neuralgia which could easily be aggravated by the cold. She in turn was worrying about us, and of course we all worried and wondered about Papa. Suddenly we heard the sound of a truck stopping outside.

"Hey, Uchida! Apartment 40!" a boy shouted.

I rushed to the door and found the baggage boys trying to heave our enormous "camp bundle" over the railing that fronted our stall.

"What ya got in here anyway?" they shouted good-naturedly as they struggled with the unwieldy bundle. "It's the biggest thing we got on our truck!"

I grinned, embarrassed, but I could hardly wait to get out our belongings. My sister and I fumbled to undo all the knots we had tied into the rope around our bundle that morning and eagerly pulled out the familiar objects from home.

We unpacked our blankets, pillows, sheets, tea kettle, and most welcome of all, our electric hot plate. I ran to the nearest washroom to fill the kettle with water, while Mama and Kay made up the army cots with our bedding. Once we hooked up the hot plate and put the kettle on to boil, we felt better. We sat close to its warmth, holding our hands toward it as though it were our fireplace at home.

Before long some friends came by to see us, bringing with them the only gift they had— a box of dried prunes. Even the day before, we wouldn't have given the prunes a second glance, but now they were as welcome as the boxes of Maskey's chocolates my father used to bring home from San Francisco.

Mama managed to make some tea for our friends, and we sat around our steaming kettle, munching gratefully on our prunes. We spent most of the evening talking about food and the lack of it, a concern that grew obsessive over the next few weeks when we were constantly hungry.

Our stable consisted of twenty-five stalls facing north which were back to back with an equal number facing south, so we were surrounded on three sides. Living in our stable were an assortment of people—mostly small family units—that included an artist, my father's barber and his wife, a dentist and his wife, an elderly retired couple, a group of Kibei bachelors, an insurance salesman and his wife, and a widow with two daughters. To say that we all became intimately acquainted would be an understatement. It was, in fact, communal living, with semi-private cubicles provided only for sleeping.

Our neighbors on one side spent much of their time playing cards, and at all hours of the day we could hear the sound of cards being shuffled and money changing hands. Our other neighbors had a teenage son who spent most of the day with his friends, coming home to his stall at night only after his parents were asleep. Family life began to show signs of strain almost immediately, not only in the next stall but throughout the entire camp.

One Sunday our neighbor's son fell asleep in the rear of his stall with the door bolted from inside. When his parents came home from church, no amount of shouting or banging on the door could awaken the boy.

"Our stupid son has locked us out," they explained, coming to us for help.

I climbed up on my cot and considered pouring water on him over the partition, for I knew he slept just on the other side of it. Instead I dangled a broom over the partition and poked and prodded with it, shouting, "Wake up! Wake up!" until the boy finally bestirred himself and let his parents in. We became good friends with our neighbors after that.

About one hundred feet from our stable were two latrines and two washrooms for our section of camp, one each for men and women. The latrines were crude wooden structures containing eight toilets, separated by partitions, but having no doors. The washrooms were divided into two sections. In the front section was a long tin trough spaced with spigots of hot and cold water where we washed our faces and brushed our teeth. To the rear were eight showers, also separated by partitions, but lacking doors or curtains. The showers were difficult to adjust and we either got scalded by torrents of hot water or shocked by an icy blast of cold. Most of the Issei were unaccustomed to showers, having known the luxury of soaking in deep pine-scented tubs during their years in Japan, and found the showers virtually impossible to use.

Our card-playing neighbor scoured the camp for a container that might serve as a tub, and eventually found a large wooden barrel. She rolled it to the showers, filled it with warm water, and then climbed in for a pleasant and leisurely soak. The greatest compliment she could offer anyone was the use of her private tub.

The lack of privacy in the latrines and showers was an embarrassing hardship especially for the older women, and many would take newspapers to hold over their faces or squares of cloth to tack up for their own private curtain. The Army, obviously ill-equipped to build living quarters for women and children, had made no attempt to introduce even the most common of life's civilities into these camps for us.

During the first few weeks of camp life everything was erratic and in short supply. Hot water appeared only sporadically, and the minute it was available, everyone ran for the showers or the laundry. We had to be clever and quick just to keep clean, and my sister and I often walked a mile to the other end of camp where hot water was in better supply, in order to boost our morale with a hot shower.

Even toilet paper was at a premium, for new rolls would disappear as soon as they were placed in the latrines. The shock of the evacuation compounded by the short supply of every necessity brought out the baser instincts of the internees, and there was little inclination for anyone to feel responsible for anyone else. In the early days, at least, it was everyone for himself or herself.

One morning I saw some women emptying bed pans into the troughs where we washed our faces. The sight was enough to turn my stomach, and my mother quickly made several large signs in Japanese cautioning people against such unsanitary practices. We posted them in conspicuous spots in the washroom and hoped for the best.

Across from the latrines was a double barrack, one containing laundry tubs and the other equipped with clotheslines and ironing boards. Because there were so many families with young children, the laundry tubs were in constant use. The hot water was often gone by 9:00 A.M. and many women got up at 3:00 and 4:00 in the morning to do their wash, all of which, including sheets, had to be done entirely by hand.

We found it difficult to get to the laundry before 9:00 A.M., and by then every tub was taken and there were long lines of people with bags of dirty laundry waiting behind each one. When we finally got to a tub, there was no more hot water. Then we would leave my mother to hold the tub while my sister and I rushed to the washroom where there was a better supply and carried back bucketfuls of hot water as everyone else learned to do. By the time we had finally hung our laundry on lines outside our stall, we were too exhausted to do much else for the rest of the day.

For four days after our arrival we continued to go to the main mess hall for all our meals. My sister and I usually missed breakfast because we were assigned to the early shift and we simply couldn't get there by 7:00 A.M. Dinner was at 4:45 P.M., which was a terrible hour, but not a major problem, as we were always hungry. Meals were uniformly bad and skimpy, with an abundance of starches such as beans and bread. I wrote to my non-Japanese friends in Berkeley shamelessly asking them to send us food, and they obliged with large cartons of cookies, nuts, dried fruit, and jams.

We looked forward with much anticipation to the opening of a half dozen smaller mess halls located throughout the camp. But when ours finally opened, we discovered that the preparation of smaller quantities had absolutely no effect on the quality of the food. We went eagerly to our new mess hall only to be confronted at our first meal with chili con carne, corn, and butterless bread. To assuage our disappointment, a friend and I went to the main mess hall which was still in operation, to see if it had anything better. Much to our amazement and delight, we found small lettuce salads, the first fresh vegetables we had seen in many days. We ate ravenously and exercised enormous self-control not to go back for second and third helpings.

The food improved gradually, and by the time we left Tanforan five months later, we had fried chicken and ice cream for Sunday dinner. By July tubs of soapy water were installed at the mess hall exits so we could wash our plates and utensils on the way out. Being slow eaters, however, we usually found the dishwater tepid and dirty by the time we reached the tubs, and we often rewashed our dishes in the washroom.

Most internees got into the habit of rushing for everything. They ran to the mess halls to be first in line, they dashed inside for the best tables and then rushed through their meals to get to the washtubs before the suds ran out. The three of us, however, seemed to be at the end of every line that formed and somehow never managed to be first for anything.

One of the first things we all did at Tanforan was to make our living quarters as comfortable as possible. A pile of scrap lumber in one corner of camp melted away like snow on a hot day as residents salvaged whatever they could to make shelves and crude pieces of furniture to supplement the army cots. They also made ingenious containers for carrying their dishes to the mess halls, with handles and lids that grew more and more elaborate in a sort of unspoken competition.

Because of my father's absence, our friends helped us in camp, just as they had in Berkeley, and we relied on them to put up shelves and build a crude table and two benches for us. We put our new camp furniture in the front half of our stall, which was our "living room," and put our three cots in the dark windowless rear section, which we promptly dubbed "the dungeon." We ordered some print fabric by mail and sewed curtains by hand to hang at our windows and to cover our shelves. Each new addition to our stall made it seem a little more like home.

One afternoon about a week after we had arrived at Tanforan, a messenger from the administration building appeared with a telegram for us. It was from my father telling us he had been released on parole from Montana and would be able to join us soon in camp. Papa was coming home. The wonderful news had come like an unexpected gift, but even as we hugged each other in joy, we didn't quite dare believe it until we actually saw him.

The fact that my father had retired from Mitsui two years before the war at the mandatory retirement age of fifty-five (many Japanese firms required early retirement to make room for their younger employees), his record of public and community service, and the affidavits from his friends were probably factors that secured his early release. As a parolee, he would have to account for every move he made until the end of the war and would not be able to leave government custody without a sponsor to vouch for him. But these restrictions didn't seem important at the time. The main thing was that he was coming home.

We had no idea when he would actually return, but the next day another messenger appeared to tell us that my father had already arrived and was waiting for us at the administration building.

My sister and I couldn't wait for Mama, and we ran ahead down the track to the grandstand. We rushed into the waiting room and saw my father waiting for us, looking thinner, but none the worse for wear.

"Papa!" we screamed, and rushed into his arms.

He had returned with two other men, and their families joined us in a grand and tearful reunion. We all had supper together at the main mess hall, and by the time we returned to our stall, word had spread that my father was home. Almost all of our many friends in camp stopped by that evening to welcome him home. It was pure joy and pandemonium as friends crowded into our tiny stall.

My father, a lively conversationalist as always, was brimming with stories of his five-month internment, and as our friends listened eagerly, the light burned in our stall long after the adjoining stalls had grown quiet and dark. From their own stalls our neighbors were listening, and one of them came the next day to tell us how much she had enjoyed my father's descriptions of life in Montana. She often listened to conversations that took place in our stall, sometimes coming later to ask about a point she had missed, or hurrying out from her stall when our friends left to see the face of a voice that had aroused her curiosity.

The night of my father's return was the first of many evenings spent in conversation with our friends as a reunited family. We may have been in a racetrack "assembly center" with four cots now crowded into a stall that had housed a single horse, but we were together once more, and that was something to be grateful for.

In the days following my father's return, we gradually heard more of what had happened to him after we left him at the Immigration Detention Quarters the day of our last visit. He and the other men transferred to Missoula had boarded buses for Oakland and then entrained for Montana. As the train moved northward, cars from Portland and Seattle were added to those from Los Angeles and Oakland, and my father later found many old friends in each contingent. The oldest man in the group was eighty-two.

It was a long forty-eight–hour ride on stiff straight-backed seats, with the blinds drawn day and night and armed guards at each exit. The men had been designated "dangerous enemy aliens" and every precaution was taken against their escape. They had been stripped of all their possessions, including handkerchiefs, and most of them traveled in the clothing they were wearing when so abruptly taken into custody. Some of the men had been apprehended on golf courses, others as they worked in their fields or as they came off their fishing boats. One man who had just undergone surgery for cancer of the stomach four days earlier had been taken directly from his hospital bed. During the course of the journey another man suffered a breakdown and his friends had to force a pencil between his teeth to keep him from biting his tongue.

Once they arrived in Missoula, the men were housed thirty to a barrack, with cots lining both sides of the room, army fashion. Here all the men, whatever their station in life, were treated alike as prisoners of war. Each was required to take his turn cleaning the barracks and latrines and working in the kitchen as waiter, cook, or dishwasher. My father, who had often helped my mother with some of her household chores, slipped easily into these new roles, rather enjoying the challenge they presented, but other men, who were more traditional Japanese husbands, found it difficult to perform what seemed to them demeaning tasks.

The men were encouraged to become self-governing, and shortly after their arrival, elected a mayor and various committee chairmen. It was typical of my father that he should be elected chairman of the welfare committee since he had had so much experience caring for the sick, the aged, and those in need. He made arrangements for meetings and speakers, and one of his first acts was to establish a church. He also organized and personally attended classes in English composition, grammar, American history, law, and even ballroom dancing, all of which were held daily and taught by internees versed in these subjects. In one of his letters he wrote, "You will be surprised to find me a good dancer when I come home!"

It was also his task to arrange funeral services for the men who died in Montana. The first was a seventy-four-year-old man who died of pneumonia. The second was the man who had been removed from the hospital following surgery. Because the remains of those who died were shipped home directly from the morgue, the interned men were permitted only to hold memorial services for them. Although many of the internees were strangers to each other, the deaths drew them all closer.

Out of the meager funds they were permitted to keep, they contributed generously to purchase flowers and candles for the services, sending the surplus to the families of the men who had died. Just as he often did at our church at home, my father sang a hymn at each of the services as his own special tribute.

All the internees' incoming and outgoing letters were subject to censorship, and many of my father's letters arrived well-ventilated with the holes left by the censor's scissors. Outgoing mail was restricted to three letters a week and my father, a great letter writer, was one of the first to be reprimanded. "I've been warned," he wrote us, "that I write too much and too long." He soon located an old typewriter which he borrowed for his letter writing to make life easier for the censors, and later had to limit his communications to brief telegrams which included such messages as, "Please give Kay freesia bouquet and hearty greetings on her birthday."

All paper was stripped from incoming packages to prevent the entry of illegal messages. Labels were removed from canned goods, wrapping removed from fruit, and boxes of chocolates were emptied on the counter so the paper cups could be discarded. The only way the men were allowed to retrieve the candy was to scoop it up in their caps, and receiving it in such a manner so diminished the joy of having it that my father soon asked us not to send any more.

It wasn't until the day before Christmas that their personal effects were released and my father could at last write with his pen instead of with a pencil. He was also allowed to have up to $15 of his cash. The government issued candy and nuts to the men, but our package was the only one that arrived in time for Christmas at my father's barrack, and he told us they saved every tag and string and scrap of wrapping paper to tack up on the walls for Christmas cheer.

Soon after the men arrived in Missoula, the temperature plunged to thirty below zero. Windows were coated with ice and giant icicles hung from the roof to the ground. The men, with their California clothing, were scarcely prepared for this kind of harsh weather and finally after a month the Army issued them some basic winter clothing. We had also spent many of our evenings knitting in order to rush some wool gloves, socks, and caps to Papa and his Mitsui friends, along with books, games, and candy. He thanked us many times for everything, saying they had warmed his heart as well as his person. "The other men envy me," he wrote, "and want me to stay here forever as long as I have such a nice family!"

Early each morning, the men gathered for group calisthenics, then they worked at their assigned tasks, attended classes, and maintained a disciplined, busy life. In the evenings, when there were no meetings, they often gathered around the coal stove in the center of each barrack to socialize.

On January 3, which was my parents' twenty-fifth wedding anniversary, we sent my father a wire with our love and good wishes. He immediately wired back, "Thanks for telegram. Extend my fondest greetings on our anniversary which almost slipped my mind as I was busy arranging seventeen speakers for tomorrow's services. Everybody well and happy. Regards to church friends. Love to all."

It sounded like Papa. We were glad to know he was keeping busy and well. Our wire, it seemed, had done more than remind him of his anniversary. It had also spread the news among his friends, and that night the men of his barrack gathered around their pot-bellied stove and had a fine party in his honor. They made Japanese broth by boiling water in an old kerosene can and then adding seasoning and squares of toasted rice cakes which had been sent to one of the men. Papa's friends from other barracks came to join in the celebration, and the ensuing festivities with much singing and speech-making touched and cheered my father immensely. He wrote us about the happy evening, and the fifty or more men who were at the party sent their greetings to my mother on the back of an old Christmas card. That card and news of the celebration in Montana gave my mother as much pleasure, I think, as the flowers from my sister and me.

All during the war years my father never forgot his friends who were not as fortunate as he and had to remain in the prisoner of war camps. They were eventually scattered to distant camps in New Mexico, Louisiana, North Dakota, and Ellis Island, and some men were moved so often that letters to them would return covered with forwarding addresses that had failed to locate them. The thought of their lonely lives in internment always saddened us.

Plate in hand,
I stand in line,
Losing my resolve
To hide my tears.

*

I see my mother
In the aged woman who comes,
And I yield to her
My place in line.

*

Four months have passed,
And at last I learn
To call this horse stall
My family's home.

YUKARI

Letters from a Justice Department Camp

Isohei Hatashita

As traumatic as the process of packing and evacuating was, some families suffered still more by the fact that many husbands and fathers were being detained in separate Justice Department camps. Some men arrested on December 7 disappeared for months or years; others were released after shorter periods of detention. Communication was limited to letter correspondence, which required special "Internee of War" stationery that was carefully scrutinized and censored by the federal government. The following letters were written by former Terminal Island, California, resident Isohei Hatashita as he was moved between a series of high-security camps to his family who were interned in Jerome, Arkansas. Although it was not his native language, Hatashita wrote his letters in English. While his use of English grammar is often incorrect, his warmth and love for his family shine through. The original letters are kept at the Japanese American National Museum in Los Angeles.

Fort Missoula, Montana
Feb. 9, 1942

Dear Wife Kazue Hatashita and family,
Yesterday as soon as I arrived Fort Missoula's camp I wired, so you know where I am now. This place is nice, not cold as I imagined even snow falled about eight inches deep last night. How are all family at home after I left? I am all right, don't worry. All officers are understanding our position, very kind, and treat us with sympathy.

It was wholesale eviction of alien Japanese fishermen in Terminal Island, far inland.

When we arrived Missoula, our group separated in three part, our group [censored] persons encamped at Missoula, last of other part of group gone for North Dakota. In the camp at Missoula are about [censored] Japanese. In one house forty persons are living and sleeping side by side. My bed,

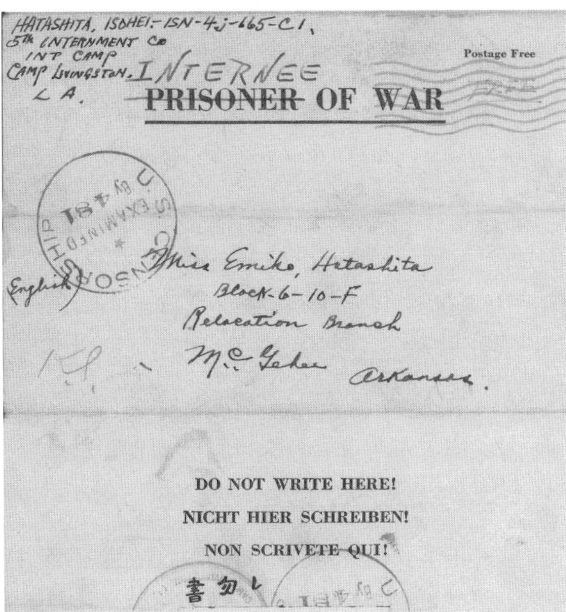

An envelope from Isohei Hatashita's mail from the Camp Livingston, Louisiana, Justice Department camp sent to his family interned in Arkansas clearly shows the censor's mark.

mattress, blankets are all new, so it's better than my twenty-years-old bed at home. [censored] I received my suits case. I want some more shirts my black shirts which I weared when I was fishing, jacket, safety razor, heavy kubimaki, looking glass, etc. [conclusion lost]

Fort Missoula, Montana
June 16, 1942

Dear daughter Emiko,
I have received you letter and glad to hear that everybody are well at there and doing fine, Kiyoko is getting fat and black with sunburn just as to see Negro fat girl is.

Emiko send me urgently your essay "To the Color" which you wrote and speached in public speaking contest when you were in high school. The hearing started, if my turn comes I want to show the hearing boards how our family's ideas is for United States of America.

Yes Emiko we will never see again our home at Island, it's past just as like a dream. Forget past and strive yourself make better and good home in future. Be good, take care,

Your father
Isohei Hatashita

5th Internment Co
Int. Camp
Camp Livingston, Louisiana
March 12, 1943

Dear daughters Emiko & Haruko,
It was fine day when you were here but after you left the weather is changed cloudy sky. [censored] I had in my mind lots of things to tell before you come but when we met, there was not be much to talk.

As soon as I came back my camp, I went physician and asked the cause that how makes spot (tonedo) on young girl's face.

He said that young age has tonedo naturally. Anyhow she has too much sugar therefore do not each much candy or sweet stuff and also fat. To take off them, take vitamin E. That is his advice so you better take and try vitamin E.

Haruko I am glad to hear your graduation and want to extend my hearty congratulations. I suppose that you are satisfied with the dress which

The husband-father of this small family was in a Justice Department internment camp. Denson, Arkansas, November 20, 1942. Photograph by Tom Parker.

Mother bought for your graduation. If I were in outside, surely I bought a million dollar-worth good one.

Be good,

your father
Isohei Hatashita

(P.S. Use lemon & drink lemonade clean internal organ all right)

Isohei Hatashita
Barrack -9
Santa Fe Detention Station
Santa Fe, New Mexico
July 9, 1943

Emiko Hatashita
Block-6-10-F
Relocation Branch
McGehee, Arkansas

Dear daughter Emiko & family,
I hearty thank your greeting card for my 62 birthday.

Last year I celebrate alone my birthday at Missoula drinking 7-up but this year I forgotten my birthday.

I know it by receiving your greeting card.

From Kimio Australia I have not heared.

General Douglas MacArthur moved on his headquarters to New Guinea and opened his offensive and is commanding his invasion forces and took Rendova Island and others on June 30 July 1, so I suppose that your brother T.Sgt. Kimio must be with the invasion forces. Tokyo claims that on the Redova Island fighting killed over ten thousands soldiers. So let us pray Kimio safety and luck.

New Mexico "in size it is the third largest state but the population is one of the smallest. Santa Fe is capital the oldest towns inhabited by white in America." [censored] The climate is very good. Ray is strong good for all patients especially [TB]. The few days we are having shower in afternoon. I am all right don't worry. Be care yourself.

Your father
Isohei Hatashita

Isohei Hatashita
Barrack -9
Santa Fe Detention Station
Santa Fe, New Mexico
Sep. 20, 1943

Emiko Hatashita
Block-6-10-F
Relocation Branch
Mc Gehee, Arkansas

Dear daughter Emiko,
Last Saturday evening 18th I received your special mail and also mother. To have good husband make your life happy one. On the contrary, if you had bad husband your future life will be unfortunate and miserable. So your definite decision for proposed marriage is very important matter to you. I wish that I could give you good advice and help what to do but I am sorry. I can't because I don't know his personality. I think everyone of us in our family does not know him very well, therefore you better confer the matter with Mother very carefully and I hope decide it. I have no objection for the decision you make. I will hearty appreciate you, you are big enough. I trust you that you will take good care yourself and know what you are doing. It is true and I feel same as I told you that you could marry to the person if he is Japanese and as long as you love him and he is healthy.

I have only worry and anxious in case you married to a soldier who is going sooner or later for battle front to fight. If there is long war and continue to fight years more every soldier must go front anyway. Your brother T.Sgt. Kimio who is now somewhere in South Pacific told us unless he is lucky never can't tell back home safely again. I think so too. I imagine that Kimio tried to marry before he goes front but they changed their mind after Yuriko went Minnesota. They reconsidered their marriage to postpone until Kimio got back home. I suppose that they have their promise that Yuriko will wait for Kimio.

CONCLUSION Dear loving daughter Emiko:

Please decide yourself with mother consent.

Inform Kaguya concerning of your marriage. He is only one to support and look after our family hereafter.

Your father
Isohei Hatashita

FROM Citizen 13660

Miné Okubo

Artist Miné Okubo was born in Riverside, California in 1912, the youngest of seven children. After receiving both her BA and MA, she won a traveling fellowship to study in Europe. Eighteen months later, the outbreak of fighting there forced her to return to California. At the time of evacuation, Okubo was working for the Federal Arts Project doing murals in mosaic and fresco for the Army in Oakland. Okubo and one of her brothers were evacuated together to the Tanforan racetrack for six months and then to Topaz, Utah, for one-and-a-half years. In Topaz, she taught art to children and worked as art editor for the camp newspaper and for Trek *literary magazine. "I was always busy. In the daytime I went around sketching. There wasn't any photographing allowed so I decided to record everything. Observing. I went around doing all these minute sketches of people and events. I didn't sleep much."*

In 1944, Okubo left camp for a job in New York for Fortune *magazine, where someone saw her camp ink-and-rice-paper sketches, and suggested that she write a book. However, she says, "It was so difficult getting it published. At that time anything Japanese was still rat poison." Her stunning drawings and narrative describing the internment experience were published as* Citizen 13660 *by Columbia University Press in 1946, making it the first book published in the United States by a Japanese American internee on the subject of internment.*

*

On warm days it was unbearable in the stalls and barracks. The stench of manure returned with the heat, and this in turn brought back the horseflies. Most of the people remained outdoors on such days, and usually I did too, but there were times when I kept on working inside.

Later, by the order of the medical authority, all windows in the stalls were hinged so that they could be opened.

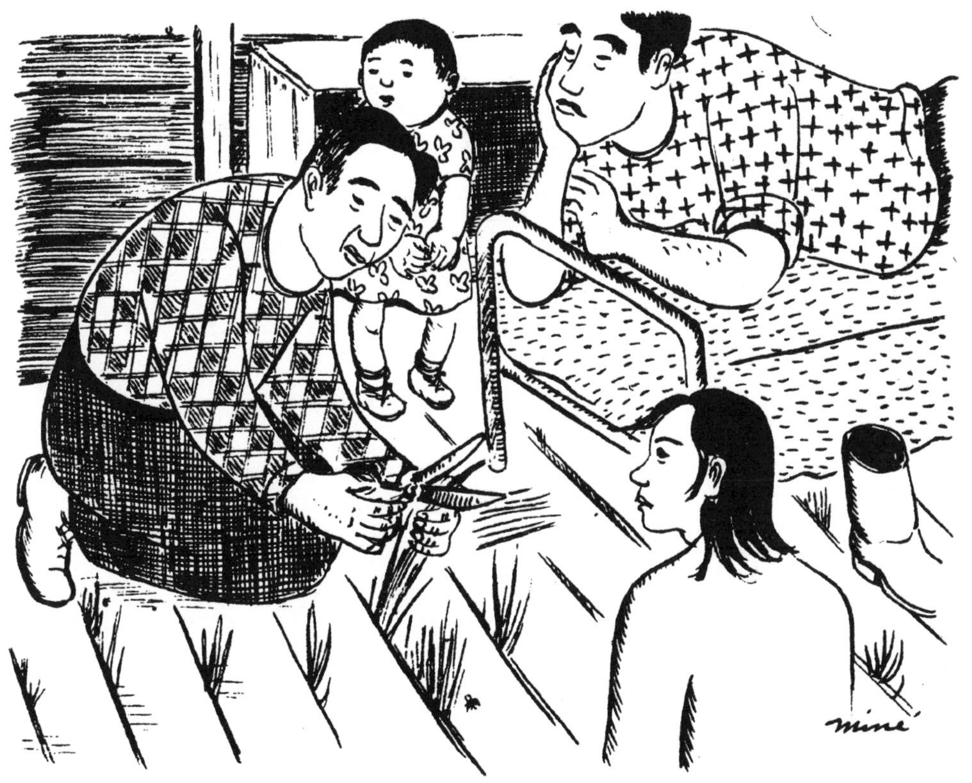

The warping of the new lumber left cracks in the floor half an inch to an inch wide. Through the cracks the tall grass came up.

There were two center-wide inspections at Tanforan. The first, on instructions from the Wartime Civil Control Administration in San Francisco, was entirely routine; it was made because the evacuees' baggage had not been thoroughly searched upon arrival. Potentially dangerous tools, such as saws and chisels, were confiscated, and Japanese phonograph records and literature were also taken away. (Bibles and religious books were later returned.)

The second inspection was conducted by the Army. At this time a still more thorough search was made. Each section was placed under guard while the search was conducted. Because of the quarantine sign on my door they almost passed me by.

We inferred from the inspections that we would be moved to a permanent center fairly soon.

Rumors about the site and date and conditions of the relocation were always arising in Tanforan to make a brief stir among the residents. But in August, relocation assumed the shape of reality in the minds of all.

Posts strung with chicken-wire appeared on the northeast corner of the camp near the back gate by the railroad siding. The entire area around the gate, including the laundry building and the toilets, was completely fenced off, leaving one section open.

Although there was no official word on specific details, residents were putting two and two together and arriving at the same conclusion—that we were going to a relocation center in Utah....

With about five hundred evacuees and fifty military police on board, the train started on its way at exactly 7:45 P.M. Our last glimpse of Tanforan Assembly Center brought smiles. Some of the residents had climbed to the stable roofs and were holding aloft huge bon voyage signs, as others waved good-bye to us.

The trip was a nightmare that lasted two nights and a day. The train creaked with age. It was covered with dust, and as the gaslights failed to function properly we traveled in complete darkness most of the night, reminding me of the blackout trains in Europe. All shades were drawn and we were not allowed to look out of the windows.

For many it was the first long journey. They were both excited and sad to leave California and the Bay region. To this day for many of them, the world is as large as from San Francisco to Tanforan to Topaz.

The first night was a novelty after four and a half months of internment. However, I could not sleep and spent the entire night taking the chair apart and readjusting it. Many became train sick and vomited. The children cried from restlessness. At one point on the way, a brick was thrown into one of the cars. The journey was otherwise uneventful. In the daytime we saw only barren desert lands of Nevada and Utah, for we had passed the beauty spots of California during the night.

I could forgive all other discomforts because of oranges and lemons. Boxes of them were set out in each of the coaches for the passengers. It was

In the late afternoon the train stopped in the desert somewhere in northern Nevada and for half an hour we were permitted to get off the train and walk around. Barbed-wire fences bounded the stretch on either side of the track and military police stood on guard every fifteen feet.

[continued from p. 93]
a precaution against illness on the train. The older people did not care for them, so I ate their share too.

The meals on the train were good after camp fare.

Restless from exhaustion, everyone was wakeful on the second night. Nothing functioned well on this old relic. The steam heat could not be turned off, so the car was overheated and stuffy. About two o'clock in the morning someone shouted, "The Great Salt Lake!" There was a general scramble to open the windows and look out. It was pitch black and I could see nothing, but I could hear the ripple of the water. An hour later the train pulled into the huge railroad station at Ogden. I have a dim recollection of seeing ice and water put on the train, but do not know how long we stopped here.

I was half awake when the train arrived at Salt Lake City. A small group of Japanese Americans had come to see their friends on the train. The big clock in the station indicated that it was already 4 A.M. We tried to sleep the rest of the morning.

The train arrived in Delta at eight o'clock, but we were all too tired to be excited. The captain of our car was fast asleep. Officials were darting about and there was some commotion. The Chief of Project Reports at Topaz came on board the train and handed to each of us the first copy of the *Topaz Times.* We chuckled as we read, "Topaz, Jewel of the Desert." The paper described the camp and gave instructions to the newcomers.

By this time the car captain was awake and was calling us to attention. We stepped out of the train and into the bus waiting alongside. Military police were on guard. When the bus was full, one of them got into the front seat. The driver stepped on the gas and the bus moved off.

FROM *Stray Clouds*

Toyo Kazato

When war broke in 1941, immigrant first-generation Japanese, or Issei, were still prohibited by law from becoming American citizens, forbidden to own land in California, and virtually powerless against discriminatory laws that affected their choices of marriage, jobs, and education. Toyo Kazato was born in Iwakuni, Japan in 1886 and arrived in the United States in 1906 at the age of nineteen. Prior to the war, she and her family farmed in Fresno, California. An educated woman, Kazato could communicate fluently in English, which many Japanese could not. Her language skills helped build the Japanese Congregational Church in Fresno. Through her poetry, she expressed the feelings of the Issei. Chigire gumo, *a collection of Kazato's poetry in Japanese, was published in Japan in 1965, and later translated into English as* Stray Clouds *by Ernie Kazato and Helen Hasegawa. Much of the longing in her work speaks of prewar days in the San Joaquin Valley and the inarticulate sadness of the war conflict that clung to the inner core of many Issei.*

PREFACE

Unlike my argumentative and gloomy self, my husband often jokes. He once said to me, "How impressive it would be to have a big gravestone when I die!... But instead of that expense, wouldn't it be better if you could collect all your scattered writings into a book. Why don't you do it!"...

I wonder in America
What have I to leave behind?
For these fifty years
I have lived
To the very limit of my strength.

These are my footprints as I have passed through a life which has tested the limits of my strength. I publish them with the prayer that my children will somehow find them useful.

The Will of Heaven and Earth

The will of heaven and earth says "trust,"
For most everything is solved
As time and days go by.

The will of heaven and earth says "forgive,"
The big heart
Embracing the whole creation!

The will of heaven and earth says "grow."
Do you see that even a tiny grass
In the fields is growing.

The will of heaven and earth tenderly heals.
Did you see that the cut end of a tree
Gradually heals?

Going to the Relocation Center

(December 1941, the war with Japan broke out. In July 1942 we were sent to Poston, Arizona to be confined).

Do they think I am
An enemy from today?
since the war has broken out?
What fierce stares people give me
All so suddenly!

As herd of sheep driven by
Swinging whips into their corral,
We are fenced behind barbed wire
With guard towers on the alert.

Where the scorpions sting
And the coyotes howl
Is this our temporal abode
Poston, Arizona, (Camp II)?

They say that beyond the woods
Where the water tank stands
Must be near the place
Where our brothers came yesterday

I can not help but weep
Thinking of our brothers
Who reached Camp II last night
During the raging storm.

They say those distant mountains
Are California mountains.
What a remote place
They have discarded us.

The sand and gravel fly.
The lightning flash and thunders roar,
And the barracks are shaken.
The people nearly lost their senses.

We knew it was to be
A desert in Arizona,
But we did not know
That we were going to be
Dazed by the burning sand storm.

If we lived long here
Where burning sands fly about,
Our tears will be all parched
And our nature will become wild.

Comforting each other saying
"Any way, another month,"
We noticed, it was
120 degrees again today!

Evening Glow

The distant mountains of cobalt blue,
The wilderness wrapped
In golden evening glow
For a moment I forgot
That I was in a desert.

It is very quiet tonight,
The breeze is gentle and soothing,
We are all out of doors
Counting the stars in amusement.

We are trying to sleep
Taking our cots out of doors
And gazing at the millions of stars above.
Even the Arizona desert is cool.

The sand is flying!
A storm is coming.
Everyone is shouting and rushing
Into the barracks with cots in their arms!

The chorus of thousands of crickets
Is in full swing at midnight
Where our dreams are easily broken
And we lay wide awake.

This Too, Is a Holy Place

The burning sun rays
And the hurling sand storm
Kept my ears deaf,
Even though many a time
I pleaded to listen.

The gentle cool breeze
Floating in the air this morn

Pleasant autumn is now here.
My feeling soothed, my mind serene
I feel the nearness of His Presence.

Since we came to Arizona
It's already three months.
At last I hear a wee Voice,
"This too is a Holy Place,
Take off your shoes."

The autumn sky is very high.
And the wild horses loud neighs.
Our boys are full of energy
They will turn this barren land
Into green and fertile fields.

The Storm Will Not Last Forever

The storm is raging,
The sand and gravel are flying.
On the way to our library work
We are almost blown off our feet.
Calling to each other,
Holding our hands together,
Clinging to each other,
We are almost blinded by the sandy gust.

It's like swimming in the ocean
Evading the tide of sandy gust.
Finally we have reached the library,
And my friend says in relief,
"How brave we have become!
We are accustomed to the storm now.
A year ago we would have shut ourselves
Watching in great fear from our barrack windows."

The storm is still raging outdoors!
The sand has blown in
Through the crevices of the barrack
And even through the coolers
Causing us to cough.
But we worked steadily,

Not even one flower could be found
In this desert!
So we made paper flowers to
Decorate the last rite of our friend.

We gathered together
And made a cross
Covered with white paper
To remember the one who passed away

The white cross reminds us
Of our friend's pure life,
And his faithful, devoted past.

He died alone in the desert,
But now, he sleeps peacefully,
Covered with the beautiful artificial flowers.

Persimmons

Wondering over the box
Sent by our American friends,
When opened, we found beautiful persimmons.

This American friend
Having pity on us in captivity
Sent us the persimmons,
Knowing that they are from Japan
And how attached to them we are.

This American who had lived
In Japan many years
Sent the beautiful persimmons
To us in captivity

We are still confined in the desert
And Autumn is nearly gone.
The persimmons are well ripened
Into such a beautiful color

In Fresno, where you would not
See a single Japanese, now,
The persimmon trees in many orchards
Must be heavy with beautiful ripened fruits.

New Year's Mochi, by Hisako Hibi. Oil on canvas, 17¼ x 21½ in. c. 1944.

FROM *Farewell to Manzanar*

Jeanne Wakatsuki Houston

Jeanne Wakatsuki Houston and her family were evacuated directly to Manzanar internment camp located in the Owens Valley of California. Farewell to Manzanar *is Houston's autobiographical account of her experiences before, during, and just after her family's internment, describing the heartbreaking details of survival in camp. She wrote the book with her husband, writer James D. Houston, and together they have won numerous awards.*

*

A Common Master Plan

I don't remember what we ate that first morning. I know we stood for half an hour in cutting wind waiting to get our food. Then we took it back to the cubicle and ate huddled around the stove. Inside, it was warmer than when we left, because Woody was already making good his promise to Mama, tacking up some ends of lath he'd found, stuffing rolled paper around the door frame.

Trouble was, he had almost nothing to work with. Beyond this temporary weather stripping, there was little else he could do. Months went by, in fact, before our "home" changed much at all from what it was the day we moved in—bare floors, blanket partitions, one bulb in each compartment dangling from a roof beam, and open ceilings overhead so that mischievous boys like Ray and Kiyo could climb up into the rafters and peek into anyone's life.

The simple truth is the camp was no more ready for us when we got there than we were ready for it. We had only the dimmest ideas of what to expect. Most of the families, like us, had moved out from southern California with as much luggage as each person could carry. Some old men left Los Angeles wearing Hawaiian shirts and Panama hats and stepped off the bus at an altitude of 4,000 feet, with nothing available but sagebrush and tarpaper to stop the April winds pouring down off the back side of the Sierras.

The War Department was in charge of all the camps at this point. They began to issue military surplus from the First World War—olive-drab knit caps, earmuffs, peacoats, canvas leggings. Later on, sewing machines were shipped in, and one barrack was turned into a clothing factory. An old seamstress took a peacoat of mine, tore the lining out, opened and flattened the sleeves, added a collar, put arm holes in and handed me back a beautiful cape. By fall dozens of seamstresses were working full-time transforming thousands of these old army clothes into capes, slacks, and stylish coats. But until that factory got going and packages from friends outside began to fill out our wardrobes, warmth was more important than style. I couldn't help laughing at Mama walking around in army earmuffs and a pair of wide-cuffed, khaki-colored wool trousers several sizes too big for her. Japanese are generally smaller than Caucasians, and almost all these clothes were oversize. They flopped, they dangled, they hung.

It seems comical, looking back; we were a band of Charlie Chaplins marooned in the California desert. But at the time, it was pure chaos. That's the only way to describe it. The evacuation had been so hurriedly planned, the camps so hastily thrown together, nothing was completed when we got there, and almost nothing worked.

I was sick continually, with stomach cramps and diarrhea. At first it was from the shots they gave us for typhoid, in very heavy doses and in assembly-line fashion: swab, jab, swab, *Move along now,* swab, jab, swab, *Keep it moving.* That knocked all of us younger kids down at once, with fevers and vomiting. Later, it was the food that made us sick, young and old alike. The kitchens were too small and badly ventilated. Food would spoil from being left out too long. That summer, when the heat got fierce, it would spoil faster. The refrigeration kept breaking down. The cooks, in many cases, had never cooked before. Each block had to provide its own volunteers. Some were lucky and had a professional or two in their midst. But the first chef in our block had been a gardener all his life and suddenly found himself preparing three meals a day for 250 people.

"The Manzanar runs" became a condition of life, and you only hoped that when you rushed to the latrine, one would be in working order.

That first morning, on our way to the chow line, Mama and I tried to use the women's latrine in our block. The smell of it spoiled what little appetite we had. Outside, men were working in an open trench, up to their knees in muck—a common sight in the months to come. Inside, the floor was covered with excrement, and all twelve bowls were erupting like a row of tiny volcanoes.

Mama stopped a kimono-wrapped woman stepping past us with her sleeve pushed up against her nose and asked, "What do you do?"

"Try Block 12," the woman said, grimacing. "They have just finished repairing the pipes."

It was about two city blocks away. We followed her over there and found a line of women waiting in the wind outside the latrine. We had no choice but to join the line and wait with them.

Inside it was like all the other latrines. Each block was built to the same design, just as each of the ten camps, from California to Arkansas, was built to a common master plan. It was an open room, over a concrete slab. The sink was a long metal trough against one wall, with a row of spigots for hot and cold water. Down the center of the room twelve toilet bowls were arranged in six pairs, back to back, with no partitions. My mother was a very modest person, and this was going to be agony for her, sitting down in public, among strangers.

One old woman had already solved the problem for herself by dragging in a large cardboard carton. She set it up around one of the bowls, like a three-sided screen. OXYDOL was printed in large black letters down the front. I remember this well, because that was the soap we were issued for laundry; later on, the smell of it would permeate these rooms. The upended carton was about four feet high. The old woman behind it wasn't much taller. When she stood, only her head showed over the top.

She was about Granny's age. With great effort she was trying to fold the sides of the screen together. Mama happened to be at the head of the line now. As she approached the vacant bowl, she and the old woman bowed to each other from the waist. Mama then moved to help her with the carton, and the old woman said very graciously, in Japanese, "Would you like to use it?"

Happily, gratefully, Mama bowed again and said, "Arigato. Arigato gozaimas. I will return it to your barracks."

"Oh, no. It is not necessary. I will be glad to wait."

The old woman unfolded one side of the cardboard, while Mama opened the other; then she bowed again and scurried out the door.

Those big cartons were a common sight in the spring of 1942. Eventually sturdier partitions appeared, one or two at a time. The first were built of scrap lumber. Word would get around that Block such and such had partitions now, and Mama and my older sisters would walk halfway across the camp to use them. Even after every latrine in camp was screened, this quest for privacy continued. Many would wait until late at night. Ironically, because of this, midnight was often the most crowded time of all.

Like so many of the women there, Mama never did get used to the latrines. It was a humiliation she just learned to endure: shikata ga nai. She would quickly subordinate her own desires to those of the family or the community, because she knew cooperation was the only way to survive. At the same time she placed a high premium on personal privacy, respected it in others and insisted upon it for herself. Almost everyone at Manzanar had inherited this pair of traits from the generations before them who had learned to live in a small, crowded country like Japan. Because of the first they were able to take a desolate stretch of wasteland and gradually make it livable. But the entire situation there, especially in the beginning—the packed sleeping quarters, the communal mess halls, the open toilets—all this was an open insult to that other, private self, a slap in the face you were powerless to challenge.

Photo Essay:
How I Spent the War

Life behind barbed wire had its many contradictions and for the internees, it was but another challenge to overcome. Many volunteered their services for a scant $12, $15, or $19 monthly salary as doctors, dentists, cooks, garbage collectors, stenographers, journalists, teachers, and block wardens. For some Issei, who spent years of zealous struggle to build a life in a new country, there came an ironic escape from the drudgery of their former lives. Hobby clubs and English language classes were organized, and for the youth, schools, sports, and activities were established. Cultivated gardens thrived and bloomed around barrack doorways.

All assembly centers and camps had community newspapers that were written, illustrated, and edited by internees who were supervised by WRA officers. The newspapers were in English with Japanese-language sections and were intended to keep evacuees informed of camp and outside activities. Of course there was censorship, both self-imposed and WRA-enforced.

In one of the more ironic turnabouts in the federal government's attitude, thousands of Nisei internees (Issei and Kibei were disqualified) were released and sent to work in sugar-beet farms in Utah, Idaho, Montana, and Wyoming to relieve a combined crisis of crop spoilage and shortage of farm labor. Most important to most internees was the need to escape camp and begin life on the outside again.

*

Pomona Assembly Center, 1942. Photographer unknown.

The assembly center, located in North Portland, was close enough for us to request a needed item or small treats from our friends. Mrs. Nelson, loaded down with two shopping bags full of cheese and cracker snacks, peanut butter, jelly, and Oreo cookies, visited us on her days off from the shipyards. She rode three buses and walked several blocks to reach the center. On one particular visit, I spied a basket of glistening strawberries in one of the grocery bags. My mouth watered.

Kiyoko carefully parceled the red jewels to each member of the family. We inhaled the sweet, tangy fragrance, and ate small bites to tantalize our taste buds and make the moment last. We kept saying, "Yumm, oooh, aaah," until no trace of the strawberries was left. Toward the end of the visit, Mrs. Nelson began to weep. Through her tears, she asked, "Why are they doing this to you? How can they do this to you? You are American citizens, born right here in Portland. It's wrong, all wrong. What is going to happen to you?"

We sat silently. We had no answers, but the memory of strawberries red and unreachable.

Sato Hashizume

Manzanar, California, April 2, 1942. Photograph by Clem Albers.

Now, after two years,
Everyone can distinguish
The sound of his own mess hall gong.
ANONYMOUS

For a few months our diet at first consisted of brined liver—salted liver. Huge liver. Brown and bluish in color weighing up to twenty pounds and would bounce if dropped.
JAMES GOTO

Laundry facility. Santa Anita, 1942. Photographer unknown.

Existing without barriers
between rich and poor
isn't it hot awfully hot?
Ryokuin Matsui

Issei men playing go, a game of military strategy and keen wits. Heart Mountain, Wyoming, January 4, 1943. Photograph by Tom Parker.

Since the day of internment
Sitting on his ass
The go player
SASABUNE

Granada, Colorado, March 6, 1943. Photograph by Pat Coffey.

If you're a teenager, you live like a teenager. You don't spend your time moping around wondering why you're there, or saying, "This is a terrible injustice." It's true, it's an injustice. But you don't dwell on it. You make the best of it.

Jerry Enomoto

An evacuee from Granada internment camp volunteers for beet topping. Keensburg, Colorado, November 5, 1942. Photograph by Tom Parker.

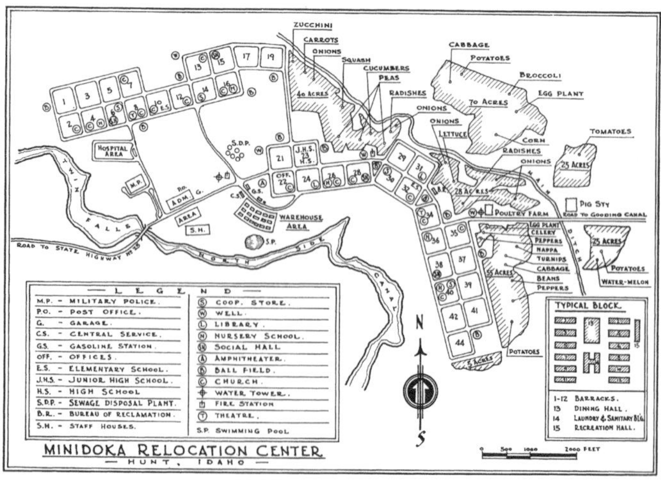

Minidoka internment camp and crops. Minidoka, Idaho, 1944.

Tule Lake, California, November 5, 1942. Photograph by Francis Stewart.

Granada, Colorado, December 13, 1942. Photograph by Tom Parker.

I used to do watercolor paintings. I don't think I ever finished one of them. I don't know whether it was unconsciously deliberate or not. There was always this big question mark. Who are we? What are we doing here? I shouldn't be out here painting pretty pictures. There's more to be said than that.

Yosh Kuromiya

Camp Harmony composite, by Kenjiro Nomura. Watercolor, 24 x 19 in. 1942.

Working on the *Tulean Dispatch* newspaper: Dick Kurihara, Martha Mizuguchi, Mas Inada. Newell, California. November 2, 1942. Photograph by Francis Stewart.

The first baby was born in camp last Monday. I wonder what it will be named. We got the news too late to headline it in the paper so had to box it in one corner. Taro certainly is having a headache with the paper. Everything has to be read and "OK-ed" by the front office. They are cautious to the nth degree.... K. says that the administration is very sensitive about radicalism or unfavorable publicity; I think that he has pretty good information that a sample of the outgoing mail is censored, but I hardly think that this is true. There are bound to be mistakes made, but they shouldn't be afraid of that as long as they are sincere. W. H. and some others write directly to WRA with their complaints and they seem to think that they get immediate action. It would be much better if they were frank with the administration here and took their problems to them; I'm sure that they would give it consideration—if they had time. Notice was issued today that no notice could be placed on any bulletin board without an official "OK." Reason??

Charles Kikuchi

A Far Country: Poems from the Arkansas Camps

While most of the camps were located in bleak deserts, two of the camps—Jerome and Rohwer—were established on swampy areas in distant Arkansas. These locations suffered bitter cold in the winter and sticky heat in the summer. Internees at the Arkansas camps were predominately from the San Joaquin Valley of California and included members of the two free verse poetry clubs, Valley Ginsha Haiku Kai of Fresno and the Delta Ginsha of Stockton. Despite the uprooting of the Japanese American community, these two clubs, led by haiku masters Neiji Ozawa and Kyotaro Komuro, survived and were active within the internment camps.

Haiku is a traditional Japanese verse form, usually written in three-line stanzas with a 5-7-5 syllable pattern. The free-verse haiku written by the internees abided by the traditional seasonal observations but did not restrict itself to a strict syllabic count.

Reading haiku has been described as having to "fill in the blanks and capture the emotion not spelled out in words." The free-verse haiku included here were translated from the Japanese and compiled by poet Violet Kazue Matsuda de Cristoforo in a extraordinary anthology of internment camp kaiko haiku entitled May Sky, There Is Always Tomorrow: An Anthology of Japanese American Concentration Camp Kaiko Haiku, *published in 1997 by Sun and Moon Press.*

*

Hearing sound of train
—AWAKE—
this endless night

TOKUJI HIRAI

Autumn foliage
California has now become
a far country

Yajin Nakao

Low cotton plants
black pickers
harvesting crop

Konan Ouchida

Friends leave one by one
autumn sun
sets behind forest

Tojo Fujita

Stepping on muddy shoe print
winter trees
yet standing

Honjyoshi Kunimori

Frosty night
listening to rumbling train
we have come a long way

Senbinshi Takaoka

FROM *To the Stars*

George Takei

Actor George Takei, a veteran of both stage and screen, is best known for his portrayal of Mr. Sulu in the television series Star Trek. *However, most fans are unaware of Takei's years spent as a child in desolation at the Rohwer, Arkansas, and Tule Lake, California, internment camps with his family. In 1994, Takei recounted his childhood internment memories in his book,* To the Stars: The Autobiography of George Takei.

CHILL WIND OF TULE LAKE

Tule Lake was—and is—a cold, windswept, dry lake bed near the northern California-Oregon border. It was the bleakest opposite of Rohwer. Where the southern Arkansas air was lush and sultry in the summertime, while crisp and invigorating in the winter, Tule Lake's higher elevation, at four thousand feet above sea level, always made the air sharp and biting, with a cold that in winter could plunge down to bone-chilling frigidity. Instead of the soft dust of Rohwer, here there was gritty gravel and cutting little shards of hard fossils and rocks. From verdant Rohwer, we had come to a harsh landscape barren of any foliage except for the spiny tumbleweeds that rolled aimlessly around the stark, flat surface. The only landmark was Castle Rock, a great brown abalone shell of a mountain that loomed bleak and solitary to the east.

Camp Tule Lake was an internment camp converted into a maximum-security segregation camp for "disloyals," those who had responded No-No to the key questions on the Loyalty Questionnaire, or those who had applied for repatriation or expatriation to Japan, or those whose loyalty was questionable "in the opinion of the Project Director." The barbed wire fence and guard towers were here, too, but unlike Rohwer, the fence was heavy wire mesh and "man-proof." The guard towers were turrets equipped with machine guns. The outer perimeter was patrolled by a half-dozen tanks and armored Jeeps. The guards were battle-ready troops at full battalion strength. All this bristly armament was positioned to keep imprisoned a people who had been goaded into outrage by a government blinded by hysteria. Half of the 18,000 internees in Camp Tule Lake were children like me.

I liked our barrack in our new Block 80. It was right across the way from the mess hall. To an always-hungry six-year-old, it was great to be just a short dash through the cold to the noisy warmth and comfort of food. But Mama hated it. She didn't like the loud clanging and banging from the kitchen that began in early morning with the preparation for breakfast and continued on until the last cleanup after dinner. She didn't like the idea of people lining up just outside our windows three times a day, every day. But most of all she complained bitterly about the smell that blew across from the kitchen—the lingering aroma of mass cooking, combined with detergents and other chemicals from the dishwashing and the acrid smell of disinfectants from the hosing down of the floor after dinner. "Stink terrible," was Mama's simple summation of the problem.

Daddy was philosophical. He said that was the trade-off. Here at Tule Lake, we had two rooms. Each room individually was smaller than the one we had at Rohwer, but combined, we had more space. We now had what we could call a bedroom and a living room.

"What trade-off?" Mama persisted. "Now toilet so far away. Children can't go so far in cold." She was right about that. Sometimes it was sheer torture dashing through the wind, muscles tightly held, to the latrine. There were occasions when I didn't think I could make it in time. I would barely get there, frenzy in my eyes, jumpy with tension, just on the verge of

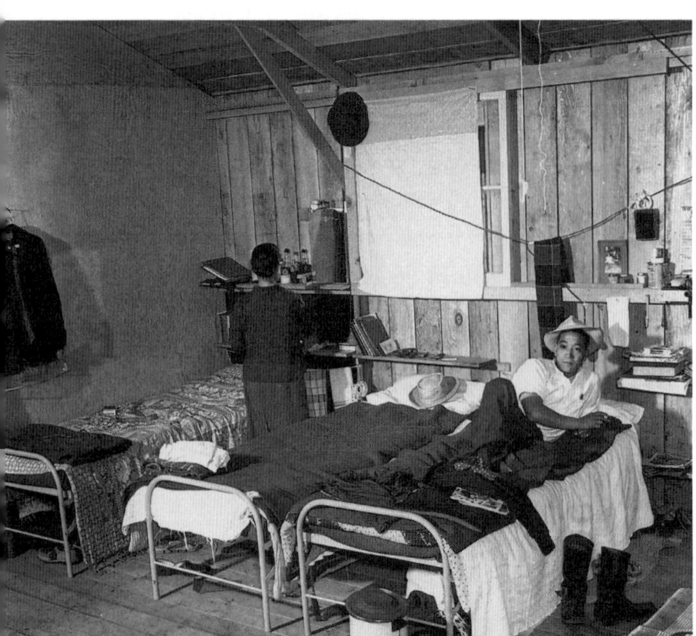

Barracks interior. Salinas Assembly Center, March, 1942. Photograph by Clem Albers.

Between ceiling slats
And thick electric
wires
Dawn comes through
unhindered
Kyotaro Komuro

bursting. Fortunately, I never had an accident, though Henry did. That was when Mama started collecting big coffee cans, which she kept in the bedroom for us kids.

There was another reason I liked being across from the mess hall. Life in camp was usually boring and monotonous. But the mess hall was the social focal point and cultural center of the block. We were closer and had better access to those great special events.

Sometimes, after dinner, movies were shown in the mess hall. A big white sheet would be hung up at one end and a bulky, black projection machine set up at the opposite end. Because we were right across the way, we always had the best seats. I saw Paul Muni in *Scarface,* Bette Davis in a movie where she suffered a lot, and the *Gangbusters* serials. Of them all, I remember Charles Laughton most vividly as the tragic monster in *The Hunchback of Notre Dame.* The movie was a transporting experience. I empathized with, of all things, this love-starved, deformed cripple whom people scorned and insulted. I discovered the fascinating world of old Paris through his pathetically misshapen eyes. I ached when he pined. I hurt when he agonized. And his final plummet down the tower of Notre Dame with the bells banging and clanging was unforgettably terrifying. I discovered the mind-expanding, world-extending, emotion-exhausting joy of the movies in the mess hall across from our tar-paper barrack.

At other times, we saw old Japanese movies about samurai and ninja and tear-jerking contemporary stories about long-suffering mothers and widows. Apparently, the sound track on some of these Japanese movies was missing. When that happened, a man from another block who specialized in these things would come and sit at the bottom of the screen. He had a dimly lit script in front of him, and he would narrate in Japanese what we were seeing on the screen. Not only did he narrate, but he played all the speaking roles as well. He would do the deep voice of the gruff samurai, then immediately become the crystalline-voiced princess, then the cackling old crone—all matching, the fast-moving drama on the screen.

At exciting high points in the movie, like a sword fight scene, he had bamboo clappers that he would slap rhythmically and his assistant would crash small cymbals. The cymbals made drama-heightening "chang" sounds and the clappers a rippling "bara-bara" sound, matching and energizing the swordplay on screen. The old folks called all samurai sword-fighting epics "chambara" movies, and I could see why. Whenever the swords started to fly, the "chang" and "bara-bara" sounds filled the mess hall.

I found the performance of the narrator completely mesmerizing. With his voice alone, he became so many different people; he suffered anguish, experienced joy, provoked fear, and stirred so many emotions—wonderfully. After the movie, I asked Daddy how one man could become so many people and experience so much. He told me these people are called benshi. In the old days in Japan when movies had no sound, these benshi provided the aural dramatic accompaniment, making the silent movies talk. He told me that a good benshi in those days was considered an artist equal to actors. I said, "I think the man we saw tonight is an artist." Daddy agreed.

Daddy was again elected block manager of our new Block 80 at Tule Lake. And again we lost him to meetings, pressing matters, and crises. And Mama again began the work of making a home for us—this time from two rooms. The living room windows got new curtains, of course, but now we had an extra bed in the living room, for which Mama made matching cover and pillows. It became our sitting couch. And she found beauty even in the tumbleweeds that rolled around outside. Mama brought them in and made austerely elegant arrangements.

Cold wind would blow up through the spaces in the floorboards and the open knots in the wood planks. Daddy covered the knotholes using lids from empty tin cans. The one luxury appointment of the living room we owed to the cracks between the floorboards. To cover them up, Daddy and Mama went to the camp canteen many blocks away and bought a square of blue linoleum spangled with white stars. It was so shiny and smooth. Henry and I loved sliding on it in our stocking feet, and Reiko shrieked with delight when Daddy pulled her around on the slippery linoleum floor. In the limited space of the other room that became our bedroom, there was no possibility of esthetic arrangement. It was jammed with five beds lined up side by side. But Mama made absolutely sure of one thing. None of the beds were kita makura—pillows to the north. This was bad luck. In Japan, dead people were laid out with their heads to the north, she told us. All of our pillows were laid to the south. Daddy was farthest away, then Mama, then a little space for entry from the living room, then in reverse birth order Reiko, Henry, and me. I was oldest so I was the farthest away from Daddy and Mama. And I had the window over me. I could stand on my bed and look out on the back side of the next barrack. The curtain over Daddy's window on the opposite side was always drawn closed. That was the side that faced the mess hall.

*

A Visit from Superman

In the 1940s, Superman was a popular comic strip appearing in daily newspapers across the country. In an episode that lasted nearly two months—from June 28, 1943 to August 21, 1943—the "Man of Steel" visited an internment camp. On June 28, Superman, in his guise as Clark Kent, reporter, and Lois Lane are sent to report on the conditions at camp. Here they are met by a square-jawed officer, Major Munsey, who shows them around and explains how kindly the inmates are being treated, how the Japanese have their own schools and newspapers, and how they are allowed to work at worthwhile projects. The government, explains Major Munsey, "has done all but lean over backwards in its desire to be humane and fair." Lois Lane is suitably impressed and notes that the government of Japan should be showing its prisoners of war similar kindness and good treatment. Clark Kent, however, has the advantage of X-ray vision and detects trouble brewing: he has seen a group of villainous-looking Japanese plan an escape, and are about to take pretty Lois Lane and the good Major Munsey as hostages.

We sincerely regret that we are unable to run an excerpt from this comic strip, and that DC Comics alone among the publishers whom we queried, was adamant in refusing us permission to reprint sensitive material. We did our best to explain that the material would be used in historical context, and that we felt its inclusion would fill out an understanding of the era. DC Comics' response, however, was that the company had a huge investment in Superman—in its "character, trademarks, logos, and related indicia"—and they would not allow us to reprint even a portion of the material.

Permission refused. Courtesy of DC Comics.

A Teacher at Topaz

Eleanor Gerard Sekerak

Eleanor Gerard Sekerak, a native Californian still living in the Bay Area, graduated from the University of California, Berkeley, prior to taking up a teaching assignment at Topaz. She was one of several hundred Caucasians who entered one of the ten internment camps as professionals, working in such diverse fields as medicine, administration, security, and of course, education. When the evacuees arrived at the assembly centers and later at the internment camps, the education program was little more than a promise. In the first few weeks the students sat on the floor with little or no equipment such as textbooks or laboratory and shop supplies. Now retired after thirty years as a social studies teacher and counselor at Hayward High School, Sekerak works in historic preservation. "A Teacher at Topaz" was first published in a groundbreaking collection of essays on the wartime incarceration, Japanese Americans: From Relocation to Redress.

I was teaching a criminology class at San Francisco City College when a field trip took us to observe a camp set up at Sharps Park by the Immigration and Naturalization Service after Pearl Harbor. This was my first contact with internment. Other contacts quickly followed: I volunteered time as an interviewer for those Oakland residents of Japanese ancestry who wished to move east before the "freeze" date set for evacuation. A hastily assembled crew worked all day and late into the night, checking destination addresses and writing travel passes. By midnight, March 29, 1942, long lines of Japanese Americans were still standing outside waiting to be processed. Dramatically, an Army officer strode in, climbed up to a huge wall clock, set the hands at 11:55 P.M. and announced, "Ladies and gentlemen, it will remain this time until you are finished—please proceed." By 4 A.M., all those who planned to relocate voluntarily had been processed and the Army gallantly escorted the weary interviewers home. For me, the evacuation had become real.

The next event, a few days later, made it even more personal. In a graduate class on the UC Berkeley campus, the professor unexpectedly informed us that one of our colleagues would be giving his final oral presentation early. Hiro Katayama bade us farewell and left the classroom—his destination Tanforan. He had stayed in class until the last possible moment on Friday, April 3.

A number of Nisei students attended Technical High School in Oakland, the location of my second supervised teaching assignment. Faculty members worried aloud about their Nisei students. What would happen, especially to the seniors removed from classes before the end of the semester? What about their plans for college? I had no Nisei in my class, but during hall duty I occasion had to admonish, almost daily, a youngster who always dashed by as though on roller skates. Once while reminding him not to run in the halls, I asked his name. "Bill Oshima," he told me.

The halls seemed very quiet after evacuation. From neither the teachers nor the students did I hear any anti-Nisei sentiment; no one identified the "enemy" with our students.

At last, the semester ended and evaluation and interviews occupied my days. One of California's most prestigious districts accepted my application for a teaching position and told me that a contract would be mailed later in the summer. That settled, I happily departed for the summer as a counselor at Camp Sunset in Bartlett, Illinois, near Chicago.

However, the teaching contract did not arrive and, finally, I wrote my dean asking him to inquire. Back came his regrets, informing me that the district had decided to hire a man. This was long before the days when one could rush into court claiming discrimination!

As I wondered what to do next, a telegram arrived from Lorne Bell, formerly a YMCA executive in the Los Angeles area and then a regional supervisor for the National Youth Administration. During the early summer of 1942, he had left the NYA to work for the War Relocation Authority [WRA]. His wire read, "If you have not signed a contract, will you consider a position at Topaz, Utah. We are in desperate need of teachers." When Camp Sunset closed, I took a crowded wartime train home, was processed for civil service employment in the San Francisco Western Regional Office of the WRA, packed, and caught a train for Utah, arriving there October 1.

It was my good fortune to have supportive, liberal-minded parents not overly concerned with public opinion. They not only encouraged me but later sent to Topaz cartons of pencils, paper, chalk, crayons, tacks, and other things necessary for a classroom but in short supply in our early days. Occasionally, a package would be stamped "Contents examined or acceptability verified under Order No. 19008 at Station B, Oakland, Calif."

I never did learn what the postal inspectors were actually looking for, but evidently FBI "clearances" were run on all WRA employees, for reports of these came trickling to us from the hometowns of staff members. My father, an electrician, was working on the Manhattan Project at UC Berkeley, all unknowing of what that was to mean! My brother, a machinist and engineer, was a civilian employee at the Mare Island Navy Yard. Both of them had security clearances, clearances that involved the FBI talking to our neighbors. When yet a third FBI check was circulated concerning the Gerard family, Mother lost her sweet disposition and gave the agent who called on her a frank opinion of such a waste of taxpayers' money. Two FBI men who were in almost full-time residence at Topaz during our first year reported my mother's interview to me with much amusement.

I had no illusions about what I would find at Topaz; Lorne Bell had warned, "This is an internment camp with barbed wire and military police." The advice at the San Francisco office of the WRA had been, "Take warm clothes; Utah winters are cold at 4,700 feet." And further, "Don't expect gourmet meals—you'll eat mass cooking in a staff dining hall." The preceding three months as a camp counselor proved good preparation for dorm life.

Mr. and Mrs. Bell met my train at Delta, Utah, a small Mormon town with wide streets surrounded by alfalfa fields. Delta was an oasis in the midst of the alkali Pahvant Desert, part of prehistoric Lake Bonneville. On the seventeen-mile drive from Delta to Topaz, the Bells alerted me to two conditions I never did become accustomed to: dust storms and the sticky, slippery mud that followed rain. With a sudden crack of wind, the dust storms seemed to whirl up and around in blinding fury, leaving a talcum-like film on everything—clothes, hair—even sifting into clenched mouths and gritting between teeth! One simply learned to endure dust and mud. However, other aspects of the high desert country made up for the unpleasant ones—the wonderful silhouette of Mt. Swazey on the horizon, the enticing sparkle of Topaz Mountain, the clarity of the stars at night, and the scent of sage after rain.

Despite our location in the middle of an alkali desert, we did enjoy one great advantage—we didn't displace any local residents. We were made to feel as welcome as was possible under the distressing conditions. We experienced none of the really nasty episodes that plagued some of the other centers, and I personally credit the basic goodness of our neighboring Mormon residents.

Within hours of arriving at the staff women's dorm, my trunk was delivered by a crew of young men, one of whom shrieked upon seeing me and dropped the trunk on his toes. It was my hall-runner from Technical High. He dashed away shouting, "Guess who's here? That strict teacher from Tech!" By noon, the whole of Topaz knew that a California teacher had arrived.

Charles Ernst, an experienced settlement-house director from Boston, dignified and imposing but warm and considerate, was our first project director. He was an excellent administrator, undaunted by the bureaucratic paperwork from Washington. With a deep concern for human values, Mr. Ernst kept representatives of the community in touch with developments.

Evening meetings to introduce new staff were one procedure. Never was an ordinary teacher made to feel more welcome. People crowded around to ask questions, shake hands, bow, and thank me for being there. When questioners learned that I was from Oakland and from UC Berkeley, out of the crowd emerged classmates from University High and a smiling Hiro Katayama who had told us "good-bye" only six months before. Thus on my first day there were three meshings with past experiences.

The next day those teachers who had already arrived met with the administrators and other faculty. For some months I was the only California-credentialed teacher, giving me enormous prestige with the resident families. This standing also gave me an "instant" tool for discipline: I had only to remark to a reluctant student, "Homework not done? I think I'll stop to talk with your folks on the way home," to see an immediate transformation to eager scholar.

Most of our first-year teachers were trained in Utah; at that time a fifth year of college for secondary credentials was not required in Utah. For this reason, the Topaz residents felt shortchanged and worried about their children's academic preparation. However, our superintendent, a Utah native, had a Ph.D. from the University of California, Berkeley, and this mollified the parents. "Appointed," i.e., U.S. Civil Service, faculty were augmented by the resident staff, many of whom had excellent backgrounds but were without formal teacher-training credits. Hiro Katayama joined us in this capacity, having been recruited by Henry Tani. Henry, himself a graduate of Stanford University in business administration, became our administrative assistant. He had organized the high school at the Tanforan Assembly Center and would later become a national staff member with the United Church of Christ.

The first Sunday at Topaz arrived and, at breakfast, the appointed staff idly talked about their plans for the day. I was the only one at my table planning to go to church. I was told, "The only church is the one the residents have." "I know," I said, "but since I went to the Rev. Tsukamoto's church in San Francisco, why not here?" As an active Episcopalian in Berkeley and in Oakland, I had met many Bay Area clergymen. So, seated on a makeshift bench in the first row of a tar-paper "rec hall," I listened to Rev. Tsukamoto's sermon and to Goro Suzuki (who later became television's Jack Soo) sing "The Lord's Prayer." During the three years at Topaz, only a few of the appointed staff attended the evacuee church.

This common commitment brought the rich rewards of deep and lasting friendships with the Nisei whom we came to love and admire. There is a special quality to these friendships, both among staff and evacuee—whenever we meet, we pick up where we left off the last time we visited. (In 1946 I married the man I went to church with that first day, one of the staff who came from Ohio to work in the consumer co-ops.)

The school buildings were far from complete when I arrived. A half-block of barracks at each end of the project was to house the two elementary

Tule Lake, California, November 4, 1942.
Photograph by Francis Stewart.

Dear Lawson,
2 Ys U R,
2 Ys U B,
I C U R
2Ys 4 Me!
YOUR FRIEND,
BOBBY

Dear Lawson,
I meet you early,
I meet you late
I meet you at
Amache Gate!
ALWAYS,
NAOMI

schools, called "Mountain View" and "Desert View." Block 32, midway in the camp, constituted the six-year high school with a total anticipated enrollment of 1,720. Residents were arriving from Tanforan as fast as barracks could be built. Priority for the available carpenter time was to go to the elementary schools; volunteer labor sped up high school construction—the students and teachers all fell to. Alumni still laugh at the memory of Miss Gerard, teetering precariously on a wobbly table, holding a sheetrock slab with both arms while hammer-wielding students banged nails on each edge—and presto, a ceiling!

As soon as the barracks were winterized, huge "pot belly" stoves were moved into the middle of a room, tables and benches brought in to accommodate thirty-six students, and we were in business—it was October 26, 1942. The lack of supplies was desperate, so a phone call to my mother (and we waited hours to place a wartime call) resulted in her calling my former teachers at University High. Thanks to their efforts outdated "surplus" texts began to arrive. "History is history, government is government," I sternly told my juniors and seniors, "you don't need a brand-new book!" Thus were we launched on an idealistic curriculum designed for us by a summer-session graduate class in curriculum development at Stanford University.

The curriculum began with the concept of the "community school," that is, the school is looked upon as an extended home, the community furnishing observations and opinion. This approach proved most valuable for students in the vocational area, and some of our students (those over sixteen years) were soon spending half their time in apprentice training or work experience. The schools in all relocation centers were to be affiliated with, and to meet the standards of, the states in which they were located. Utah had long been active in the vocational education field, so advisory committees were organized and planning help generously given. Consultants from the state board of education and even the board itself visited us.

The curriculum designed for us was based on a "core" of general education in agriculture, commercial, or college preparatory, and, in addition, a guidance program in which every teacher was expected to have a role. Our sequential theme for the entire school system was to be "Adaptation of Our Socioeconomic Arrangements to the Control and Direction of Technological Development." We were provided with illustrations of how to adapt this theme to the various grades, e.g., in grade one, "How can the yard at school be made more useful and beautiful?" In reality, the yard was dust (or mud) with huge piles of coal, and not a leaf could be coaxed from that alkali soil. In grade eleven, it was suggested, "How may the community take advantage of improved transportation and communication to make better living conditions for its people?" Our transportation consisted of walking the gravel roads of a one-mile square; no one went to Delta unless by special pass and by riding in an army truck.

In the beginning, faculty meetings were an exercise in how to tolerate frustration, as we wrestled with the "how to" of a core curriculum in a community school with few supplies and practically no library. Then we ran into opposition from the community itself—the parents did not want an experimental curriculum. They wanted their children to be prepared for college and to lose no academic ground because of the evacuation. So, with apologies to Stanford's Professor Paul Hanna, we modified the curriculum procedures by combining social studies and English as the "core" for the 1942–43 school year.

The first semester we covered federal, state, county, and city government and administration. An update on the creation and administration of wartime agencies was included. Then an intensive study of the WRA calling our project a "federally created municipality" followed. Staff members came to class to discuss the various phases of the administration of Topaz, and students took field trips and participated in an actual week of work experience in one phase of the community.

In May 1942 our community participation took a very active form when all seniors and their teachers went into the fields to plant onions and celery in areas of tillable ground scattered beyond the alkali deposits. Thereafter, whenever crooked celery stalks appeared on mess hall tables, much merriment ensued concerning whose responsibility it was to have produced such a deformity.

The second semester each student decided on the town in which he wished to resettle, and we set up a community survey of this locality and state. Using a Russell Sage publication, *Your Community* by Joanna Colcord, they sent for materials (writing model letters), did primary and secondary research, and wrote a term paper in college manuscript form summing up their results. At a recent reunion, there was amusement as alumni recounted that they had arrived at their chosen resettlement destinations knowing more than the natives.

Underlying all this was my personal determination that standards of behavior and of learning and performance were in no way to be lessened. As I faced my first day I wondered how I could teach American government and democratic principles while we sat in classrooms behind barbed wire! I never ceased to have a lump in my throat when classes recited the Pledge of Allegiance, especially the phrase, "liberty and justice for all."

In our opening discussion, the students and I agreed that the whole evacuation process had been traumatic but could not last forever—and we could not permit academic achievement to be interrupted. So they arrived at class on time, with homework completed, worked diligently, took their exams, and otherwise observed normal classroom standards. (We had one exception: the day the first snow fell, the California Bay Area students and their teacher rushed to the window to watch.) All the normal life of a typical high school was set up: school chorus, student newspaper, yearbook, student government, drama, athletics, dances, and the usual senior week activities. Borrowing caps and gowns graciously loaned by the University of Utah, 218 seniors marched across the dusty windswept plaza to outdoor graduation exercises on June 25, services complete with an invocation and a begowned faculty.

Just as we thought we were settling down to a stable community, there was an uproar in the news media outside the camps over student resettlement, Nisei registration for the draft, and the anti-administration incidents at the Manzanar, Poston, and Tule Lake centers. As a consequence, "applications for leave clearance" to permit evacuees to go farther east were combined with registration of every man of military age into a single questionnaire. The controversial questions were worded for simple "yes" and "no" answers. Question 27 concerned a person's willingness to serve in the armed forces and question 28 asked for unqualified allegiance to the U.S. and the forswearing of allegiance to Japan. All activities were suspended for a week while staff members interviewed the adult residents to complete the questionnaires. To the Issei, question 28 was impossible to answer because they were not allowed to become American citizens; for them the wording was later changed. "No" answers to either or both questions were given by Issei desiring repatriation or by Issei and Nisei desiring to verbalize a protest against evacuation.

More interviews followed, and anxiety flourished as family loyalty and faith in and hope for the future were all called into doubt. It was a very unsettling experience for staff and residents alike. There were many meetings, many committees, and much speech making. I thought at the time that my students and the whole Topaz community remained amazingly calm. Months later reports surfaced that there had been scattered threats against the staff; I was deeply touched to learn that two of my most stalwart students had spent several nights on guard outside my room in the Block 2 barracks.

September and October 1943 found us facing the actual transfer (called "segregation") of a small minority classified as a result of the questionnaire. They were either repatriates or voluntary segregants who were accompanying their families. After tearful farewells, the buses bound for the Tule Lake Center pulled out and I waved off several of my best students.

On one occasion, I chaperoned the first experimental group of senior girls and young women to work for the summer in a tomato cannery near Ogden.

We started with light-hearted attitudes, anticipating hard work but making money. The grim realities of migratory agricultural life met us when we found utterly unacceptable, unsanitary, and crowded housing conditions plus an employer who couldn't or wouldn't consider any improvements. I had to appeal to nearby military to place me in phone contact with our project director. Upon hearing of the conditions, he ordered us back to Topaz, explaining to grateful parents that their daughters were not to be exploited.

To thank me for heading off a potentially embarrassing incident for the WRA administration, the director assigned my roommate and me an apartment in the new staff housing. Until that time we had lived in barracks rooms just as the evacuees did. Unlike some centers, at no time were there barriers between staff and evacuee housing. From then on, our apartment became a center for visitor and student meetings and parties.

Third Winter in Topaz 1944, by Hisako Hibi. Oil on canvas, 16 x 20 in. January 1944.

My first roommate, Emily Minton, community activities director, was married at Topaz in December 1942. Her husband, Norman Center, arrived from San Francisco carrying Reverend Tsukamoto's altar candlesticks, and Goro Suzuki sang "I'm Dreaming of a White Christmas" at the reception. Mary MacMillan, my second roommate, taught at the high school until she left for graduate work in Nashville, Tennessee. "Mary Mack," much beloved by the students, would later go to postwar Hiroshima to teach. Third to move in was Muriel Matzkin, a biology teacher from New York. Muriel and I later went to Washington, D.C., to help close out the WRA. Later Muriel married Milton Shapp and became "first lady" of Pennsylvania.

Good-byes to those actually relocating to jobs out of the evacuation zone were far happier than parting with those destined for Tule Lake. When the first large group of families left for resettlement in the East, and not just on seasonal leave, staff and friends crowded around the gate to say their farewells. Voices raised in song—"God be with you till we meet again"—as tears ran unashamedly down dusty cheeks.

Happiest of all leave-takings were those when students left for college. Many educators, such as my faculty colleagues at Technical High, had worried about the evacuee students who were then in college or planning to enter in the spring of 1942, and about those who would be graduating during the war years. During the early summer of 1942, some thirty deans and registrars met to consider the problem. With the eventual cooperation of over three hundred colleges and universities, they established five requirements: (1) The student had to be accepted academically by the college while still in camp; (2) students could attend any school approved or "cleared" by the War and Navy Departments; (3) students had to be able to provide for themselves financially for one year; (4) they had to be assured of a welcome in the college community; and (5) all students had to provide an autobiography.

The fourth stipulation created problems, as many of the large universities had war-related projects on their campuses; as a consequence, the need for an agency to handle a multitude of details became obvious. John J. McCloy, assistant secretary of war, and Milton Eisenhower, the first director of the WRA, requested that the American Friends Service Committee coordinate the activities of all interested groups, such as the churches, the YMCA, the YWCA, and the Fair Play Committee. The result was the National Japanese American Student Relocation Council funded by church boards and two philanthropic foundations. Thomas R. Bodine was appointed to the position of field director, and thereby hangs a tale of true dedication and commitment. Tom Bodine was a member of the Society of

Friends and brought to the position the personal resources of extraordinary patience, understanding, and tremendous good cheer. He had charm, compassion, integrity, and aplomb with which to cajole, console, and counsel evacuee students and their parents, relocation center high school faculty, foundation boards of directors, and college presidents.

When we finally built a school auditorium at Topaz, had an adequate library, fielded uniformed athletic teams, and had "settled in," Tom made us realize the stagnation of the human spirit that was occurring behind barbed wire. Spurred by him, we set up a student relocation office; our first was run very efficiently by the gracious Louise Watson. It later became a part of the high school, and I was called the "student relocation advisor" so as not to offend the high school "guidance counselor." We organized our own scholarship fund to which both residents and outsiders contributed. (Once, when a dental problem forced me to make a quick train trip home, my only other engagement during that one-day visit was to talk with a group of teachers. Asking me to please wait, they withdrew and returned with a check for a thousand dollars. "If Hayward students are awarded scholarships, tell them Hayward High teachers gave the money, otherwise we are to be anonymous," they said.)

The scholarships awarded, plus a $25 leave grant made when an evacuee departed camp, helped establish the student's financial ability. However, jobs, housing, and community acceptance were the concern and responsibility of the National Japanese American Student Relocation Council. By summer 1945, at least 3,000 students had been placed in various kinds of post-secondary education, having been relocated from all ten centers.

Topaz's closure was official on October 31, 1945, and I left immediately for Washington, D.C. My responsibility there was to handle correspondence concerning student records, especially transcripts, as the relocated students had entered schools all over the nation. Several months later, when all seemed quiet on the school front, Dr. John Provinse and I went to lunch with an official from the National Archives. We turned over the educational records from all the centers, everything in good order and all students accounted for.

Now, when at class reunions (the Topaz Class of 1945 has five-year reunions and the '43–'44 classes recently held a forty-year affair attended by 400 persons) I happily acknowledge the gratitude and applause of "my" alumni; and I am deeply aware of all those upon whom I leaned. Tom Bodine and his "support system" picked up and guided the alumni so that

Poston, Arizona, June 5, 1942. Photograph by Francis Stewart.

today our reunions are attended by a host of distinguished professionals and a multitude of wonderful, decent people from all over the United States.

Also supporting my efforts were fine colleagues, such as my principals Drayton Nuttall and Golden Woolf, superintendents John Carlisle and LeGrand Noble, project directors and assistants Lorne Bell, Roscoe Bell, Charles Ernst, and Luther Hoffman. Behind them stand my parents, my own instructors from high school and college, my faculty peers and dear friends. I was a link in that great chain. Henry Brooks Adams said, "A teacher affects eternity; he can never tell where his influence stops." It was my privilege, my joy to have been a teacher at Topaz.

A Young Nisei's Diary

Stanley Hayami

Stanley Hayami was an eighteen-year-old student from Los Angeles who attended high school at the Heart Mountain, Wyoming internment camp. He left behind an intimate diary from 1942 to 1944 in which he recorded a spectrum of youthful dreams of becoming an artist-writer, and doubts ranging from the quality of his schoolwork to the meaning of democracy. Hope pervades the diary, as Hayami writes, "My heart says that if I believe, I will go far. My mind reminds me that I can indeed go far, but only so far as my IQ and race handicap will allow me to go. Thus you have me, a person who at this moment is quite undecided and uncertain, but who thinks he sees the light and decision springing up ahead." Hayami left Heart Mountain in June 1944 to join the U.S. Army and was tragically killed in combat in Northern Italy on April 23, 1945, while trying to help a fellow soldier. He was eighteen years old. The diary, which is illustrated with pen and ink drawings by Hayami, is part of the National Resource Center collection at the Japanese American National Museum in Los Angeles.

*

November 29, 1942

Today I am writing my first entry in this journal. It is no special day, but I have to start someplace.

Right now Walt is listening to Gene Krupa so I don't feel much like writing. Sach is talking with Ma + Pa about leaving camp and going to College & if so what school.

Today I went to sunday school and then saw a football game. It was really cold out there watching that game — there was snow on the ground + it was snowing slightly.

Well I'll be darned they've finally decided to let Sach go to college; its to be Washington U. In St. Louis. Mo. Shes majoring in dress design.

Frank isn't home right now like he always isn't. He's probably playing for the dance tonite. I don't understand Frank very well, in his few stops at our house (+ mean room) which he's supposed to be living in, he managed to get mad at me sometime last week & I guess he's still mad.

Well thats about all for now I guess. Gotta get up early tommorow & get braced for the great bad news — Report cards.

1

Dec. 8, 1942

Today, last year I went to school exited, scared (tho I had no reason to be) and sort of embarrassed. When I went to class everyone was talking about it and I felt a little conspiquous as if everyone was looking at me. The rest of the kids said hello to me as usual and all tried to keep off the topic of war. However I didn't feel much like talking about anything that day. All during English Class my English teacher had the news broadcasts on. One report was coming from Manila and was cut short as Jap. planes began flying over. After I got home I did little else except listening to news reports.

Today I took my physical exam.

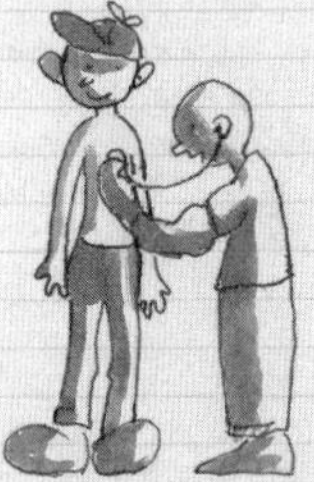

Dec. 12, 1942

Sorry I did not write the last night or so, it is because I was studying for my chemistry test

Tomorrow at Los Angeles U.C.L.A. plays U.S.C. to determine who goes to the Rose bowl. Gosh I wish I were home so I could see that game. Oh well Its going to be some game anyway. Bill Stern is going to broadcast that game. I hope UCLA wins. If they win and if they go to the Rose Bowl it'll be the first time they will go.

Dec. 13, 1942

Well UCLA finally ~~was~~ beat USC. Score was 14-7 and was it exciting! Had me gasping for breath on every play.

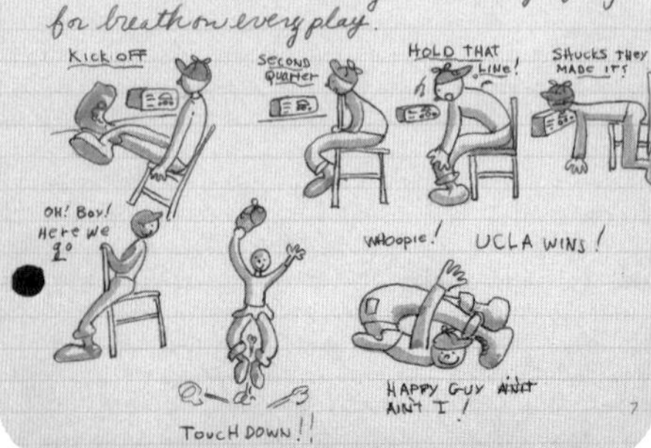

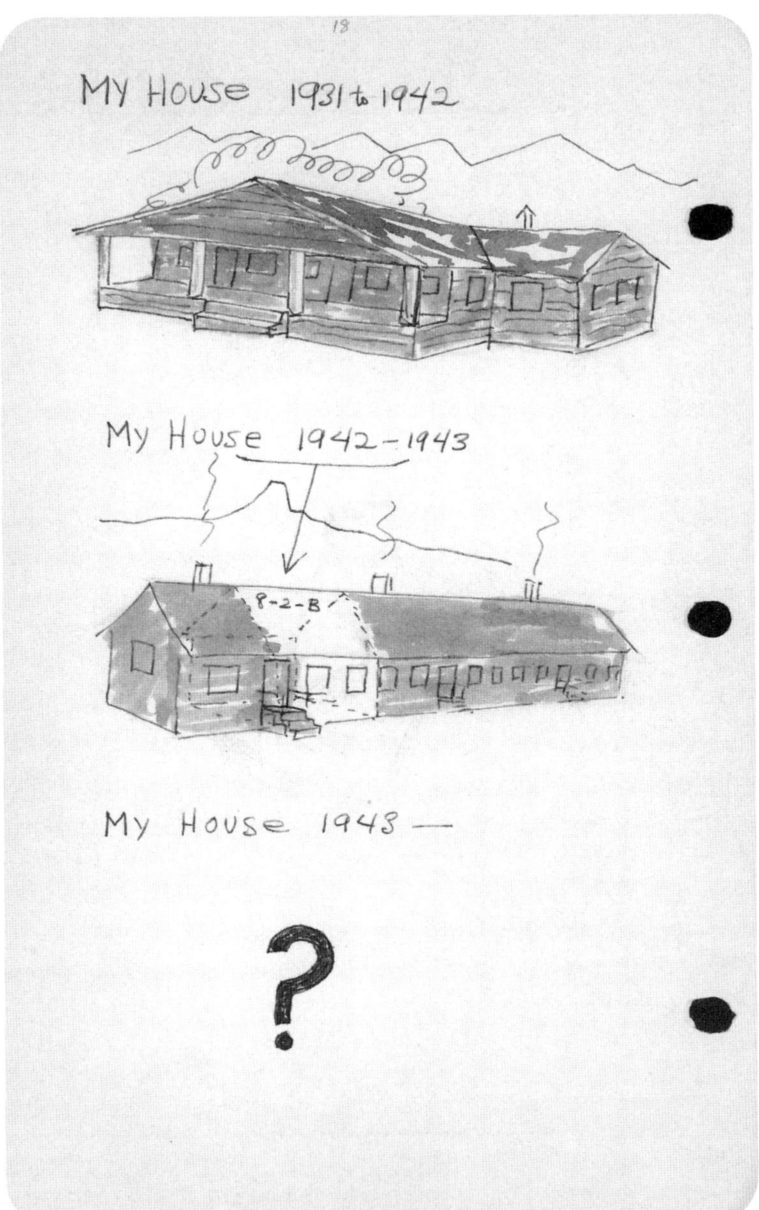
18
MY HOUSE 1931 to 1942
My House 1942-1943
8-2-B
My House 1943 —
?

Recollections of Heart Mountain

Peter Simpson

The irony of moving potential saboteurs off the West Coast into the interior states was not lost on the citizens and politicians who lived in the communities where the internment camps were eventually built. If they were dangerous on the West Coast, why were they less dangerous in the interior? Governor Ralph L. Carr of Colorado has been described as the one mountain-state governor receptive to relocation of the Japanese in his state, claiming in a February 28, 1942 radio address that "If any enemy aliens must be transferred as a war measure, then we of Colorado are big enough and patriotic enough to do our duty. We announce to the world that 1,118,000 red-blooded citizens of this State are able to take care of 3,500 or any number of enemies, if that be the task which is allotted to us."

Few written recollections by citizens where internment camps were built exist today except in oral-history form. In a rare exception, a collection of recollections on Japanese American internment in Wyoming, entitled Remembering Heart Mountain, *was published in 1998 by Western Historical Publications. The following excerpt is from contributor Peter Simpson, a professor of history at the University of Wyoming. His brother, Alan Simpson, who joined him on numerous visits to the Heart Mountain internment camp, later entered politics and became a Wyoming senator.*

I am a fourth-generation Wyomingite whose family home has been in Cody, Wyoming for more than eighty years. Born in Cody in 1930, I lived in that town all of my growing-up life and attended the public schools there. I need to paint a picture here because I think it is important to show how I felt at the time World War II broke out and the Heart Mountain Relocation Center was constructed. I think it is important and instructive in terms of what it was like to come to grips with a cultural chasm of many, many miles, not just the physical distance between Heart Mountain and Cody. It was an educational experience, perhaps outstripping anything that I had learned in the school system at the time and I want to revive that for the reader....

When the war broke out I was eleven and my brother Al was ten. The common causes and the common enemy which brought us together were all that anyone talked or thought about. In many ways it was a unifying factor and in many ways, like it did across America, it produced an economic upturn. The depression years began to fade and the cause of all-out war was upon us.

My father was Defense Council Chairman, which was simply the head of civil defense for Park County, Wyoming. Dad ran as a Republican for the United States Senate in 1940 but was defeated by the incumbent Democrat, Joseph C. O'Mahoney, in a race that was not even close. It was a landslide with Franklin Roosevelt at the helm and an impending crisis. My father was disappointed by that loss and doubly disappointed when he also found he could not rejoin the Army. He had been a young lieutenant in World War I. Since he was not taken into the Army in World War II, he focused his attention on the home front. My most vivid early memories were of things he did and activities my parents were involved in on the so-called "home front" in the little town of Cody. You would not imagine there would be an immense amount of fervor, but the intensity of the war effort permeated that small town like it did every other community in America....

The most powerful memory that I have of the entire war was the visits that I took, as a young boy, to the Heart Mountain Relocation Center. I do not think there is a soul in Park County who can ever forget it. It is surprising that the center was not better known in Wyoming. It seemed a major part of our lives. My first experience related to Heart Mountain came when I was walking down the street one day. As an eleven- or twelve-year-old I can remember the sign in Merle Rank's barber shop—it was a big sign that said, "No Japs Allowed." I can remember seeing them elsewhere in Cody too. So my first memory as a young boy in that fiercely patriotic, homogeneous town with stories and propaganda coming across the airways, in the newspaper, and on Movie-Tone News was fear and concern, maybe very much like the Scots in the northern part of the British Isles when their parents wanted them to be good, would say "Watch out, or the Vikings will get you." There was something of that in the air for us early on in the war.

The fierce patriotism of Wyomingites was reflected in the high percentage of young men and women who went to the service. It was nearly the highest percentage rate per capita in the nation. In this isolated little state, with its parochial concerns, it had a wellspring, very powerful sentiments related to the war and we were participants in that sentiment.

It seemed like an inordinately threatening thing to have a Japanese relocation center put up just a few miles from the hometown. Most of us, and this seems incredible looking back on it, but most of us as young kids growing up were actually encouraged and even soothed by news that there would be military police and protective barbed wire around the camp. We were curious enough to take trips out after it was built and saw the barbed wire and the guardtowers firsthand, in front of us. It made one clear impression on both Al and me, as twelve- and eleven-year-olds at that time, that we needed to be protected and that the internees were alien and potentially hostile. That is what the camp symbolized and what it conveyed. When I hear now of the protest by the internees to the construction of the barbed wire fence around the camp back then, I can empathize with them. They knew what the symbol would mean as well.

I am an Episcopalian and was an acolyte, together with Al, in the Episcopal church. (The little poker church in Cody, the one that was built when Buffalo Bill and five cronies got together in a poker game and decided the pot had gotten so big that they ought to try to do something good with it rather than give it to one of their rapscallion friends who might win. So they decided that the winner should put the money toward the construction of a church. To assuage the conscience of those renegades they built the Episcopal church. There must be it place in heaven for people who do the right things for the wrong reasons.) I was shocked to hear our minister, John McGlaughlin (who we would have literally followed to the moon), when he said, "Boys, I want you to help pack up the vestments, sacred vehicles, and utensils. We are going to go out to the relocation center and hold a service." I could hardly wait to grab Mom and Dad afterwards and say, "This guy is going to take its out to the alien camp. We are in mortal peril." My parents were surprisingly complacent. I thought, "Where is the protection when you really need it?"

Two days later we were in a car on our way down that old dirt, graveled, partly-paved farm road. I will never forget going through the gate and coming into what seemed like an absolutely alien, strange, horrifying, and difficult world. We stuck very close to the minister and to each other. We did not want to offend anybody. I remember unconsciously bowing more than I have ever bowed in my life, before or since.

We went to a very plain, tar-papered recreation hall. There was a table at one end of the hall, and as I recall, no windows. We put it a cross on the table and gathered things together. I remember sitting up close, right in the front. I sat stock still and watched as the congregation came in. As the service progressed, I was fascinated to see that not only did everybody there speak the same language I did, they actually knew the service better than I did. It was during this interesting cross-cultural experience, and I remember in my nervousness, that I made a major mistake. You had to give the wine to the minister first and the water second. In my nervousness, the water went first, and I remember a wry guy, probably in his fifties, looking at me and giggling. After that Sunday, it was never quite as easy to fit the people of the Heart Mountain Relocation Center into the stereotype of the enemy abroad.

We went four times to do that in the space of one year. I found that by the fourth time (there were six of us who were acolytes in the church) we were competing with each other to see who might be able to go to the camp because of the interesting stories we would bring back. We would tell other kids what it was like, and it fascinated them. Eventually John McGlaughlin made sure that not only the six acolytes went, but many of the younger members of the congregation as well. He was a smart guy. He knew that if the children and young teenagers went to the camp there would be lessons taught that he might not be able to teach the older members of the congregation. The older members of the congregation were split concerning the trips we had been taking to the camp. Some of them approved of it. Others disapproved, but were silent, while others who disapproved were very vocal.

The next most vivid experience in my education as a thirteen-year-old was the result of another great youth leader, Glenn Livingston (an elementary school is named for him in Cody), who was the Scoutmaster of Troop 250 in Cody. He was a remarkable man. Glenn Livingston did the same thing as John McGlaughlin. He said, "Men of Troop 250," (we always snapped to attention) "we are going to have a jamboree at the Heart Mountain Relocation Center." "What?" "We are all going to go out there and we are going to spend an entire day at the relocation center with the Boy Scouts of Troop 379."

We were going to go out and have a jamboree with Troop 379 at the Japanese relocation center. We arrived at Heart Mountain at eight o'clock in the morning. It seemed to take forever to reach the relocation center and it probably did in the old cars with the roads the way they were. The first speaker was the Scoutmaster from Troop 379 and again, to the astonishment of many young men who had not had the advantage of going to the camp with their minister, the guy spoke perfect American English. That was a big revelation for some of Troop 250's most stalwart members. Next, Glenn Livingston gave a talk. Both Scoutmasters made an impression on us because they both spoke about the preparation of young men for life and about the war in very patriotic terms.

Following the initial talks by the Scout leaders, we worked on merit badges. I remember a very skillful young Japanese boy who must have been practicing tying rope knots out in California. It was more than a little bit embarrassing that a guy from the "Cowboy State" could not do the first damn knot and this guy was spinning them out like he could do them in his sleep. We exchanged projects, did merit badges, and had quite a morning. I did notice that we stayed pretty close to our Caucasian Cody friends and the Japanese stayed pretty close to theirs. We seemed to be making formal exchanges rather than informal exchanges. I am not sure whether it was planned or how that worked out, but it did help us to ease into the events of the day.

By noontime we were sitting pretty much mixed together in the recreation hall over a hot meal. In the afternoon we broke up into less formal groups and I was paired with a young Japanese American who liked art and so did I. He drew a picture of Tarzan that was terrific. We then went outside and tossed the football around. It could have been out there on Bleistein Avenue in Cody. It was cold and there was snow on the ground. It looked just as God-forsaken at the camp as it did in Cody. My Japanese friend had a dandy sense of humor. He said at one time during the ball throwing. "I'm so cold, even my goose pimples got goose pimples." I laughed like he was Bob Hope. I thought that was the funniest damn thing I had ever heard. I followed him around the rest of the day waiting for his next one-liner.

After tossing the football around, my friend took me to one of the tar-paper shacks and we went inside. His mother was making tea but she also had hot chocolate and cookies. I remember how gracious she was and how good the hot chocolate tasted after our tossing the football. After the hot chocolate my friend took me a few yards down along the front of the tar paper barrack and we went into another room where his grandmother lived. My friend's grandmother was a very dignified little lady. Though the outside of the barrack was poor and bedraggled looking, the inside was a scene of Oriental opulence with tapestries hanging on the walls and a little shrine in the front of the room. It was almost like a religious experience. Though she could not speak English, my friend told me that his grandmother said she was glad I was there and that she hoped I was enjoying the day. Meeting my friend's family was a memorable experience.

That night after the dinner, they had games including Blind Man's Bluff, which must have been played differently in California than we had ever played it in Wyoming. Instead of just touching the person, the guy in the middle—who was wearing the blindfold—was armed with a rolled up newspaper that he would use to take whacks at the people who touched

A view of the barracks and Heart Mountain. Heart Mountain, Wyoming, c. 1943. Photographer unknown.

him. If you could not get away, you would get clubbed with the newspaper. One particular guy and I did very well at that game until we came across a little Japanese fellow who I think only weighed 120 pounds. He was not very big. At twelve years of age I was taller than everybody, but I was certainly not as mature. The little guy, to my horror, had hair on his legs. He was stocky and armed with this damn newspaper, and he beat the hell out of me. I had a terrible time. I did not want any part of him after that and my friend had disappeared. I do not know where he went; he might have set me up. After the game ended the little guy peeked out from under his blindfold. I call still see that goofy grin on his face, when he saw my red nose and watering eyes.

I had at least six experiences at the relocation center. The last one, and perhaps the most telling, did not have anything with conversations or with an interconnection with anybody at the relocation center. It was a trip that Mom and Dad had to take to Heart Mountain for an errand. I remember that when we came to the gate on the way home, Dad stopped the car and got out to talk to somebody. As we sat waiting in the car I looked over my right shoulder and saw a soldier and his girlfriend standing under the guard tower. He had one arm around her. He had a red Fifth Army patch on his shoulder (my favorite army). I will always remember that picture. I can see it not just in memory, but in Technicolor. The red patch, that fellow with sort of a jaunty look, looking at a kid in a car, a proud look, smiling, and I involuntarily waved. He did not wave back; he just smiled as we drove away.

That might have been the beginning of the first independent, intellectual, challenging political and philosophical thought that I had about this whole thing. That thought stemmed from six experiences, a friend in the camp, a Boy Scout beating, a church muff and an occasion of discontentment and unsettling feelings. It dislodged my comfortable stereotyping and left me, for the first time, without a ready-made answer to questions of national right and wrong. I grew up in those years, and my growing up became conscious that day. I have only one regret out of all of that. I wish I would have kept my Boy Scout friend's name so I might have kept in touch with him. My brother, however, did find one of his Boy Scout jamboree friends, Norm Mineta. He and Al shared the experience in the Congress of the United States where Norm, the former Mayor of San Jose, serves as congressman from California. They have a fast friendship to this day.

I found myself at UCLA recently looking at relocation pictures in an exhibit there. I was looking mostly at the faces of people in the photos to see how visibly the tragedy might have been written on them. Though I never saw it in their faces, I could see tragedy in every grain of the pictures.

The distance between Cody and Heart Mountain was twelve-and-one-half miles, but it seemed like the longest trip in the world for a young boy between two cultures and two separate times.

Behind Barbed Wire, Heart Mountain, Wyoming, c. 1943. Photograph by Hansel Mieth and Otto Hagel.

III

At daybreak
stars disappear
where do I discard my
dreams?

Neiji Ozawa

Statement to the Commission

Elaine Black Yoneda

Contrary to common belief, the internment of enemy aliens during World War II was not limited to Japanese Americans, the West Coast, or even the United States. Simultaneous forced evacuation and incarceration occurred in Alaska, Canada, Mexico, and Central America, as well as parts of South America, Haiti, and the Dominican Republic. Nor was the internment experience limited to the Japanese alone. Several thousand Americans of German and Italian ancestry and Aleutian island natives were classified as enemy aliens and forced to move.

Within the camps, boredom, frustration, and political friction both between the administration and internees and between different generations of Japanese internees grew into physical harassment and violence. Protests, strikes, and riots over living and working conditions and other political disputes broke out. As the elder Issei were disqualified from holding most prestigious leadership positions in camp because of their alien status, resentment towards the younger Nisei generation grew uglier. Anyone considered too friendly with the white administration or suspected of providing information to WRA intelligence agencies was considered an inu—literally, dog or informer. Under these conditions, daily life became intolerable as morale and dignity dissolved into fear.

Elaine Black Yoneda was born in Connecticut and raised in a predominately Jewish section of Brooklyn, New York. In the 1930s, Yoneda became increasingly interested in socialist activism in California, and eventually joined the International Labor Defense and the Communist Party. Following a demonstration in 1931, her future second husband, Karl "Hama" Yoneda was arrested and beaten by police. Elaine rushed to the jail, posted bail, and took the badly-injured Japanese American to a doctor. They were later married in a ceremony held in Washington state, where interracial marriages were tolerated.

After the attack on Pearl Harbor, Karl and their two-year-old son, Tommy, were to be interned along with other Japanese Americans. Elaine was not officially included in the relocation order because she was white, but she insisted on accompanying her husband and child into the Manzanar internment camp. Caucasian, Korean, Chinese, Mexican, and African American spouses of Japanese were among those swept into camps following evacuation orders that didn't take interracial marriages into account.

After the war, the Yonedas continued their usual political activities; she pursued equal-pay issues, spoke at Negro History Week, protested nuclear war, and was a member of Local 29, AFL-CIO Office and Professional Employees Union. Before her death, Yoneda was an active supporter in the campaign for Redress-Reparations for Japanese Americans. Yoneda is the subject of a biography entitled The Red Angel: The Life and Times of Elaine Black Yoneda, 1906–1988, *published in 1991. The following excerpt is from her testimony of camp experience and her account of the events leading to the Manzanar Riot, a mass uprising of Manzanar internees in protest of camp conditions and politics that left two internees dead and at least ten injured. The unrest began on December 5, 1942, when Japanese American Citizen League (JACL) leader Fred Tayama was severely beaten. Tayama later identified several of his attackers, who were taken into custody. The next day, crowds assembled to protest the jailing of the accused, which led to intervention by the military police who sprayed tear gas and began firing live ammunition into the crowd. Yoneda's testimony was written for the Los Angeles hearings held by the Commission on Wartime Relocation and Internment of Civilians in 1981.*

*

My name is Elaine Black Yoneda. I am a retired office worker residing in... San Francisco with my husband, Karl, a retired longshoreman. I am a native of New York City and will be seventy-five years of age in September.

When the bombing of Pearl Harbor occurred, Karl, a Kibei, born in Glendale, California (raised in Hiroshima), and then nearly three-year-old son, Tommy, my fourteen-and-a-half-year old daughter, Joyce (by a former marriage), and I were living in the San Francisco Fillmore district, on the fringe of Japantown.

Both of us were known activists in labor, civil rights, and antifascist organizations for many years prior to Pearl Harbor. I was Pacific Coast vice-president of the International Labor Defense (ILD) and Congressman Vito Marcantonio was its national president. I held the position of vice-president from 1937 until the evacuation and was the secretary of the San Francisco International Longshoremen's and Warehousemen's Union (ILWU) Ladies Auxiliary. Therefore, hopefully, my written and oral statements will bring out factors and events about pre-evacuation and Manzanar camp experiences of a more diverse nature than most presented to the Commission.

About 7:45 A.M. on December 8, 1941, three FBI agents came looking for Karl. I let them in without inquiring whether they had a search warrant, something I would have demanded if Japan's military attack on the United States had not taken place. When I informed them Karl had gone to his longshore job on Pier 45, (he was a member of the ILWU), they were skeptical and had me call the Union Hiring Hall for confirmation.

The agents searched our small upper four-room flat, taking nothing, and made snide remarks as they looked through some Chinese War Relief cards I was addressing for our Christmas and New Year's messages. They called them "a good cover for pro-Japan activity."

I was attempting to cooperate but was irate at that remark, as well as the travesty of their searching for Karl. I told them, "You're barking up the wrong tree looking for Karl as a possible enemy of democracy. You're wasting valuable time which allows fascists in our midst to disappear from the scene or clean up their acts."

Soon after this they left. Later I was informed by two neighbors that additional FBI agents with submachine guns had been posted on roofs facing the front and rear entrances to our home.

At noon I learned from a co-worker of his that Karl had been picked up on the dock and taken to the Immigration Detention Center on Silver Avenue. I called the union attorney, George Andersen. He said he would start habeas corpus proceedings within forty-eight hours if Karl wasn't set free. On the evening of the 9th, he was released. Karl told me about the 100 or so Issei and four Nisei who were also confined in the center. We immediately went to the Western Union office where he dispatched a telegram to President Roosevelt offering his service to the United States Armed Forces. He also visited his draft board but to no avail.

Jobs got scarcer for Karl and in February, 1942, the Army ordered "no one of Japanese ancestry be allowed to work on the waterfront." This, despite the fact that the ILWU and others vouched for him as a long-time fighter against Japanese militarists, and who had been a union picket captain when ships loading scrap iron for Japan were picketed by thousands of Chinese and other antifascists in 1937 through 1939.

Karl and I attended the Tolan Congressional Committee Hearings—"Problems of Evacuation of Enemy Aliens and Others from Prohibited Military Zones"—held in San Francisco on February 21 and 23, 1942. The hearings went on even though the President had already signed Executive

Order 9066 on the 19th. But how many knew about this or what it forebode for the Japanese American West Coast residents and communities?

The most outstanding testimony at those hearings, I believe, both orally and written, against evacuation, bigotry, and racism, was that of Louis Goldblatt, then secretary of the California State Industrial Union Council ...presently retired ILWU International secretary-treasurer.... It is still germaine to the temper of the times and the unjust evacuation this commission is now investigating.

Karl gave a written statement to the committee, which they titled: "Japanese American Loyalty to the United States."

Meanwhile, we discussed our future course as a family. With the prospect of no work, car payments on a new Studebaker, plus rent and food to be met, where and to whom could we turn to help solve our dilemna? Karl heard undercurrents in Japantown that volunteer Japanese American construction workers, for a camp to be built in Manzanar, were being recruited by Los Angeles Maryknoll priests. They were the liaison to the U.S. Army. Without any further questions we decided to move to Los Angeles. There my children and I could live with my parents while I got war-related work and Karl volunteered for a construction job.

Though we were aware the impending "evacuation" was a violation of constitutional and human rights, we also knew that if it suited the ruling U.S. leaders, they would use the Armed Services and their guns without hesitation to round up all those of Japanese descent, as was done to the Native Americans after passage of the 1830 Indian Removal Act.

Thus, we did not speak out against the edict; nothing must be done by us to impede the war effort. The immediate main task was to defeat the enemy—the fascist Axis (Germany-Italy-Japan), for if they won the war, there would not be a shred of democracy left in this country or anywhere on this earth. We could thrash out the question of rights after victory. That was our rationale as we prepared to go to Los Angeles.

On March 8, we had the sad duty to attend the funeral of world-renowned labor leader (and our son's godfather), Tom Mooney. Karl was one of the honorary pallbearers and I spoke at the graveside service.

We were able to store most of our furniture, documents, and books with union friends. In mid-March, we drove down to my parents' home. Karl contacted the Maryknoll priests and signed up to go to Manzanar, in Owens Valley. On March 23, 1,000 men and a few women "volunteer evacuees" of Japanese descent left for Manzanar. Eight hundred, including Karl, boarded a train at the Santa Fe depot with whatever belongings they could carry. The other 200 gathered at the Pasadena Rose Bowl, and in a long-car caravan—

from an old Ford to a new convertible, which were loaded with all sorts of personal possessions—were escorted by Army personnel to the camp.

My parents, Joyce, Tommy, and I were at the depot to see Karl off. Newsreel cameras, radio recorders, magazine and news reporters were milling all around, as were the armed military and some Maryknoll priests and nuns. Reams of coverage appeared that afternoon and all the following week. When I have occasion to re-read the *Los Angeles Evening Herald Express* of March 23, 1942 and look at the picture of Karl kissing our son good-bye published therein, the qualms, anguish, and uncertainty of that day and the future come to mind.

Karl went with high hopes of helping to build a place livable for those who were to arrive later, at the same time continuing to pressure for acceptance of his enlistment into the U.S. Armed Forces.

The Army personnel and Maryknoll fathers told the volunteers there was no need to worry about personal possessions or holdings they left behind, for their families would be the last ones ordered out of Military Area No. 1, allowing for ample time to dispose of or store belongings.

Suddenly on the evening of Sunday, March 29, the radio blurted out: "Attention, Attention, all those of Japanese ancestry whose breadwinners are in the Manzanar Reception Center: You are hereby ordered to report to the Civil Control Station at 707 South Spring Street tomorrow from 8:00 A.M. on for processing to leave for Manzanar by noon, April 2, or be in violation of General DeWitt's Civilian Exclusion Order No. 3."

I sat stunned in disbelief. Had I heard correctly? What of the promise of the "last ones out" and here it was only six days since their departure? But soon the announcement was repeated.

I then immediately called Army Headquarters but was told to call back after 7:00 P.M. for an answer to my query: "Does General DeWitt's Manzanar order include a three-year old Eurasian child living with his Caucasian mother and grandparents?" When I called again I was given the Maryknoll phone number and told to call there. I do not recall the name of the priest I spoke to. He kept repeating to my one question: "Does DeWitt's order include a three-year old...?" "You do not have to go, Mrs. Yoneda, nor will you be allowed to go, but your son must go on the basis of the Geneva Accords. That is, the father's ancestry counts and 1/16th or more Japanese blood is the criteria set." I assured him Tommy was at least 50 percent and that he might even be more Asiatic because my parents came from a region which had been overrun by Genghis Khan and his hordes.

After relating the conversation to my parents, I told them if Tommy had to go I would go too, come hell or high water, but Joyce would stay with them. They agreed my decision was correct. Tommy, since he was five weeks old, needed special care because of extreme food and medication allergies and now suffered from asthma as well.

On Monday morning Tommy and I took our places in the long line already formed outside the station. Suddenly an Army officer and a priest came running to where we stood, telling us to "go right in, not to wait in line." I protested but was ushered inside anyway. There the captain refused to give me two application forms and the Maryknoll father kept saying: "We will have a Children's Village where our well-trained sisters (nuns) will take care of your son. You needn't, nor will you be allowed to go. It will be too hard for you." This made me irate and my determination to go became stronger. I turned to the officer with my voice rising and said: "As sure as we are standing here, my husband will be in a khaki uniform like yours before the year is out and I'll be there with our son to see him off." Then turning to the priest, I exclaimed loudly: "Father, for all you know I may be an atheist, but I took an oath to love, honor, and cherish, NOT OBEY, for or better or worse, and that means something to me. I'll be with my child and husband and never mind the too hard bit."

After again demanding two forms, they were handed to me. I completed the applications and was given a typhus shot, but I would not allow Tommy to get one; that would have to wait until a doctor was in attendance because of a possible reaction. I also informed them we would take the first train on April Fool's Day.

The first letter from Karl, a special delivery, came Tuesday, March 31. In it he implored I not attempt to visit him yet. The barren barracks with unpaned windows, lack of toilet facilities and the harsh gravelly dust storms all would have bad effects on Tommy. Visits could wait awhile though he sorely missed us. He also wrote that work was not what had been promised, nor did he yet know what the wage scale would be. He also mentioned some "characters" among the volunteers. A couple were very unsavory, die-hard, pro-military, emperor lovers.

On Wednesday, April 1, at 6:45 A.M., we reported to the railway station. There was much suppressed excitement, bewildered old and young men and women, babes in arms, and small children running around. Tommy was exuberant at the thought of seeing his daddy, jumping up and down repeating to my parents, Joyce, and me: "I'm going to see my daddy again." Maryknoll personnel were there as well as armed soldiers posted all around.

When the soldiers lined up at each car step, we knew it was time to go aboard with only the baggage we could carry. Some, women especially, had very little with them because of the children they had to carry. I managed two suitcases and Tommy carried a few toys in a bag. We all seemed determined to refrain from crying as good-byes were bid to relatives and friends. When and where would we see each other again? The train pulled out at 9:30 and arrived in Lone Pine toward sunset. There we were transferred to buses for the eight-mile ride to Manzanar.

What chaos when the buses pulled inside the barbed wire. A number of the early evacuees, including Karl, had volunteered to help arriving families, presumably from Bainbridge, Washington, when lo and behold they discovered some of their own families among the arrivals.

Karl at first demanded to know: "Why have you disregarded my plea not to visit yet—do you want to make Tommy sick?" I merely pulled out a copy of DeWitt's Order No. 3 and handed it to him.

After stuffing straw into three mattress tuckings, we were put into Block 4, Barrack 4, in a room with six other people. Though there were already watchtowers with searchlights manned by armed Military Police, there were no toilet or washing facilities—only one cold water faucet at the east end of each barrack and at the west end of the block were six portable toilets, actually for use by the construction crews. Incidentally, the construction crews were all white men; Karl and other volunteers were refused construction-helper jobs as promised by the Maryknoll personnel.

Tommy was happy, jumping around and hugging his daddy. After reading Order No. 3, Karl's remorse at the way he had greeted me was intense. We had a good, silent cry in each other's arms. Both of us, with a shot-induced, swollen, feverish arm, spent a most restless night.

The next morning upon going outside we found the faucets frozen. For hours we were unable to brush our teeth or wash our hands, even after use of the portables. It had been a cold night and it took until noon for the faucets to thaw out. This situation went on for a week. In the meantime, quarters were reassigned. If you were a family of four or more you could bunk together up to seven persons in a so-called "apartment"—a room twenty-by-twenty-five feet. We, being only three, were assigned to Block 4, Building 2, Apartment 2, to share with a seventy-five-year old blind man and his fifteen-year-old nephew, the overflow from Apartment 1, where the other seven members of the Nishimura family were housed.

Our apartment contained five old iron army cots, five straw mattresses without sheets, and only two scratchy army blankets each. Two beds were placed near the entrance wall, three at the other end, and an oil heater. There were no chairs, nothing to use for partitions nor closets. Dust from windstorms covered us, coming in through the knotholes. We soon named our quarters "Tommy's Dust-Out-Inn." We were often kept awake by the uncle scratching open sores on his legs but he wouldn't go to a doctor.

When the latrines were opened, they consisted of five toilet bowls in a row with another five back to back—no partitions or doors. One corner was to have some shower heads installed and another corner had five wash-basins. Their green lumber walls had many "Peeping-Tom" holes until covered with tar paper.

I began encountering frustrated, horrified faces, primarily among teen-aged girls, as they came into the latrine, especially if Tommy was with me. Some would run away crying. Did they have the "Manzanar runs" or their menstrual periods, I wondered?

A couple of days of this convinced me something had to be done. After discussing this with Karl, I went to the Administration Building on April 10. There I saw Mr. J. M. Kidwell, service division director, to whom I related the situation, demanding that doors, partitions, and shower curtains be provided. He shrugged his shoulders and said, "It is Army specifications," Pounding his desk I replied, "To hell with specifications. If you don't do something soon, there might be mass hysteria and maybe even some suicides!"

On April 18 hot water for the showers and the laundry room became a reality. Soon there were shower curtains, partitions, and doors for the toilets.

Untitled, by Estelle Ishigo. Pencil drawing, 5¾ x 3¼ in. 1943.

Karl was appointed Block 4 Leader. "Blockhead" was the expression commonly used by most evacuees. Wages were at the semi-skilled rate of $16.00 per month for a forty-eight–hour work week.

On May 8, I went to work as an assistant librarian and recreation overseer in the Block 12 Library and Recreation Building. Wages started at $12.00 per month, the unskilled pay for the same number of hours, but was soon upgraded to $16.00 because of library work experience I had in the late 1920s. The extra income was needed to purchase special food and vitamins prescribed by the Stanford Hospital Clinic for Tommy and to buy his corrective shoes which wore out frequently due to the gravelly ground. The soybean and corn or rice flour bread cost $.75 per loaf, the cookies $1.00 per pound, plus postage from San Francisco. In July we had to stop the order for the baked goods. It was coming in moldy due to the extreme heat—over 100 degrees in the shade for days on end—and it took four days for delivery.

My parents sent us some bed sheets for use on our cots and for curtains around them. They also sent blankets, a two-burner electric plate, and a garden hose. The stove was to prepare other special food purchased from Lone Pine or the camp store, when it opened, if the camp menu was too far off Tommy's diet. The hose was to wash down our room to keep it as dust-free as possible, and for the lawn between Buildings 1 and 2, which we started from seed sent to us by a friend. The lawn thrived once we could water it regularly.

Karl picked up four empty nail kegs for seats, and every scrap piece of lumber and bent, discarded nails he could find was used to build some shelves, a table, and chest. Tommy's bouts with severe asthma and other illnesses caused many visits and confinements to and from the camp hospital. The doctor ordered our straw mattresses be thrown out. These were replaced by three army quilts.

My parents and daughter came on May 9 to visit us. At first we could only meet at the camp guardhouse. After a couple of months of protest to the administration, they could come to our "apartment," and even stay overnight after notifying the Administration Office of the date and approximate time of arrival. Their car had to be left near the guardhouse. Later, many of our friends also visited us with cameras and took pictures without any restrictions.

Early in May a small group of a dozen or so men calling themselves the Manzanar Black Dragons appeared. They were mostly Kibei, working as scavengers or repair crews, riding around on a trash truck, displaying a pirate flag: a black cloth with a white painted skull and crossbones and another enscribed in Japanese, "Manzanar Black Dragon Association."

James Oda, a Los Angeles active union member and outspoken antifascist was their first known beating victim. They also tried to ram the truck into wooden steps where Karl and Tokie Slocum (a well-known U.S. World War I hero) were sitting. Luckily, they were able to jump aside. The steps were demolished. Complaints were lodged with the administration staff, but they did nothing, not even having the culprits remove the obnoxious pro-Japan Black Dragon flags from government property. In fact, Ned Campbell, assistant camp manager told Karl: "You are all Japanese and will have to live together."

Karl and I had requested and received San Francisco primary election ballots, which we completed and returned to the San Francisco Registrar of Voters on June 5.

In June a new work project was established in Manzanar. It was war connected, producing camouflage nets, and only U.S. citizens could work on them. Taking a leave of absence from the library, I started work on the nets on June 22. It was hot, smelly work in a wall-less, barrack-length shed. Workers had to wear nose and mouth masks and take salt pills. When a dust storm started we had to leave the area. There were no shelters available. Again, I started at the $12.00 rate but soon became a pattern maker, and the pay increased to $16.00.

Leaflets dated June 24, 1942, in Japanese and signed by the Patriotic Suicide Corps (probably the Black Dragons using another name), and another dated June 26, signed by the Manzanar Black Dragons were tacked inside the doors of the men's latrines, urging Nisei not to be fools, to stop working on war equipment, etc.

The Black Dragons rode around on the truck, still displaying the distasteful flags, urging Issei not to permit their children to work on the nets. From time to time, Ben Kishi, Kibei Black Dragon leader, goaded youngsters to throw rocks at the net workers. I went home with bruised legs a few times.

On July 15, Karl's thirty-sixth birthday, he sent off a letter to the ILWU about the possibility of enlistment into the "Dock Battalion" which he had read about in the union newspaper. This also proved fruitless. The following week he and Koji Ariyoshi decided to circulate a petition to President Roosevelt urging the opening of a second front and allowing Nisei to volunteer and/or be drafted into all U.S. Armed Forces. (Ariyoshi was a Hawaiian Nisei "strandee" in San Francisco on December 7 as he awaited a berth home on a merchant ship. He had just obtained his master's degree in journalism from the University of Georgia and had come to Manzanar as Karl's cousin). I typed the stencil, which was run off at the *Manzanar Free Press* office. They circulated it and on August 5 forwarded it to President Roosevelt with an accompanying open letter. This action made headlines and editorials which appeared in many U.S. newspapers, but brought no response from the White House.

On July 31 I had to take what became a seventeen-day leave from work because of a painful rash and swollen arms due to the dyes used in the net strips. About sixteen others also had reactions.

Rumors of all sorts were circulating including one that the Black Dragons had prepared a "death list." When I returned to the net project, I found one of the "unsavory, pro-Japan characters" Karl had written about in his March letter, working there. His last name was Uyemoto but he was known throughout the camp as "General Araki" because for months, he wore his mustache fashioned after Japan War Minister General Araki's. "Why was he there?" I asked myself. A couple of days later, he came to work with it trimmed into a Hitler-style mustache. I observed him talking to four teen-aged boys. They then walked over to my station and "playfully" threw rocks at me. A bloody forehead was the result. After the August 20 stoning, Karl and I went to the front office to report the names of the instigator and attackers that I knew. Ned Campbell was in the office and he informed us Camp Manager Nash was in San Francisco. We left the information with him and we hoped that Nash would return with a new policy on the growing Black Dragon menace. We also sent a letter to the FBI asking them to clean out the handful of fanatics who were making life more miserable than it already was and hindering the U.S. war support efforts as well.

Election for Block Leader was held August 21 and Karl was defeated. He continued on a night checking job....

On August 23, there was a knock on our door. I called out, "come in." A voice asked, "Yoneda-san, may I come in." Karl answered "yes" and in trooped fourteen Kibei. Among them were Ben Kishi and Harry Uyeno, (the two I knew by name) talking menacingly in Japanese, which I do not read, speak, nor understand to this day. I looked out a window and saw more of their ilk staked outside. The fourteen were in our room over an hour arguing and making threatening gestures toward Karl. Tommy sat cowering on his cot as I tried to calm him....

Tommy's asthma grew worse and his attacks more frequent. We were given permission to make our room smaller by moving Apartment 1's wall inward into our area by five feet. The two Nishimuras, their cots and straw mattresses joined their family—a total of nine persons in a twenty-by-thirty foot room! We hoped this move would help to lessen Tommy's health problems. Windows could be kept closed nights, no more straw dust nor smell, etc. I went back to work on the nets, taking special care to shield my arms.

Group after group of men and a small number of women, including Koji Ariyoshi and his bride, Taeko, went out on temporary leave to Idaho and Montana to help save the sugar beet crop. Soon Koji wired Karl to help recruit additional workers. We decided Karl should also go. The nursery school had not reopened and I stopped work since Tommy could not be left alone.

Karl, with about 100 others, left for Idaho on October 6. After seeing him off, Tommy and I stopped at Block 1, Barrack 14 when we saw its door ajar. The nursery school and kindergarten were to be housed there. It had reopened that day and Tommy enjoyed playing with the other children. The next morning we returned to the school with some toys to add to its meager supply. While talking to one of its aides, I learned the kindergarten section needed a helper. I went for a job interview, was hired and started to work there on the 8th. I felt this would be very helpful, as I could be nearby should Tommy get an asthma attack, yet not be constantly with him, and I would be doing something useful.

Joe Kurihara, Hawaiian Nisei and World War I veteran (a behind-the-scene Black Dragon advisor with whom Karl had had many confrontations), accompanied by two Kibei, came over late that afternoon looking for Karl. Kurihara did the talking: "We came with a proposition for Karl." They did not tell me nor did I ask what it might be. I just told them it had to wait until his return from Idaho.

More war saving stamps for Tommy, packages of toys and candy arrived from Karl, plus a crate of delicious Idaho apples, which were shared with some neighbors and friends. After a pay day, he sent two war bonds. Tommy was thrilled over all this attention. He drew pictures for his daddy, had me print messages he dictated and tried to copy. He also made sure I enclosed them with my letters to Karl. I wrote about camp happenings and rumors. One of the latter grew persistently louder—a military recruiting team was headed this way....

Instead of rumor, I soon learned from a reliable source that, indeed, Colonel Kai Rasmussen of the Military Intelligence Service [MIS] Language School would be in Manzanar soon on a recruiting mission. I wired Karl on November 13 to come back quickly if he wanted to see the Colonel. He returned on the 18th with more war saving stamps and cash in his pockets—sugar-beet toppers were paid the prevailing farm wage.

Untitled, by Estelle Ishigo. Pencil drawing, 5½ x 7½. 1943.

The MIS team did arrive November 28, 1942. Black Dragons busily cruised around urging Nisei not to enlist. About fifty applied but only fourteen Nisei and Kibei, including Karl (the oldest) passed the bilingual test. They were immediately inducted as buck privates in the U.S. Army for Pacific Warfare service. We held a lively celebration that night with many well-wishers dropping by. My parents who had been visiting that weekend, took a few of our belongings with them in anticipation of Tommy and my early return to Military Area No. 1.

About ten to twelve men began sulking around our barracks; three of them followed Karl and me for a couple of hours. Karl asked Camp Police Chief Gilkey for protection but none showed up. Therefore enlistees Koji Ariyoshi, Louis Obikane, James Oda, and others took turns guarding us with baseball bats until the day of departure, December 2.

Their families and friends were kept inside the barbed-wire fence by MPs posted along the exit, as the fourteen commenced their journey to Camp Savage, Minnesota. No one was allowed near the bus, not even for what might turn out to be a last embrace, considering their dangerous commitment. Everyone, including men, had tears in their eyes. Tommy cried out: "Daddy, don't leave me. I want to go with you and help beat up the Nazis." Suppressed sobs could be heard as the bus pulled away.

Early that evening I had to take Tommy to see a doctor. He had cried most of the day calling for his daddy, had the runs, and his temperature was 103. The doctor, suspecting dysentery, ordered him into the hospital. He was kept there until mid-afternoon of the 5th. The diagnosis was simple diarrhea....

I received a wire from Karl Saturday morning. They had arrived in very cold and snow-covered Minnesota.

During lunch on the 6th [...] heard about the vicious beating given Fred Tayama the night before and what had happened at the hospital while he was being treated, and that a suspect, namely Harry Uyeno, was under arrest. Tayama was the former Los Angeles Japanese American Citizens League chapter president and one of the founders in July of the Manzanar Citizens Federation along with Karl, Koji, and six others. He had just returned from attending the National JACL Conference held in Salt Lake City, Utah, where a resolution had been adopted requesting Nisei be drafted into the U.S. Armed Forces.

Though Karl was in the U.S. Army, our son, whose fourth birthday would occur on January 10, was classified a "potential dangerous enemy" and could not return to Military Area No. 1 without a special permit issued by General DeWitt. We could have gone to Minnesota at our own expense but I had to consider Tommy's health and the uncertainty of length of time Karl would be there. Thus, on the afternoon of December 6, Tommy and I headed for the Administration Building to inquire if his pass had been received, not knowing that what was to turn into the "Manzanar Riot" was in progress in front of the office—a most frightening experience!

I heard Joe Kurihara speaking to a crowd of about 1,000 in Japanese (it sounded strange even to my ears and later I was told it was "pidgin" Japanese). He mentioned the name "Yoneda" a couple of times but I didn't know in what context. Mr. Chester, administration staff member who understood Japanese, came over to me and said, "Elaine, they are in an ugly mood and Joe is saying that Yoneda ran away from them to hide in the Army but Yoneda's son is still here so we can still 'get him'." I stood there stunned in disbelief. Then Ben Kishi took the podium and he, too, mentioned "Yoneda" about three times.

Satoru Kamikawa, Issei UC graduate and a *Manzanar Free Press* Japanese Section reporter, came running over. He repeated what Chester told me, adding: "Go back to your apartment, lock yourself in, and don't even go out for meals."

With Tommy in tow, I ran to the Camp Police Station requesting protection at our apartment but none was offered. We proceeded at a run to [our apartment], barricading the door with the inside bolt and the table.

Yo Ukita came over towards dusk and said she would try to get us some food and spend the night, although things were tense out there. An hour later she returned but was unable to stay because her father had forbidden her to do so due to threats to him and the rest of their family.

At nine that night I became aware of movements outside, then loud banging on kitchen utensils came from Mess Hall No. 4. After midnight, anguished screams came from the direction of the Ito apartment in Barrack 1. Not able to contain myself, I warned Tommy not to make any noise nor put on a light. I moved the table and ran across to the Itos'. There I heard the horrifying news that their youngest son, James, a signer of the petition to President Roosevelt, was shot and killed by an MP as he headed to his Administration Building night job. Mother Ito, James' sister, Martha Kano, and I embraced in tears. They said: "You had better go back to Tommy. We know you and Karl are not guilty of James' death as some are saying. Please watch out."

At 4:30 A.M., December 7, unable to withstand the growing anxiety for our safety, I tied a scarf on Tommy's head, and put on his coat with its shiny lining outside to give him a little girl's appearance. With nothing but my son and purse in hand, I began running in the darkness toward the Administration Building.

I did not know martial law had been declared. Near the west end of Block 4, Barrack 1, a voice called out: "Halt, who goes there?" A soldier appeared with a drawn bayonet-equipped rifle, flashing a light in my face. He asked: "What are you doing on this side of the fence?" He mistook me for a "hysterical wife" from the MP encampment a mile away. After I explained our plight and his having heard about the fourteen Japanese American enlistees, he took us to the next guard and so on down the line until the office building was reached. It was surrounded by troops clustered around machine guns. After yet another explanation, this time to an Army officer, we were then escorted into an office by a soldier.

When Campbell saw us, he said, "Oh, I forgot about you." (He knew full well we were on the Black Dragon death list.) In the largest office, desks had been pushed against the walls and two long rows of army cots had been placed in the remaining space.

Nearly sixty "pro-Americans," men, women, and children, had already been transported there for protection. They were trying to sleep fully clothed.

At daybreak we were all taken by army trucks to the MP encampment and crowded into the small, two-room dispensary building for meals and "rest." Late that afternoon our good San Francisco friends, Tom Yamazaki, Issei UC graduate journalist, his Nisei wife, Ruth (both antifascists), and two young daughters arrived at the MP quarters. Yo Ukita and six other members of her family were also brought in. She indicated it would be all right for her to remain with us. But her father insisted they all go back to Block 4 and the Army took them back. (It would be five years before we were to meet again.) I inquired about the whereabouts of Koji's pregnant wife but no one seemed to know. The next day an administration employee told me Taeko was okay and hoped to leave for Minnesota soon.

After three days of requesting an opportunity to obtain a change of clothes for Tommy and me (some of the others taken into protective custody had baggage with them), we were escorted by an armed soldier in a jeep to [our apartment].

A crowd, all wearing black armbands, soon gathered. Our escort kept knocking on the door urging us to hurry. Changing our clothes as quickly as possible, I packed two suitcases and Tommy again held a bag of toys. I had been told to bring back only what I could carry for all of us would soon be moved again.

Halfway back to MP quarters I suddenly realized that I had forgotten my purse. Our driver called for and was given reinforcements. He had qualms about returning to Block 4. Upon reaching the barrack, we found three young boys, Mas Nakajo, George Fukumoto, and Seigo Murakami's son, trying to break off the door lock. They fled when we appeared and I retrieved my purse in a hurry. This proved to be the last time we were to see [our apartment] and the belongings we left behind.

On December 10, some sixty-seven were convoyed to an abandoned Civilian Conservation Corps (CCC) camp in Death Valley. Most buildings were in need of repairs; windows and toilet bowls had been smashed. We all rolled up our sleeves to clean up and patch up as best we could. Fred Tayama (his head bandaged from the beating) and his brother Tom, former restaurant operators, became our cooks. What a change from Block 4's fare. A package of candy through Manzanar came from Karl but no letters.

Life at the CCC camp was one of waiting and more waiting for my son's pass and Karl's letters while I worked as one of the kitchen crew. A lecture and slides on the beauty of Death Valley, as well as short, guided tours of the area by Death Valley Park personnel were accorded us.

Tommy landed in the makeshift hospital with a high fever and crying for his daddy.

E. R. Fryer, San Francisco WRA regional director, drove in on December 15 and told me he would try to rush Tommy's permit. The next day eighteen letters and cards from Karl and four from friends were delivered via Manzanar. They were all written prior to December 7 and it was obvious he and the others did not know we were in Death Valley, although I had written about the events that had taken place and of our removal to the Valley.

I heard from a new Manzanar arrival that Karl and others had wired various heads of governmental agencies inquiring about their families' well-being.

Campbell and Fryer returned from Manzanar the evening of the 16th and informed me to pack and be ready to depart for Los Angeles the following morning. However, along with Tommy's permit there was a letter of instructions: (1) I must complete an affidavit each month (to be supplied by General DeWitt's office), attesting to the fact Tommy had or had not been in any fight because of his ancestry; (2) He had done nothing to endanger national security; (3) I was to report all address changes; (4) He was to always be in a Caucasian's custody, namely his mother! I demurred at point 4, inquiring: "If Tommy was to spend weekends or what have you with any of our Chinese, Filipino, or Negro friends, would he be in violation of his right to be in Military Area No. 1?" Campbell admonished me: "You always raise unnecessary questions." I replied: "Not unnecessary; I'm just trying to avoid any misunderstandings that might lead to his return to a concentration camp." At this, Fryer tore up the instructions, remarking: "Just get those affidavits in and keep General DeWitt's headquarters informed of any address change, no matter how temporary."

Campbell told me the office had received a long wire from Karl demanding protection for his family from mob violence and that he, Campbell, wired back a reply that we were safe and well cared for. He failed, however, to inform Karl that the brunette wife he had kissed goodbye less than three weeks ago was now "silver-haired." (This, no doubt, an aftermath of the Manzanar Riot and the residue of the other Black Dragon confrontations I had.)

We bid farewell to the others with wishes that they would soon get out to more fruitful lives. Ruth, Tom, and I tearfully parted, promising to keep in touch. A thought flashed through my mind—would we ever get together again? (Later, Tom became a Japanese language instructor for the Armed Forces. In 1945 he joined the U.S. Occupation Army in Japan. There he was killed in an aircraft accident. We remained close friends with Ruth until her untimely death in 1975.)

Campbell drove us to Lone Pine where I purchased bus tickets with our funds. My parents met us at the terminal.

It must be borne in mind that all the above occurred before the unfair 1943 loyalty questionnaire issue; that we were not JACL members then, but had been (and still are) antifascists cooperating with them to help fight the fascist Axis and its inherent genocidal tenets....

Incidentally, the notarized reports and change of address notices to DeWitt continued until October, 1944. This was even after Karl had seen active no-man's-land duty in the North Burma Battle of Myitkyina. (He had been assigned to the China-Burma-India OWI Psychological Warfare Team and served until November 11, 1945.)

Tommy and I soon returned to San Francisco, where I worked on a coffee warehouse belt line, obtained through the ILWU Local 6 hiring hall, for three months. Then we visited Karl during the Easter Week of 1943. Returning to San Francisco I immediately obtained a secretarial job in the Oakland office of the United Electrical, Radio, and Machine Workers of America Union (UE Local 1412, CIO.) This was war-related and from late 1943 until April of 1946, I was its office manager.

In the meantime, Tommy's condition, because he had not been under constant care of a trained allergist, was escalating. He spent a month under observation at the San Francisco French Hospital, and from October 1944 to mid-June 1945, was in the Stanford Convalescent Children's Hospital in Palo Alto with asthma and suspected rheumatic fever. Testing showed his high fevers and stomach disorders were the result of consuming food that caused internal hives to form. His diet was reduced to only sixteen items and he was given allergy shots three times a week. Thus it took several more years of testing and many more hospitalizations until some respite was attained. All at our expense; the Army and Red Cross were too busy to care for him due to the heavy load of casualties coming through this area. In June 1945, through my position with the UE, we were covered under the Kaiser Permanente Health Plan which lessened our medical costs.

We firmly believe our son's condition would not have become so severe had he been able to continue under the care of Stanford's allergy department instead of going into hiatus for nearly a year due to "evacuation."

The occurrences relating to Manzanar and Death Valley are taken from my diary. I kept it because Karl and I believed that the issue of the internment of those of Japanese ancestry, without hearing or trial, would have to be addressed some day and I should be prepared to participate in the process. As events evolved, where some of us were further victimized by the failure of governmental officials to put a stop to the Black Dragon activities in Manzanar, the need seemed even greater. Their anti-U.S. and "Long Live the Empire of Japan," etched in 1943 into wet cement around the former camp reservoir site, can be seen even today.

The question is often asked, were there any psychological affects? Yes, Tommy had nightmares, waking up crying and demanding to know: "What will happen to my daddy if the enemy gets ahold of him? Why didn't he go to fight Hitler instead of where the mean ones like those who came to our room in camp were?" My answer—"He's a soldier and had to go where ordered"—seemed to satisfy him, although his crying spells continued. After he overheard a conversation with friends about Karl's determination to serve in the Pacific, the nightmares increased in intensity.

We moved to Sonoma County in 1946 to try our hands at chicken farming. Tommy was in the second grade. The effects of internment lasted for a long time. For example, his pain and confusion when he saw a swastika in a classmate's home and was taunted anti-Japanese and anti-Semitic insults. He knew this was wrong, yet he questioned whether he should confront his friend or "keep his mouth shut."

Later, in the McCarthy era, when he was eleven and in the sixth grade, after a civics class, he came running home and asked: "Will I have to go into another concentration camp because my other grandparents came from Russia?"

In 1952, insult was added to injury in direct relation to the "evacuation." The Department of Justice Claims Division, after we agreed to settle our modest loss claim of $1,355.00 (the Studebaker, five cartons of books, pictures, and other documents) for $1,010.00, in turn notified us [the sum] would be reduced to $677.50 based on compensational items. This document contained a stamped addendum—"Above amount excludes interest of one spouse deemed ineligible." Thus, the payment we received was for only $460.00. We could have started appeal proceedings but felt it would be a futile and costly undertaking.

Though I had been housed, fed the same as all evacuees, and paid the meager sum of $12.00 or $16.00 per month for a forty-eight-hour work week, I was denied a share of our joint losses....

We never received a clothing allowance, nor reimbursement for the special foods, vitamins, and corrective shoes we supplied for our young child so that he could retain some semblance of health.

In 1957 we first became members of the Sonoma County JACL chapter. When we moved back to San Francisco in the 1960s, we transferred to a Bay Area chapter. We were active in obtaining trade union support for the successful Title II of the McCarran Act repeal and presently for union support for Redress/Reparations for Japanese Americans and Aleuts, now pending before this commission.

I feel very strongly there is a great need for redress as well as monetary reparations, free from any tax, to all those who endured confinement in a U.S.-style concentration camp. If some do not want payment, they could have the prerogative to assign their award to a community undertaking or charitable institution.

But most of all, we must see that it is made impossible for such racist, repressive edicts to be issued and used ever again against any group of people in these United States.

July 17, 1981
[signed]
Elaine Black Yoneda

Insufficient Care

Mabel Ota

Perhaps the greatest problems in the assembly centers and internment camps were inadequate medical facilities and care. Evacuee doctors and nurses and outside medical help were recruited to work in camp hospitals, often with minimal equipment and supplies. One Caucasian nurse at Heart Mountain remembers making do with extremely limited facilities, "We made mustard plasters in wash basins to put on the chests of the little pneumonia patients, and for diarrhea we used the water that rice had been cooked in." Soon after Mabel Ota was interned at Poston, Arizona, she gave birth to a daughter who suffered brain damage. Her account of the harrowing experience along with a description of her elderly diabetic father's decline in camp was published in 1984 in And Justice for All , *a compilation of oral histories.*

*

I was born in San Diego. I went to Calexico Elementary School, Calexico Junior High School, and graduated valedictorian from Calexico High School; and then I went to UCLA. I went out to UCLA, but I couldn't get in any of the dorms. They didn't allow Orientals in any of the dorms at UCLA, and so I ended up staying at the YWCA in Boyle Heights and commuted back and forth all those years. I got married in April 1939, graduated from UCLA in June, and then I looked for a job.

First I worked in a market as a cashier and then I took a civil service exam for the city. I passed it and got a job with the city in the Fingerprint and Identification Bureau. I had been working there for a short time when Pearl Harbor was attacked and they said it wasn't convenient to have Japanese working in that division, so I got transferred to the Jefferson Branch Library for six weeks and then I was terminated. They didn't give me a reason for it but I knew why. It was because I was Japanese.

My parents had written to me and asked my husband and me to come down to Calexico and help them sell the store, all the merchandise and so forth. We got permission to leave, and we went down there and helped my father. We advertised a closing-out sale in a local paper, and we sold everything at nominal cost and at a great loss. We had to because we didn't know what was going to happen to us or where we would be sent.

It was really sort of unbelievable. You know, when you go to college you have very high ideals of democracy, and when you have your rights taken away, it is really a shock. I kept saying all along, we're American citizens and the government couldn't possibly put us into camps. I really didn't believe it would happen until it did.

But I didn't become bitter. I guess we learn to roll with the punches. My parents were very stoic about it. You know, they never showed anger or bitterness, so I guess we sort of adopted their attitude. I guess we thought we should still be loyal and show that we are loyal by obeying. It wasn't anything that the Japanese Americans Citizens League said; it was just how we felt ourselves. In El Centro we found out that we were going to be evacuated to Poston, and then they sent out a notice requesting Nisei or any Japanese Americans to volunteer to go first to help open up the camp. And so Fred and I volunteered. We thought that it would probably help us get out sooner if we showed that we would cooperate. We were already thinking of getting out of there.

They said we could go up in our own car, so I piled all kinds of things in that car. The young fellow who was a gasoline attendant in Hoytsville, who knew me because I got gas there and my family got gas there, had offered to buy our car. When we told him we had to go to Poston, he offered to drive us there. He drove us, and we had to stop at Blythe for lunch. When we went in the restaurant, they refused to serve us. He didn't buy anything either. We thought that was awful and so we walked out of that restaurant, I remember. But there was kindness from some. Like this fellow, he drove us all the way to Poston and helped us unload, and then he paid us for the car in cash and he drove the car back.

There was only one obstetrician in that camp of ten thousand people, at the beginning anyway. And many of the women there were in their childbearing years like myself. Once a month I went in for a checkup. Then my husband, Fred, received this offer to leave to go to New York to become assistant manager of a cooperative. He left and the baby was supposed to come in May, so he said he would be back in time for the birth of the baby. But she came one month early, and when I went to the hospital, the nurse said the doctor had collapsed during the course of the previous day or night. He had delivered two babies and he had been on his feet all that time without help, so he collapsed and had gone back to the barracks to sleep.

I was in this room by myself and the nurse would come and check me every once in a while. I had a very long labor, almost twenty-eight hours.

The nurse who was checking me would listen to the heartbeat of the baby, and finally she said the heartbeat was getting very, very faint and she was going to have to call the doctor. But you know, for twenty-eight hours the doctor didn't come to see me. So then the doctor came and checked me and then he informed me that, yes, they were going to have to use forceps to pull the baby out because they couldn't perform an operation because there was no anesthesiologist in camp. So that was the way they were going to do it.

They took me to the delivery room and gave me a local and I could see the knife to cut me. Then he used these huge forceps, and I kept watching that clock. He really had a hard time yanking her out, but I was conscious all the time. So it was really a horrible experience. And then I remember looking at the baby and saying, "Gee, I thought babies were bright red when they were born." This one was very pale and she gave one faint cry and they rushed her to the incubator and said she was very weak. Then I didn't get to see her for three days because they said she was too weak to be moved. When I did see her on the third day I noticed that she had scabs on her head where the forceps had been used. There's one spot where hair has never grown.

I'm convinced that she suffered permanent brain damage at birth, and I've read a lot of publications and medical books and they say that if you have hard labor and oxygen doesn't get to the fetus for one minute or something, it causes damage. There was another lady who had a baby about the same time and her baby started sitting up at six months or so. Well, my baby couldn't, and so I could see that her development was behind. Other children start walking, say at around a year, and Madeline couldn't walk. She couldn't walk until she was twenty-two months, so I know she was way behind in her development.

She was born in April. I wanted to join Fred, but the camp doctor said, "Oh, you can't travel with her, she's too weak. You'll have to wait until she's at least six months." So I waited until November and joined him in New York.

My father, who was at Gila, was a diabetic and so in our family we never had desserts because diabetics are not supposed to have a lot of starch or sweets. He always limited himself to one bowl of rice and he had whole wheat bread. He had always raised all kinds of vegetables in the backyard, fresh vegetables, because they were so essential to his diet. When we lived at camp, the diet at the beginning was really terrible—just starches, whatever they could ship in, and hardly any vegetables or fruits. One meal I think there were nothing but bread, potatoes, spaghetti, and macaroni. I looked at it, and I said, "My gosh, there's nothing but starch." I remember having breakfast, oatmeal, and it was full of those little black bugs, and I remember taking all those bugs out of that bowl and it made a black ring around the bowl.

The food, I'm sure was related to my father's death, but you see, they didn't diagnose it correctly. They put him in the hospital. I got a letter from my mother who said, "He's in the hospital, come quickly." I went back and she said, "They said it's not diabetes." And so I went to the hospital to see him and they said he's suffering from melancholia. And they said we have no way of treating him here, but we can arrange for him to go to the Phoenix Sanitarium, where he can get shock treatment, and maybe he'll come out of it. But they said, it will be at your own expense, because they didn't have any money to do that. We had some money from the sale of the grocery store, and so my mother said, "Well, let's go there."

The sanitarium was outside of Phoenix, and my father was there and was given shock treatments, but be was only there for about six weeks and then the doctor called the camp and said, "Come, your father is going to pass away." We went back and he passed away a short time after we arrived

Transfering the infirm was a complicated matter. Arrival at Heart Mountain from Tule Lake, September 1943. Photograph by Bud Aoyama.

there. We got to see him before he died; and when I talked to the doctor the next day he said, "He didn't really have melancholia. It was brought on by his diabetes." The camp had only given him a urine test. They had not given him a blood analysis test, you see, and the urine test would come out okay. The diabetes wouldn't show up, but they had never given him a blood test and the doctor assumed that the camp had made the correct diagnosis, and he accepted it. So he went through all that for nothing. But his death certificate definitely says, "Died from diabetes," so he went into a diabetic coma, that's what it was, and then he died. If he didn't go to camp I'm sure he would have lived to a ripe old age because he was very careful watching his diet. The person himself has to do it, and he was always very careful.

I think the government was very wrong. This is why, although it is a very painful subject, I decided that I need to tell my story so that this kind of thing won't happen again. If people don't tell, no one will know the kinds of things that happened to loyal American citizens. I always considered myself loyal all through those years, and so it was a real shock that a loyal American citizen could be incarcerated like that and treated like a criminal. Maybe I should feel some anger or bitterness towards the government, because if the evacuation had not happened, then the tragedies in my life wouldn't have occurred. But, you know, you always have to roll with the punches, and I always look on the good side too.

Winter Night Sentry: Poems from the Justice Department Camps

Deprived of their liberty, many internees isolated in the Justice Department camps turned to haiku to articulate their longing for their wives, families, and homes, as well as their feelings of disillusionment over the war. Most of the haiku included here were written by the inmates of the Lordsburg and Santa Fe camps.

*

In the shade of summer sun
guard tapping rock
with club

Shiho Okamoto

Son joined the army
walked great distance
alone in the sagebrush

Sho Nakashima

Desert rain falling
spitting blood
then fall asleep

Neiji Ozawa

Festival of Souls
probably no water for them
in the cemetery this year

Yotenchi Agari

In the distance
early white clouds of fall
talk of transfers

Soichi Kanow

Winter night
sentry whistling
in the darkness

Shiho Okamoto

Internees at a Justice Department detention camp. Santa Fe, New Mexico. No date. Photographer unknown.

FROM *Hawaii End of the Rainbow*

Kazuo Miyamoto

Nearly 158,000 persons of Japanese ancestry lived in Hawaii when Japan attacked Pearl Harbor. Despite the logical assumption that the greatest danger of Japanese espionage would be among the Japanese living in Hawaii, fewer than 2,000 Japanese Americans—barely one percent of the Hawaiian population of ethnic Japanese—were taken into custody; even fewer were shipped to mainland WRA internment camps. Immediately following the Pearl Harbor attack, Hawaii was put under martial law. However, after much discussion, the War Department concluded that evacuating many Japanese from the Hawaiian Islands was impractical due to shipping difficulties and the labor shortages that would arise should the Japanese be removed. A year after Pearl Harbor, only fifty-nine families had been evacuated from Hawaii.

Kazuo Miyamoto was born in Kauai in 1897, attended Stanford University, and studied medicine at Washington University Medical School in St. Louis, Missouri. He practiced medicine in Honolulu before and after World War II. His Hawaii End of the Rainbow *is a history of the Japanese American people in Hawaii that covers wartime reactions and the deportation of Japanese internees who were arrested as suspected enemy aliens.*

*

...Mrs. Haru Arata was in the kitchen early. From that night on there was to be no light after sundown. A complete blackout and curfew order was out for the civilians. But no home was prepared for such an emergency measure and the only alternative was to go to bed early. It was nearing a time of the year when nights could be long even in Hawaii. The sun set at 6:00 P.M.

Just sandwiches or rice and tea with pickled vegetable for those that wished a light, simple dish. Nobody had much of an appetite. The day was bright and sunny but toward evening it cooled rapidly. There was no moon. In no time the entire city was dark. The streets were deserted except for official cars that silently coursed back and forth with shrouded headlights.

Sporadic firing could be heard from many quarters of the city. Jittery civilian guards must be firing at any moving object. It was risky to be stirring outside.

At seven o'clock, Seikichi Arata was in pajamas. It was early to go to bed but it was a nerve-racking day and he was very tired. Just to stretch and relax would do him good. Just then there was a knock at the front door. Sadao went to the door.

"Is Seikichi Arata at home?"

"Yes, he is."

"Please call him here." There were two men and they produced badges. They indicated that they were from the police department.

"I'll go call him," and Sadao went to the bedroom to fetch his father.

"We are from the police department and want to take you to headquarters for questioning," explained the Caucasian member.

"For what?" asked Sadao.

"Oh, just a few questions. He will be detained only a few hours," soothingly explained the police officer.

"Then I have to change clothes," said Seikichi and turned to go to the bedroom.

"I'll go with you," said the officer as he entered the room and remained there while Seikichi dressed.

Haru Arata instinctively felt something was wrong and followed the two. She took out his heaviest serge suit, added a few handkerchiefs, a comb, and his pair of glasses. "You may or may not need any money, but just in case, I am putting two $10 bills in your pocket. These officers say it will only be for a few hours. We hope you will be back in the morning. Take care and be careful. Now officer, please drive slowly."

"OK mama-san. He will be all right."

Seikichi stopped in the doorway. "Sadao, I'll leave everything to you. Take good care of all." Somehow he felt it was going to be longer than a few hours. The two men helped him from each side to descend the front steps. Just to be escorted in such a manner gave him the feeling that his liberty was being curtailed: that he was being spirited away. In some inexplicable way he felt in his bones that this was like being kidnapped.

When they reached the street, there was a touring car with a man at the wheel. "All right, let's go, Joe," commanded the "haole" man.

"Papa-san, hands please," and when Seikichi raised his hand to a horizontal level he felt the cold steel of handcuffs applied to his wrist.

Shocked to his bones, Seikichi felt a cold anger rising in his chest. "Why this degradation! Can't these two giants see that a puny five-footer at seventy years of age would not even consider escape? Why, in decency's name handcuffs?" He was seated between the two men on the back seat. He reclined and closed his eyes. When he opened his eyes because the car came to a stop, he found that all traffic was being scrutinized at a roadblock at the junction of Liliha and King Streets. Several men in plain clothes and military police with fixed bayonets were peeping into and inspecting cars that approached. The driver of each car stepped out to show identification badges to the sergeant in charge. Everything was done in subdued flashlight.

The touring car proceeded toward the waterfront and finally turned to the right and stopped in front of a building. It was not the Police Station. It was the Immigration Station. Seikichi was led into a room where six army enlisted men were processing arrivals. The handcuffs were removed and he was led to a desk by the detective who laid a blue card on the desk. It bore the name "Arata, Seikichi, alien." This name was checked on the list of names that filled several pages.

When he entered there was a bald, timid, and whimpering man in pajamas and wrapped up in a blanket. Evidently he was not given much time before he was snatched away from his sick bed. "I am sick, I have a fever of 101. Very chilly. I must have my medicine. My blood pressure is high and I must have medicine." To this plea the sergeant said nothing. There was no consideration. His duty was to process these prisoners into this ready-made prison. Sick or dying, nothing beyond handkerchiefs and glasses were allowed. Medicine was not a permissible item.

"Now go over there and face the wall. Put both hands above your head and keep your hands on the wall." Seikichi did as he was ordered, while one of the sergeants searched his pockets and took out the wallet and fountain pen. These were confiscated and placed in a large Manila envelope marked with his name.

"All right, old man. Go up the stairway. It is dark. Hold on to the side railing. It is perfectly safe," said the not unkind sergeant. Then he yelled facing the second story. "Another prisoner!" Seikichi was ordered from home with the assurance that it was going to be an interrogation lasting a few hours; the truth of the matter was that he was now a prisoner.

Up the stairway, he was careful to cling to the metal railing. At the top a soldier took him by the arm and talked to a guard that stood outside a door. The guard opened the door and pushed him into a room that was stuffy and reeking with the odor of human bodies. There was a continuous mumbling sound and there were some bodies on the floor. When his eyes became accustomed to the darkness he was able to discern the outline of three tiers of iron beds. It occurred to him that since he was not the first, he would not be the last. He had better look for a place to sleep if he were to rest at all. Most of the beds were occupied but on the farther end, he found empty spaces on the uppermost tier. He clambered aloft warily to avoid stepping on the persons on the lower two levels. Without taking off his coat, he stretched out on the mattress.

It was a strange feeling. He closed his eyes. It did not matter much because even with his eyes wide open there was nothing visible in this pitch dark night. He reviewed the turn in events of the last thirty minutes.

It was a short half hour, but during that interval a revolutionary change in human status had come over him. Never had he dreamed before that he would ever run afoul of the established laws of the country. He considered prisoners a different breed of men. He was an honest and upright citizen of the community. But then, here he was with that appellation preceding his name. In the seventy years of his life this episode could be the culmination and an inglorious end: to be considered a shame by his children and grandchildren. The low voices of the people in the room were strained, but devoid of any anger or hysteria. The conversation centered on the events of the day rather than the arrest which brought them together.

Almost every quarter hour the door opened to let in new arrivals. "Mr. Kagami, how is Waialua Way?" came a voice from near the door. Evidently the newcomer was recognized.

"Four of us were brought in from Waialua by the FBI. Whereas ordinarily it is a one-hour travel, today we were five hours on the way. There was another attack by Japanese planes after dark. Police stopped the car and crawled under it. We four sat on the side of the ditch, but nothing happened," related the new arrival and Seikichi listened to the talk as he had nothing else to do. His mind ceased to function and he was in complete passivity. Somebody opened the windows. It was discovered the following morning that in a room built for eighty persons, one hundred and eighty had been crowded in. The stifling oppressiveness resulting from the stagnation of air was somewhat ameliorated by the open windows, but in the wee hours of the morning it became chilly.

At about two o'clock, a commotion took place as twelve barefooted fishermen wearing raincoats were thrown into the room. These men were out fishing that morning, had been machine-gunned by planes, and were glad to be alive.

With every arrival there was conversation and the continuous hushed talk prevented any sustained sleep. When day dawned at six o'clock, the outline of faces became more distinct. Remarks such as these were heard all over the room.

"You, too! What a night! When did you arrive? I was escorted by in an MP in the late afternoon. The Caucasian MPs were very gentlemanly and there was no rough talk."

"I came after dark. Oriental detectives came after me. I was watering the lawn wearing tennis shoes. Because I was told that this questioning was to take only several hours I did not even change clothes. I have thin summer pants and tennis shoes. It certainly was cold this morning. I wonder how long the several hours is going to stretch out?"

"Soldiers came after me. They had fixed bayonets and appeared fearsome but they were gentle. We were having supper when they arrived but they allowed me to finish my meal. I was allowed to change into a suit and hearing what you went through, perhaps I was the best treated," smiled a groceryman from Pawaa.

With the break of dawn, people began stirring and most headed for the lavatory. It adjoined the large dormitory and was open at all times, but contained only two flush bowls and two wash basins. To economize on water a gadget usually found on steamers was attached to the faucets. One had to grab the two flaring out-turned thumbs to turn on the water. Thus to wash

Untitled, by Sadayuki Uno. Oil on canvas, 20 x 24 in. 1944.

one's face, the left hand had to grasp these blades to let water out while washing with the right hand. While the new immigrants from ships were accustomed to such devices, why the architect installed such a miserly gadget in water-plentiful Honolulu was beyond anybody's comprehension. With 180 men to use this limited facility, the room was packed continuously.

At about 9:00 A.M., the door opened and an MP stuck his head in and announced, "You will be taken out of the room to have your breakfast. Form in a single line and make it snappy!" The inmates lined up and marched into the hallway and descended a long straight stairway that led into the inner court of the Immigration Station. There were three MPs with bayoneted rifles stationed along this hall and stairway to direct and keep the file of men against the wall. They used the sharp instrument at a menacingly short distance from the men urging them forward.

To Seikichi Arata, this was the most degrading and humiliating experience he had ever gone through, but this was only the first experience of such a nature he was destined to undergo. He heard one of the soldiers growl, "What the hell! Let's get a machine gun and mow these bastards down. Lot of time wasted and good food thrown away." Seikichi could not help feeling sorry about the whole situation. Perhaps this soldier lost a brother or friend in the blitz. Naturally he had seen the sunken ships in Pearl Harbor. It was natural for one to become angered at the wanton destruction. Perhaps his own grandson, Edward, was feeling the same indignation as this lately arrived soldier to the islands.

The line passed a table out in the open courtyard and each was to pick an army aluminum mess kit and be given two slices of bread with strawberry jam. Each was to help himself to coffee which was in a large, thirty-gallon container. The coffee was so hot it nearly burned Seikichi's lips and tongue. Most just drank coffee. Ironically, Japanese carpenters were busily constructing barbed-wire extensions above the ten-foot wall surrounding the inner court. The twenty minutes allowed out in the open air was a treat after the stuffy, cramped room. Men walked back and forth stretching their stiffened joints, and shaking hands with friends who were also caught in yesterday's raid. A shrill whistle blew and they were lined in single file and returned to the same room.

At about noon, Shoichi Asami's name was called and he was led downstairs. Because his name began with an A, there was a faint hope in everyone's mind that "hearings" had begun in alphabetical order and soon all would be returned home. All knew almost everyone else and there was none in the crowd that would have acted inimically to the security of the United States.

Mr. Asami returned after a short while. "There was no hearing. I was questioned about certain matters concerning the Nippu Jiji Publishing Co. But while I waited there, I overheard talk that there was a Japanese naval officer taken captive in yesterday's attack. I wonder how it happened but the talk was pretty excited about this captive." This was the group's first news concerning the operator of the midget submarine with whom they were to travel and share hardship for many months.

At about three o'clock, the door was again opened and the single-file procession proceeded down to the inner court where two slices of bread, corned beef, and a cup of coffee were served. As the room could no longer admit newcomers, the men were able to arrange themselves so that as many as possible could sleep on the bunks. On Seikichi Arata's three-tier bunk, three slept in place of the regular two. Two on the edges slept with their heads in one direction and the middle person had his head at the opposite end. This arrangement was all right as far as stretching their bodies was concerned, but being kicked in the face during the night was not very pleasant. On some lower bunks four slept across two beds.

That night, December 8, there was a turmoil in the next room until dawn, just as there was with their incarceration the previous night. Germans and Italians were being hauled in and the door kept banging as a new arrival was shoved in. The following morning, Seikichi counted about sixty men and twenty women when the new arrivals were marched out for their meals. There were only a dozen Japanese women incarcerated. During the night, there were about fifty more Japanese apprehended and these were quartered in a room in the opposite wing. When these arrivals came out for their meals, the old-timers, with mixed emotions, looked down upon them from their window.

"He's come too. Well, well, we'll have company and fun too," joyfully exclaimed one observer.

"There's Yamada. He was very active in community affairs. He led the drive for the Japanese Red Cross and help for the wounded's families. I was wondering why he was not in the 'blue card' list." His remarks were not devoid of a certain triumphant glee in seeing a mishap overtake a competitor.

"Just the same I am sorry that he has joined us, because I heard his wife is bedridden from apoplexy. For that matter there are several here that should have remained at home. Mr. Komeya, now eighty-four, was in bed for the last two years. Dr. Mori is also about that age. He has diabetes and can hardly walk. That man from Ewa cannot walk from joint trouble. I don't know how the FBI picked us out of the mass, but if you qualify and I am considered suspect, then there are thousands more that should be here," said Seikichi Arata. He was thoughtful. The whole pattern of procedure was not clear. How extensive was this roundup going to be and on what evidence was it based? For as long as he could remember he was never questioned once by the authorities.

A journalist nearby added, "We are all in the 'blue card' class. Those not in this category have not been invited, that's all."

"But look at some of these young men. I don't know them well. They are Nisei I am sure. Doesn't American citizenship protect them?" Seikichi was thinking aloud.

The journalist took up the thought, "Whether you heard or not I don't know, but yesterday's radio announced that Governor Poindexter conferred with Washington, D.C. and turned the government over to the military. Hawaii is now under martial law and run by General Short."

"What does this change of government mean?"

"It means that the usual protection for civilians is now suspended. You have heard of the writ of habeas corpus that was evolved in England in the people's struggle against the aristocracy? You have not? Well, it is a guarantee that we small potatoes are given: that our liberties will be protected and we cannot be imprisoned without cause for any length of time. I don't know to what extent the martial law will supplant civilian law. I don't think martial law ruled any American community for a long time because Americans

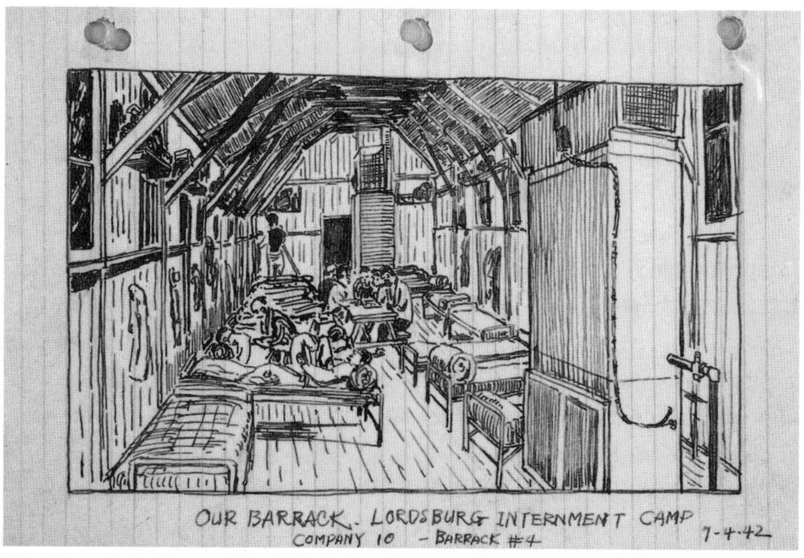

Our Barrack by George Hoshida. Ink and watercolor, 9½ x 6 in. July 4, 1942.

are very proud and jealous of the writ of habeas corpus. From a legal standpoint, the people of Hawaii will be at the mercy of the military. A dark age in Hawaii has come. Yet a military governor is an American raised with an education no different from any other civilian, and his military lawyers are grounded in Anglo-Saxon law. I cannot see how these men will defy the usual concept of human rights. But I think the courts of law will function very swiftly under martial law."

"That means then that all of us are now subject to martial law?"

"That I am pretty sure. Even without martial law, aliens are subject to detention and segregation. This is a customary procedure among warring nations. A country at war must look after security from within. We as enemy aliens can be detained as long as America decides to keep us behind fences."

On Tuesday morning after breakfast, the sergeant came into the room and read the names of about half of the men. These were ordered out of the room; where to nobody knew, but it was better than being locked up. Seikichi Arata's name was not on the list. For the first time in two days the remaining ones, being relieved of congestion, felt that they could at least sleep in comfort. Brooms and mops were handed to them and a general clean-up was undertaken with vigor. People were glad to do something. The atmosphere seemed to get cleaner and fresher after the sudden exodus, and the common urge was to stretch at full length and catch up on sleep. Just about the time when they woke from their nap, in mid-afternoon, the sergeant reappeared and called off a list of names. Seikichi was among them.

These men were taken out to the lawn in front of the side entrance facing Pier 2 amidst a drizzling rain that soaked them to their skin. Few had coats and there was no shelter. The list was checked twice. They were then ordered to board covered trucks which took them to Pier 6, the Naval Wharf. During this trip they were guarded by soldiers with fixed bayonets, three to a truck. Two armored cars were sandwiched among the vehicles. On the wharf, the men were lined up and again checked as to number and then ordered to board a large scow. A steam tugboat towed it. Fifty men that comprised this group were ordered to crouch down on the floor of the flat boat, while half a dozen soldiers with shotguns stood menacingly fore and aft with the muzzles pointed at the men huddled together in the center.

Perhaps one of the young soldiers could not help but crack a joke, in spite of the situation being anything but jocular, when he said, "You are all being taken out into the Pacific Ocean and will get scuttled to feed the sharks." This was bad enough, but the Germans had machine guns trained on them when they were ferried across later. A coast guard cutter was moored nearby, and its crew lined the rail watching these poor captives led away.

The radio of the coast guard cutter was turned on and its loud speaker blared forth President Roosevelt's message to Congress announcing the declaration of war against the three Axis nations. It recounted the treachery of the Japanese in attacking Pearl Harbor while peaceful negotiations were being conducted at Washington. Since these men were ignorant of the events taking place in the world, this was the first news of the spread of the war to a worldwide scope. Honolulu looked like a deserted city. At the waterfront, the usual traffic at that time of day was conspicuous by its absence. It looked like a Sunday afternoon.

The tugboat pulled the barge out into the harbor and took it straight across to Sand Island which is situated on the west side of the harbor entrance. When the first contingent left the room in the morning, somebody said that they were to be shipped to an "island," and many thought it would be Molokai. Since pineapple crates are hauled from Molokai and Lanai on these barges, the destination could have been that island. When it turned out to be Sand Island everyone let out a sigh of relief.

A detachment of soldiers awaited them at the crude landing and the captives were marched two abreast. A dozen soldiers armed with shotguns flanked both sides. It was just getting dark but everything was still visible. In front of Seikichi Arata walked Mr. Komeya, eighty-four-years-old, who had been routed out of his sick bed. He could hardly walk, let alone keep up with the rest. Seikichi called the guard's attention to his plight. The captain came over and told the old man to step out of the line, for a truck was going to take him to the destination.

Just then a cold shower drenched them to their skin. It was a short march and a welcome exercise for most of them, but the tragic spectacle of a beaten group of men guarded with lethal weapons forlornly marching to an unknown destination in the gathering dusk was objectively and poetically felt by Seikichi even as a participant. It is said that Japanese love tragedy—love to shed tears over drama and stories—and they seem to have the peculiar quality of "enjoying pain." For any motion picture or drama to be a financial success among the Japanese there must be included in its plot scenes and episodes that wring the tear glands. Seikichi was detachedly imagining the scene of "retreat from Moscow of Napoleon's men" that he had once seen in a picture book. Surely the only common factor was the dejected manner of the marchers, but somehow he felt poetically elated. The procession ended at the headquarters of the Sand Island garrison made up of low, Spanish-type architecture.

The prisoners were lined up in single file in the hallway, which was lit by a very dim green light, for the windows were all covered by black board.

"Take off all your clothes and shoes. Hold them in your hands." As they stood without a stitch on their shivering bodies, a captain appeared and addressed them through an interpreter.

"You are now prisoners of war. I have been ordered to see that you are kept here. Strict discipline will be maintained, but I do not intend to be inhuman. Whether I shall be able to pursue this course and succeed in my purpose will depend on your behavior. I have respected the Japanese people in the past. I have studied your people a little and I think I know you. But after Sunday I know that we have a worthy opponent in the Japanese Army and Navy." Captain Coughlin, spare and straight, was well over six feet, and his bearing was very military.

The immediate reaction to this speech of introduction was favorable and the men accepted the ensuing humiliating search of their person and belongings without resentment. It was a manly talk, straight and succinct. They were ordered to stand before several non-commissioned officers, to place their belongings on the desk. Money and valuables were placed in an envelope and after a search, clothes and shoes were returned. When ten or twelve put their clothes on, they were led outside. It was pitch dark. No light could be used and so they held on to each other's hands and followed a soldier. After walking about a quarter mile, they met their friends who had preceded them in the morning. These people had put up tents all day. The new arrivals were handed two blankets and assigned tents for the night.

When Seikichi Arata went to his tent there was no cot. Because of the rain the ground was wet and since Sand Island is only slightly above sea level, brackish water seeped through the ground. The sergeant found cots for them and led them to the dining room for some sandwiches. The attack of mosquitoes was persistent and annoying, but before Seikichi knew it he was fast asleep. He was exhausted mentally. It was an eventful day.

Autobiography of an Italian Internee

Ezio Pinza

One of the contradictory aspects of the Japanese American internment was that the United States declaration of war against the Axis nations (Japan, Germany, and Italy) did not result in mass exclusion of German or Italian aliens. While the War Department did consider whether the power of Executive Order 9066 should be used to extend to the roughly 80,000 Italians, Germans, and former Germans expatriated by the Nazi government who were living on the West Coast, mass movement of Germans and Italians was generally opposed as being too costly and logistically difficult. On an individual basis however, Italians and Germans, like the Japanese, had been under surveillance by the FBI since 1939. By February 16, 1942, the Justice Department had seized 2,192 Japanese; 1,393 Germans, and 264 Italians. Close to 250 German and Italian individuals were interned for up to two years in camps in Montana, Oklahoma, Tennessee, and Texas. Like the Japanese, Italians and German aliens were also forced to move inland beyond Military Zone No. 1, away from their homes and livelihoods.

Ezio Pinza, born in Rome in 1892, was a world-famous Italian basso opera singer residing in New York in the 1940s with his wife and daughter. This excerpt from Ezio Pinza: Autobiography, *written with the assistance of Robert Magidoff, follows his arrest and detention at Ellis Island together with other Japanese, German, and Italian aliens who were rounded up on the East Coast after the declaration of war.*

As it does every spring, the Metropolitan Opera was planning a tour early in 1942. Along with the many other Italians in the company, I applied for permission to join the traveling group. Days passed, weeks, and no answer. There was no refusal, but no permission either, whereas most of my colleagues had received theirs without delay. It was clear to me that something had gone wrong. I even had my suspicions of what it was—the fierce jealousy of a fellow bass—but I could not bring myself to believe that he would stoop to treachery. Now my thoughts kept drifting to him.

On Thursday, March 12, 1942, at eleven o'clock in the morning, two well-dressed young men entered my house through the back door without ringing the bell. Doris had gone to the village to shop. The seven-month-old Clelia was in her room with the nurse. I was at my desk in the living room, writing out some checks. The two men came in and walked straight up to me.

"Are you Ezio Pinza?" one of them asked sharply.

"Yes, I am. What can I do for you?"

"In the name of the President of the United States, you are under arrest!"

There was such iron in his voice that I rose involuntarily. For one fleeting moment, I had the illusion of myself behind bars, handcuffed, condemned, lost to the world for all eternity. A sound came from Clelia's room. Was she crying or laughing? I don't remember, but the sound brought me back to reality.

"Would you mind waiting until my wife comes back from the village?" I asked. "It won't be long."

"There's plenty of time," one of them said, "We intend to search your place, anyway. Here is the warrant."

"And Now for You Two!" by Cloyd Sweigert, May 28, 1942.

This cartoon, which appeared in the *San Francisco Chronicle*, underlines the intention of Lt. Gen. DeWitt to do to German and Italian Americans what he had already done to Japanese Americans.

"I know who sent you," I suddenly blurted out.

"Who?" one man said.

I named the Met singer. One of the men made a note, without giving any indication of whether he knew the name. Then the two young men systematically set about searching our house. They missed nothing—every closet, every drawer, every scrap of paper was examined—while I sat helpless. After a long while one approached me and asked where I had hidden my ring with the swastika.

"Do you mean my tortoise-shell ring?" I asked them. "It was brittle and broke up years ago. I threw away the pieces. It was not a German swastika anyway."

The men made no comment, but wrote down my words and went on with the search. Their function, I understood, was not to interrogate or discuss my case with me, but to search the house and take me away. I was silent from then on.

They were still at it when Doris came home. The two FBI men said that I could talk to her all I wanted and paid no further attention to us.

Young, inexperienced, and immature in so many ways, my Piccola ("the little one," as I called Doris in Italian) quickly overcame the initial shock and began to ask questions and make suggestions that were calm, direct, realistic. There was nothing except her very, very pale face to show that she was engaged in anything other than the businesslike conversation between husband and wife on the eve of a normal parting. I knew that, as an enemy alien under arrest, I would be able to do next to nothing on my own behalf. This meant that the fight for my release would be completely in Doris' hands, and it braced me to see that those hands, which I thought had been made solely for me to kiss, were steady.

The search finally came to an end. The one thing the FBI men found of sufficient interest to take along with them was the bill of sale for my motorboat. We were about to leave when one of them noticed a framed letter, written in Italian, hanging on a wall alongside autographed photos of some of my friends and colleagues. Pointing at the letter, he said, "What is this?"

"A letter written by Verdi. One of my prize possessions."

"Who?"

The question, coming as it did from an exceedingly keen-looking young man, was so unexpected that Doris and I exchanged glances and smiled. It was a good sign that we smiled, I thought, an omen signifying that I would come back soon, a free man. I did come back, and I was free, but that did not happen soon at all.

The men took me to the Foley Square Courthouse, where I was searched, photographed, fingerprinted and questioned. Then, the same two men took me to Ellis Island on a private boat, to prevent publicity, and there they surrendered me to uniformed guards and said in farewell, "Good luck, Pinza!"

There were 126 of us, Italians, Germans, Japanese, milling around in the enormous barrack-like room on Ellis Island. Most of us were bewildered and frightened, desperate for solace and despairing at our helplessness. Our misery was still further intensified by the untidiness to which we were reduced: all suspenders, belts, shoelaces, and other objects that might help a would-be suicide had been taken away from us.

Many of the internees recognized me and wondered why I had been brought in, for I had never taken part in political activity. Whatever the degree of their own guilt, they all were touchingly solicitous of me, especially the Italians. They introduced me to a card game called scopa and welcomed me as a partner whenever I wished to play.

The men I was with came from different walks of life: workingmen, professional soldiers, and intellectuals. One man was a member of a noble German family, who, far from resenting the incarceration, as most of us did, justified it in conversations with me as a necessity dictated by centuries of experience with enemy espionage. Sophisticated, superior and, I can wager, unhappy in his personal life, he discussed our plight with the detachment of a scientist speaking of insects. Every living cell in my body cried in protest against that approach. Let the guilty be punished, but I—I wanted to go back to my family, the opera house, the daily routine of playing with Clelia, puttering around in my victory garden, rehearsing, facing the audience! Instead, there were the guards, the open latrine, the dull food, the weary monotony of prison life—a monotony broken by sporadic questionings and by Doris' weekly visits. She had only a few brief minutes each time, into which she crowded news of our child and home, and reported on her efforts to obtain my release—all within the earshot of a guard....

At first I thought that mine was a simple case of an anonymous denunciation which could be disproved easily, because I knew I was innocent of any wrongdoing against my adopted country, in thought as well as in deed. A good lawyer, a few affidavits, would turn the trick, I was sure; but the rigidity of legal procedures, the nature of the questionings to which I was subjected and the obstacles Doris kept encountering soon opened my eyes to the magnitude of the blow that had befallen me.

Doris' natural first step was to telephone my friends and associates, Constance Hope, Edward Johnson, and Marks Levine. All three were horrified and asserted their confidence in my integrity, and a readiness to anything in their power on my behalf. Just as unanimously, they recommended that Doris retain the services of a reputable lawyer and that the fact of my detention be kept out of the newspapers until the authorities reached a decision.

Easier said than done. Every newspaper in New York carried the story of my arrest under sensational headlines, the very next morning. Even the *New York Times* front-paged it as a "hot" story, with my photo thrown in:

Ezio Pinza Seized as Enemy Alien;
FBI Takes Singer to Ellis Island

The very thoroughness of the press coverage proved to be the silver lining in the cloud: it won me a powerful ally. Mayor Fiorello LaGuardia, a patient of Dr. Leak's [Doris's father, a dentist], remarked to him in the course of a telephone conversation, "There's something crooked about this business. Someone was terribly anxious to tip off the papers. Let me know if there's anything I can do for Mr. Pinza."

I heard of this remark the very next day from my father-in-law himself. Luckily, he had been treating my teeth at the time of my arrest, which gave him the right to a pass two or three times a week to complete his job. He was therefore able to keep me in touch with developments far more regularly than Doris could.

The law firm to which she turned for help, on Constance Hope's advice, was that of Greenbaum, Wolff, and Ernst, headed by the well-known champion of liberal causes, Morris Ernst. He agreed to represent me, but only on the understanding that, in view of the wartime situation, his ultimate client was the United States government, and that he was free to withdraw from the case at any time he became convinced that my freedom was not thoroughly warranted. This meant, in effect, that he and his associates would sit in judgment of me before wholly identifying themselves with my case, and would continue to sit in judgment throughout its course. Neither Doris nor I hesitated. A lawyer who is convinced of his client's innocence, we knew, is a hundredfold more effective than one who is not. Whatever doubts Ernst entertained at the outset were dissipated by the facts that emerged during his inquiry, and by Bruno Walter's plea for him to undertake my defense. My old friend, himself a foe and victim of totalitarianism, rallied to my side the moment he heard of my arrest.

The decision taken, Ernst assigned one of his firm's brightest young men, Harold Stern, to handle my case—a most happy choice. Tireless, resourceful, and a man of integrity, Harold was to become, with the years, a personal friend and a trusted business associate.

By the time he came into the picture, however, it was almost too late. A hearing of my case had been held on March 24, twelve days after my arrest, and the decision of the Board was against me.

To understand the full gravity of my situation, you must bear in mind that the Bill of Rights, not always applicable to U.S. citizens in time of war, is nonexistent so far as an enemy alien is concerned. In being summoned to a hearing, he is presumed guilty until he can prove his innocence, and is expected to answer charges of which he is kept in ignorance. It is up to him to refute detractors whose identity and allegations are withheld from him, and to show that his release is not inimical to the best interests of the United States. This, at a time when he has no way of knowing whether the evidence he offers is to the point or is utterly irrelevant. The hearing is held before a Board of three reputable private citizens, from which the defendant's lawyers are barred, unless called in as witnesses. If the Board fails to reach unanimity in clearing the accused, he is sent to a detention camp for the duration.

The Board consisted of Dr. George Schuster, president of Hunter College; Edward Collins of the Fifth Avenue Coach Company; and Dr. Henry Van Dusen, then president of the faculty at Union Theological Seminary. There was never any doubt in my mind that these men, selected to weigh the testimony and reach a verdict, were fair-minded American citizens doing a necessary job, yet how could I, or any other person whose happiness and career depended on the outcome of a hearing conducted under such circumstances, help finding it all strange and forbidding?

Shocked by the arrest, demoralized by the prison-like life in the barracks, and ignorant of the charges against me, I put on the worst show of my life at the hearing. My English, imperfect under the best circumstances, must have been positively murderous as I stuttered, mumbled, and repeatedly proclaimed my innocence—the least recommended and most unconvincing method of defense, for who would acknowledge his guilt under those circumstances?

Several days later I was informed of the Board's failure to acquit me. As I learned subsequently, only one of the three judges was not convinced of my innocence, but that was sufficient to condemn me to a camp until the war's end, with no visitors allowed, and only one letter a month from home. That was the end. The end of family, of love, of opera, of sweet life itself. Only a mere formality stood between me and incarceration for God knows how many years: the signature of the United States attorney general, Francis

Biddle, approving the Board's decision. He had, of course, the power to order a second hearing, but thus far, we were told, he had not exercised it in cases involving enemy aliens. I therefore listened without hope or enthusiasm to various plans of carrying on the fight, outlined to me one day by Doris, the next by her father, the third by Harold Stern.

I did not discourage them, naturally. What I did was far worse. Bewildered by the verdict and by the legal processes I did not understand, I yielded to apathy, to a kind of hypnotized listlessness which kept frustrating them at every step.

The strategy, as worked out by Stern, aimed first at obtaining Francis Biddle's order for a second hearing; next, testimonials from unimpeachable character witnesses, that might outweigh the allegations of my slanderers; and finally, finding out the nature of the charges against me in order to enable me to meet them, should we succeed in gaining the hearing. I could help little in connection with Biddle's order or testimonials, but Stern depended almost exclusively on me in his efforts to trace the charges. Yet I was of no help whatsoever.

"Please try!" Stern appealed to me. "Recall the questions you were asked; analyze them. What were they after—the FBI, the Board? What precisely did they want to know?"

The men who had been questioning me since my arrest were cagey, yet I had some vague ideas. All I needed was to make an effort and work it out in my mind, but this seemed beyond my power to do.

"How can you expect me to fight windmills?" Stern would shout in desperation, and turn to Doris for help. She pleaded with me, tears in her eyes, but I was like an ox unresistingly led to slaughter. I behaved as though I had lost all interest in the case. Or in anything, for that matter. Before the hearing, I used to delight in the fruit and cheese which Doris was allowed to bring for me, to supplement the wholesome (lots of meat, milk and butter) but monotonous fare at Ellis Island. Now I hardly touched Doris' food. I listened dutifully to her stories of baby Clelia's intelligence and happy vitality, but they no longer aroused that sharp longing which might have awakened me to alert participation in the struggle for my freedom. Blocked myself, I was blocking those who tried to help. Nothing short of a miracle, it seemed, would turn the trick for me, and a miracle did happen, wrought by none other than my little Clelia.

She was a most cheerful baby, a ready smile on her face at all times and for anyone who might come along. She was also a healthy child, but one morning she woke up vomiting, then lay pale and silent, hardly showing signs of life. Doris immediately called Dr. Elsworth Smith, an old friend of the Leak family, who had taken care of Doris herself since she was nine months old, and who was now our pediatrician. Dr. Smith found Clelia suffering from intussusception (the telescoping of the small intestine into the larger one), and rushed her off with Doris to a New York hospital equipped for an immediate operation. The operation itself, he said, was not complicated, but there was the danger of shock, which might be fatal.

While Doris was on her way to New York, her mother informed the Ellis Island authorities of the emergency, requesting them to send me to the hospital so that I could be on hand during the operation. They responded with utmost sympathy, dispatching me immediately in the company of a guard. I met Doris in front of the hospital, took the prostrate child in my arms, and carried her in. Alerted by our doctor, the hospital personnel had everything ready for the operation, but first Clelia was given barium by enema. Dr. Charles Blakemore, the famous surgeon, watched the progress of the liquid through a fluoroscope to find the point of blockage, simultaneously exerting gentle pressure on Clelia's abdomen with his fingers. Miraculously, the manipulation unknotted the intestines, making the operation unnecessary. Clelia came to life and started to cry, and soon the sparkle returned to her eyes, the color to her cheeks. Doris picked up our daughter and handed her to me. Clelia looked at me and smiled happily. I cried. Then drew Doris toward me, and kissed them both. The guard, who had orders to take me back the moment my presence was no longer needed, turned to look out the window and waited until I told him I was ready to go.

I leave it to psychologists to explain why the shock of this experience should have proved more effective than Doris' pleas, Harold's logic, and my own realization of the danger confronting me. Whatever the reason, the fact remains that my memory and power of analysis began to function from that day on. Alert and cooperative, prodded by Harold at every step, I was able to gather the various clues inherent in the questionings and to pinpoint the following accusations:

1. I owned a ring with the Nazi swastika on it.
2. I had a boat equipped with a radio that received and sent out secret messages.
3. I was a personal friend of Benito Mussolini.
4. I proudly bore the nickname "Mussolini."
5. I sent coded messages from the stage of the Metropolitan Opera House during the Saturday matinee radio broadcasts. The code was allegedly based on a system of changed tempi in my singing.

6. In 1935, I had organized a collection of gold and silver for the benefit of the Italian government.

Harold was shaken by the cumulative effect of the implied charges, the deadly intent behind them, and the peril to me, should I be unable to disprove them. The year was 1942, you will recall, when the enemy was riding high, and the military situation was fraught with the gravest danger. The mood of the country was dominated by suspicion and lack of forgiveness.

One by one Harold went over the accusations against me:

1. The "Nazi" ring referred to was that Pago Pago [Samoan] tortoise-shell ring I have mentioned earlier, with the primitive inverted swastika.
2. I had sold the boat soon after Pearl Harbor, simply because gasoline was not available for pleasure boats. The common ship-to-shore radio that came with the boat was not functioning, and I did not have it put in order, as any radio mechanic could verify with no difficulty.
3. I had never met Mussolini, and never tried to.
4. No one called me "Mussolini" at any time. That was the nickname of another Metropolitan basso, the distinguished Virgilio Lazzari, who, in fact, resembled the dictator. Harold obtained a photo of the singer, which was shown to the Board.
5. This is the most ridiculous of all charges, considering the fact that it emanated from sources well versed in music. No singer can change tempi of an opera. They are set by the conductor, and the conductor alone.
6. The only charge that had some basis in fact concerned the collection of gold for Italy. I had no hand in organizing the collection, but I did contribute a plain gold ring. However deeply I regret the contribution, the regret is in no way to be interpreted as evidence of fascist leanings on my part, or as an admission of participation in an act directed against the United States. The time was 1935, the year of Italy's invasion of Ethiopia. Most of us Italians in the U.S.A. saw the conflict as merely a war between their mother country and a land named Ethiopia. I came to know better, but I did not then.

Among the letters submitted to the Board was one by the assistant conductor at the Metropolitan, Giacomo Spadoni, who, like myself, contributed to the collection. In his letter Spadoni stated:

> I have always been antifascist and am now a naturalized citizen of the United States since 1923....Many Italians in 1935 were on the side of Italy as a country against Ethiopia. I think I am fair in saying that all Italian people or people of Italian descent in this country, citizens and noncitizens, in 1935 felt the same way. Fascism or Mussolini or the form of the Italian government had no bearing on the incident. I feel sure that the question of being or not being a fascist never crossed anyone's thoughts.
>
> I have known Ezio Pinza for many years and am certain that he feels that the United States is his country and that he would do anything he could to help it even against Italy.

Like Morris Ernst, Harold was troubled by the incident of the gold collection, and undertook a through investigation to resolve their own doubts in one way or another. As Ernst was to write in a memorandum to the Board on April 25, 1942:

> These doubts arose through rumors I had heard, which may have come to the attention of your Board, alleging that Mr. Pinza had organized some kind of a collection of gold for the Italian government. I checked on these rumors to the best of my ability and I believe they are entirely without any significance. I am convinced he did not organize any such activity. On the other hand, there is no doubt that he, together with thousands of other Italians, long before the United States was involved in the war, made a contribution of gold in aid of Italy against Ethiopia; the particular contribution which was the only one that I have been able to discover, was the result of a virtual mass meeting of all Italians connected with the Metropolitan Opera House. Mr. Pinza was one of the mass. My inquiry indicates that not a single Italian at the Opera House declined to join this mass, that many of the contributors were also noncitizens, and that the effort itself was organized by citizens of Italian origin whose allegiance to the United States at this time of war is above suspicion.

It seems unnecessary to burden you with quotations from the many, many letters and testimonials written at the time by various people on my behalf. But one brief note must be cited, for it bears directly on the most dangerous charge against me: activity as an agent of the enemy. The writer was Carlo Tresca, the most violent antifascist Italian in the United States. Addressed to the attorney general, his letter reads:

> The undersigned, Carlo Tresca, editor of the antifascist publication *Il Martello,* believes he knows all the dangerous agents of Mussolini, all the fascist propagandists, and all the potential fifth columnists of Italian descent.
>
> The undersigned is of the opinion that Ezio Pinza never has shown himself to be, directly or indirectly, an agent of fascism or of Mussolini.

Tirelessly searching through my records, Harold produced evidence of my singing without remuneration for the benefit of organizations above reproach or suspicion, including the U.S. Treasury Department (aiding its Defense Bonds drive), the Red Cross, the International Ladies Garment Workers Union (at a convention which adopted a strongly worded anti-totalitarian resolution), and the Friends of New Music.

Our work on the preparation of my defense was completed with the arrival of a letter signed by Wilfred Engelman and Giacomo Spadoni, pinpointing my main accuser and his motivation:

> We, the undersigned, do hereby testify that on several occasions of recent date we have heard an American bass state that he personally is responsible for exposing to the FBI Ezio Pinza's political conversations of the past three years, adding that he (the American bass) never had an opportunity to sing because Ezio Pinza was the first basso of the Metropolitan.

The slow pace of the bureaucratic machine had hitherto worked in our favor. Now that our defense was as complete as we could possibly make it, time was heavy on our hands, especially mine. You will recall that the Board had made its adverse decision on March 24. Attorney General Biddle could, with one stroke of his pen, condemn me to the detention camp or decree a new hearing. On April 2, LaGuardia informed Dr. Leak that the necessary papers finally had been forwarded to Washington, and my father-in-law, accompanied by Doris, went there in the hope of prevailing upon Biddle not to close the case. Day after endless day, they sat in the anteroom where the attorney general's chief assistant, Ugo Carusi, kept informing them that the papers had not reached his desk. When they finally did, at six in the afternoon of April 7, Carusi assured Doris that he would see to it that Biddle gave his personal attention to the matter. But Doris insisted that the attorney general receive her and Dr. Leak, so they could present their arguments in favor of a new hearing. Biddle sent word that he could not see them. At this, Doris broke down. The strain of the past weeks and the endless hours in the anteroom had proved to be too much. She insisted hysterically that an American citizen has the right to speak to the attorney general, and she was determined to exercise that right. Poor Carusi had to make another trip to Biddle's office, only to return with the message that the attorney general was swamped with work on similar cases and that mine would have to await its turn.

Doris returned home, but she could not rest, fearing that the overworked Biddle might not read the various documents with sufficient care, that some vital detail might escape him, that he might automatically accept the Board's verdict. Bruno Walter wrote a moving letter to Biddle, and also called on LaGuardia with Doris, appealing to the Mayor to help her. LaGuardia wrote a personal message to Biddle. The very next day, on April 13, the attorney general received Doris and Dr. Leak. There was an icy politeness in his manner, but he listened attentively.

As loyal Americans, they told him, they were not asking for my release—only for another hearing to establish my guilt or innocence. This the attorney general granted. The hearing was held on April 28, at the federal court in New York.

The curious thing about the hearing was that I took almost no part in it. Several witnesses were called, including Marks Levine and the Metropolitan Opera singers Thelma Votipka and Wilfred Engelman, all three of whom were exceedingly generous in their remarks about me; but the star of the show was Doris. She spoke for fully an hour and a half, exposing the plot and refuting the charges. She also emphasized my essentially apolitical nature and stressed the Board's responsibility for my destruction as an artist, which was bound to follow a conviction.

Had I thought there was the smallest grain of truth in the charges against you," she later told me, "I would not have been able to do what I did."

What she did was to effect my release.

We were not informed of it immediately; and, indeed, I was not allowed to return home until June 4, nearly three months after I had been taken into custody, with instructions to report regularly to a parole officer in my area, and to our physician, Dr. Smith, who would act as sponsor. I was completely free to pursue my profession, except that I still had to apply for permission each time my work involved a trip away from home. After the first flurry of excitement and statements to the press, I settled down to a quiet summer devoted to my family, the victory garden, and to the planning of a comeback. Some friends urged me to denounce those at the Met who were known to have had a part in the plot that had caused me so much anguish. My constant reply was, "'God will punish them in His own time and way.'" Unfathomably, He has. I cannot say any more without disclosing the identity of the persons involved, thus adding to their suffering.

Pinza's widow, Doris, has informed the editors that what was eventually published of Ezio Pinza's experience was not entirely accurate. Throughout Pinza's term in prison, Doris and Harold Stern worked frantically for his release. On April 12, New York Mayor Fiorello LaGuardia did telephone and arrange for a meeting with Attorney General Biddle, who they found to be polite but not encouraging. However, he later granted them a second hearing in which the evidence presented cleared Pinza.

FROM *Adios to Tears*

Seiichi Higashide

Unknown to most Americans, the scandal of Japanese internment during World War II extended beyond the U.S. border. Over the duration of the war, approximately 2,200 Latin American citizens and residents of Japanese ancestry in thirteen countries in Latin America were arrested, shipped to and interned in the United States by the American government. Of those brought to the U.S., 1,800 of them were Peruvian Japanese, representing 80 percent of the Latin American Japanese interned. Most of these people were interned at Crystal City, Texas. Several months before the bombing of Pearl Harbor, the U.S. government had discussed internment of the Japanese in the event of war with Latin and Central American nations, under the condition that the United States would bear all expenses and assume full responsibility should any claims arise. The primary issue behind the seizure of the Latin American Japanese was not security, but the use of hostages that could be traded for Americans trapped in Axis countries. More than 800 Latin American Japanese eventually served the government's purpose and were exchanged for U.S. civilian prisoners by deportation to Japan. Adios to Tears *was originally written in Japanese and published under the title* Namida no Adios. *The translated English edition was released by E & E Kudo, Inc. in 1993 and will be reprinted in 2000 by the University of Washington Press.*

THE BLACKLIST

...It was December 24, 1941. On that unforgettable day, two major Peruvian newspapers, *El Commercio* and *La Prensa,* published a lista negra, a "blacklist" of approximately thirty "dangerous Axis nationals" residing in Peru. Of the thirty, approximately ten were Japanese.

Shivers passed through me. "Can this really be true?" I thought. My name was included in the list. We learned that the list had been leaked to reporters by a local U.S. agency. Although it had no connection with the Peruvian government, that did not alleviate our concerns.

Why was my name on the list? I could not understand. I had only been in Peru for about a decade, and what I had accomplished was quite insignificant. Our business was flourishing, but there were many others who had attained grander business successes who were not on the list. If not that, I thought perhaps it was because I had been president of the Ica Japanese Association for two terms. But, upon closer examination, the other Japanese on the list did not share such a background.

I could not think of other reasons. I had not committed any crimes. I had not participated in any propaganda activities for the Japanese government and, of course, had not engaged in espionage or underground activities. I could not understand what criteria had been used to compile the list.

Later, the newspapers published similar lists several more times and names of Axis nationals associated with major enterprises began to appear. Comparing the subsequent lists with the first, it could be seen that the initial list was different in nature. At the time I was not fully aware of this point, but when I consider it now it seems clear that rather than being influential persons or leaders within their respective communities, those on the first list were Axis nationals who had involved themselves deeply with the local Peruvian establishment.

When looked at from that perspective, I can see many reasons for my being included in the list. Whether it was fortunate or not, from the time I took over the Otani Company in Canete I had gradually widened my sphere of acquaintances to include those in the non-Japanese Peruvian society at large. Because my name was difficult to pronounce, they simply addressed me as "Ingeniero" and accepted me into their social groups.

For business purposes, too, I had felt it necessary to have connections with those in upper levels of Peruvian society and had made conscious moves in that direction. Because of this, I had formed social relationships with prominent figures in political and business circles and with leaders in law enforcement agencies.

My participation in such social activities was purely for business and social reasons, but U.S. agents may have perceived my behavior differently. The U.S. had been concerned about the existence of a sizeable group of individuals within the national Peruvian leadership who were pro-Japanese. Although I was not close to anyone in the national Peruvian leadership, I did have a number of acquaintances at the provincial level of leadership. It may have been that those in U.S. intelligence agencies had seen my activities within the larger Peruvian society, even at the provincial level, as having more "dangerous motives" than simple business and social relationships.

A Quick Change to Become an "Employed Manager"

Whatever the reason, the reality remained that I had been placed on a blacklist. I felt pessimistic as I pondered our future. Yet I also could not help feeling, with a certain grim pride, that at the age of thirty-two, I had gained enough notoriety to be included on a U.S. blacklist. It seems that the chief of the Ica municipal police also viewed the list in that light. Waving the newspaper, he rushed into our shop. Extending his hand to me, he said, "Congratulations, congratulations!"

But it was not a situation we could take lightly. At least as it related to our shop, everything seemed hopeless. My being on the blacklist meant that anyone who traded with me would surely be seen as suspect. I could not expect anyone to do business with us. It was only a matter of time, it seemed, before we would be pushed to bankruptcy. I had been prepared for unfortunate developments, but I had never dreamed I would be among the first to be stricken with such misfortune....

A plan eventually came to mind. I decided that we should immediately terminate our business licenses and close our shop. We would then reapply for business permits in my wife's name and start up as a new shop. Although she was of Japanese ancestry, my wife was born in Peru and was a full-fledged Peruvian citizen so there would be no problems if the business was in her name.

By a lucky coincidence, we had registered our marriage in Japan but not in Peru. In Peru, my wife was legally still single. According to Peruvian law we were completely unrelated.

Under those conditions, I felt that such a plan might work. Even if it failed, I thought it was at least worth trying. I immediately notified the appropriate agencies, terminated the licenses, and closed our shop. To the general public it seemed that I had gone into isolation because of the blacklist.

My wife, however, applied for business licenses under the name of Angelica Yoshinaga and we prepared to open a new shop. After about ten days the approvals came forth and the new shop was opened. We changed everything—from its name to its account books. We took every precaution so no connections could be made with the earlier business. I felt it was a fine response to our situation. In this way I became my wife's "shop manager."

Disquieting Tides

Having thus responded to our first difficult situation, we tried to appear as calm as possible and quietly continued our lives. But, disquieting tides rose up to touch us in differing ways and with differing force.

One day, soon after the beginning of 1942, the chief of detectives from the nearby police headquarters stopped by as usual in the morning and began enthusiastically discussing developments in the war. When the conversation reached a lull, he casually said, "I'm sure you have a driver's license. If you have it with you, could I take a look at it? There's something I want to be sure about."

There was nothing especially different about his appearance or behavior and I had nothing to be suspicious about so I handed over the license. He flipped it over front and back several times and examined it intently. Then he said, "I'm sorry, I'll have to borrow this for a while. Actually, we have an order from Lima Police Headquarters to send the license to them immediately. I don't think they'll keep it long. When it's returned, I will personally bring it over to you."

This was, of course, a very smoothly handled order to remain within the local area. I had been placed under travel restrictions. As soon as the chief of detectives left the shop I called a number of community leaders to inquire if something similar had occurred to them. None, however, had even heard of such an incident. The matter was related to the blacklist, I concluded, as only I had been targeted. It was a seemingly small matter, but it filled me with anxiety.

Days passed, and I remained bothered by that incident. Then new and more serious political developments suddenly came upon us. On January 24, 1942, the government of Peru severed diplomatic ties with Japan and immediately began to deport leaders in the Japanese community.

Soon, disturbing reports began to arrive from Lima. We heard that Japanese diplomats in Peru had been confined to a hotel in Chosica, and that the president of the Central Japanese Association, the owners of Japanese language newspapers, the principal of the Lima Japanese school, and other leaders of the Japanese community in the capital had been arrested and detained at a school called Leoncio Prado.

Finally, a great storm had begun to wreak its damage on the community. The storm that began in the capital soon found its way to the smaller cities in the provinces....

Deportation Orders

...About the middle of March 1942, I was...served deportation orders. The first exchange ship still had not departed. The chief of the Ica police came to our shop and said, "Mr. Higashide, we just had a communication from central office in Lima ordering you to appear there." It could only be bad news, I knew, but at that stage when diplomatic ties with Japan had already been severed it would have served no purpose to make any desperate struggle. I immediately made preparations and left for Lima, alone.

I spent the night at a hotel and early the next morning reported to the Lima Police Headquarters as ordered. I thought I might be detained on the spot, so I entered with much anxiety. To my surprise, the person who met me was extremely polite. That well-bred officer, who at a glance could be seen to have a high position, very calmly explained the situation to me. It was as I expected; I was to be deported....

I decided I would return to Japan alone and leave my wife and children in Peru. At the time, I felt certain Japan would win the war, so I did not believe we would be separated permanently from each other. After the war ended, I thought, I would return to Peru and be reunited with them.

While I was involved with preparations, I learned that the first exchange ship had left on April 14, 1942. "Well," I thought, "we will be next." About the same time, however, we received a report that another shipload of repatriates had been detained in Lima and that they were awaiting the next ship. I had no idea what the true situation was. I had been prepared to receive orders to board ship at any time, but that did not come even after an extended period. Then, two months after the first ship left, it was reported that the second exchange ship left port on June 15, 1942.

When I heard the report, I felt that by some good luck I might not be repatriated. Perhaps my deportation order was lost in the confusion. But I could not be too optimistic or secure with only such thoughts. About that time, information was passed about that the entire Japanese population in the United States was being moved inland from coastal areas. Rumors also flew about that the Japanese in Peru would all be removed to inland mountain areas. We even heard that all Japanese in Peru would be sent to the United States....

Is There Law or Justice? The Peak of Oppression.

From the end of 1942 through the beginning of 1943, Peru began to show symptoms of major social upheaval. Because of the war, the Peruvian economy had come to almost a complete halt. In urban areas, we began to see groups of unemployed men loitering about.

Peru's biggest export item at that time was cotton. Japan, which had been the second largest importer of Peruvian cotton next to the United States, had suddenly been eliminated as a trading partner. Exports to Europe had already reached a low point because of the earlier start of the war in Europe.

It was not surprising that the start of the Pacific War brought much confusion to the Peruvian economy. That economic confusion was eventually reflected in various aspects of politics and society in Peru and everywhere symptoms of instability could be seen.

The resident Japanese were easy targets amidst that confusion and were targeted as scapegoats. Feelings against the Japanese ran extremely high. Whether it was relocation or deportation, the methods used to carry them out grew completely undisciplined. People on the deportation lists were arrested without their identification being confirmed. It was common for families not to know of arrests, and for persons to be held at undisclosed locations. In extreme cases, people were arrested off the street without questioning and were placed on ships for deportation....

Rumors flew among them that they would be taken to an inland, mountainous area of Peru, where they would be massacred. Matters were so confused by that time, it would not have been strange if that had actually happened. The procedures and discipline of the Peruvian authorities had deteriorated to that point....

By this time, repatriations to Japan had completely stopped and resident Japanese were all being sent to relocation camps in the United States. American authorities apparently intended to transfer all "enemy aliens" residing in South America to the United States for the purpose of exchange, if necessary, for Americans held in Japan. From the latter half of 1942 through the beginning of 1943, deportation ships bound for the United States left many times from Peru.

One could be arrested without a word of warning and taken to the inner courtyard of the Lima Police Headquarters, where heads were counted and, with no questions or notification of destination, one would be placed on deportation ships. It was wartime and one could see that arrangements for deportation ships might not be met or that such ships might enter port without prior notice. But to go out to arrest any persons simply to meet quotas once the ship was anchored was simply without reason or justice. Because of this, a large number of persons not on the U.S. lists of deportees were nevertheless sent to the United States.

People sought to resist such blatant injustices through any means possible. Some sought to avoid deportation by offering bribes, some paid "substitutes" to take their places, and, in larger cities, some covered their tracks and joined the ranks of "whereabouts unknown."

I was supposed to leave Callao harbor at the end of February 1943, but I, too, outwitted the authorities to escape that fate.

Bravo! A True Daughter of Japan

On February 22, an acquaintance in Lima placed a long-distance telephone call to us. Based on reliable information, he said, "Early this morning, a number of plain-clothes detectives left Lima toward the southern area. Please be careful." Thanks to that phone call I was able, by a hair's breadth, to slip out of the hands of the authorities and to hide myself successfully.

By that time, all telephones in Japanese homes and shops had been confiscated. Our house, however, was an exception. When we opened our new shop under my wife's name, we had also transferred our telephone account to her name. At our shop we still had the use of our telephone as before.

After receiving the telephone report, I flew out of the shop to pass the information on to a number of friends. I then hurried home. I had intended to stay quietly in our home to observe developments, but when I came back to the shop a detective was already there awaiting my return.

I rushed into the shop, but was quickly made aware of the situation by my wife's eye movements. I instantly became a "customer" and moved about the shop looking at items. With an unconcerned look, I casually left the shop. From a distance, I observed what happened at the shop. Eventually, the detective became impatient and left. I quickly entered our living quarters and kept out of sight.

According to my wife, the detective had warned, "I'll be back." I hid myself inside of our house and remained as quiet as possible. My wife calmly said she would continue to say, "He hasn't returned!"

After a while, the detective did return. Without any trace of nervousness, my wife said, "He still hasn't returned." The detective again went off somewhere. He repeated this a number of times, always asking, "Has he come back?" My wife, showing splendid courage, continued to say, "No, he still hasn't returned."

The detective became very impatient. He eventually said, loudly, "If your husband does not come back by sunset, I will take you into custody and send you to Lima. You had better start making preparations for that. Do you understand?" He no doubt felt he could frighten her enough to reveal my whereabouts, but my wife would not budge. "He still has not returned. Please wait a while," she said and deliberately picked up our three-month-old second son, Arturo, to appeal to the detective's sympathy.

Hidden within our living quarters, I could overhear the threats, but I was sure the detective was bluffing. Even if Peru could be said to be an "uncivilized country," they would never arrest my wife in my place. But in those severely deteriorated social conditions, it was not unthinkable. When the detective left, I said to my wife, "If they actually attempt to take you into custody, I shall give myself up."

My wife, however, remained absolutely calm and said, "No, I shall go. I don't expect they will place a woman with a three-month-old child in confinement with a group of men. At least, not as a 'substitute.' At worst, I will be taken to Lima. If I were to be deported, even the North Americans would not know what to do with me."

She spoke with such magnificent courage. I had heard about the wives of Japanese warriors who, when they had reached a resolution, became even more calm and objective than their spouses. Here, it was true that my wife had achieved such a state. Terms such as the "way of the warriors" or "true daughter of Japan" could be expected to be meaningless to her, but this "true daughter of Japan" who had been born in Peru superbly met those qualifications. She immediately filled a suitcase with clothing and other necessities. Thus, prepared to leave whenever necessary, she awaited the outcome....

Later, a clock rang eleven times. The detective returned yet again. Confirming that I had not returned, he stared at my wife and children and at her hasty preparations for departure. Then, without a word, he left the shop. We waited, but he did not come back. His absence, however, only made us more anxious. When he did return, I thought, it would be the final move. I would certainly be taken into custody. My imagination was filled with pessimism. "He's probably busy arranging transportation to Lima," I thought.

An hour had creeped by when someone entered the shop. "Senorita, everyone has left. It is all right!" It was the chief of the Ica police from across the street. I was so relieved that all my strength suddenly left me and my eyes brimmed with tears. The long night had finally ended. My wife had held on and had carried us through.

I later learned from the police chief that he had seen me slip into our living quarters and was aware of my whereabouts. But he had taken the attitude, "This is not under our jurisdiction," and had simply observed what was going on. When I heard this I was grateful that I had befriended those in the general Peruvian community....

I was very lucky that the detective from Lima did not know how I looked. I had been "saved" mainly because the arrest had been left to a detective under the direct control of the National Police Superintendent, Mr. Teran. If the arrest had been assigned to the Ica provincial police or to the Ica municipal police it would have been accomplished immediately. Whatever the case, I had been greatly favored.

I could not expect, however, that such good fortune would continue forever....

Life Underground

Although we had survived the "arrest incident" in February 1943, I still faced a grave situation. Circumstances had reached a stage where my only alternative was to go completely into hiding. When I considered places where I could hide myself, however, I needed to keep in mind my family and shops. Because of them, I did not want to go too far away. Ultimately, I decided to go into hiding in my own home.

I know it sounds odd, but I had thought it through and had made definite plans. I would excavate a place under the floor of a room in our living quarters. Whenever necessary, I could hide myself there. With great secrecy, I took up the floor planks and dug out an underground cubicle measuring about six feet on each side. I furnished it with a simple bed, a small desk, and a shortwave radio.

I was prepared to remain in hiding for short periods of time. Secretly, I also devised a way of connecting the antenna of my shortwave radio via underground wires to an antenna at a neighboring school. I stored some emergency food, made arrangements for containment of bodily wastes, and completely camouflaged the entry to the underground "room."

When my preparations were ready, I suddenly "disappeared." Quite literally, I went "underground" in my own home. The only ones aware of my location were members of my family and our live-in employees. I considered allowing my situation to be known to a few close friends and neighbors, but, remembering a Japanese maxim that "the first step in deceiving an enemy is taken among allies," I decided to take complete caution.

My wife told everyone who asked, "Ever since that attempted arrest, I don't know where my husband went."... I kept abreast of developments by listening every day to shortwave broadcasts from Japan and reading every word of the newspaper, *El Commercio.*

I did not have much to occupy my time, so everyday I made detailed comparisons of the U.S. reports of war developments published in the *El Commercio* and the shortwave reports that came in from Japan. In that way I devised my own analysis of what was happening.

In the beginning, I did not even dream Japan would be defeated, but from my daily analyses of reports I could eventually see developments turning against Japan. For example, I came to see through Japanese reports when they used such terms as "the expected decisive battle" or "a decisive advance." It was the same for reports from the European front. It was clear that every day brought the Axis powers closer to defeat.

With the war going in its favor, I began to believe that the United States would no longer persist in arresting someone such as I in an outlying provincial area of Peru. But, having managed to escape detection thus far, I decided to endure my situation a while longer....

We continued in this manner for six months. During that time there were many incidents that aroused our precautions and we were haunted by the thought, "Can this be it?" In general, however, these were mostly minor incidents, such as reports that someone was looking for me or that a telephone call had come from someone we did not know. Still, they caused much anxiety for the entire household.

There being no major difficulties for some time, however, I began to feel that it might be safe to "reappear." It had been six months since the last "deportation ship" had left. I had not heard of another ship leaving and had not heard of any new oppressive actions against Japanese. It had been many months since I last heard of a Japanese being arrested and detained. Furthermore, an Allied victory was assured, so I felt that American authorities would not push for the arrest of persons such as I at that point.

Concluding that the crisis had passed, I decided to show myself to the outside community. Thus, as suddenly as I had disappeared, I again reappeared in Ica. I did not make a big deal of it, but I was very happy to be able to move about in the community once again. I was even more grateful for the warm greetings that everyone had for me....

A Sudden Arrest

For several months our lives continued without incident. The war was still on, so some uneasiness remained in the back of my mind. In general, however, I did not pay particular heed and began to conduct myself in a more open manner, not much different than the time before the war. But, one day, I was suddenly reminded of the fact that Japan was still at war. I can never forget—it was January 6, 1944.

It was a Sunday, and we had taken the family out for a picnic at Lake Huacachina. Lake Huacachina was a small expanse of water located at the lowest point of a basin that looked like an ancient volcanic crater. It was known for its cold, green waters that had some salt and sulfur content. Above its waters rose exquisite sand dunes, where people enjoyed a form of sand skiing. It was a wonderful, peaceful Sunday. We had leisurely spent the entire day there and returned home late that evening.

We had just sat down at the table for a late supper when it began. There was a knock on the front door. Previously, if it was not a special pattern of knocks, we would not have opened the door until I entered the underground cubicle. But we had enjoyed many months of an open and peaceful life, so we had forgotten those precautions. One of our employees, Victor, opened the door without hesitation. It was a fatal mistake.

Instantly, five men entered our home and one said, "We are from Lima Police Headquarters. Seiichi Higashide is under arrest." There was no opportunity to feign ignorance. Among the five was a detective from the Ica police office who knew me well. As I had been concerned about earlier, the central police headquarters in Lima had requested the cooperation of the Ica provincial police....

Accompanied by the five detectives, I was taken to the local police headquarters. I was startled to learn that my friend, the pro-Axis police chief, was not there. It was unthinkable that he would leave without telling us, but he was gone. "He must have been temporarily diverted from the arrest with some assignment," I thought. I was certain that if the police chief had been there, this would not have occurred. I lamented my bad luck, but there was nothing I could do.

That night I was detained in the holding area at the police headquarters. My family thought I would be sent immediately to Lima, so they all came to the headquarters. When they learned I was to leave the next morning, they went home for the night. After an uneasy night, at first light I was told, "It's time to go."...

Disgusting, Smelly Meals

Wearing a fine suit, I arrived at police headquarters at exactly five P.M. as ordered. I calmly confronted the investigating officer who had come over to take me in. I made it a point to look directly at him. I vividly recall that it was the investigating officer, rather than I who was being questioned, who avoided eye contact. After he confirmed my identity he said, "You will be held here for a while."

No matter how many times I asked for reasons and the nature of my offense, he would not answer me. Without any explanation, I was taken by a guard and was pushed into a cell.

The facility was wretched beyond imagination. The cell block was a three-story concrete building. The first floor was for murderers and thieves, the third floor held "political subversives," and the second floor was "reserved" for Japanese deportees. My cell was a concrete box about six feet wide and about ten feet deep. The entry, facing a walkway, had a movable framework of iron bars. During the day, the gate-like framework of iron bars was raised and we could go out onto the walkway and into other cells. At night, however, the bars were lowered and locked. If we had to eliminate bodily wastes we were told to do it "wherever you want" in our cells.

It was completely disgusting. The wastes that accumulated during the night were hosed out with water every morning, but because this had been repeated over many years the stench had permeated the concrete and remained permanently. When I was pushed into the cell my first reaction was to that powerful smell.

It was somewhat bearable during the day, but at night after the iron bars were lowered one could smell the stench of urine everywhere. By early morning, the stinging ammonia fumes were so strong that one could barely breathe or open one's eyes.

The prison meals were beyond belief. When it was time for meals each prisoner was given a large empty tin can; someone then came over and slopped out an unrecognizable mixture into the cans. We were expected to eat that. The indescribable odor of the mixture brought me to the point of vomiting. I was brought to feel even a strange admiration at the accuracy and aptness of the commonly used Japanese term, "a smelly meal." In the cell block there was no menu. Everyday—in the morning, at noon and in the evening—the "mixture" was ladled out.

The Japanese detainees, however, were blessed. We could not escape the stench of the cellblock, but we did not have to eat the prison meals. Through the kindness of an unknown benefactor, o-bento boxed meals were brought in for us three times a day from a nearby Japanese restaurant. Someone had made continuing inquiries about the number of Japanese detainees in the cell block and had arranged to have meals sent in to us. Later, of course, I arranged to pay the restaurant for my meals, but I was touched and grateful for the warm concern of those in the Japanese community.

Days passed. I knew I would be placed on a ship and sent somewhere, but I had not been told when that would happen nor what my destination would be. I expected I would most probably be sent to the United States. Beyond that, no matter how much I considered the possibilities, I could not be sure what to expect.

After about a week of prison life my family unexpectedly came to Lima. As a "special consideration," the Japanese detainees in Lima were allowed to meet family members twice a day—once in the morning and again in the afternoon—in an inner courtyard of the police headquarters.

My wife and children suddenly appeared there. According to my wife, she had received reliable information that I would be sent to the United

States in the near future, so she had hurriedly hired a taxi and had come to Lima with the children. My wife arranged to stay at a friend's home in Lima and came with the children twice every day to visit and to bring in things that they knew I liked. Even as we visited, however, we knew that I would be deported, so we could not raise ourselves to a happy mood.

Departure in the Middle of the Night—A Rising Anger

Without warning, on the morning of January 18, three or four days after my family began visiting me, we were told that we would board ship that day.

That happened to be my birthday, so my family planned to have a quiet birthday party in the courtyard of the police headquarters. My wife and children who had come to the courtyard all greeted me with "Happy Birthday!" but my situation had changed so abruptly it was not a time for congratulations. My wife quickly rushed out to buy clothing and personal items I would need when I boarded the ship. During the afternoon visiting hours she brought in two large trunks packed with those items....

Surrounded by American soldiers carrying rifles with fixed bayonets, we were lined up four abreast and marched over to the gangway to board. MPs were on all sides of us and it was clear that elaborate precautions had been taken. It was then that I truly came to understand that I was a "prisoner of war." The ship was a small freighter that had been hastily militarized with the placement of a number of cannons on it.

When we were all on board the ship, we were made to strip naked and everything that we had brought on board was examined. Then, an officer appeared and began a long and detailed explanation in Spanish of the rules and regulations we were to follow. He ordered complete compliance and repeated that any infractions would be met with severe punishment. It was quite a long presentation, but no one made a sound; not even a cough or a shuffle came through the intent silence. Eventually, his speech ended. As ordered, we went down into the hold of the ship and were locked in....

The ship lurched heavily and slowly began to move. Locked within its hold, I suddenly became very angry. I had earlier felt a deep hatred toward wars, but now I grew angry at the cowardliness of the Peruvian government. If Peru had been a direct enemy of Japan, I would have understood my situation. Peru had severed diplomatic ties with Japan, but it was still a third party to the dispute. Even if it had been pressured by the United States, what country with any pride and independence would have said, "Yes. We shall comply," and hand over innocent people? If it were only those with Japanese citizenship, a case might have been made. But the Peruvian government had given in to American pressure even to the point of deporting naturalized citizens and Peruvian citizens who had been born there.

In a civilized and respectable country, if one were there with proper approvals, it could be expected that even tourists would be given legal protections. If that could not be guaranteed, I thought, then no protest could be made when Peru was called "an uncivilized, third-rate country." I had always protested when I heard Peru called "a third-rate country" or an "uncivilized country," but now I felt justified in using such terms myself.

Americans in the United States also were not blameless. From the time I was a child I had read many books about America. I had felt that America was an ideal country that should be taken as a model for whole world. Why, then, had that country moved to take such unacceptable measures? Where was the spirit of individual rights and justice that had filled the Declaration of Independence and the U.S. Constitution? If I termed Peru, even provisionally, a "third rate country," was not America, in this instance, no different?

Even if under emergency wartime conditions, was America not in violation of individual rights? This was not, I felt, only a matter of international law, it was a broader issue of human rights. Of course, undeniably, the Axis nations perpetuated similar outrages. Yet, I felt, could I not hope that America alone would not do so?

Temporary Detainment by the U.S. Military

We were not allowed to even step out of the hold of the ship. We had no way even to confirm the position of the sun or stars, so we had no way of determining where the ship was heading. We assumed that it was heading northward toward the United States, but we had no way of confirming it. Then, three days after we began our journey, the ship suddenly slowed and eventually stopped.

It was too soon, even on a direct route, to have reached the United States. Had something happened? In the hold of the ship speculation ran rampant. The ship did not move for a long time. Then, from somewhere, a touch of raw, warm air began entering the hold. In two or three hours the hold became unbearably warm. It must be Panama! I felt sure we were in Panama.

Later, the steel door was opened and we were ordered to disembark. Holding our hands up to shade our eyes, we climbed onto the deck. I took in a deep breath of fresh air. The air was warm but was nevertheless a refreshing respite from the stale air breathed by so many people in the hold

Japanese Peruvians in a federal high school classroom at the Crystal City Justice Department Camp, Texas, 1944. Photograph by Violet Nozaki Tsujimoto.

of the ship. It was truly delicious, I thought. I looked out in all directions. Our surroundings were clearly in a tropical area. I was sure it was Panama.

Before we disembarked, we were given our luggage. The two trunks... had been brought on board as my wife had hoped. We were told to carry our own luggage and I was immediately caught short. It would be impossible for me to carry those two cumbersome, oversized trunks for a long period.

I considered abandoning one of them. But, praying that our destination was not far away, I placed one on my shoulder, grasped the other with my free hand, and staggered forward. Luckily, we were directed to large military trucks not too far away. I got on a truck with a sigh of relief. Swaying back and forth with the movements of the truck, we were taken somewhere.

The trucks came to a stop in front of what seemed to be temporary barracks in an area reserved for American military forces in Panama. We had not been told where we were, but, in any case, there were several temporary barracks and in each we could see rows of fourteen or fifteen cots. As soon as the trucks stopped, we were lined up in formation in front of the barracks. We received a detailed explanation of rules and regulations and a strict warning about unacceptable behavior.

Speaking fluent Spanish, the officer before us explained the daily schedule. Finally, he repeated twice that there must be complete compliance with orders and that any infractions would be severely punished. As was the case after boarding the ship, we listened with absolute attention and were again reminded that we were prisoners of war. We were given small, numbered badges and allowed to break formation. We were to enter the barracks and find our cots according to the numbers on the badges.

This was how we began our life at the temporary detention camp in Panama. In our shipload of deportees there were a number of people of German ancestry. There were a total of twenty-nine Japanese; of these five or six were naturalized Peruvians and one or two were Nisei who had been born in Peru.

It was clear that our group was different from the earlier Japanese deportee groups. Previously, groups of 150 or 200 persons had been detained for one or two days and immediately sent out. In our case, even when the Peruvian authorities knew the arrival date of the ship, it had taken more than two weeks to round up twenty-nine persons. Thus, in our group there were no substitutes or persons with mistaken identities. Everyone was a major figure. Thus, as could be expected, there were many older people. I was the youngest in our group.

*

A class action lawsuit (Mochizuki et al. v. United States) filed in federal court in 1996 resulted in a settlement in which the U.S. government acknowledged its wrongdoing to the Latin American Japanese in a letter of apology, but provided only $5,000 in redress payments, compared to the $20,000 paid to each surviving Japanese American internee under the Civil Liberties Act.

A WRA Center Lexicon of Japanese American Terms

In 1945, just months before the war's end, this report was compiled of common Japanese-English words used by the first-generation Issei, their American-born children the Nisei, and the Japan-educated Kibei at the Tule Lake internment camp. Although the use of the Japanese language, both written and spoken, was never officially forbidden in the internment camps, there is no question that intense pressure to "be American" emphasized the use of English and the adoption of American customs and values. An analysis of the lexicon reveals the degree to which people will adapt their language to their circumstances.

War Relocation Authority, Community Analysis Section
Community Analysis Notes No. 15, July 18, 1945

Introductory Note

Many words and phrases result from the evacuee's effort to express himself most tellingly. The Issei adopt those English words which express their thoughts more compactly than the Japanese equivalents, while the Nisei choose those expressive Japanese terms which strike their fancy, when not drawing directly on an ability to use or develop American slang. The result is words and phrases part English and part Japanese. A knowledge of both languages is necessary to appreciate completely the richness and succinctness of the words and phrases so compounded.

The whole tendency in language at the Tule Lake Center seems to be toward a shorter, more expressive speech which is neither good English nor good Japanese, but is certainly good "talk." The trend is similar to that which occurred in Hawaii. However, at Tule the trend is held in check by the more solidly-built English of the Nisei. The gradual disuse of English by the Issei in the center increases the development of Japanized English.

The merging of the two language styles may fill the need for a special center language. The center is an abnormal community with distinctive characteristics, it is not a corner of Japan, nor is it in the mainstream of American life. Such a separate community develops its own vocabulary, assimilating into it the type of humor, sarcasm, and attitudes which reflect the daily life of the center.

Terms Used by Issei and Kibei

These terms are more common at Tule Lake with its higher percentage of Issei and Kibei than elsewhere. Yet most Nisei would "catch" the meaning.

bon hedo Used like "bone-head" or "lunk-head" but has slightly different meaning. The "bon" comes from bonkura which means a shiftless or indolent fellow. Bonyari means in a daze.

dedo boru Used for "dead ball." It means hit by a pitched ball instead of the proper meaning of a ball which goes into the plate off the bat.

gamu setto Means end of a game, in baseball. Comes from term used in tennis.

bakku netto Means back-stop.

goro Means ground-ball. Goro-goro is an onomatopoetic word describing the sound of something rolling; also "thunder."

tonnel Refers to the error in which a ball passes through player's legs.

doron gamu Means "game called off" because of rain; possibly from the Japanese for "drowned out," although it is sometimes used also for games called on account of darkness.

yangu Describes a young person unversed in anything practical. The term is used in addressing such. Like "bub" in English.

ponkin Used like "pumpkin head."

sulo poku "Slow poke." However, Issei think of poku as referring to pork. Pigs are slow animals, of course.

chon Means bachelor. Comes from Korean. As such, almost a term of disapproval.

chokkuru To cheat. Comes from chokku chee (Chinese).

chokku chee kind Means "something underhanded." Used by Nisei as well.

tekkiya Means job. Comes from gardeners of southern California who "took care" of so many gardens. To lose one's tekkiya means to lose one's job.

tekushi de yuku Means "to walk." Tekushi means "taxi;" de means "with;" yuku means to "go." Since there are no such things as taxis in camp, such a statement isn't taken at face value. It is a term expressing attitude toward center life.

seco han Means "second hand." Used in derogatory fashion about girls of questionable character.

tote shan Totemo means "very." Shan comes from "schön," in German. Thus, "very pretty."

demo From "demonstration."

puro From program, professional, or proletariat.

senchi From sentimentalism

Issei studying advanced English at night school class. Heart Mountain, Wyoming. January 11, 1943. Photograph by Tom Parker.

In the general case, without study the national language where we live, it's quite hard to digest its culture. At the present time I am not able to attain such a higher purpose, but really very hard even to speak daily salutation in English with my American friend....But it is harder than I expected. I am one of the poorest student in my class, where may be numbering about twenty of us. To read the reader or to practice the conversation I am a sample of stupid stammerer....As I recognize my self I am an inferior student among my class mate. When I attend in my English class, I am shy and coward like a sheep which are drawing to the slaughterhouse. When the lesson is over, I feel myself all the time heavy sweat wet my back. It seems to me to reach my goal in English is quite long away.

Shoji Nagumo

agi From agitator.
ero From eroticism.
buru From bourgeoise.

Terms Often Used by Issei

These terms reflect the Issei interest in sports, in food, and in the common objects of camp life.

Sports:

basuketto boru	basketball	*sofuto boru*	softball
besu boru	baseball	*hitto*	hit
picha	pitcher	*kecha*	catcher
fasuto besu	first base	*sekendo besu*	second base
sado besu	third base	*homu besu*	home plate
fauru boru	foul balls	*stu-raiku wan*	strike one
stu-raiku tsu	strike two	*stu-raiku sree*	strike three
outo (aoto)	out	*outo fieda*	outfielder

Food:

mesu	mess hall	*buroni*	bologna
beru	bell	*weini*	weiners
miluku	milk	*egisu*	eggs
raisu	rice	*fishi*	fish
buredo	bread	*keiki*	cake
bata	butter	*pai*	pie
supa	soup	*rosu*	roast beef

Others:

mappu	mop	*lunba*	lumber
baketsu	bucket	*pento*	paint
tabu	tub	*bottoru*	bottle
doa	door	*brashi*	brush
windo	window	*hosu*	horse (carpenter's "horse" as well)
kyampu	camp	*katen*	curtain
stovu	stove	*lakku*	lock
canten	canteen	*buraku*	block
banku	bank	*wado*	ward
ofisu	office		

Expressions Used by the High School Nisei

These terms reflect the usual bobby-sox interests. Some terms reflect the war period, and at least one, "Pearl-harbored," reflects attitudes close to center psychology.

attractive girl:
- slick chik
- whistle bait
- sharp
- rare dish
- dilly
- dream puss

attractive boy:
- heaven-sent
- drooly
- swoony
- mellow man
- hunk of heart break

not attractive girl:
- sad sack
- goon
- rusty hen
- spook
- dog biscuit

not attractive boy:
- dog face
- void-coupon
- too safe
- stupor-man
- sad sam

girl with sex appeal:
- drape shape
- frame dame
- black out girl
- ready Hedy (from Hedy Lamarr)

boy with sex appeal:
- yea man
- groovy
- twangi boy
- go-giver

prude:
- touch-me-not
- moth-ball
- mona lizard

good dancer:
- pepper-shaker
- rhythm-rocker
- cloud-walker
- jive-bomber

girl who necks with anyone:
- toujour la clinch
- goo ball
- smooch date
- sausage (everybody's meat)
- mug bug
- share-crop
- necker-chief

a boy who's fast:
- b.t.o. (big time operator)
- wolf on a scooter
- active duty
- educated fox

girl crazy:
- skirt-nerts
- dolly-dizzy
- skirty-flirty
- dame-dazed
- witch-wacky

boy crazy:
- slack-happy
- khaki-wacky

to be in love:
- twitter-pated
- moon-bit

to be jilted:
- robot-bombed
- blow a fuse
- shot down in flames
- defrosted

"Bedroom Demonstrations," by Jack Matsuoka. Pen and ink, 11 x 14 in. 1971.

Walls in Camp II housing were as thin as paper and riddled with holes that seemed to refuse to stay plugged. Some young couples found that this lack of privacy cramped their bedroom style. Others didn't give a damn and put on first-rate demonstrations for kids who made an enthusiastic audience.

JACK MATSUOKA

teacher's pet:
gone-quisling
palm-greaser
P.C. (privileged character)

grinder:
brain box
book bug
book beater

strict parents:
crab-patch
curfew-keeper
picayunic

grades in high school:
90- "you're in the groove"
80- "you're in the solid"
70- "you're in the passive"
60- "you're off the beam"
50- "you're horrific"

an easy course in school:
gravy train

favorite word:
fuzzbuttons (for something good)

terrible:
sub-zero
salty
sklonkish (from "skunkish")

good food:
lush-mush

"Pearl-harbored"
for anything "sudden, unexpected and unpleasant." A favorite term for evacuation or for exams sprung in English school....

Older Nisei General Center Terms

Aliases for block managers:
block heads all centers
stooge (esp. Poston)
messenger boy Tule Lake

Divisions, sections, groups:
G men garbage crew
Moving and Hauling Co. Relocation office or division
Tule Lake GI's Hokoku Seinen Dan boys in hachimaki and sweatshirts
Tule Lake WACS Joshidan girls in pigtails and middies

Terms Applied to Social and Political Life of Center

"Dog license" Gate pass to Administration area (from colony to Administration area). Also for ID tag to be worn at all times.

Inu Literally, Japanese translation of "dog." Expression applied to so-called stool pigeon of administration.

Kyan-Kyan Japanese expression for a bark of small dogs. Applied to small "inus" or dogs.

Dogs are barking again Expression used when supposedly secret information intended only for the colony is acted on by the Administration.

Mug Picture identification badge issued by the Army. Also dog license—see above.

Waste time Expression meaning the dislike of some activity.

Lose fight Expression of disgust or hopelessness. Not worth it. (Often applied to Japanese School by some Nisei.)

Have you got a roll? Cigarettes?

Let's go to the shack Club house.

Did you went? Instead of using correct tense (go).

Shall we went? Instead of using correct tense (go).

"The mean!" Same as "you don't say!"

"Borrow" To steal lumber or take some necessity.

Yogore Self-derogatory term used by certain rough elements. Also used as an epithet by some. Yogoreru means to get dirty. Applied to certain gangs.

Red Kamaboko (U.S. Kamaboko) Kamaboko is a fish cake semi-cylindrical in shape; hence, sliced bologna cut in half.

Slop suey Chop suey, but served in one dish with rice, salad, etc.

Tule Lake Tuxedo Farmers' overalls, mechanics' overalls, or any overalls or Levis of the mechanics or farmers in Tule Lake....

Yule Greetings, Friends!

Globularius Schraubi

In the climate of Japan-hating mainstream culture and camp censorship, there was little room for literary expression. The sly (and brilliant) "Yule Greetings, Friends!" was a rare example of satire and protest, published in the inaugural issue of the Topaz literary magazine Trek *under the outrageous pen name "Globularius Schraubi, M.A." Building a unique and complex "Japa-Merican" etymology and "Evacuese" dialect for the purpose of the essay, Schraubi managed to criticize while slipping past censors. Historian Susan Schweik wrote that the "lines, with their dizzying array of puns on 'tail' and 'tale,' depend upon a buried allusion to the Japanese word inu ('informer' and, literally, 'dog'), a term used by some members of the community to brand others (often Nisei leaders) seen as accomodationist traitors to their own people. In the word 'tail/tale-wagging' which circulates evasively are collapsed a number of possible forms of tainted or dangerous speech: collaboration with camp authorities ('telling tales'); overeagerness to please camp authorities ('wagging tails'); malicious gossip accusing others in the camps of betrayal ('wagging tongues')." In this piece, we have distinguished the fabricated Japa-Merican words with italics. Globularius Schraubi's true identity remains a mystery to this day.*

H. L. Mencken once wrote a book entitled "The American Language," and described in it the magnificent slanguage and haranguage of this garrulous nation. It was a masterpiece of scholarliness unusual for even our much-read Henry, and, revised a few years ago, still remains a classic of Ameringlish philology.

The book is especially memorable in this day and age, the age of dislocation and relocation, for it devotes an entire chapter to a study of the language of the Japa-Mericans. The Japa-Mericans, as everyone knows, are the members of that quaint tribe of the West whose chief cultural attainment is a choreographic orgy known as the *bon odor* or "Tray Dance," performed in the streets of the tribal colony by the younger set to the tune of such colorful ballads as *naniwa bushi,* or "What, Warrior?"

The most significant part of this chapter in Mencken's book is the fact that it discusses neither the *Japa* jargon nor the *Merican* tongue current in the pueblos. Instead it discusses the English language, or, to put it more precisely, words appearing in the English language, as they are used in the Empire of the Rising Son. Just how this particular topic is related to the American language is somewhat of a puzzle, and the thing has caused much embarrassment to all the Sons, since the Menckenites have often invaded the tepees before the Sons were ready to rise, and in their attempt to waken them, have greeted them good-naturedly, "Good-o moanin-goo, Suki Yaki Son!" The situation got to be so bad that a prominent philologist of Tokyo on a tour of the pueblos was prompted to sigh in amazement and horror, "Ach, Mencken, Drinken, a Sot!"

But let us leave His Linguistic Majesty alone. By now the Tojocrats of Tokyo have evacuated all the English words, including the precious four-letter ones, from the Empire, and the Japa-Mericans are no longer to be seen lurking in the Buchanan-Post sector of the War of Words. With the pretended, as well as real, objects of the chapter entirely gone, we linguists may now look at our eminent Mencken with an indulgent smile and wynken, blynken, and nod at him.

What concerns us at the moment is the alingual status of Japa-Mericans in the Areas into which they were recently imported and where they are now concentrated. The term "alingual," as used here, should not be construed, of course, to mean that they are dumb or that they do not speak, even though they may be speechless under the circumstances. In fact there is a good deal of tongue locomotion going on in all the Areas. Just how they wag their tongues, and in what tongues, is a subject of profound speculation in philology and socio-psychiatry.

Dead men tell no tales. Dogs tell tales with their tails. Good dogs, however, wag them not at all when at a crucial moment, and as a result the merit of a dog is judged by the time, place, and manner of their tail-wagging. The best of them are enrolled, therefore, in the Tail-Waggers' Association together with such celebrities as Bette Davis. And, of course, the basis for judging the merit of little girls is the way in which they wag their pig-tails. When they grow up they are judged by the way in which they wag their tongues.

As stated previously the state of tongue locomotion in the newly established Areas, otherwise known as Little Nip Pons or Nip-Pounds—not that they are shelters for nipping canines—is alingual. By this scientific term we

Trek literary magazine cover from December 1942. Drawing by Miné Okubo.

mean that the tongue as wagged in these localities has not yet been philologically catalogued. It might be said that possibly it belongs to a family of tongues composed of Kagoshimese, Hiroshimese, and Zuzuic, with a liberal dash of Englisc and Amerikanski. Similarities between Zuzuic and the language of the Zulus are purely coincidental.

A theory has been advanced by some of our leading linguists to the effect that this tongue, now so popular in the Pounds, or Areas, should be named

Evacuese. In this essay the term will be used frequently for its simplicity, clarity, and alinguality.

The Evacuese language as spoken at the present time differs little from the language, or languages, of the Japa-Merican tribal colonies.

Japa-Merican speech had two characteristic syntaxial styles, namely Japa-Merican and Merican-Japa. Evacuese also contains similar categories, though we have noticed a gradual disintegration of Japa-Merican and its merger with Merican-Japa, an event of tremendous significance in the history of the tongue of the Nip-Pounds.

In a Merican-Japa sentence its subject is entirely omitted except when it is not needed. In this latter case "ewe" may be used to indicate the second person singular pronoun, while "mee" (which is an onomatopoeic word derived from the voice of a pussy cat) may take the place of the first person singular. This is more or less a matter of etiquette and implies that the speaker considers himself as gentle as a kitty, while calling his companion by the name of another gentle animal. That a kitty may scratch and bite does not enter into consideration. The suffix "la" (pronounced *rah)* indicates the plural forms, producing "ewela" and meela" (pronounced *ewe-rah! mee rah! rah, rah, rah!).*

Verbs never conjugate. If they do accidentally, they conjugate in any old way, without the slightest embarrassment or consideration for number, person, tense or pretense, and always end in *na, ne, no* or *batten.* This last comes from the English word "batten" which means "to fatten" or "to prosper at another's expense"—a well known pastime among the better class of Evacuese speakers.

The following is a list of words from Merican-Japa with their English equivalent:

English	*Evacuese (Merican-Japa)*	*Etymology*
barracks	*buraku*	Japanese word meaning "tribal colony."
block	*buraku*	Same as above.
city hall	*Sh-ch hole*	*Sh-ch* means "pawn;" that is, "chessmen of lowest rank moving in file but capturing diagonally." The term is used in admiration of the P.H.P., or Philanthropic Parliament, which is the city assembly, composed of the cleverest and wisest of the rank and file of the

		Nip-Pons. The abbreviation should not be confused with Pearl Harbor Patriots. *Hole* here means "a place."
co-op	*kop*	*Kopek* meaning "coin."
dining hall	*mes-ho,* or *meshi hole*	Derivation ambiguous.
fifty	*hefty*	A middle-aged lady.
foreman	*foeman*	A term of endearment.
kitchen	*ketchin*	From the Japanese word *ketchin-bo* which means "the boss of a kitchen" or a "stingy person."
shower-house	*shah house*	"House good enough for a *Shah.*" Not to be confused with the onomatopoeic word *sha* which signifies the sound made by running water.
sign, to	*shine na*	Derivation uncertain.
steal, to	*chock-chee na*	*Choked cheek*—"tongue in cheek."
soap	*sop*	"To soften, or soak in liquid."
superintendent	*suppon-ten*	*Suppon* means "turtle" and *ten,* "jelly" in Japanese. A "jelly turtle," a term of endearment.
tea	*chee*	Something to put in "cheek."
topaz	*Toppats*	*Top-hats*—another term of admiration and endearment for the leading gentry of an Area.

The Merican-Japa syntax permits complete freedom of expression. "How do you like it here?" may be transposed to "You like it here. How do?" In many cases a sentence may be reduced to its absolute minimum. When this is done, no one asks questions. No one answers them. They only glare at each other. This style of alingual communication is known as a "war communiqué" in which neither side says anything but still fights on just the same.

In Japa-Merican which, as we pointed out before, is going through the process of disintegration and of merging with Merican-Japa, the construction of a sentence is much simpler. Its verbs have no tense of any kind whatsoever no matter what happens.[1] Some sample sentences follow:

"Show last night?

"Show, show. Jew?"

"Naa, pitcherz no goo."

"What pitcher?"

“Don know.”

As in the language of that Empire, the name of which is entirely unmentionable, every person is referred to as a Son—rising or sitting, it is not clear. This term, Son, is neither male, female, nor otherwise. All men over nineteen are addressed as *odge son* and all women over sixteen are called *obba son* except in case of married women who are called *baa son* or *baa baa*—a term of endearment for ewe. These words do not inflect, regardless of age, gender, complexion, or even telephone number.

The inflection of adjectives is as follows: *goo* (or *goody),* better, more better, best, more best, most best, bestest.

Notchit, derived from “notch it,” is often erroneously translated as “not yet.” Its true significance is found in the following conversation which has been reported by a usually reliable source:

“Hah menny days half we bin here? Half ewe figure it out?”

“Naa, Notchit.”

It is not necessary to point out that Robinson Crusoe made a calendar for himself while in exile by making notches on a piece of wood. Likewise the Robin Son Kuruso’s of the various Areas spend their days making notches on a piece of two by five. Sometimes they make wooden clogs as by-products.

Twety means twenty. This is sometimes pronounced “twery” or “twely” or “lwely.” The second syllable is entirely nasal. When the word is spelled “twenty,” the *n* is silent. Thus:

“Hah ole ah ewe?”

Roy Takeno, editor of the *Manzanar Free Press.* Manzanar, California, 1943. Photograph by Ansel Adams.

"Lwely."

"Jew go tuh high schoo?"

"Yea."

The *yea* is Shakespearean.

The term "second generation" *(Nisei* in Merican-Japa) means "first generation" in English. "First generation" *(Issei* in Merican-Japa) means "immigrants." But the "second generation" does not necessarily mean "immigrants." This is a non-Euclidean proposition.

Kibei is not a Japa-Merican word. It means in Zuzuic "to come," quoted from the famous passage: *Yukubei ka, kibei ka, sore ga mondai,* or "to go or to come, that is the question."

The following was recorded at the *kop* store.

"Obba son. Bolluv hair ole chaw dye, yo! Dat won. Dis side, yo! Tan-Q. Hah much, obba son?"

"Lwely tree cen."

"Dats too much, neigh. Can chew fine som'n chee-puh?"

"Naa. Too bad, yo. Lwely tree cen chee-pest, yo. Matter key na sigh neigh!"

We have explained the term *Son. Chaw dye* means "dear," "darling," "honey." *Neigh* is a word which should be gone into rather thoroughly.

It is equivalent in value to the French "n'est-ce pas" or the English "eh, what?" though it is used in a less precise manner. The word originated at Tanforan, Santa Anita, and other racetracks in which the Evacuese language was born. (Which goes to show that the language is not only sacred but also colorful, aromatic, and full of sporting spirit.) As every good horseman knows, good horses neigh when they are pleased. *Neigh,* therefore, is a word of rejoicing; and why not rejoice in view of the stable nativity of the language? Lexicographically speaking, the word means "eh, what?" as well as "please" and "darling."

Matter key na sigh neigh! is rather difficult to translate. It is an abbreviated way of saying something quite complicated. The nearest we can come to a literal translation would be: "No matter if you sigh or neigh; so long as we have the key to the jernt you can't have what you want."—which shows how concise and convenient the Evacuese language is.

Some more passages:

"Odge son, tonight's supper pretty goo, neigh!"

"Ah goo da, neigh, oy she neigh."

In the sentence, *Obba son, baku today go to canteen and bought can soup, de shor'?* we can see a Coptic influence, probably through Zuzuic. *De shor* stands for "sure." It might be added that the hissing sound inserted between sentences, as explained in a recent issue of *LIFE,*[2] is practically extinct in Merican-Japa and Japa-Merican, and is substituted by a click of the tongue typical of Coptism. Now and then this is supplemented by a nasal hiss of a liquid character, especially in case of young children.

Baku means "I" and has to do with the current war. Adolf Hitler, or *Hit-la* (singular), as he is called in Evacuese, kept on gutturally mumbling something about Baku for years, if you remember. "Deutschland musst Baku haben," he said in his Austrian dialect, which of course means "Germany needs me," for *Hair Hit-la* never talks about anything but himself or his own *Shangri-la* (singular). *Baku* thus came to mean "mee," first person singular.

Similarly, *a pants, a slacks,* and *a panties* are commonly heard at the *kop* store, dry goods department. Surely no one buys "a trouser" or "a panty." Yet "trousers" and "panties" are, or should be, singular. Hence *a pants* and *a panties.* Logic is characteristic of the Evacuese language.

It might be mentioned here that *nani* is a word to indicate certain delicate objects such as a string from a violin when used as a garment or the House of Culture and Rest which is found in each residential block. "I left my *nani* in the *nani,*" and "Your *nani* is showing, honey," are often heard in the various Areas. This latter example, by the way, was quoted by Shakespeare and other dignitaries of British literature, as for instance,

> "It was a lover and his lass,
> With a hey, and a ho, and a hey *noni-no,*"

And by another great poet who wrote:

> "Hey nonni, nonni, nonni,
> Hotcha cha."

Hotcha cha of course refers to a beverage.

We have already discussed the word *neigh.* This word, when used by certain belles who toil not, but who, though dumb, are exponents of sweet nothings, becomes *huh.* Just how *neigh* can become *huh* is something which even Grimm would find difficult to explain. But in this age of science and progress any good horse can tell us the reason.

"Matter key na sigh, huh?" is perfectly good form, and such expressions as "Ewe hadjer breakfast, huh?" and "Dat's Sue, huh!" are commonly heard. From a developmental point of view the word might be considered as a form of hissing, *soo* and *hah,* which are so common in the older Merican-Japa jargon, and which are now substituted by a Coptic click.

Some pieces of literature have been translated into Japa-Merican from Kagoshimese, Zuzuic, and other dialects of Merican-Japa. One of them typifies the very sweet manner in which *huh* is used:

Merican-Japa (Zuzuic)	*Japa-Merican*
Neigh, neigh, I stay Chaw dye, neigh!	*Huh, huh, love me,* *Darling, huh!*
Neigh, neigh, I stay Chaw dye, neigh!	*Huh, huh, love me,* *Darling, huh!*

It is unnecessary to point out again that *chaw dye* means "darling." It has nothing to do with the color of Copenhagen chaw, for belles and wives are calling their boys and husbands in Merican-Japa: "Chaw dye, neigh, chaw dye neigh!"

Which reminds us to mention the gift-giving season now impending. It has been definitely established that the Japa-Mericans are the originators of the joyful event, which is associated with nativity in a stable, the shepherds looking up at the bright star, and all the sages in khaki pants. One of the sages gets up on his straw mattress, listens to the sounds of the belles in the next room and cries out, "Ewe-la, greetings!"

From this expression came the phrase, "Yule Greetings, Friends!"

Globularius Schraubi, M.A.

*

The biographical information appended to the essay "Yule Greetings, Friends!" reads: "The initials attached to GLOBULARIUS SCHRAUBI's name do not mean master of arts; they do not even mean master of asses. In fact, they signify nothing; he puts them there because he likes them.

Schraubi, incidentally, has written a large number of poems in blank verse. Naturally, these being blank, have never been found worth printing."

ENDNOTES:

1. The only authorized use of the past tense is seen in the conversation: "Half ewe sin Rose dis moanin?" "Yea. I did." *Sin* in this case is not a noun.
2. "Along with ritual of *o* and *Son* and the various complementary word forms, the Japanese go in for a great deal of hissing, especially when talking to superiors. "Honorable Boss Son (hsst!) honor humble and insignificant me by drinking honorable tea (hss!) with me and no-good-wife-not-worthy-to-look-up-to-your-shoes (hsst!) in my falling-down house (hsst! hsst!)" This particular *hss!* is considered very elegant. It isn't produced like an ordinary hiss but consists of a sharply indrawn gulp of air. The sound is about the same as that made by a noisy soup eater." (sss! huh! sss! huh!) Life.

The Legend of Miss Sasagawara

Hisaye Yamamoto

Hisaye Yamamoto and her Issei parents were interned at Poston, Arizona. While there, she worked for the camp newspaper, the Poston Chronicle. *After the war she worked for three years for the* Los Angeles Tribune, *a newsweekly that served the African American community. Beginning in 1948 she published work in national journals including* Partisan Review, Kenyon Review, Harper's Bazaar, *and anthologies such as* The Best American Short Stories of 1952 *as well as numerous Japanese American publications. Her stories were published together as* Seventeen Syllables and Other Stories *in 1988. She was born in 1921 in Redondo Beach, California and currently resides in Los Angeles. Her short story, "The Legend of Miss Sasagawara," addresses the controversial issue of mental breakdowns as a result of the combined fear, uncertainty, and monotony that pervaded camp life.*

Even in that unlikely place of wind, sand, and heat, it was easy to imagine Miss Sasagawara a decorative ingredient of some ballet. Her daily costume, brief and fitting closely to her trifling waist, generously billowing below, and bringing together arrestingly rich colors like mustard yellow and forest green, appeared to have been cut from a coarse-textured homespun; her shining hair was so long it wound twice about her head to form a coronet; her face was delicate and pale, with a fine nose, pouting bright mouth, and glittering eyes; and her measured walk said, "Look, I'm *walking!*" as though walking were not a common but a rather special thing to be doing. I first saw her so one evening after mess, as she was coming out of the women's latrine going toward her barracks, and after I thought she was out of hearing, I imitated the young men of the Block (No. 33), and gasped, "Wow! How much does *she* weigh?"

"Oh, haven't you heard?" said my friend Elsie Kubo, knowing very well I had not. "That's Miss Sasagawara."

It turned out Elsie knew all about Miss Sasagawara, who with her father was new to Block 33. Where had she accumulated all her items? Probably a morsel here and a morsel there, and, anyway, I forgot to ask her sources, because the picture she painted was so distracting: Miss Sasagawara's father was a Buddhist minister, and the two had gotten permission to come to this Japanese evacuation camp in Arizona from one further north, after the death there of Mrs. Sasagawara. They had come here to join the Rev. Sasagawara's brother's family, who lived in a neighboring block, but there had been some trouble between them, and just this week the immigrant pair had gotten leave to move over to Block 33. They were occupying one end of the block's lone empty barracks, which had not been chopped up yet into the customary four apartments. The other end had been taken over by a young couple, also newcomers to the block, who had moved in the same day.

"And do you know what, Kiku?" Elsie continued. "Oooh, that gal is really temperamental. I guess it's because she was a ballet dancer before she got stuck in camp, I hear people like that are temperamental. Anyway, the Sasakis, the new couple at the other end of the barracks, think she's crazy. The day they all moved in, the barracks was really dirty, all covered with dust from the dust storms and everything, so Mr. Sasaki was going to wash the whole barracks down with a hose, and he thought he'd be nice and do the Sasagawaras' side first. You know, do them a favor. But do you know what? Mr. Sasaki got the hose attached to the faucet outside and started to go in the door, and he said all the Sasagawaras' suitcases and things were on top of the army cots and Miss Sasagawara was trying to clean the place out with a pail of water and a broom. He said, 'Here let me flush the place out with a hose for you; it'll be faster.' And she turned right around and screamed at him, 'What are you trying to do? Spy on me? Get out of here or I'll throw this water on you!' He said he was so surprised he couldn't move for a minute, and before he knew it, Miss Sasagawara just up and threw that water at him, pail and all. Oh, he said he got out of that place fast, but fast. Madwoman, he called her.

But Elsie had already met Miss Sasagawara, too, over at the apartment of the Murakamis, where Miss Sasagawara was borrowing Mrs. Murakami's Singer, and had found her quite amiable. "She said she was thirty-nine years old—imagine, thirty-nine, she looks so young, more like twenty-five; but she said she wasn't sorry she never got married, because she's had her fun. She said she got to go all over the country a couple of times, dancing in the ballet."

And after we emerged from the latrine, Elsie and I, slapping mosquitoes in the warm, gathering dusk, sat on the stoop of her apartment and talked awhile, jealously of the scintillating life Miss Sasagawara had led until now and nostalgically of the few ballets we had seen in the world outside. (How faraway Los Angeles seemed!) But we ended up as we always did, agreeing that our mission in life, pushing twenty as we were, was first to finish college somewhere when and if the war ever ended and we were free again, and then to find good jobs and two nice, clean young men, preferably handsome, preferably rich, who would cherish us forever and a day.

My introduction, less spectacular, to the Rev. Sasagawara came later, as I noticed him, a slight and fragile-looking old man, in the block mess hall (where I worked as a waitress, and Elsie, too) or in the laundry room or going to and from the latrine. Sometimes he would be farther out, perhaps going to the post office or canteen or to visit friends in another block or on some business to the Administration buildings, but wherever he was headed, however doubtless his destination, he always seemed to be wandering lostly. This may have been because he walked so slowly, with such negligible steps, or because he wore perpetually an air of bemusement, never talking directly to a person, as though, being what he was, he could not stop for an instant his meditation on the higher life.

I noticed, too, that Miss Sasagawara never came to the mess hall herself. Her father ate at the tables reserved for the occupants, mostly elderly, of the end barracks known as the bachelors' dormitory. After each meal, he came up to the counter and carried away a plate of food, protected with one of the pinkish apple wrappers we waitresses made as wrinkleless as possible and put out for napkins, and a mug of tea or coffee. Sometimes Miss Sasagawara could be seen rinsing out her empties at the one double-tub in the laundry that was reserved for private dishwashing.

If any one in the block or in the entire camp of 15,000 or so people had talked at any length with Miss Sasagawara (everyone happening to speak of her called her that, although her first name, Mari, was simple enough and rather pretty) after her first and only visit to use Mrs. Murakami's sewing machine, I never heard of it. Nor did she ever willingly use the shower room, just off the latrine, when anyone else was there. Once, when I was up past midnight writing letters and went for my shower, I came upon her under the full needling force of a steamy spray, but she turned her back to me and did not answer my surprised hello. I hoped my body would be as smooth and spare and well-turned when I was thirty-nine. Another time Elsie and I passed in front of the Sasagawara apartment, which was really only a cubicle because the once-empty barracks had soon been partitioned off into six units for families of two, and we saw her there on the wooden steps, sitting with her wide, wide skirt spread splendidly about her. She was intent on peeling a grapefruit, which her father had probably brought

Nine-year-old Ayako Nakamura and six-year-old June Ibe. Poston, Arizona. June 4, 1942. Photograph by Francis Stewart.

to her from the mess hall that morning, and Elsie called out, "Hello there!" Miss Sasagawara looked up and stared, without recognition. We were almost out of ear-shot when I heard her call, "Do I know you?" and I could have almost sworn that she sounded hopeful, if not downright wistful, but Elsie, already miffed at having expended friendliness so unprofitably, seemed not to have heard, and that was that.

Well, if Miss Sasagawara was not one to speak to, she was certainly one to speak of, and she came up quite often as topic for the endless conversations which helped along the monotonous days. My mother said she had met the late Mrs. Sasagawara once, many years before the war, and to hear her tell it, a sweeter, kindlier woman there never was. "I suppose," said my mother, "that I'll never meet anyone like her again; she was a lady in every sense of the word." Then she reminded me that I had seen the Rev.

Sasagawara before. Didn't I remember him as one of the three bhikshus who had read the sutras at Grandfather's funeral?

I could not say that I did. I barely remembered Grandfather, my mother's father. The only thing that came back with clarity was my nausea at the wake and the funeral, the first and only ones I had ever had occasion to attend, because it had been reproduced several times since—each time, in fact, that I had crossed again the actual scent or suspicion of burning incense. Dimly I recalled the inside of the Buddhist temple in Los Angeles, an immense, murky auditorium whose high and huge platform had held, centered in the background, a great golden shrine touched with black and white. Below this platform, Grandfather, veiled by gauze, had slept in a long grey box which just fitted him. There had been flowers, oh, such flowers, everywhere. And right in front of Grandfather's box had been the incense stand, upon which squatted two small bowls, one with a cluster of straw-thin sticks sending up white tendrils of smoke, the other containing a heap of coarse, grey powder. Each mourner in turn had gone up to the stand, bowing once, his palms touching in prayer before he reached it; had bent in prayer over the stand; had taken then a pinch of incense from the bowl of crumbs and, bowing over it reverently, cast it into the other, the active bowl; had bowed, the hands praying again; had retreated a few steps and bowed one last time, the hands still joined, before returning to his seat. (I knew the ceremony well from having been severely coached in it on the evening of the wake.) There had been tears and tears and here and there a sudden sob.

And all this while, three men in black robes had been on the platform, one standing in front of the shining altar, the others sitting on either side, and the entire trio incessantly chanting a strange, mellifluous language in unison. From time to time there had reverberated through the enormous room, above the singsong, above the weeping, above the fragrance, the sharp, startling whang of the gong.

So, one of those men had been Miss Sasagawara's father.... This information brought him closer to me, and I listened with interest later when it was told that he kept here in his apartment a small shrine, much more intricately constructed than that kept by the usual Buddhist household, before which, at regular hours of the day, he offered incense and chanted, tinkling (in lieu of the gong) a small bell. What did Miss Sasagawara do at these prayer periods, I wondered; did she participate, did she let it go in one ear and out the other, or did she abruptly go out on the steps, perhaps to eat a grapefruit?

———

Elsie and I tired one day of working in the mess hall. And this desire for greener fields came almost together with the Administration announcement that henceforth the wages of residents doing truly vital labor, such as in the hospital or on the garbage trucks that went from mess hall to mess hall, would be upped to $19 a month instead of the common $16.

"Oh, I've always wanted to be a nurse!" Elsie confided, as the block manager sat down to his breakfast after reading out the day's bulletin in English and Japanese.

"What's stopped you?" I asked.

"Mom," Elsie said. "She thinks it's dirty work. And she's afraid I'll catch something. But I'll remind her of the extra three dollars."

"It's never appealed to me much, either," I confessed. "Why don't we go over to garbage? It's the same pay."

Elsie would not even consider it. "Very funny. Well, you don't have to be a nurse's aide, Kiku. The hospital's short all kinds of help. Dental assistants, receptionists.... Let's go apply after we finish this here."

So, willy-nilly, while Elsie plunged gleefully into the pleasure of wearing a trim blue-and-white striped seersucker, into the duties of taking temperatures and carrying bedpans, and into the fringe of medical jargon (she spoke very casually now of catheters, enemas, primiparas, multiparas), I became a relief receptionist at the hospital's front desk, taking my hours as they were assigned. And it was on one of my midnight-to-morning shifts that I spoke to Miss Sasagawara for the first time.

The cooler in the corridor window was still whirring away (for that desert heat in summer had a way of lingering intact through the night to merge with the warmth of the morning sun), but she entered bundled in an extraordinarily long black coat, her face made petulant, not unprettily, by lines of pain.

"I think I've got appendicitis," she said breathlessly, without preliminary.

"May I have your name and address?" I asked, unscrewing my pen.

Annoyance seemed to outbalance agony for a moment, but she answered soon enough, in a cold rush, "Mari Sasagawara, Thirty-three seven C."

It was necessary also to learn her symptoms, and I wrote down that she had chills and a dull aching at the back of her head, as well as these excruciating flashes in her lower right abdomen.

"I'll have to go wake up the doctor. Here's a blanket, why don't you lie down over there on the bench until he comes?" I suggested.

She did not answer, so I tossed the army blanket on the bench, and when I returned from the doctors' dormitory, after having tapped and tapped on the door of young Dr. Moritomo, who was on night duty, she was still standing where I had left her, immobile and holding onto the wooden railing shielding the desk.

"Dr. Moritomo's coming right away," I said. "Why don't you sit down at least?"

Miss Sasagawara said, "Yes," but did not move.

"Did you walk all the way?" I asked incredulously, for Block 33 was a good mile off, across the canal.

She nodded, as if that were not important, also as if to thank me kindly to mind my own business.

Dr. Moritomo (technically, the title was premature; evacuation had caught him with a few months to go on his degree), wearing a maroon bathrobe, shuffled in sleepily and asked her to come into the emergency room for an examination. A short while later, he guided her past my desk into the laboratory, saying he was going to take her blood count.

When they came out, she went over to the electric fountain for a drink of water, and Dr. Moritomo said reflectively, "Her count's all right. Not appendicitis. We should keep her for observation, but the general ward is pretty full, isn't it? Hm, well, I'll give her something to take. Will you tell one of the boys to take her home?"

This I did, but when I came back from arousing George, one of the ambulance boys, Miss Sasagawara was gone, and Dr. Moritomo was coming out of the laboratory where he had gone to push out the lights. "Here's George, but that girl must have walked home," I reported helplessly.

"She's in no condition to do that. George, better catch up with her and take her home," Dr. Moritomo ordered.

Shrugging, George strode down the hall; the doctor shuffled back to bed; and soon there was the shattering sound of one of the old army ambulances backing out of the hospital drive.

George returned in no time at all to say that Miss Sasagawara had refused to get on the ambulance.

"She wouldn't even listen to me. She just kept walking and I drove alongside and told her it was Dr. Moritomo's orders, but she wouldn't even listen to me."

"She wouldn't?"

"I hope Doc didn't expect me to drag her into the ambulance."

"Oh, well," I said. I guess she'll get home all right. She walked all the way up here."

"Cripes, what a dame!" George complained, shaking his head as he started back to the ambulance room. I never heard of such a thing. She wouldn't even listen to me."

Miss Sasagawara came back to the hospital about a month later. Elsie was the one who rushed up to the desk where I was on day duty to whisper, "Miss Sasagawara just tried to escape from the hospital!"

"Escape? What do you mean, escape?" I said.

"Well, she came in last night, and they didn't know what was wrong with her, so they kept her for observation. And this morning, just now, she ran out of the ward in just a hospital nightgown and the orderlies chased after her and caught her and brought her back. Oh, she was just fighting them. But once they got her back to bed, she calmed down right away, and Miss Morris asked her what was the big idea, you know, and do you know what she said? She said she didn't want any more of those doctors pawing her. *Pawing* her, imagine!"

After an instant's struggle with self-mockery, my curiosity led me down the entrance corridor after Elsie into the longer, wider corridor admitting to the general ward. The whole hospital staff appeared to have gathered in the room to get a look at Miss Sasagawara, and the other patients, or those of them that could, were sitting up attentively in their high, white, and narrow beds. Miss Sasagawara had the corner bed to the left as we entered and, covered only by a brief hospital apron, she was sitting on the edge with her legs dangling over the side. With her head slightly bent, she was staring at a certain place on the floor, and I knew she must be aware of that concentrated gaze, of trembling old Dr. Kawamoto, (he had retired several years before the war, but he had been drafted here), of Miss Morris, the head nurse, of Miss Bowman, the nurse in charge of the general ward during the day, of the other patients, of the nurse's aides, of the orderlies, and of everyone else who tripped in and out abashedly on some pretext or other in order to pass by her bed. I knew this by her smile, for as she continued to look at that same piece of the floor, she continued, unexpectedly, to seem wryly amused with the entire proceedings. I peered at her wonderingly through the triangular peephole created by someone's hand on hip, while Dr. Kawamoto, Miss Morris, and Miss Bowman tried to persuade her to lie down and relax. She was as smilingly immune to tactful suggestions as she was to tactless gawking.

There was no future to watching such a war of nerves as this; and besides, I was supposed to be at the front desk, so I hurried back in time to greet a frantic young mother and father, the latter carrying their small son who had had a hemorrhage this morning after a tonsillectomy yesterday in the out-patient clinic.

A couple of weeks later on the late shift I found George, the ambulance driver, in high spirits. This time he had been the one selected to drive a patient to Phoenix, where special cases were occasionally sent under escort, and he was looking forward to the moment when, for a few hours, the escort would permit him to go shopping around the city and perhaps take in a new movie. He showed me the list of things his friends had asked him to bring back for them, and we laughed together over the request of one plumpish nurse's aide for the biggest, richest chocolate cake he could find.

"You ought to have seen Mabel's eyes while she was describing the kind of cake she wanted," he said. "Man, she looked like she was eating it already!"

Just then one of the other drivers, Bobo Kunitomi, came up and nudged George, and they withdrew a few steps from my desk.

"Oh, I ain't particularly interested in that," I heard George saying.

There was some murmuring from Bobo, of which I caught the words, "Well, hell, you might as well, just as long as you're getting to go out there."

George shrugged, then nodded, and Bobo came over to the desk and asked for pencil and paper. "This is a good place..." he said, handing George what he had written.

Was it my imagination, or did George emerge from his chat with Bobo a little ruddier than usual? "Well, I guess I better go get ready," he said, taking leave. "Oh, anything you want, Kiku? Just say the word."

"Thanks, not this time," I said. ""Well, enjoy yourself."

"Don't worry," he said. "I will!"

He had started down the hall when I remembered to ask, "Who are you taking, anyway?"

George turned around. "Miss Sa-sa-ga-wa-ra," he said, accenting every syllable. "Remember that dame? The one who wouldn't let me take her home?"

"Yes," I said. "What's the matter with her?"

George, saying not a word, pointed at his head and made several circles in the air with his first finger.

"Really?" I asked.

Still mum, George nodded in emphasis and pity before he turned to go.

How long was she away? It must have been several months, and when, towards late autumn, she returned at last from the sanitarium in Phoenix, everyone in Block 33 was amazed at the change. She said hello and how are you as often and easily as the next person, although many of those she greeted were surprised and suspicious, remembering the earlier rebuffs. There were some who never did get used to Miss Sasagawara as a friendly being.

One evening when I was going toward the latrine for my shower, my youngest sister, ten-year-old Michi, almost collided with me and said excitedly, "You going for your shower now, Kiku?"

"You want to fight about it?" I said, making fists.

"Don't go now, don't go now! Miss Sasagawara's in there," she whispered wickedly.

"Well," I demanded. "What's wrong with that, honey?"

"She's scary. Us kids were in there and she came in and we finished, so we got out, and she said, 'Don't be afraid of me. I won't hurt you.' Gee, we weren't even afraid of her, but when she said that, gee!"

"Oh, go home and go to bed," I said.

Miss Sasagawara was indeed in the shower and she welcomed me with a smile. "Aren't you the girl who plays the violin?"

I giggled and explained. Elsie and I, after hearing Menuhin on the radio, had in a fit of madness sent to Sears and Roebuck for beginners' violins that cost five dollars each. We had received free instruction booklets too, but unable to make heads or tails from them, we contented ourselves with occasionally taking the violins out of their paper bags and sawing every which way away.

Miss Sasagawara laughed aloud—a lovely sound. "Well, you're just about as good as I am. I sent for a Spanish guitar. I studied it about a year once, but that was so long ago I don't remember the first thing and I'm having to start all over again. We'd make a fine orchestra."

That was the only time we really exchanged words and some weeks later I understood she had organized a dancing class from among the younger girls in the block. My sister Michi, becoming one of her pupils, got very attached to her and spoke of her frequently at home. So I knew that Miss Sasagawara and her father had decorated their apartment to look oh, so pretty, that Miss Sasagawara had a whole big suitcase full of dancing costumes, and that Miss Sasagawara had just lots and lots of books to read.

The fruits of Miss Sasagawara's patient labor were put on show at the block Christmas party, the second such observance in camp. Again, it was a gay, if odd, celebration. The mess hall was hung with red and green crepe paper streamers and the greyish mistletoe that grew abundantly on the ancient mesquite surrounding the camp. There were even electric decorations on the token Christmas tree. The oldest occupant of the bachelors' dormitory gave a tremulous monologue in an exaggerated Hiroshima dialect; one of the young boys wore a bow-tie and whispered a popular song while the girls shrieked and pretended to be growing faint; my mother sang an old Japanese song; four of the girls wore similar blue dresses and harmonized on a sweet tune; a little girl in a grass skirt and superfluous brassiere did a hula; and the chief cook came out with an ample saucepan and, assisted by the waitresses, performed the familiar dojo sukui, the comic dance about a man who is merely trying to scoop up a few loaches from an uncooperative lake. Then Miss Sasagawara shooed her eight little girls, including Michi, in front, and while they formed a stiff pattern and waited, self-conscious in the rustly crepe paper dresses they had made themselves, she set up a portable phonograph on the floor and vigorously turned the crank.

Something was past its prime, either the machine or the record or the needle, for what came out was a feeble rasp but distantly related to the Mozart minuet it was supposed to be. After a bit I recognized the melody; I had learned it as a child to the words,

> When dames wore hoops and powdered hair,
> And very strict was e-ti-quette,

Yaeko Yamashita (in doorway) watches Fugiko Koba trying a new pair of geta sandals especially useful in dust. Manzanar, California. April 2, 1942. Photograph by Clem Albers.

When men were brave and ladies fair,
They danced the min-u-et....

And the little girls, who might have curtsied and stepped gracefully about under Miss Sasagawara's eyes alone, were all elbows and knees as they felt the block's 150 or more pairs of eyes on them.

Although there was sustained applause after their number, what we were benevolently approving was the great effort, for the achievement had been undeniably small. Then Santa came with a pillow for a stomach, his hands each dragging a bulging burlap bag. Church people outside had kindly sent these gifts, Santa announced, and every recipient must write and thank the person whose name he would find on an enclosed slip. So saying, he called by name each block child under twelve and ceremoniously presented each eleemosynary package, and a couple of the youngest children screamed in fright at this new experience of a red and white man with a booming voice.

At the last, Santa called, "Miss Mari Sasagawara!" and when she came forward in surprise, he explained to the gathering that she was being rewarded for her help with the block's younger generation. Everyone clapped and Miss Sasagawara, smiling graciously, opened her package then and there. She held up her gift, a peach-colored bath towel, so that it could be fully seen, and everyone clapped again.

Suddenly I put this desert scene behind me. The notice I had long awaited, of permission to relocate to Philadelphia to attend college, finally came, and there was a prodigious amount of packing to do, leave papers to sign, and good-byes to say. And once the wearying, sooty train trip was over, I found myself in an intoxicating new world of daily classes, afternoon teas, and evening concerts, from which I dutifully emerged now and then to answer the letters from home. When the beautiful semester was over, I returned to Arizona, to that glowing heat, to the camp, to the family; for although the war was still on, it had been decided to close down the camps, and I had been asked to go back and spread the good word about higher education among the young people who might be dispersed in this way.

Elsie was still working in the hospital, although she had applied for entrance into the cadet nurse corps and was expecting acceptance any day, and the long conversations we held were mostly about the good old days, the good old days when we had worked in the mess hall together, the good old days when we had worked in the hospital together.

"What ever became of Miss Sasagawara?" I asked one day, seeing the Rev. Sasagawara go abstractedly by. "Did she relocate somewhere?"

"I didn't write you about her, did I?" Elsie said meaningfully. "Yes, she's relocated all right. Haven't seen her around, have you?"

"Where did she go?"

Elsie answered offhandedly. "California."

"California?" I exclaimed. "We can't go back to California. What's she doing in California?"

So Elsie told me: Miss Sasagawara had been sent back there to a state institution, oh, not so very long after I had left for school. She had begun slipping back into her aloof ways almost immediately after Christmas, giving up the dancing class and not speaking to people. Then Elsie had heard a couple of very strange, yes, very strange things about her. One thing had been told by young Mrs. Sasaki, that next-door neighbor of the Sasagawaras.

Mrs. Sasaki said she had once come upon Miss Sasagawara sitting, as was her habit, on the porch. Mrs. Sasaki had been shocked to the core to see that the face of this thirty-nine-year-old woman (or was she forty now?) wore a beatific expression as she watched the activity going on in the doorway of her neighbors across the way, the Yoshinagas. This activity had been the joking and loud laughter of Joe and Frank, the young Yoshinaga boys, and three or four of their friends. Mrs. Sasaki would have let the matter go, were it not for the fact that Miss Sasagawara was so absorbed a spectator of this horseplay that her head was bent to one side and she actually had one finger in her mouth as she gazed, in the manner of a shy child confronted with a marvel. "What's the matter with you, watching the boys like that?" Mrs. Sasaki had cried. "You're old enough to be their mother!" Startled, Miss Sasagawara had jumped up and dashed back into her apartment. And when Mrs. Sasaki had gone into hers, adjoining the Sasagawaras', she had been terrified to hear Miss Sasagawara begin to bang on the wooden walls with something heavy like a hammer. The banging, which sounded as though Miss Sasagawara were using all her strength on each blow, had continued wildly for at least five minutes. Then all had been still.

The other thing had been told by Joe Yoshinaga who lived across the way from Miss Sasagawara. Joe and his brother slept on two army cots pushed together on one side of the room, while their parents had a similar arrangement on the other side. Joe had standing by his bed an apple crate for a shelf, and he was in the habit of reading his sports and western magazines in bed and throwing them on top of the crate before he went to sleep. But one morning he had noticed his magazines all neatly stacked inside the crate, when he was sure he had carelessly thrown some on top the night before, as usual. This happened several times, and he finally asked his family whether one of them had been putting his magazines away after he fell asleep. They had said no and laughed, telling him he must be getting absent-minded. But the mystery had been solved late one night, when Joe gradually awoke in his cot with the feeling that he was being watched. Warily he had opened one eye slightly and had been thoroughly awakened and chilled in the bargain by what he saw. For what he saw was Miss Sasagawara sitting there on his apple crate, her long hair all undone and flowing about her. She was dressed in a white nightgown and her hands were clasped on her lap. And all she was doing was sitting there watching him, Joe Yoshinaga. He could not help it, he had sat up and screamed. His mother, a light sleeper, came running to see what had happened, just as Miss Sasagawara was running out the door, the door they had always left unlatched or even wide open in summer. In the morning Mrs. Yoshinaga had gone straight to the Rev. Sasagawara and asked him to do something about his daughter. The Rev. Sasagawara, sympathizing with her indignation in his benign but vague manner, had said he would have a talk with Mari.

And, concluded Elsie, Miss Sasagawara had gone away not long after. I was impressed, although Elsie's sources were not what I would ordinarily pay much attention to, Mrs. Sasaki, that plump and giggling young woman who always felt called upon to explain that she was childless by choice, and Joe Yoshinaga, who had a knack of blowing up, in his drawling voice, any incident in which he personally played even a small part (I could imagine the field day he had had with this one). Elsie puzzled aloud over the cause of Miss Sasagawara's derangement and I, who had so newly had some contact with the recorded explorations into the virgin territory of the human mind, sagely explained that Miss Sasagawara had no doubt looked upon Joe Yoshinaga as the image of either the lost lover or the lost son. But my words made me uneasy by their glibness, and I began to wonder seriously about Miss Sasagawara for the first time.

Then there was this last word from Miss Sasagawara herself, making her strange legend as complete as I, at any rate, would probably ever know it. This came some time after I had gone back to Philadelphia and the family had joined me there, when I was neck deep in research for my final paper. I happened one day to be looking through the last issue of a small poetry magazine that had suspended publication midway through the war. I felt a thrill of recognition at the name Mari Sasagawara signed to a long poem, introduced as "....the first published poem of a Japanese American woman who is, at present, an evacuee from the West Coast making her home in a War Relocation Center in Arizona."

It was a tour de force, erratically brilliant and, through the first readings, tantalizingly obscure. It appeared to be about a man whose lifelong aim had been to achieve Nirvana, that saintly state of moral purity and universal wisdom. This man had in his way certain handicaps, all stemming from his having acquired, when young and unaware, a family for which he must provide. The day came at last, however, when his wife died and other circumstances made it unnecessary for him to earn a competitive living. These circumstances were considered by those about him as sheer imprisonment, but he had felt free for the first time in his long life. It became possible for him to extinguish within himself all unworthy desire and consequently all evil, to concentrate on that serene, eight-fold path of highest understanding, highest mindedness, highest speech, highest action, highest livelihood, highest recollectedness, highest endeavor, and highest meditation.

This man was certainly noble, the poet wrote, this man was beyond censure. The world was doubtless enriched by his presence. But say that someone else, someone sensitive, someone admiring, someone who had not achieved this sublime condition and who did not wish to, were somehow called to companion such a man. Was it not likely that the saint, blissfully bent on cleansing from his already radiant soul the last imperceptible blemishes (for, being perfect, would he not humbly suspect his own flawlessness?) would be deaf and blind to the human passions rising, subsiding, and again rising, perhaps in anguished silence, within the selfsame room? The poet could not speak for others, of course; she could only speak for herself. But she would describe this man's devotion as a sort of madness, the monstrous sort which, pure of itself, might possibly bring troublous, scented scenes to recur in the other's sleep.

One Happy Family

Toshio Mori

Toshio Mori was born in Oakland, California in 1910. Although his profession was a flower grower and wholesaler, he wrote throughout his entire lifetime. His first collection of short stories, Yokohama, California, *was set to be published in 1942, but with the onset of World War II, publication was delayed. The book finally appeared in 1949. Another collection of short stories,* The Chauvinist and Other Stories, *was published in 1978, and a novel,* Woman from Hiroshima, *was released in 1980.* Unfinished Message, *a selection of Mori's writings, will be published in 2000. While interned at Topaz, Mori worked on the literary magazine,* Trek, *in which the following short story was published.*

The postman's familiar footsteps were audible to the little American Japanese boy and his mother. It was nine in the morning. The improvised mailbox rattled and they heard the postman going away. Ben, the seven-year-old son, ran to the door but his mother was quicker. She took the letter and brought it in the house.

"Is it from daddy?" Ben asked his mother.

The seven-year-old son stood below her as she intently read the letter. He pulled her apron when she did not answer.

"Is it from daddy, mama?" he asked again.

The mother looked away from the letter and then sat down. "Yes Ben. It is from daddy," she said quietly.

The room became silent again, and the silence of the house shook little Ben's persistence. His lips opened to say something sharp because his mother would not confide in him. He looked at the quiet figure of his mother and his resentment faded away. Yes, she was keeping something from him but she was sad. He could not be angry at her when she was so sad.

"Ben," his mother began, "Your father is, I've often told you, away on a long vacation. The letter says that his trip will probably be long but it may be short too. It depends entirely on his business. Daddy says for you to be patient and be a good boy, a good fighting American boy."

For a moment Ben's brown Japanese eyes twinkled and his face lit up. Then a frown clouded his face. "What kind of a business did daddy go on? Why did he have to go away?"

His mother did not reply. She stared at the blank wall a long while.

"Mama, did daddy run away?" Ben asked his mother.

"No, no!" the mother replied quickly. "Daddy would never run away."

She reached for her knitting bag and began knitting a sweater that was too big for Ben and too mannish for herself. Ben watched her quick, skillful fingers move swiftly, and then he saw them gradually lose their speed until her fingers barely moved.

Suddenly he cried, "I know! He's dead! Daddy's dead!"

The mother raised her hands and gasped, "Ben! Don't say that again!"

"He's dead, mama. He's dead."

His mother shook her head vigorously. "Ben, you must believe me. Your father is alive. He is on a vacation. You must take mother's word for it."

"He's dead. I know," Ben said.

"No, Ben," she said quietly.

Ben faced his mother triumphantly. He knew his dad was alive. His letter had come, hadn't it? Yet, mama was hurt. He saw her hurt look when he made guesses about dad. He must be on the right track. All of a sudden his eyes opened wide, and he knew why his father was not home, why his mama must suffer and become sad. He remembered the headlines of the city papers, he recalled that day when a strange group of older boys at school called him a Jap and chased him home. America was at war with Japan, but he could not understand. What had war to do with their home, with his quiet father who had worked hard for a living? His daddy must have done an awful thing to be sent away.

Ben heard his mother sigh and glanced up. He looked at her lost face and sighed too. "Mama, did he do something bad? Is he a bad man in America?"

His mother gave a cry so sharply that Ben sat up straight, and then he saw that her eyes were wet. He looked away, triumphant for a moment. Knowing he had found out the truth at last, he felt big and wise like a grown-up man.

His mother came over and put her arms about him. Her eyes were soft and her hand on his head was soft. "He is innocent, daddy is. Please remember that, Ben. Don't ever be ashamed of him. Believe in him."

"Why was he taken away, mama?" he asked.

Mother shook her head slowly. "He was taken as a suspect but he is not guilty. He was taken because America doubted him and he had no explanation. And please, Ben dear, never become bitter. America is for us plain people. Believe in America. Bitterness is not for the common man. When you grow up you will realize that this war was fought to destroy bitterness, sadness, and fear."

Ben could not understand her words. He wondered if everything would turn out right. He became doubtful of ever seeing his dad. If he had a wishbone like his friend, Frankie Brown, back home he would wish for the world to turn out right. That was all he would wish for, and realizing his helplessness he buried his face in her apron and sobbed softly.

High over his head he heard the soft words, and the tender stroking of a hand. "Stop crying, Ben. He will come back when the government investigates his case. He will be back free."

The world swam before his closed eyes as he clung tightly to her skirts. The little boy continued sobbing because even a mother cannot soothe and comfort one at times.

A Thousand Stitches

Henry Sugimoto

Born in Wakayama, Japan in 1901, Henry Sugimoto emigrated to the United States in 1919 to join his parents in Hanford, California. Upon graduation from Hanford High School, he enrolled at UC Berkeley, but later transferred to the California College of Arts and Crafts in Oakland, where he received his B.F.A. in 1928. In 1929 he left for Paris, where he studied at the Academie Coroasrossi and exhibited at the Salon d'Automne. When he returned to the United States, he married and continued to paint and exhibit. With World War II, Sugimoto and his family found themselves interned at the Fresno assembly center and later at the Jerome and Rohwer internment camps in Arkansas. During his confinement, he taught art. Using sheets, pillowcases, and mattress bags, he improvised canvases to stretch and paint on. After the camps closed, the Sugimotos moved to New York, where Sugimoto found work illustrating books and translating captions into Japanese, before landing a job as a textile designer. He has published a book of his camp life paintings in Japan, has been honored by the Japanese Emperor with a medal for his contribution to Japanese culture in America, and has received several medals from the Japanese government for his contribution to art. Although a substantial and important body of Sugimoto's work from the internment period has survived, he admits that the losses of evacuation were great. "I lost all my hundred paintings left in gallery. A hundred paintings all gone. I think maybe they auctioned my paintings. All gone."

*

Untitled, by Henry Sugimoto. Woodblock print on paper. 8 x 9½ in. No date.

Thousand Stitches to My Son, by Henry Sugimoto. Woodblock print on paper. 8 x 9½ in. No date.

According to a traditional Japanese custom, when a soldier went to battle, his mother prepared a sash covered with one thousand stitches, each sewn knot contributed by an individual well-wisher. This good luck charm was believed to keep the soldier free from any harm.

Untitled, by Henry Sugimoto. Woodblock print on paper. 8 x 9½ in. No date.

Innocent Babies (Nisei), by Henry Sugimoto.
Woodblock print on paper. 8 x 9½ in. No date.

IV

"Disloyal"
With papers so stamped
I am relocated to Tule Lake.
But for myself,
A clear conscience.

Muin Ozaki

A Challenge to American Sportsmanship

Eleanor Roosevelt

By October 1942, over 110,000 evacuees were being detained in United States government internment camps although no individual charges had been made against any single person. As the tide of war panic began to subside, some members of the government, including War Relocation Authority Director Dillon Myer, began to express the belief that the internment of citizens and resident aliens of Japanese descent had not been a good idea. Added to this, many officials became concerned about the realities of the situation. The high costs of running the camps, and difficulties brought about as the morale of internees continued to deteriorate led government officials to question their next move. Some wanted to begin disbanding the camps. Others were concerned that subversive activities among Japanese Americans were still a threat. Officials began to try to address both concerns, to develop an effective leave program and to develop a method of screening the disloyal from the loyal.

In early 1943, questionnaires entitled "Statement of United States Citizenship of Japanese Ancestry" were distributed to everyone in the camps over the age of seventeen. These questionnaires were distributed with two purposes in mind. First of all, the WRA used the questionnaire as a means of assessing the loyalty to the United States of Issei and Nisei alike. Second, in a change of policy, the War Department wanted to identify loyal Nisei to volunteer for military service. For those not eligible for military service (women and all Issei) the questionnaire was entitled "Application for Leave Clearance," thus suggesting that the process of allowing loyal internees to return to normal civilian life had begun. While perhaps originally intended to bring the internment of Japanese Americans to a swifter end, the loyalty-review program was to become the most divisive, tragic episode of the internment.

First Lady Eleanor Roosevelt was widely viewed as an energetic and dedicated advocate of common people, earning the love of millions throughout the world. On April 23, 1943 she made a camp inspection at Gila River accompanied by Dillon Myer, where according to WRA reports, she was "greeted by crowds of enthusiastic evacuees." In a very public attempt to eradicate fears of the "Jap problem," Mrs. Roosevelt wrote the following essay to inform the general American population of a loyalty-assessing questionnaire that was to be distributed amongst the Japanese. "A Challenge to American Sportsmanship" appeared in Collier's *magazine on October 16, 1943.*

*

I can well understand the bitterness of people who have lost loved ones at the hands of the Japanese military authorities, and we know that the totalitarian philosophy, whether it is in Nazi Germany or in Japan, is one of cruelty and brutality. It is not hard to understand why people living here in hourly anxiety for those they love have difficulty in viewing our Japanese problem objectively, but for the honor of our country, the rest of us must do so.

A decision has been reached to divide the disloyal and disturbing Japanese from the others in the War Relocation centers. One center will be established for the disloyal and will be more heavily guarded and more restricted than those in which these Japanese have been in the past. This separation is taking place now.

All the Japanese in the War Relocation centers have been carefully checked by the personnel in charge of the camps, not only on the basis of their own information but also on the basis of the information supplied by the Federal Bureau of Investigation, by G-2 for the Army, and by the Office of Naval Intelligence for the Navy. We can be assured, therefore, that they are now moving into this segregation center in northern California the people who are loyal to Japan.

Japanese Americans who are proved completely loyal to the United States will, of course, gradually be absorbed. The others will be sent to Japan after the war.

At present, things are very peaceful in most of the Japanese Relocation centers. The strike that received so much attention in the newspapers last November in Poston, Arizona, and the riot at Manzanar, California, in December were settled effectively, and nothing resembling them has occurred since. It is not difficult to understand that uprooting thousands of people brought on emotional upsets that take time and adjustments to overcome.

Neither all of the government people, naturally, nor all of the Japanese were perfect, and many changes in personnel had to be made. It was an entirely new undertaking for us, it had to be done in a hurry, and considering the

First Lady Eleanor Roosevelt, accompanied by Dillon Myer, National Director of the War Relocation Authority, visits the Gila River Relocation Center. Rivers, Arizona, April 23, 1943. Photograph by Francis Stewart.

After many months of operating relocation centers, the War Relocation Authority is convinced that they are undesirable institutions and should be removed from the American scene as soon as possible. Life in a relocation center is an unnatural and un-American sort of life. Keep in mind that the evacuees were charged with nothing except having Japanese ancestors; yet the very fact of their confinement in relocation centers fosters suspicion of their loyalties and adds to their discouragement. It has added weight to the contention of the enemy that we are fighting a race war: that this nation preaches democracy and practices racial discrimination....

There are approximately 40,000 young people below the age of twenty years in the relocation centers. It is not the American way to have children growing up behind barbed wire and under the scrutiny of armed guards.

DILLON MYER, MARCH 1943

number of people involved, I think the whole job of handling our Japanese has, on the whole, been done well.

Influx from the Orient

A good deal has already been written about the problem. One phase of it, however, I do not think has as yet been adequately stressed. To cover it, we must get our whole background straight.

We have in all 127,000 Japanese or Japanese Americans in the United States. Of these, 112,000 lived on the West Coast. Originally, they were much needed on ranches and on large truck and fruit farms, but, as they came in greater numbers, people began to discover that they were competitors in the labor field.

The people in California began to be afraid of Japanese importation, so the Exclusion Act was passed in 1924. No people of the Oriental race could become citizens of the United States by naturalization, and no quota was given to the Oriental nations in the Pacific.

This happened because, in one part of our country, they were feared as competitors, and the rest of our country knew them so little and cared so little about them that they did not even think about the principle that we in this country believe in: that of equal rights for all human beings.

We granted no citizenship to Orientals, so now we have a group of people (some of whom have been here as long as fifty years) who have not been able to become citizens under our laws. Long before the war, an old Japanese man told me that he had great-grandchildren born in this country and that he had never been back to Japan; all that he cared about was here on the soil of the United States, and yet he could not become a citizen.

The children of these Japanese, born in this country, are citizens, however, and now we have about 47,000 aliens, born in Japan, who are known as Issei, and about 80,000 American-born citizens, known as Nisei. Most of these Japanese Americans have gone to our American schools and colleges, and have never known any other country or any other life than the life here in the United States.

The large group of Japanese on the West Coast preserved their national traditions, in part because they were discriminated against. Japanese were not always welcome buyers of real estate. They were not always welcome neighbors or participators in community undertakings. As always happens with groups that are discriminated against, they gather together and live as racial groups. The younger ones made friends in school and college, and became part of the community life, and prejudices lessened against them.

Their elders were not always sympathetic to the changes thus brought about in manners and customs.

There is a group among the American-born Japanese called the Kibei. These are American citizens who have gone to Japan and returned to the United States. Figures compiled by the War Relocation Authority show that 72 percent of the American citizens have never been to Japan. Technically, the remainder, approximately 28 percent, are Kibei, but they include many young people who made only short visits, perhaps as children with their parents. Usually the term Kibei is used to refer to those who have received a considerable portion of their education in Japan.

While many of the Kibei are loyal to Japan, some of them were revolted by what they learned of Japanese militarism and are loyal to the land of their birth, America.

Enough for the background. Now we come to Pearl Harbor, December 7, 1941. There was not time to investigate families or to adhere strictly to the American rule that a man is innocent until he is proven guilty. These people were not convicted of any crime, but emotions ran too high. Too many people wanted to wreak vengeance on Oriental-looking people. Even the Chinese, our allies, were not always safe from insult on the streets. The Japanese had long been watched by the FBI, as were other aliens, and several hundred were apprehended at once on the outbreak of war and sent to detention camps.

Approximately three months after Pearl Harbor, the Western Defense Command ordered all persons of Japanese ancestry excluded from the coastal area, including approximately half of Washington, Oregon, and California, and the southern portion of Arizona. Later, the entire state of California was added to the zone from which Japanese were barred.

Problems in Relocation

At first, the evacuation was placed on a voluntary basis; the people were free to go wherever they liked in the interior of the country. But the evacuation on this basis moved very slowly, and furthermore, those who did leave encountered a great deal of difficulty in finding new places to settle. In order to avoid serious incidents, on March 29, 1942, the evacuation was placed on an orderly basis, and was carried out by the Army.

A civilian agency, the War Relocation Authority, was set up to work with the military in the relocation of the people. Because there was so much indication of danger to the Japanese unless they were protected, relocation centers were established where they might live until those whose loyalty could be established could be gradually reabsorbed into the normal life of the nation.

To many young people this must have seemed strange treatment of American citizens, and one cannot be surprised at the reaction that manifested itself not only in young Japanese Americans, but in others who had known them well and had been educated with them, and who asked bitterly, "What price American citizenship?"

Nevertheless, most of them realized that this was a safety measure. The Army carried out its evacuation, on the whole, with remarkable skill and kindness. The early situation in the centers was difficult. Many of them were not ready for occupation. The setting up of large communities meant an amount of organization which takes time, but the Japanese, for the most part, proved to be patient, adaptable, and courageous.

There were unexpected problems and, one by one, these were discovered and an effort was made to deal with them fairly. For instance, these people had property and they had to dispose of it, often at a loss. Sometimes they could not dispose of it, and it remained unprotected, deteriorating in value as the months went by. Business had to be handled through agents, since the Japanese could not leave the camps.

An Emotional Situation

Understandable bitterness against the Japanese is aggravated by the old-time economic fear on the West Coast and the unreasoning racial feeling which certain people, through ignorance, have always had wherever they came in contact with people who were different from themselves.

This is one reason why many people believe that we should have directed our original immigration more intelligently. We needed people to develop our country, but we should never have allowed any groups to settle as groups where they created little German or Japanese or Scandinavian "islands" and did not melt into our general community pattern. Some of the South American countries have learned from our mistakes and are now planning to scatter their needed immigration.

Gradually, as the opportunities for outside jobs are offered to them, loyal citizens and law-abiding aliens are going out of the relocation centers to start independent and productive lives again. Those not considered reliable, of course, are not permitted to leave. As a taxpayer, regardless of where you live, it is to your advantage, if you find one or two Japanese American families settled in your neighborhood, to try to regard them as individuals and not to condemn them before they are given a fair chance to prove themselves in the community.

"A Japanese is always a Japanese" is an easily accepted phrase and it has taken hold quite naturally on the West Coast because of some reasonable or unreasonable fear back of it, but it leads nowhere and solves nothing. Japanese Americans may be no more Japanese than a German American is German, or an Italian American is Italian. All of these people, including the Japanese Americans, have men who are fighting today for the preservation of the democratic way of life and the ideas around which our nation was built.

We have no common race in this country, but we have an ideal to which all of us are loyal. It is our ideal which we want to have live. It is an ideal which can grow with our people, but we cannot progress if we look down upon any group of people among us because of race or religion. Every citizen in this country has a right to our basic freedoms, to justice, and to equality of opportunity, and we retain the right to lead our individual lives as we please, but we can only do so if we grant to others the freedoms that we wish for ourselves.

FROM The Betrayed

Hiroshi Kashiwagi

Playwright and poet Hiroshi Kashiwagi was born in 1922 in Sacramento, California. He was one of the first artists to write beyond the stereotype of the Japanese American internee as a helpless, innocent victim and to explore the more complex reality. The following is an excerpt from a recent full-length play, The Betrayed, *which acts out the arguments for and against answering the Loyalty Questionnaire's two most controversial questions, numbers 27 and 28:*

> *Number 27: Are you willing to serve in the armed forces of the United States on combat duty wherever ordered?*
>
> *Number 28: Will you swear unqualified allegiance to the United States of America and faithfully defend the United States from any or all attack by foreign or domestic forces, and forswear any form of allegiance or obedience to the Japanese emperor, or any other foreign government, power or organization?*

How to determine one's loyalty, when loyalty exists not only to one's country but to one's family, friends, personal values, and conscience became a matter of paramount importance for Issei and Nisei alike. In the following excerpt from The Betrayed, *the two sides of this debate are illustrated in two young Nisei still in camp. For many, the internment was a betrayal of their beliefs in democracy and the United States itself. As the play goes on to show, the fact of that betrayal leads inexorably to one individual's betrayal of another, until everyone is a traitor and everyone is betrayed.*

SCENE 2

(At the firebreak during a dust storm; both Grace and Tak are in heavy GI mackinaws with their collars turned up; Grace is wearing a kerchief. They are huddled close, trying to protect themselves from the dust swirling about them.)

Grace: What are we doing here?

Tak: Well, we're together and there's no one outside in this storm.

Grace: Privacy at last.

Tak: Yeah, with a curtain of dust.

Grace: I guess everyone's inside trying to keep out the dust, covering windows and plugging up holes. But it's no use, the sand comes through the walls and it'll be everywhere—on the beds, tables, chairs, windowsills, clothing…and gritty underfoot.

Tak: And in your eyes and nostrils too. (He spits.) Look at that—black. What a hellhole they put us in.

Grace: I'd hate to go back now. Mother will be in tears and father will be cross.

Tak: Who can blame them? This is no place for humans.

Grace: It's the best reason for wanting to leave.

Tak: Yeah.

Grace: Tak, let's go outside.

Tak: We are outside.

Grace: I mean out of here, out of this hellhole.

Tak: Grace, are you all right?

Grace: Of course, I'm all right. Why do you ask?

Tak: Well, it's hard to stay sane in these conditions.

Grace: (laughs) I'm all right. Don't worry about me.

Tak: Remember, there's the fence and the soldier up in the guard tower with itchy fingers and a Jap near the fence would be a nice, easy target.

Grace: I meant walk out through front gate with the full blessings of the authorities. Then we'll be free, free to go anywhere we want.

Tak: You don't mean anywhere.

Grace: Well, no. But out of here. Tak, if you want to go to college, you can.

Tak: Wait a minute Grace, are you talking about the registration?

Grace: Yes, they're going to let us leave here; in fact, they want us to leave. That's why the questionnaire.

Tak: It's more complicated than that.

Grace: How can it be? If we're loyal Americans, what's so hard about declaring it; that's what they want to know.

Tak: This storm, this hellhole, do you like it? Is this any way to treat Americans? I'm not going to sign anything just because they want me to.

Grace: I didn't know you felt that way.

Tak: Well now you know.

Grace: You're not one of those fanatics who are pro-Japan, are you?

Tak: No but I know some people who are.

Grace: You do?

Tak: They have a right to feel that way. My uncle's one of them; his wife and children are in Japan. I try not to listen to him. (There's a sudden gust of wind and both are nearly obscured by the dust.) It's impossible to talk out here with all this dust.

Grace: Tomorrow, why don't we meet at the *Dispatch* office?

Tak: I'm not comfortable there.

Grace: No one will be there after work.

Tak: Yeah sure.

Grace: I'll talk to Fred, tell him I'll be working late.

Tak: Who's Fred?

Grace: Fred Williams, the Reports Officer.

Tak: Your boss?

Grace: Sort of.

Tak: What about the gate? How will I get through?

Grace: Here, take my pass; they know me so I won't need it.

Tak: I don't know about this…

Grace: Oh come on, Tak. It'll be quiet there…and we'll be alone.

Tak: Alone?

Grace: Yes.

Tak: I'll be there.

(Lights dim to darkness.)

SCENE 3

(At the *Dispatch* office, late afternoon, next day. There's a knock and Grace lets Tak in. The room is furnished with a table, a couple of chairs, and a bulletin board upstage. A typewriter is on the table.)

Tak: Hey, there's something different about this place. What is it? (looks around) I smell an Englishman.

Grace: Maybe Fred's English. Don't worry he's not here, nobody's here. (Tak goes around sniffing.) Tak, you're like our dog.

Tak: You have a dog here?

Grace: He belongs to Fred, a burly St. Bernard, gentle as a baby. He's our mascot. His name is—

Tak: Don't tell me. Tiny.

Grace: How did you know?

Tak: Simple. Just like the *Dispatch,* no imagination. (laughs)

Grace: Would you like some juice? I think we have some in the refrigerator.

Tak: How about a hamburger and milkshake.

Grace: Sorry the best I can do is coffee.

Tak: You gotta do better than that.

Grace: Well then, let me see how about canoeing?

Tak: Canoeing?

Grace: Yes, on Lake Washington. (She gets up on the table; motions him to join her; he climbs up.) Easy, you're on a boat, remember.

Tak: Oh yeah…safe?

Grace: I think so. Got your oar?

Tak: Uh huh.

Grace: This is how you do it. You go deep in the water, full paddle up, keeping your weight parallel to the water. Got it? (They paddle.) Yes, yes, now switch. (They switch.) This way you stay in a straight line. Yes. (They paddle, switching. She spies something in the distance.) What's that?

Tak: Where?

Grace: Over there.

Tak: Ah…fish? (suddenly) Invasion! The Rising Sun! (They paddle frantically; Tak starts to fall, taking in water.)

Grace: Tak, get up. (She helps him up.)

Tak: You saved me, thank you.

Grace: You're welcome. (They paddle a bit more, then she puts out her hand. Tak realizes the ride is over, helps her down.) Thanks for the ride.

Tak: Anytime. (Grace exits L, returns with a glass of juice.)Lots of space here.

Grace: I'll give you a tour later; the lounge is back there. The editorial room is beyond Fred's office but I do most of my work here.

Tak: Did he write the registration order?

Grace: Who, Fred? (Tak nods.) No, that came from Washington.

Tak: (finishing his juice) The mess crew and about twenty other guys in our block decided not to register.

Grace: When did that happen?

Tak: Last night at our block meeting.

Grace: And your decision?

Tak: To go along with them.

Grace: How does your family feel?

Tak: My mother's worried, she wants to keep the family together. She depends on me too much.

Grace: And your father?

Tak: I don't know; he's in a hospital outside. He's leaving the decision up to me.

Grace: You'll be going against orders, if you don't register.

Tak: I know.

Grace: They can put you in jail.

Tak: Hey, we're already in jail.

Grace: But they can put you in the stockade. You want to risk that?

Tak: I thought I'm an American.

Grace: Yes, you are, you're loyal to your country and of course you'll defend it. That's all they want to know, why can't you tell them that?

Tak: Why should I?

Grace: You're just making it difficult for yourself.

Tak: Grace, you're being so Japanese.

Grace: You said I was too hakujin, now you're saying I'm too Japanese.

Tak: I mean you're so accommodating. When you used to go to your parties, your fancy hakujin parties that you talked about—

Grace: What has that got to do with this?

Tak: I bet you brought the most expensive gift, I bet you were the best mannered and the most agreeable person there. And the ladies said, "Oh you Japanese are so polite."

Grace: What's wrong with being polite?

Tak: I bet you even stayed late to help clean up.

Grace: Tak, you're a boor!

Tak: What's that?

Grace: An animal! (beat) Tak, what's the matter with you?

Tak: There's a lot you don't know about me, Grace. I'll tell you something. When I used to ride the bus to school, there was this guy who would snap my ear from behind. Well, I looked straight ahead, never turned around, even though my ear was burning. I knew he wanted to start something and I wouldn't give him that satisfaction. But I was also afraid, afraid of the barrage of "Japs" that would rain on me if I did anything. I could feel the sting going away but inside I was sick and miserable because I had to take it.

Grace: And refusing to register is your way of fighting back?

Tak: Yeah, for all the insults I've taken, for all the times I was called a Jap. (beat) Hey, it's a good feeling. I never knew it could be so good. (voice rising) It's liberating. Is that the right word Grace?

Grace: Tak be reasonable. Not registering is like saying "no" to the questions. You'll be labeled a "disloyal," you'll be put in jail or even sent to Japan. You don't want that, do you? Think about it, Tak.

Tak: I can only think of Howard.

Grace: Howard?

Tak: Yeah the bully who used to torment me. Every time he saw me, he would laugh at me. He had those long arms; one time when I was passing by, he socked me right in the chest. My chest ached for months; I thought it would never go away.

Grace: Maybe he liked you?

Tak: Liked me?

Grace: Have you ever thought of that?

Tak: How could he like me?

Grace: People have strange ways of expressing themselves sometimes.

Tak: You mean hakujin?

Grace: Not necessarily.

Tak: (after a moment) What are you gonna do…about the questions?

Grace: My father's been after me to register.

Tak: But he was arrested by the FBI and held as a dangerous alien, why would he want you to register?

Grace: He thinks it's the right thing to do; I've been making excuses and holding out.

Tak: Waiting for me?

Grace: I've never gone against him.

Tak: Well, don't start now because I'm not going to register.

Grace: Sometimes, I wish we had never met.

Tak: The camp brought us together…

Grace: We're so different…what's going to happen to us?

Tak: I don't know.

Grace: (after a moment) Let's pretend nothing's happening out there, let's pretend we're back in Seattle.

Tak: Yeah?

Grace: You drive up in a car…

Tak: What car?

Grace: You have to have a car to go on a date.

Tak: Oh yeah.

Grace: We'll have dinner at a nice restaurant…let's see where could we go…ah the Olympic Hotel.

Tak: Is that good?

Grace: The best in Seattle.

Tak: (In the restaurant, looking around) Have you been here before?

Grace: Yes, I come here every now and then. (They sit.)

Tak: Who's that guy in the funny suit?

Grace: He's the waiter.

Tak: (loudly) I rather go to a drive-in movie.

Thanksgiving Day Harvest Festival. Rivers, Arizona, November 26, 1942. Photograph by Francis Stewart.

Last night, I took a walk around the camp. It was a very beautiful moonlight night and just right for romance, but I found myself wondering if this was my home. I saw spotlights in the towerhouse shining up and down, the police car prowling with no lights, the outline of the barbed wire fence across the ditch, the lights in the Administration building, the cars going in and out.

I heard the sentinel on duty walk back and forth, back and forth; I heard the frog crying in the creek and then heard the wild geese flying overhead; I heard the dog bark in the distance and the sound of the runaway horse. I heard the squealing of the pigs in their pen, and the baby crying in some barrack. I heard the slam of the door in the wind, and someone singing down the road, and another playing a harmonica. I heard the radio softly playing into the night. I heard laughter of a girl, then a voice of the man. I saw lights slowly go out, and the camp settle down to its slumber.

T. D.

Grace: (quieting him) After our elegant dinner.

Tak: (holding up a glass) How about some wine?

Grace: That's a water glass.

Tak: Oh...

Grace: Besides, you'll need an ID to prove you're 21.

Tak: (holding up Grace's pass) I've got this pass that proves I'm you. (He laughs as Grace takes the pass from him; they finish dinner.)

Grace: Wasn't that a lovely dinner?

Tak: It was okay. Now we'll get a hamburger after the movie. At the movie, we'll sit close together and I'll put my arm around you and tell you how beautiful you are. (He kisses her; after a moment Grace breaks away.) What's the matter?

Grace: Nothing.

Tak: Did I do something wrong?

Grace: No.

Tak: What is it, Grace?

Grace: You know why they put us in camp, don't you? Because they didn't trust us. Well, the registration is a way out for us; it's a way we can prove we're good Americans.

Tak: We're not good Americans?

Grace: They want proof.

Tak: Why do we have to prove ourselves over and over again? Aren't we good enough the way we are? I'm sick of saying yes, to everything. Yes, I'll go to camp. Yes, I'll register. Yes, I'll declare my loyalty. Yes, I'll serve in the Army and prove I'm a loyal, patriotic American.

Grace: People are making a commitment to go to war and putting their lives on the line. It takes courage to make such a commitment.

Tak: I know it takes courage.

Grace: Then why were you mocking it?

Tak: I wasn't mocking anything; I was just making a point. I'm proving my loyalty by fighting for my rights.

Grace: Tak, how do you feel about the draft? You know the question asks if you're willing to serve in the Army.

Tak: I know what the questions ask. Grace, what are you driving at? That I'm trying to evade the draft, that I'm afraid of killing and dying, are you saying I'm a coward?

Grace: No.

Tak: But you thought it. It's all right! (in a gentler tone) It's all right. Maybe you're right; I don't know, it's so mixed up. I know I don't like the idea of killing, never have.

Grace: On that morning we left Seattle the residents fixed breakfast for mother and me…

Tak: To go to war, you have to be convinced it's right…

Grace: and we all sat together and ate together.

Tak: there can't be any doubt, you can't even think about it…

Grace: The table was beautifully set…

Tak: just march to the drumbeat.

Grace: lace tablecloth, our best silver and chinaware, crystal.

Tak: I think I can be trained to be a soldier, learn to kill and be killed.

Grace: They even had flowers and they played my favorite Baroque music.

Tak: Just listen to the drumbeat.

Grace: I can almost hear it now. (music in the background)

Tak: On the day before we left, I slaughtered a flock of my Rhode Island reds I had raised from chicks. I didn't want to sell them and I didn't want to leave them…

Grace: We didn't know when we would see each other again.

Tak: so I chopped off their heads. Blood spattered on my hands…

Grace: They said they would be waiting for us.

Tak: I could feel the powerful struggle for life and I could feel that life going out.

Grace: Now I'm not so sure.

Tak: (to Grace) I don't want to break with you; I don't want to do that. Grace, I love you.

Grace: I love you too, Tak.

Tak: Let's close out everything…just you and me.

Grace: And promise never to part.

Tak: Yes. (They embrace and kiss; lights fade to darkness.)

Campus Report

Lillian Ota

Of the 110,000 evacuees, about 70,000 were Nisei, and of those about 3,300 were enrolled in colleges and universities at the time of evacuation. Over the duration of the war, another 5,500 left the camps to pursue their education through a project known as the National Japanese American Student Relocation Program, which was organized by Quaker leader Clarence E. Pickett.

Lillian Ota was one of the first Japanese Americans who were to leave camp through the program. She left Tanforan Assembly Center on scholarship in August 1942. Before evacuation, she was a junior Phi Beta Kappa at the University of California, Berkeley, where she was on the editorial staff at the Daily Californian *student newspaper. While interned at Tanforan, she served as the women's editor of the* Tanforan Totalizer *camp newspaper. "Campus Report" originally appeared in* Trek *magazine.*

Wellesley, Mass.

Go through the red tape of student relocation, then go to the nearest railroad station, and you're on your way to some midwestern or eastern college.

Most likely, you won't encounter any trouble from the other passengers on the train. They'll either ignore you or go out of their way to make you comfortable. That's been the experience of students who have already left assembly and relocation centers. I was one of the first to leave for college.

Only one person inquired of my race. She was a middle-aged woman who had once taught, so she told me, at some university in China. She praised the Chinese people and I agreed with her. She then intimated that it was a good thing the "dangerous Japanese" in this country were "interned," referring to the evacuation of Issei and Nisei into assembly and relocation centers.

Next, she queried, "What part of China did your parents come from?" When I replied that I was an American of Japanese descent, that I was on

Valediction yearbook,
Manzanar High School, 1945.

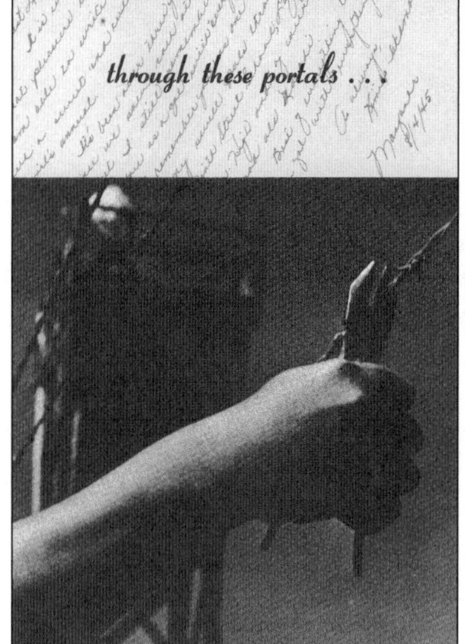

. . . to new horizons

my way to Wellesley College, the alma mater of Madame Chiang Kai-shek, and that I was on a generous scholarship, she became even more pleasant towards me. A few weeks after I reached Wellesley, she sent me a nice traveling bag from Pittsburgh.

During the first few days you'll be invited by the college to teas and receptions. Before long you'll lose the awkwardness you might first feel at such doings after the months of abnormal life in evacuation centers. If any Caucasian church groups, such as the Quakers, had anything to do with your release from the centers you'll probably be invited to teas and dinners at the homes of friends of people that helped you get out to college. You won't remember all the persons you meet at the social affairs, but gradually you'll build up your own set of chums.

You can almost count on being invited to the home of one of your fellow students for some weekend or holiday. I went to Connecticut to visit another student for the Christmas weekend. The train trip was dull and uneventful, except that an ensign who happened to sit across from me in the diner offered me a big piece of cheese, which I politely refused, since I don't care for cheese. The visit with my friend's family was delightful. To be able to get a glimpse of a typically "average American" family was quite something after months of living in barracks and dormitories.

Probably you'll be invited to join a Cosmopolitan club or some such "international" club on the campus. Aside from joining the "Cos" club, I haven't noticed that my being a "Jap" has made much difference on the campus itself.

Oh yes, I had one nasty "grilling." One student accused practically all the Japanese in this country of being in some or way connected with the "sabotage and espionage network." I argued against the misconception in the best way I could, but didn't finish my spiel as I had to return to my dormitory before lockout time. Later I sent her a copy of the *Pacific Citizen.* She then acknowledged that she had been wrong.

Several times I've been in Boston and the neighboring small towns. People stare at me, but not so much as to make me feel uncomfortable. Often I hear them whisper to each other "...Chinese...Japanese...?" Only once did someone yell at me and that was when a Boston drunkard shouted, "Oh, Chinis pliss." The only people that really stare and stare, although merely in curiosity, are other Orientals, mostly Chinese.

It is scarcely necessary to point out that those who have probably never seen a Nisei before will get their impression of the Nisei as a whole from the relocated students. It won't do you or your family and friends much good to dwell on what you consider injustices when you are questioned about evacuation. Rather, stress the contributions of these people to the nation's war effort. Mention the great number of Nisei in the United States Army, the way the Manzanar Boy Scouts protected the American flag from a pro-Axis mob, how the evacuees are engaging in wartime agriculture, and you will do the Japanese in this country more good than talking about "discrimination."

College isn't exactly an escape to the Ivory Tower it might have been a year or so ago. Just as on the outside, you are conscious that a war is going on. There aren't so many men students as in bygone days. Some schools have closed entirely or refused new admissions so that the Army and Navy might use the campuses as training centers. You're asked not to use the dorm elevators or needlessly use up electricity in other ways. There are practice blackouts which have a neat habit of coming on the night before important exams. Officer procurement agents from the armed services will come to the campus, but you know you haven't much chance of being accepted. Nevertheless, you can always participate in the war effort by rolling bandages, smashing tin cans, or helping the farmers out with their crops.

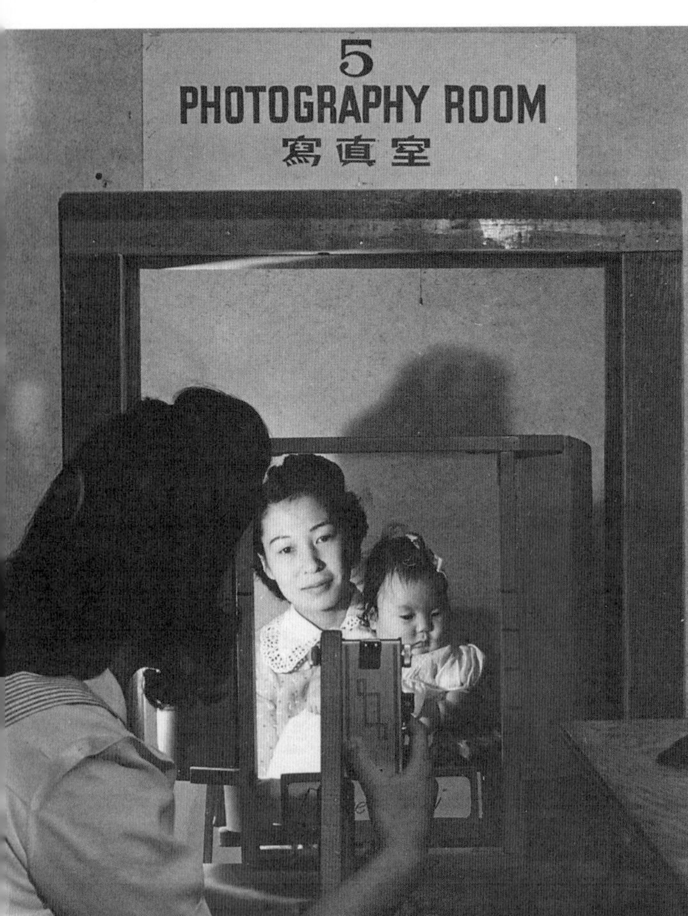

Identification Photo. Heart Mountain, Wyoming, March 16, 1944. Photograph by Hikaru Iwasaki.

Yuki Shirakawa, Relocation Department Photographer, takes a picture of Mrs. Tom Oki and daughter Dinne for the file and identification card, as the Okis have applied for indefinite leave. Procedure included fingerprinting all internees, including the baby.

The going might be a little tough in getting used to the classes at another college, but you'll make adjustments by the end of a couple of weeks.

Living accommodations will of course vary. The boarding houses can be good, bad, or just so-so, but generally the dormitories operated by the college are very comfortable. In the best dorms, there are maids who wait on the table and clean up the students' rooms every day.

You don't have much money? If you can't meet the annual tuition of about $1000 in the best private colleges, there are the less expensive, but just as good, state colleges of the Midwest. Perhaps you can get some scholarship. Due to the universal labor shortage, it isn't so terribly difficult to pick up a part-time job. However, it'll be hard to go through college entirely on your earnings.

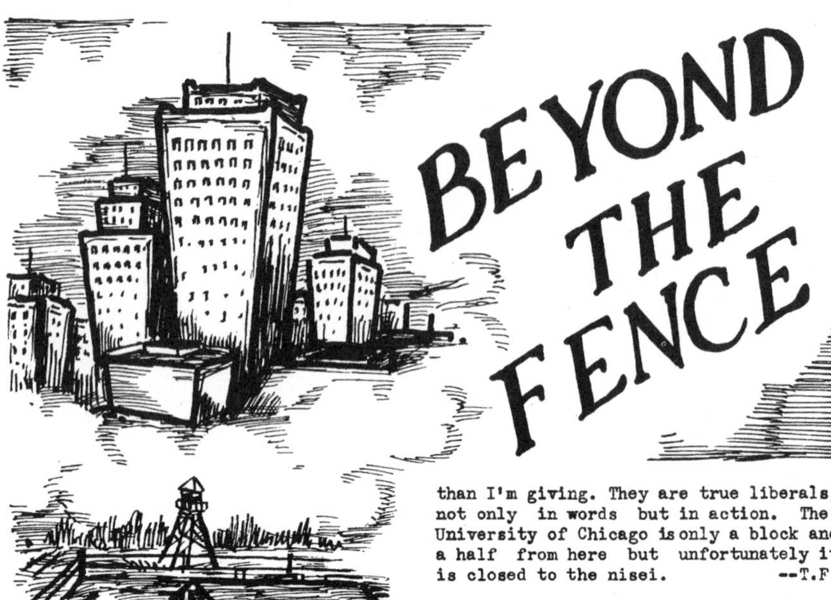

Center residents have received many letters from evacuees resettled outside. The following are excerpts from some of the letters:

Chicago, Ill.
Feb. 20, 1943

Four weeks of residence in this big city has not dimmed my original enthusiasm for it. Reception everywhere has been most heartening. I have taken in stride even the bitter cold. Couple of weeks ago I experienced my first heavy snowfall and I was thrilled beyond expression. A dreary grey city was magically transformed into an ethereal loveliness. Such views almost obliterate in one's consciousness the terrific strife in which the world is enveloped.

I am working in a wonderful home of a professor and his wife and three girls. I couldn't be more happily situated. They exercise every regard for my interest; I feelas though I'm taking far more than I'm giving. They are true liberals, not only in words but in action. The University of Chicago isonly a block and a half from here but unfortunately it is closed to the nisei. --T.F.

Denver, Colo.
Feb. 24, 1943

We left Heart Mountain on Jan. 30 and came to Denver. We had to buy a house here as it was impossible to rent one. The house is an old six-room affair in an old Jewish district, not far from the downtown section. Our immediate neighbors (just as in Los Angeles) are Jewish and Mexican Americans. No "Boochies" live in this district,--mostly Jewish.

The freedom and privacy are wonderful. Center life already seems far away and like a bad dream. People are impersonal and nice, both on the train and bus, and here in Denver--no unpleasantness so far. --M.M.

River Forest, Ill.
Jan. 28, 1943

I pulled into Windy City on the 15th of this month. I am now working as a houseboy for a doctor who lives about 12 miles from the "Loop", Chicago. This job is really tedious and monotonous, and I get lonely, but it's worth the price of freedom. I'll be here temporarily; in the meantime, looking around for something better.

Letters from relocated internees. *Denson Magnet*, 1944.

I swear there are all kinds of jobs here. Most of the nisei who came here before evacuation have some fairly good jobs.

In Chicago I have met a fair cross-section of former Pacific Coast nisei---nisei all the way from San Diego on the south to Seattle on the north. Those who migrated here from the west are really the more intelligent ones. --B.K.

New York, N.Y.
March 1, 1943

New York is just as exciting now, in spite of the dim-out, as it was in its hey-day.

Were New York women always this beautiful? Or, is it just that any slim-legged, lean-flanked blond with an obvious bosom (euphemism for breasts) looks good to me after 10 months in camps?

But sidewalks (no mud puddles) and a room to myself and the right to choose my own menu or to starve, if I prefer, and other freedoms really feel good. And people to talk with--people who speak the same language--and books and good music --they're good.

I went to a meeting for Toledano (Mexican labor leader) which featured cultural good-neighborliness with Latin America and met Canada Lee (played Bigger Thomas in "Native Son"), Langston Hughes and Aline MacMahon (now appearing in "Eve of St. Mark"). At the meeting (I didn't meet the following) were also Tito Guizar, who sang songs--plus all the consuls of the Latin American countries.

Had more fun at an Italian night sponsored by the Common Council for American Unity (which publishes "Common Ground"); I went with Margaret Anderson, editor of "Common Ground", and Rose Williams, assistant to Margaret Anderson. Met Jerre Mangione, author of "Mount Allegro", who spoke--Vivian Della Chiesa, who sang--and Martinelli, who didn't sing, but who led us in singing, "Happy Birthday to You" to Maria Coress who played the piano. So I can truthfully say that I sang with Martinelli. Much wine and light talk afterwards. --E.S.

Chicago, Ill.
March 5, 1943

A thousand pardons for the long delay in answering your letter of November. I've been very busy, as I work evenings, too, modeling at various art schools and studios. Recently, my sister came out here to join us, and there are the three of us living together.

As for work for women, there are plenty of jobs here in Chicago, and I understand that it isn't difficult at all to get placed in office, sales, factory, or domestic work, or any kind of work that a white girl can qualify for. However, don't come out with the idea of making money, because the jobs that are open are the ones that the Caucasians are now leaving for better paying defense jobs. Living conditions are high and rents exorbitant due to the influx of thousands upon thousands of office workers, transferred from Washington, D.C. Defense workers are pouring into Chicago from all parts of the country, and nisei evacuees like myself are coming into Chicago daily.

Our place is practically a USO Center for both nisei civilians and soldiers, both male and female. Last Sunday there were 24 visitors and since the beginning of the year, 105 visitors. My landlady raises the roof, but what can we do?

A group of us are planning to attend "Peter & the Wolf", "Romantic Age", and "The Fantastic Toyshop". I'm especially anxious to see the first for Sono Osato, the ballerina, is in it. Dorothy Toy (the former Dorothy Takahashi of Los Angeles) and her sister Helen, and Paul Jew were in Chico Marx's show at the Blackhawk Hotel for two weeks and then moved to the Oriental theater. They are very good and well received, judging from the applause. --M.K.

Seabrook Farms Employee identification buttons. Photographer unknown, no date.

In 1944, Seabrook Farms was the largest vegetable farm and food processing facility in the world. Between 1944 and 1946, more than 2,500 individuals (approximately 600 families) left WRA internment camps nationwide to relocate to Seabrook, New Jersey.

I left [Amache] in 1943, in the latter part of December and I stopped various places like New York, Chicago.... On the train to New York...I went to a smoke room and picked up a Readers Digest *and it was a current issue, I guess somebody forgot it there. Anyway, I picked it up and there was an article in there about Seabrook, New Jersey. They're going to get a contract from the government to supply that service with frozen foods and things like that. When I reached New York, I inquired about that article in the* Readers Digest *and they told me why don't you go down to Philadelphia WRA and inquire about it there....And [I] came here....*

I stayed for about three or four months....In the summer they have these harvest and production, harvest various vegetables and freeze it and put it away. In the winter they bring these out and package it for various retail groups, like chain stores and things like that, depending on the order, and that's what I did, repack during the winter....

Some people came and gave up in a week and were disgusted and left.... Some of the people came and stayed for years.

George Sakamoto

Preface to *No-No Boy*

John Okada

The Loyalty Questionnaire could not have been more untimely or insensitive. The shock of being uprooted from communities and relocated, and the many difficulties of camp life were hardships for residents in all the camps. The Loyalty Questionnaire, arriving as it did in the guise of a step along the way to release, became a means of dividing friends and families from each other as people tried to grapple with the implications of the answers they would give. Question number 28 in particular was perceived as unfair and illogical for the Issei, who, having survived the uprooting from their homes and businesses and having been forced into a life behind barbed wire, were now being asked to forswear their Japanese citizenship and to register unqualified loyalty to the United States, a country which refused them citizenship. A "Yes" answer would essentially render the respondent a person without a country. As a result, hordes of Issei and their families signed up for repatriation to Japan as a way of avoiding the loyalty questions. For the Nisei repatriates, this meant a loss of U.S. citizenship. The gravity of the loyalty controversy would fracture families caught between choosing where their allegiances lay and the political consequences following their choices. Although individual cases varied, in general those who answered "Yes" to both question number 27 and number 28 were fingerprinted, photographed, and released upon registration. However, a significant number of internees answered "No" to both questions, or gave no answers at all.

John Okada's novel No-No Boy *was published in 1957, and was then all but forgotten. It dealt with the consequences for a Nisei who answered "No/No" and spent the later years of the war in prison for his action, only to return home to Seattle to a bitter, depressed, and angry Japanese American community which vehemently shunned anyone who had protested the Loyalty Questionnaire. Five years after Okada's death in 1971, the Combined Asian American Resources Project reprinted* No-No Boy. *This reprint edition sold out two printings, each of three thousand copies. The University of Washington Press has continued to keep* No-No Boy *in print with two additional printings.*

*

December the seventh of the year 1941 was the day when the Japanese bombs fell on Pearl Harbor.

As of that moment, the Japanese in the United States became, by virtue of their ineradicable brownness and the slant eyes which, upon close inspection, will seldom appear slanty, animals of a different breed. The moment the impact of the words solemnly being transmitted over the several million radios of the nation struck home, everything Japanese and everyone Japanese became despicable.

The college professor, finding it suddenly impossible to meet squarely the gaze of his polite, serious, but now too Japanese-ish star pupil, coughed on his pipe and assured the lad that things were a mess. Conviction lacking, he failed at his attempt to be worldly and assuring. He mumbled something about things turning out one way or the other sooner or later and sighed with relief when the little fellow, who hardly ever smiled and, now, probably never would, stood up and left the room.

In a tavern, a drunk, irrigating the sponge in his belly, let it be known to the world that he never thought much about the sneaky Japs and that this proved he was right. It did not matter that he owed his Japanese landlord three weeks' rent, nor that that industrious Japanese had often picked him off the sidewalk and deposited him on his bed. Someone set up a round of beer for the boys in the place and, further fortified, he announced with patriotic tremor in his alcoholic tones that he would be first in line at the recruiting office the very next morning. That night the Japanese landlord picked him off the sidewalk and put him to bed.

Jackie was a whore and the news made her unhappy because she got two bucks a head and the Japanese boys were clean and considerate and hot and fast. Aside from her professional interest in them, she really liked them. She was sorry and, in her sorrow, she suffered a little with them.

A truck and a keen sense of horse-trading had provided a good living for Herman Fine. He bought from and sold primarily to Japanese hotel keepers and grocers. No transaction was made without considerable haggling and clever maneuvering, for the Japanese could be and often were a shifty lot whose solemn promises frequently turned out to be groundwork for more extended and complex stratagems to cheat him out of his rightful profit. Herman Fine listened to the radio and cried without tears for the Japanese, who, in an instant of time that was not even a speck on the big calendar, had taken their place beside the Jew. The Jew was used to suffering. The writing for them was etched in caked and dried blood over countless generations upon countless generations. The Japanese did not know. They were proud, too proud, and they were ambitious, too ambitious. Bombs had fallen and, in less time than it takes a Japanese farmer's wife in California to run from the fields into the house and give birth to a child, the writing was scrawled for them. The Jap-Jew would look in the mirror this Sunday night and see a Jap-Jew.

The indignation, the hatred, the patriotism of the American people shifted into full-throated condemnation of the Japanese who blotted their land. The Japanese who were born Americans and remained Japanese because biology does not know the meaning of patriotism no longer worried about whether they were Japanese Americans or American Japanese. They were Japanese, just as were their Japanese mothers and Japanese fathers and Japanese brothers and sisters. The radio had said as much.

First, the real Japanese Japanese were rounded up. These real Japanese Japanese were Japanese nationals who had the misfortune to be diplomats and businessmen and visiting professors. They were put on a boat and sent back to Japan.

Then the alien Japanese, the ones who had been in America for two, three, or even four decades, were screened, and those found to be too actively Japanese were transported to the hinterlands and put in a camp.

The security screen was sifted once more and, this time, the lesser lights were similarly plucked and deposited. An old man, too old, too feeble, and too scared, was caught in the net. In his pocket was a little, black book. He had been a collector for the Japan-Help-the-Poor-and-Starving-and-

World War II political cartoons, c. 1942. Cartoonist unknown.

Flooded-Out-and-Homeless-and-Crippled-and-What-Have-You Fund. "Yamada-san, fifty American cents; Okada-san, two American dollars; Watanabe-san, twenty-four American cents; Takizaki-san, skip this month because boy broke leg"; and so on down the page. Yamada-san, Okada-san, Watanabe-san, Takizaki-san, and so on down the page were whisked away from their homes while weeping families wept until the tears must surely have been wept dry, and then wept some more.

By now, the snowball was big enough to wipe out the rising sun. The big rising sun would take a little more time, but the little rising sun which was the Japanese in countless Japanese communities in the coastal states of Washington, Oregon, and California presented no problem. The whisking and transporting of Japanese and the construction of camps with barbed wire and ominous towers supporting fully armed soldiers in places like Idaho and Wyoming and Arizona, places which even Hollywood scorned for background, had become skills which demanded the utmost of America's great organizing ability.

And so, a few months after the seventh day of December of the year nineteen forty-one, the only Japanese left on the West Coast of the United States was Matsusaburo Inabukuro who, while it has been forgotten whether he was Japanese American or American Japanese, picked up an "I am Chinese"—not American or American Chinese or Chinese American but "I am Chinese"—button and got a job in a California shipyard.

Two years later a good Japanese American who had volunteered for the Army sat smoking in the belly of a B-24 on his way back to Guam from a reconnaissance flight to Japan. His job was to listen through his earphones, which were attached to a high-frequency set, and jot down air-ground messages spoken by Japanese Japanese in Japanese planes and in Japanese radio shacks.

The lieutenant who operated the radar-detection equipment was a blond giant from Nebraska.

The lieutenant from Nebraska said: "Where you from?"

The Japanese American who was an American soldier answered: "No place in particular."

"You got folks?"

"Yeah, I got folks."

"Where at?"

"Wyoming, out in the desert."

"Farmers, huh?"

"Not quite."

"What's that mean?"

"Well, it's this way...." And then the Japanese American whose folks were still Japanese Japanese, or else they would not be in a camp with barbed wire and watchtowers with soldiers holding rifles, told the blond giant from Nebraska about the removal of the Japanese from the Coast, which was called the evacuation, and about the concentration camps, which were called relocation centers.

The lieutenant listened and he didn't believe it. He said: "That's funny. Now, tell me again."

The Japanese American soldier of the American Army told it again and didn't change a word.

The lieutenant believed him this time. "Hell's bells," he exclaimed, "if they'd done that to me, I wouldn't be sitting in the belly of a broken-down B-24 going back to Guam from a reconnaissance mission to Japan."

"I got reasons," said the Japanese American soldier soberly.

"They could kiss my ass," said the lieutenant from Nebraska.

"I got reasons," said the Japanese American soldier soberly, and he was thinking about a lot of things but mostly about his friend who didn't volunteer for the Army because his father had been picked up in the second screening and was in a different camp from the one he and his mother and two sisters were in. Later on, the Army tried to draft his friend out of the relocation camp into the Army and the friend had stood before the judge and said let my father out of that other camp and come back to my mother who is an old woman but misses him enough to want to sleep with him and I'll try on the uniform. The judge said he couldn't do that and the friend said he wouldn't be drafted and they sent him to the federal prison where he now was.

"What the hell are we fighting for?" said the lieutenant from Nebraska.

"I got reasons," said the Japanese American soldier soberly and thought some more about his friend who was in another kind of uniform because they wouldn't let his father go to the same camp with his mother and sisters.

FROM *Beyond Loyalty*

Minoru Kiyota

For the Kibei, those Japanese Americans born in the United States but partly or entirely educated in Japan, the issue of answering the Loyalty Questionnaire was a crowning insult to the discrimination they faced as truly aligned with neither the more American Nisei nor the more Japanese Issei. The U.S. government viewed Kibei as dangerous elements, closer to the Issei in their alliance with Japan. At the same time, many Nisei shunned their contemporary Kibei, which further alienated these American-born citizens caught in an already explosive social hierarchy.

Minoru Kiyota has taught Buddhist studies and kendo at the University of Wisconsin, Madison for more than three decades. His autobiographical account, Nikkei Hangyaku, *or* Beyond Loyalty: The Story of a Kibei, *was translated into English by Linda Kepinger Keenan, and first published in 1999 by the University of Hawai'i Press.*

I wanted so badly to get out of Topaz. And good news was surprisingly soon in coming. It came in the form of an announcement from the WRA that students would be able to apply for permission to leave the camp to continue their studies. I went to the administration office immediately to submit my leave application. About a month later I received a summons for an interview. This invitation was not, however, from WRA officials as I had anticipated. It was from the FBI. When I saw that, I had a certain premonition about it.

Trembling, I reported to the administration office.

"Take a seat, please," I was told.

The investigator was a rather paunchy middle-aged man. He smiled as he spoke in a deep, powerful voice. I always feared the smile of a Caucasian. You never knew what lurked behind that pleasant face. Apprehensive, I took the proffered seat without saying anything.

"You were educated in Japan, right?" he began.

"I spent four years there."

"So—you're a Kibei," he stated.

I knew well the negative connotations of the term Kibei, and that the FBI were keeping an especially close watch on the Kibei. I hesitated a moment before answering, thinking over the implications of his question. In that I had been educated in the States, was completely fluent in English, and was comfortable in the American milieu, I was a Nisei. By the same logic, inasmuch as I had been educated in Japan, was fluent in Japanese, and was comfortable in the Japanese milieu, I was also a Kibei. I wondered exactly what my interrogator understood by the term Kibei, but—intimidated as I was under the circumstances—I dared not ask him to clarify.

Evidently my failure to respond promptly made a bad impression on the FBI agent, for his smile suddenly vanished and he became agitated.

"You dirty Jap!" he shouted, pounding the table in front of me with his pudgy fist.

I paled. He continued to shout. Not quite sure what was happening, I was terrified.

"I suppose you'd be *glad* if Japan won this war, wouldn't you?" he said accusingly.

I just sat there with my mouth open at that absurd suggestion, for I knew very well from my boyhood experience in Japan how poor the Japanese were. How could Japan win a war against a rich and powerful country like the United States?

"Well, why don't you say something?" he shouted.

Again he banged the table sharply, then sat on it, glaring down at me from his perch.

Finally, I found my voice.

"I am an American citizen," I said.

It had taken all my effort to say that much, and my voice trembled as I spoke. It was no longer fear, however, that made me tremble. It was the wretched feeling of having to endure such humiliating insults from this man. Utterly oblivious to any human feelings I might have, he continued to throw out questions, his voice harsh and thick with ridicule.

"What were you doing while you were in Japan?" he asked.

My voice became harsh as well.

"I was a child. I went to school there from the time I was eleven until I was fifteen. That's on my leave application, if you'd read it!"

"And what were you doing in San Francisco?"

"I was in high school," I replied.

"Not school. What kind of organizations did you belong to?"

"I didn't belong to any organizations."

"It will do you no good to lie," he warned.

"I did not belong to any organizations," I repeated.

"Liar! You were a member of the Butoku-kai,[1] were you not?"

"I just took some kendo lessons. I guess the San Francisco Kendo Club was affiliated with the Butoku-kai, but I never knowingly became a member of that."

"I am not asking you what you *knowingly* did. I am telling you that the Butoku-kai is a reactionary organization. What kind of training did they give you? What sort of orders did you have when you came into this camp?" he asked.

"I took kendo lessons as a sport!" I retorted.

"Why do you lie? The head of the Butoku-kai is General Araki Sadao. What orders did Araki give you? Orders to commit sabotage, right? You speak Japanese—you're a perfect candidate for sabotage. You're a Kibei, and a member of the Butoku-kai. You are a dangerous individual! And you are *not* getting out of this camp!" he concluded, shouting.

By this time, I was shaking with a hatred that boiled up from deep within me, and I no longer cared whether or not I got out of the camp. It was all right with me if I never went to college at all. My future didn't matter anyway. If I had possessed a knife at that moment, I have no doubt that I would have plunged it into the FBI man's heart. From my kendo training, I knew how to kill another and to kill myself in the tradition of the ancient samurai. And kendo had trained in me the determination to accomplish what I willed. I knew that I could kill him, and myself. Such was the intense hatred and rage that the FBI agent provoked in me.

I have no memory of leaving that office. Once outside, I began to wonder how the American government could be so suspicious and afraid of a youth like myself, a minor who had not yet even graduated from high school. Why on earth was the government persecuting me? Why wouldn't they let me out of the camp to go to college? I tried to puzzle it out rationally. The only reasons the man had given, though, were that I was a Kibei, that I had taken lessons in kendo, and that I was a member of the Butoku-kai!

In those few hours, all my hopes for this world, my trust in other human beings, and my confidence in myself were utterly decimated.

"The FBI is cruel! They're tyrants! They're abusing their power!" I was screaming inside.

That afternoon I paced up and down the dusty roads of Topaz, feeling completely and utterly alone. Enviously, I watched a hawk soaring high in the sky, free to fly wherever it wished to go. Finally I found a deserted corner of the camp where, away from the curious eyes of others, I could release my feelings in tears of vexation and rage. I could not help recalling my boyhood days in Japan. Innocently chasing dragonflies and cicadas in the garden in Hiratsuka, playing with Pooch, swimming with my classmates, stealing watermelons with the bad boys—those had been the best years of my life. I had never had such freedom in San Francisco. Life there had been a much more serious business for me. Once I entered high school, I became all too keenly aware of the realities of the struggle involved in living as a member of a minority in this society—and those realities had pressured me to work as hard as I could at my studies.

High school in San Francisco had also been a period of social isolation for me. Alone in a corner of the school yard during the lunch hour, I would sit quietly, eating the simple sandwich I had made for myself and observing with a cool eye as my Caucasian classmates enjoyed lunch together, chatting and joshing with one another. And my Nisei classmates had always eaten their lunches in a certain spot, in the same group, repeating the same simpleminded conversations. I had not been accepted by that group either, for I was a Kibei. I don't care what they do, I had told myself. I reacted against them with contempt, becoming more and more attracted to the Japanese tradition that had been the source of so much solace to my soul. In fact, I had begun to take great pride in that tradition.

They don't know anything about Japanese tradition at all, I had thought. They don't understand it, but *I* do.

Still, I could not altogether deny the fact that I had been lonely. I had had no friend with whom to share confidences or discuss the future. More and more, I had turned inward. Kendo lessons had given me a physical outlet for my resentful feelings, and Mrs. Sano had helped to soothe my troubled spirit through the Japanese literature she had read with me. But, all in all, high school in San Francisco had been a lonely time for me.

Darkness fell in Topaz.

The howls of coyotes from outside the camp's enclosure were almost tangible in the night. Every few moments the eerie beam of the searchlight from the watchtower swept across my feet and moved on.

That evening, idly flipping through the pages of the book of Chinese verse that I kept beside my bed, I found these lines:

> Behind his words he tends the dark flame that annihilates bones;
> In his smile he stealthily sharpens a rapier to pierce the other through.

That's what it is, I thought, reflecting on the day's events. America misleads people with its clever words about freedom, only to persecute them in the end. America preaches equality as its loftiest ideal, smiling as it leads people to their destruction, I concluded.

I would never forget my hatred of that FBI agent. I cursed the government of the United States, which had thrown me into this camp—I would curse it forever. In my powerlessness, this was the only means I had to express my defiance toward those in power.

Morning came. I decided I would quit going to school for good, no matter how close I was to graduating. This time it was not just because I found it unbearable to listen to the teacher's hypocritical preachments about civics and American history. It was because I knew how excruciating it would be to watch my classmates complete their studies with prospects of going on to college and to witness their elation when they received permission to leave the camp. Now I knew that I would not be leaving the camp. I would not be going to college. I was distraught. I despaired of ever finding a way out of here.

It was at this point that I began to think seriously of escape.

I recalled our arrival in the camp. The little freight station called Delta had been about thirty minutes away by bus. I should stay away from there for sure. Local people would know as soon as they saw my Asian face that I was an escapee from Topaz, and they would lose no time in informing the authorities. I would avoid Delta, then, and head north into the desert. I would skirt around population centers altogether, moving along the southern edge of Salt Lake at night and then into Ogden. That was about 150 miles from the camp. It should take me about ten days to get that far.

The desert is bitter cold at night in the winter and is beastly hot in the summer, so I figured it would be best to make my break sometime in the spring or early summer. I would need a magnet for my compass. I had spotted a surveyor's instrument at a construction site in the camp and one night went to the worker's shed, broke open the instrument, and stole the magnet. I would need at least five leather water bags—or botas, as they were called—to carry enough water. These, too, I began to take one at a time, at intervals, from the construction site. At each meal in the mess hall I saved a portion of my rice, dried and salted it, and stored it in a bag. I knew that I would perspire in the desert so I would need to replace the salt in my body if I were not to collapse.

I whittled a hardwood stick to make a weapon for protecting myself against wild animals in the desert. Coyotes are shy, so I knew that I didn't need to worry about them. Wolves can be vicious, but I figured that if they attacked me in a small pack of two or three I could handle them. With that in mind, I practiced kendo every night—targeting a low object and hitting it vertically, whirling around instantly and making a horizontal slash, then stepping back to make another vertical hit. There was no way, though, to protect myself from rattlesnakes that might slither up while I slept—I just had to hope I wouldn't encounter any. But I equipped myself with a first-aid kit just in case.

Finally, I began to think about what would happen once I got through the desert. If I could slip into Ogden under cover of dark, then I could get on an eastbound freight train. Once I got farther east, I should be able to buy sandwiches or something in the stations. All races of people lived in the eastern industrial cities, and, in any case, the exclusion order didn't apply in that part of the country. I envisioned that I would live in one of those cities, get a job there, and attend school at night.

The problem was how to get out of the camp. I certainly could not escape in broad daylight, for the soldiers in the watchtowers were constantly on the lookout. It would have to be done at night. But even at night, they continually swept the perimeter with searchlights from the towers. I tried to estimate the range of the searchlights. They illumined a stretch of about two hundred yards at five-minute intervals. I thought I could make it if I could get past the range of the inner searchlight, cut through the wire fence with pliers, then move quickly beyond the range of the outer searchlight.

Again I visited the shed at the construction site, this time to steal a strong pair of pliers. I practiced cutting steel wire of the same thickness as the fence, but discovered it would take me well over ten minutes to cut a hole in the fence that was large enough to crawl through. I practiced and practiced, but still I could not get the time under nine minutes. Just thirty seconds of cutting with those pliers and my hand was so numb I could barely move it. I realized that if it took me that long to cut the fence, then I couldn't possibly avoid being caught in the sweep of the inner searchlight. I was sure in any case that the soldiers in the guard tower would immediately notice a hole that big in the fence. Besides, I was afraid that if they caught me in the act of escaping, they might well shoot me on the spot. (Later I learned that I was not far wrong on that count. On April 11, 1943, James Hatsuki Wakasa, age sixty-three, was taking a perfectly innocent morning stroll near

Hatsuki Wakasa, Shot by MP, by Chiura Obata. Sumi on paper, 11 x 1¾ in. April 11, 1943.

the fence inside the camp when he was fatally shot by a guard from a watchtower about three hundred yards away.)

I gave up the plan of cutting my way out through the fence.

I now recalled the enormous sewer pipes in the city of Paris that I had once seen in a movie in San Francisco. It wasn't likely there were any sewer pipes that large in the camp, but perhaps there would be some kind of pipe big enough for me to crawl through. During the daylight hours I searched diligently for the openings of any pipes inside the camp, but none that I found were large enough for a person. Apparently camp sewage was discharged through rather narrow pipes to a spot about half a mile away. So escape through a pipe would not be possible either.

I had seen those basement rooms that some residents dug out under their living quarters. They worked on them very openly, and no one thought anything about it when they saw a pile of dirt outside the barracks. But if I were to dig a tunnel, say from our living quarters all the way to the outside of the fence, the pile of dirt would be so gigantic it would be sure to invite suspicion. And if I did succeed in escaping through a tunnel leading to the outside from our quarters, it would bring certain trouble for Mother. So a tunnel escape was out of the question, too.

I thought and thought about it.

Then one day, as I was walking near the camp entrance, I spotted a truck full of men in work clothes leaving the camp. I asked a middle-aged man where they were going. He said that the camp had a farm about five miles away, and that the men on the truck were going to work there. I headed straightway for the camp employment office and signed up as a farm worker. What a beautifully simple way to get out of the camp! I smiled to myself and forgot all about the previous obstacles I had encountered.

I drew a deep breath as the truck carried me and the other farm workers out the front gate. It was the first time I had left the confines of the camp since they put me here. The very air seemed full of hope. As the truck moved along the road, the barracks of the camp receded into the distance until they looked like so many tiny matchboxes.

The truck bounced along for about twenty minutes over the narrow, dusty road to the farm. There were no soldiers anywhere in sight. We were surrounded by desert, of course, so they probably figured there was no place to run and hide. But that was where they were wrong. Still, an escape would require meticulous planning. And, before anything else, I needed to develop a feel for the surrounding terrain. I decided to take my time and perfect my plan without rushing things.

Someone was waiting for us with a fire burning when we got to the farm. The workers all walked over to the fire to warm themselves, and there I saw a tanned, robust young Kibei from Hawaii. Near the fire he had an old wooden plank that he proceeded to prop up at one end with a small stick. To the bottom of the stick he attached a string, which he led off some distance to the side. He pulled a piece of bread from his pocket and broke it into small pieces, scattering them about under the board. Within five minutes a dozen sparrows had gathered to feast on the bread. The boy then jerked the string, dropping the board, and the men all shouted and dived after the sparrows. The boy from Hawaii casually shoved the birds he snared into his pocket. Then, one by one he took them out and plucked their feathers. He rinsed the naked birds in water, placed a wire mesh over the fire, and began to roast them. When they were done he picked one up and ate it with great relish. The other men followed suit, preparing and roasting their sparrows to eat. I just stood there watching. Then the boy handed me one of his roasted birds.

"Try it. It's tasty," he urged.

I took a bite of the thigh. I couldn't truthfully say it was tasty, but everyone was having such a good time roasting and eating the sparrows that I found the whole thing immensely enjoyable. I smiled again.

The young man was about my age, but hard work had given him a physique and maturity that I still lacked. Everyone called him Yoshida. He had a friend two or three years older named Yoshino, who was also from Hawaii. Neither of them could speak a word of English but they had a kind of unsophisticated charm. Because they were Kibei who had returned to Hawaii from several years of schooling in Okinawa just before the war broke out, they were regarded by the U.S. government as particular security risks. Thus, they had been sent to this concentration camp on the mainland even though most Japanese Americans in Hawaii were not interned. I liked the two of them, and they seemed to like me as well.

Yoshida and Yoshino were friendly with a third young man originally from Okinawa named Nakasone. One day Nakasone suggested to Yoshida, Yoshino, and me that we steal a pig. This suggestion rekindled my own youthful fondness for such pranks. The four of us remained at the farm after the usual quitting time that day, telling the others we would be working late that night. We laid our plans. I had little to contribute as a novice at this particular endeavor, but each of the others readied a rope.

After dark, we stole into the hog house on a neighboring farm. Yoshida grabbed the back legs of a hog while Yoshino got the front legs and tied them up. Meanwhile, Nakasone firmly bound its nose and mouth. Their movements were so swift and simultaneous that the pig was easily bound before it had a chance to make a noise. It must have weighed over two hundred pounds. The four of us struggled to carry the heavy bound animal to a tree about a hundred yards away. Nakasone hung the pig's rope-bound hind legs over a branch of the tree. As it swung there upside down, he swiftly slit its throat and the warm blood began to gush out. The three young men sat on the ground and lit their cigarettes. As much blood as possible had to be drained from the animal before it could be butchered, they explained.

After they all finished their cigarettes, Nakasone cut the pig down and they proceeded swiftly to cut off its head and legs, split open the belly, and rip out the entrails. It was truly a skillful job. I just stood there observing the whole process in silent admiration until they pressed me into service as well, instructing me to dig a deep hole at the spot where the blood had drained onto the ground. Then the bloodstained soil, along with the pig's head, legs, entrails, and any other parts that would take too long to cook, were all dumped into the hole and buried to eliminate all evidence of the slaughter.

Back at our farm, my companions lit their cigarettes once more for a well-deserved rest. Then they went to work again, carefully cutting up the parts of the hog that could be easily cooked and wrapping them in waxed paper. We dug a deep hole near the shed, buried the waxed-paper packages there, and placed a large stone on top so that our treasure would not be stolen by coyotes or wolves. Neither the manner of butchering nor the method of storage was particularly sanitary, but this was not the time or place to be concerned with such niceties.

It was the wee hours of the morning before we got back to the camp. It had been a thrilling evening.

The next day all of us working at the farm ate our fill of stone-roasted pork. Nakasone bewailed the fact that we couldn't roast the pig whole, but all in all it was a very pleasant day.

The manager of the farm project was an Issei man in his sixties, a soft-spoken fellow with a powerful build. He taught me very carefully how to do all kinds of things—to plant potatoes, to transplant tomato and celery seedlings, to drive a tractor. I learned firsthand just what backbreaking

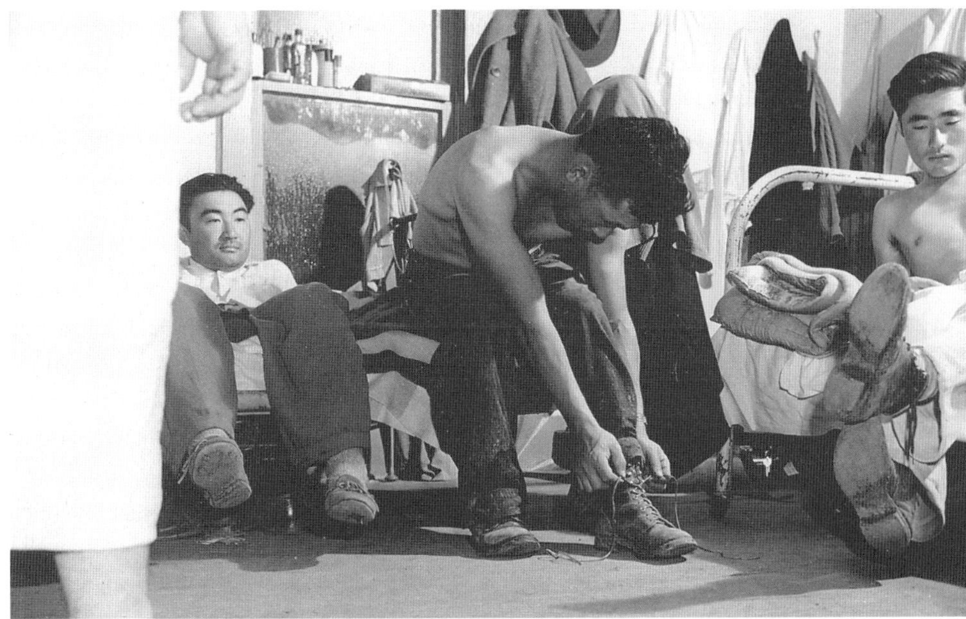

Chihiro Sugi, Asao Philip Nakaoka, and Takayuki Tashima. Keensburg, Colorado, November 3, 1942. Photograph by Tom Parker.

labor it is to transplant seedlings or plow a huge farm. But hard work did have its compensations. The three rice balls I wolfed down every day at lunch time were more delectable by far than the sandwiches I used to eat all alone in the corner of that school yard in San Francisco.

Summer was on its way. The manager began to give me, the city boy, work that was less strenuous but that carried greater responsibility. In one leap, I was put in charge of the irrigation ditches. I drove a small truck all around the farm, and when I discovered a break in one of the ditches I would plunge into the water with a shovel to fix it.

With the truck at my disposal, I took the opportunity to investigate thoroughly the territory surrounding the farm. Once I even accompanied the manager and the Caucasian supervisor to the train station in Delta to pick up some fertilizer and farm implements. While there, I discovered that eastbound trains did make stops in Delta, and I concluded that this would be my best route of escape after all. I checked the layout of the station and glanced over the train schedule, committing it to memory to note down at a later opportunity. Eastbound departure times varied depending on the day of the week but were generally between four and six in the morning. All were freight trains headed for eastern industrial areas by way of Ogden. The boxcars looked securely locked, so the only "open seating," so to speak, would be on the coal cars.

I readied my compass, botas filled with water, food, clothing, and even blankets, and hid them in a shed at the farm, awaiting my chance. Then one night I stayed at the farm after the others left, on the pretext of doing some necessary night work. To make certain it was safe, I went first to check the outer perimeters of the farm. Having made sure that no one was about, I went back to get my provisions. By this time it was already beginning to get light—I had to hurry.

But just as I started down the road in the truck I glanced out over the fields and was startled to see in the distance that one of the large scallion fields was entirely flooded with water from an overflowing irrigation ditch. Had I altogether forgotten to close the sluices at the end of the day yesterday, or was there a sudden influx of water from upstream? I hurried to close all the gates, rushing up and down every road on the farm, then proceeded to shovel the water out of the field. It took me hours. By the time I finished, it was morning and I gave up all hope of escaping that day.

Presently, the truck carrying the other workers arrived for the day. I hurried over to tell the manager.

"Sir, I did a terrible thing," I confessed.

My words tumbled over one another as I explained how the ditch had broken, flooding the field, and how I had shoveled it out. I hung my head with shame and apologized. The manager laughed loudly at my excessively downcast expression.

"Why, that sort of thing happens all the time!" he reassured me.

Then he got into the truck with me and we went to take a look at the situation. The gates were all closed by this time, and the drainage outlets neatly repaired. Assuming that I had stayed up all night just to fix the outlets, the manager praised me so generously that I was really embarrassed. I knew very well that the whole thing had happened only because I was so absorbed in my escape plans that I failed to check the water level upstream.

At lunch time, I sat down beside the manager and apologized to him again.

"I'm really sorry about that mess," I said.

"You don't need to apologize. Everybody makes mistakes. You just keep up the good work. You do amazingly well at this work for a city boy!" he said encouragingly.

Indeed, as he sat there next to me, the manager seemed to be genuinely enjoying his lunch, altogether unconcerned about my lapse. I was tremendously relieved. I resolved that I would not make another mistake like that one.

I had great respect for the farm manager. The oversight of this huge farm required careful attention to all its many aspects, but he had such a firm grasp of the entire operation that in an emergency he could quickly make the appropriate decision. Moreover, he encouraged people, gave them responsibility, and had excellent judgment when it came to putting the right person in the right place. When a job was well done, he saw to it that the workers got all the credit for the results. When something went wrong, however, he took the responsibility himself and never blamed the others.

The men working on the farm were all either Issei or Kibei who spoke little or no English. Their conversation tended to be dominated by prewar reminiscences. Whenever I broached the subject of what might happen after the war, they would smile and say, "Who knows?" It wasn't that they didn't know, though. They were afraid. When they were evacuated from the West Coast they lost the farms they had labored to build up over many years, so they knew that after the war they would have to begin again from scratch. But they did not want to think about that right now.

"What do you think you'll do, though, Minoru-kun?" they asked.

"I want to go to college," I told them.

Despite the situation in which I now found myself, I still had not given up my determination to finish school. I remained convinced that the only way to make a decent life for myself in America was to get an education.

"You're right. If we were educated, we wouldn't have spent our whole lives working like peasants," the manager muttered.

"But farmers do honorable work, don't they?" I asked.

The manager just grinned and patted me lightly on the shoulder. He got up slowly, dropped his cigarette, ground it out with his boot, and headed back to work. Perhaps my youthful earnestness recalled to him the aspirations of his own youth. He had been born and raised in Meiji-period Japan and came to America right after the Russo-Japanese War in the early 1900s. People said he had no family and no property of his own. Apparently he had experienced something of the seamier sides of life—he was no stranger to alcohol, gambling, or women. He was a man well acquainted with the pain of living, with the ironies of life, and a heavy, lonely shadow always seemed to trail in his wake. But he would never dream of demeaning another human being.

The three young Kibei from Hawaii continued to sit there with me.

"What are you going to do in college?" one of them asked curiously. College was an alien world to these young men.

"Well, first I want to study Western philosophy. Then after I graduate from college in the States, I want to go to Japan and study Asian philosophy. I want to do something to create better understanding between Japan and the United States."

Suddenly embarrassed at revealing so much of my own inner thoughts and ambitions, I fell silent. But the others were unperturbed. They looked at me with new eyes.

"You study hard and do that, okay?" one of them said.

"You won't forget about us when you're famous, though, will you?" another kidded with a grin.

The three stood up to go back to work. Like the farm manager, these were not the kind of people who would ever criticize or hurt anyone. They were a little unsophisticated, but they were humble, hard-working young men.

I remained sitting there for a while after the others returned to work. I *do* want to hurry up and go to college, I thought. When can I get out of here? When will I ever be able to go to college? Will all *my* plans end up as empty dreams, too? I wondered.

I slipped my hand into the pocket of my work pants and took comfort from the touch of a small, well-worn paperback book I carried there. It was the biography of Benjamin Disraeli—born a despised Jew, he was an adventurer who overcame poverty and illness and rose to become prime minister of the great British Empire.

Ten days had passed since the break in the irrigation ditch. Once more I remained at the farm overnight. This time I was very careful to check the sluice gates and ditches. All was as it should be. Once more I gathered my gear and started off through the darkness in the truck. I drove with the headlights off, for I knew the roads well enough. I headed for a mosquito-infested alfalfa field about a mile from the Delta station and there I parked the truck. Shouldering my gear, I walked silently through the dark toward the station. There was the freight train standing just where it was supposed to be. I climbed into one of its coal cars, made an indentation for myself in the midst of its black contents, and spread out the blankets I had brought to conceal myself and my belongings. As I settled in to wait for the train to begin its journey, I looked up at the stars twinkling in the early summer sky.

At last I was out of the camp! My heart was already in the East. When I get there, I'll be able to study! I thought, elated.

And the FBI can go to hell! I added bitterly.

Self-portrait, by Sadayuki Uno. Oil on canvas, 24 x 20 in. 1944.

Thirty minutes went by. I began to feel a little calmer. But then something started to bother me: How would the manager at the farm explain my escape to the white supervisor? They might interrogate him pretty harshly. It could affect the other workers, too—those men who'd been such good friends to me. Maybe they wouldn't be allowed to leave the camp to work on the farm anymore. Or perhaps they would be sent to a special detention center, locked up as criminal accomplices of the escapee. The men would surely hate me for what I had done. They would question my integrity.

Slowly I folded my blankets, gathered my belongings, and forced myself to begin the long walk back to the truck.

Frustration seething within me, I gunned the motor and raced the truck through the darkness. Tears fell on my hands as I gripped steering wheel. My body shook with uncontrollable sobs.

"*Damn* the FBI! *Damn* the FBI" I screamed over and over inside the truck as I drove back to the farm.

I heard a whistle in the distance. It was daybreak. Time for the train to depart.

In February 1943, a few months before my brief escape from the camp, an explosive manifesto had arrived in Topaz. All residents would be required to complete a government questionnaire, a copy of which was posted on the notice board in the mess hall. Entitled "Application for Leave Clearance," the implication was that those who completed the questionnaire satisfactorily would be allowed to apply for release from the internment camps and be free. The most crucial question included in this document was number 28:

> Will you swear unqualified allegiance to the United States of America and faithfully defend the United States from any or all attack by foreign or domestic forces, and forswear any form of allegiance or obedience to the Japanese emperor, or any other foreign government, power or organization?[2]

I paled when I read these words. I had to think what to do. I did not want to answer such a question. The point was not whether I was loyal to the emperor of Japan or loyal to the United States. The point was the excessive coercion being exercised against me—an American citizen—by the U.S. government. That government had incarcerated me against my will, taken away my freedom, prevented me from getting an education, subjected me to the intolerable humiliation of an interrogation by the FBI, caused me to despair of ever leaving the camp, and now—on top of all this—it was trying to coerce me into pledging my unconditional loyalty to it. I did not want to yield to that kind of oppressive force. Then, to underscore the government's demand, the WRA administration warned camp residents that those who did not respond to the loyalty question would be subject to a $10,000 fine or twenty years in prison. Much later it was revealed that this threat was nonsense fabricated by the WRA without any legal basis whatsoever. It is a cruel hoax when a government chooses to practice that kind of deception on its own citizens.

The loyalty question was initially intended for all camp residents, with complete disregard for the fact that those in the older generation were still Japanese citizens and that citizens of any country who are living abroad when a war breaks out might legitimately retain feelings of affection and loyalty toward their own homeland. Even the thickheaded U.S. government bureaucrats finally realized how absurd it was to demand that the Issei declare their undivided loyalty to America—particularly given the fact that the laws of this country had denied these same Japanese immigrants the right of naturalization. Thus the government eventually dropped its demand that noncitizens answer question number 28.

It was a fundamentally different issue for us Nisei, however. We were Americans. We did not have Japanese citizenship, so it was not at all surprising that the majority of our generation responded "yes" to the loyalty question. Still, even in our case, it was hardly a simple yes-or-no matter. We were members of the same ethnic minority as the Issei, and together we had a long history of being persecuted as Asians in the United States. Moreover, our two generations were naturally related as members of the same households, as parents and children. It is not surprising that some Nisei felt compelled to refuse to declare their loyalty.

The dilemma of loyalty versus disloyalty that faced internment camp residents was not just an idle topic for dinner table conversation, a simple choice between two alternatives. To choose the one (pledging one's loyalty to America) meant hoping for the total destruction of the other (Japan), and here lay the cruel ramifications of the issue. To pledge our loyalty to America meant collaborating in the killing and wounding of people who lived in Japan, a denial of a personal connection based on a shared culture. This denial was the source of particular anguish for Kibei like myself who were American by birth and citizenship but who had also lived and studied in Japan.

Issei, Nisei, Kibei—all had to live through this war between the United States and Japan, each in his or her own particular situation experiencing an individual anguish. It is impossible to say who made the "right" decision at the time and who the "wrong." We all had to endure a period that was rife with ironies, and each of us had to act with integrity in accord with the dictates of conscience.

Of course—as in any group of people—there were some who seemed to lack this quality of integrity, who based their decisions more on opportunism than anything else. One such person was the principal of a San Francisco Japanese-language school. When a prince of the Japanese Imperial family had come to the United States in the prewar years, this principal invited him to visit his school and did his best to encourage a spirit of emperor worship among the other Japanese Americans. Again, when the Japanese Imperial Navy's tanker put into port, the same man invited the Japanese naval officers to his school and loudly advocated the community's support for the Japanese military. Strangely enough, however, soon after the war broke out, this same principal accepted a job as a Japanese-language instructor working for the American military, training U.S. intelligence forces for the war in the Pacific. At that point he boasted to all who would listen that *he* was supporting the struggle against "fascist Japan, imperialist Japan, aggressor Japan." It seems that there will always be those in every age and nation who feel that integrity, when inconvenient, is a dispensable commodity.

Even young Nisei children got entangled in the discussions about loyalty and disloyalty.

"Mama, I'm an American. I want to hurry up and get out of this camp and be free," says the little girl.

"Me, too!" chimes in her little brother.

"What do you mean?!" the mother replies. "I'm Japanese. If the Japanese Army lands in San Francisco, I'll go out and greet them with the Rising Sun flag!"

"If you carry a Japanese flag, Mama, I'll carry the Stars and Stripes and fight those Japanese soldiers!"

Such were the absurd interchanges that the loyalty issue provoked between Issei parents and their American-born children. But if the Japanese Army had indeed landed in San Francisco, what would have become of this family?

There was another scenario that was at the same time less hypothetical and a great deal grimmer. In a number of Japanese American families, one son living in Japan was drafted into the Japanese Army while another son in the States enlisted in the United States Army. Thus it came about that brother was pitted against brother—as enemies fighting one another on the ephemeral stage of a global war. This was not some fictional scene from Dante's *Inferno* or an imaginary description of the Buddhist hells related by the monk Genshin in his *Essentials of Deliverance.* It was a real situation created by a war between Japan and the United States in the very twentieth century that advocates love for humanity and prides itself on rational, scientific thinking. Brothers screaming at one another about loyalty and fidelity while devouring one another in the name of "justice"—what is this if not a scene from hell?

The war in the Pacific created some very strange scenes in the camp at Topaz—scenes curiously similar to some I had witnessed on the streets of Japan during the Sino-Japanese War. A soldier's mother would go from door to door begging other women to contribute one stitch apiece to a "thousand-stitch belt" for her son who was going to war. Each fervently hoped that this traditional good-luck charm would ensure her son's safety on the battlefield. Even though some in the camp scoffed at these women, they would persist until they acquired all of the one thousand stitches for their sons' belts. Whether or not their American-born sons ever actually wore those belts as they went into battle is another question. But many a nightly tear was undoubtedly shed by these young men on their army-issue pillows when they thought of the love that their Issei mothers had sent with them as they went to war armed with this traditional protective charm. This was the tragic dilemma of the Nisei soldiers: Even as they took up arms against the homeland of Japanese tradition, they realized they themselves were heirs to that same tradition.

The Nisei in Topaz held meeting after meeting to explore and discuss among themselves the ramifications of the loyalty question. Extremist elements among the Kibei in the camp had been rather quiet, but with this new provocation from the government they became vocal once again. The pro-Japan group tried everything they could do to discourage other Nisei from cooperating with the U.S. government. They would barge into Nisei meetings, heckling, ridiculing, and threatening the participants. It was an extraordinarily tense atmosphere in which the Nisei had to decide what they should do.

At one of the meetings, a group of very rational young Nisei men were working to draft a declaration of their intent to comply in every respect with the laws and regulations of the U.S. government, to fight against imperialism, and to meet their obligations as good American citizens. As I sat listening to the debate, I became so disturbed by the tenor of the discussion that I could no longer contain myself. Their arguments only magnified the sense of indignation I had been feeling, particularly since that humiliating interrogation by the FBI agent. I raised my hand and was recognized by the polite young Nisei presiding over the proceedings.

"I have two objections to all of this," I stated. "First of all, the term 'imperialist' is very ambiguous. It would be easy enough to demonstrate that America, too, is imperialistic. Second—as to meeting the obligations of a good citizen—what on earth does 'good' mean here? And exactly what *are* those obligations? When you make a blanket promise to 'meet your obligations as a good American citizen,' aren't you just committing yourselves blindly to doing whatever the U.S. government orders you to do?" I asked.

The young chairman's gentlemanly attitude suddenly vanished and he responded with anger to my outburst. "There is a war going on, you know!! We don't have the luxury to deal with all these abstract, philosophical questions you're talking about. The point is, we have to prove to the U.S. government that we're loyal Americans. We *have* to make the government see that we're sincere!"

Obviously there was no point in my pursuing this argument any further, so I held my peace and left the meeting. True, the things I'd said were rather abstract. I didn't make any practical suggestions about what we ought to do in the situation we were facing. But I really did feel that the questions I'd raised were the crux of the matter. I wasn't so much concerned about what we ought to do right here and now as I was about the war itself. It galled me that the other Nisei just accepted the war without question and were simply calculating what they should do to ensure their own future best interests.

After I left the meeting, the group drafted a resolution of their intent to declare their loyalty to the United States government and to cooperate in every way possible with the war effort. This declaration passed by a majority vote of those present that evening and was duly forwarded to the camp administration.

A few days after that meeting, as I was leaving the mess hall one evening, I was accosted by the mother of the young Nisei man who had argued so vehemently against me the night of the meeting.

"Minoru-san, you are still young. You are too idealistic. My son is enlisting in the U.S. Army because this is his country. He is a courageous young man—he's no coward. When this war is over, we'll see who was right," she declared.

Having no desire to discuss the matter with this woman, I turned on my heel and walked away.

"It's ridiculous, all this talk about who is courageous and who is a coward! History will be the judge of that!" I muttered to myself.

I felt more and more isolated. I found that I could sympathize neither with the ingratiating, opportunistic attitude of the Nisei, nor with the violence of the radical pro-Japan Kibei group. I knew no one who shared my feelings.

I began to see the loyalty question as my only opportunity to take a stand against oppressive government authority. I decided that I would no longer allow myself to be led around by the nose doing as I was told by the U.S. government. Accordingly, I responded with a decisive "No" to the loyalty question. At this time I was yet a minor, just nineteen years of age and totally oblivious to the far-reaching consequences of giving such an answer on the government's questionnaire.

One of the consequences of my refusal to declare my loyalty to the government became clear enough in short order, however. I was informed that because I had answered "No" to question number 28, I was now considered to be a member of the dangerous, anti-American element. As such, I would presently be transferred out of the Topaz Relocation Center to the Tule Lake Segregation Center located in northern California.

Thus it was that I bade farewell to the residents of Sand Capital Topaz, to my Nisei friends, to the Issei and Kibei who had befriended me at the farm—and to my mother. My father, who was also interned at Topaz, was subsequently given leave clearance and later died.

It was autumn 1943.

ENDNOTES

1. Martial Arts Association
2. Commission on Wartime Relocation and Internment of Civilians, *Personal Justice Denied* (Washington, D.C.: The Commission, U.S. Government Printing Office, 1982), 192.

Let Us Not Be Rash

THIS department has been queried as to our opinion in regard to the petition movement in war-born relocation centers. Our reply is simple. We are in full sympathy with the general context of the petitions forwarded to Washington by the Amache Community Council and the Topaz Ciizens Committee. We do not necessarily agree on all the points raised, however.

Insofar as the movement itself is concerned, the Nisei are well within their rights to petition the government for a redress of grievances. Beyond that, it would be treading on unsure footing. We must not forget that we are at war. This department does not encourage resistance to the draft.

It is reported that five at Amache and thirty at Hunt are guilty of resisting the draft. There will probably be more before this matter is finished. We cannot conscientiously believe that by these sporadic actions anything concrete and fundamental can be achieved. Those who are resisting the draft are too few, too unorganized and basically unsound in their viewpoints.

EXPATRIATION is not the answer to our eventual redemption of democratic and constitutional rights. Unorganized draft resistance is not the proper method to pursue our grievances. Expressions and feelings of disloyalty, purely because democracy seems not to have worked in our particular case, are neither sound or conducive to a healthy regard of our rights.

We agree that the constitution gives us certain inalienable and civil rights. We do not dispute the fact that such rights have been largely stripped and taken from us. We further agree that the government should restore a large part of those rights before asking us to contribute our lives to the welfare of the nation—to sacrifice our lives on the field of battle.

BUT those who have grown bitter with the evacuation must not forget that "eternal vigilance is the price of liberty." We have not been vigilant. We cannot condemn democracy for our present unhappy predicament. Democracy is not only a form of government, but it is also a spirit. If there is no spirit of democracy in our governmental leaders, we would not have democracy in action. Let us therefore not condemn democracy but the men who manipulate public affairs and the masses who sympathize and condone undemocratic ideals.

We should at all times stand firm on our God-given rights. We should let our voices be heard whenever an attempt is made to abridge such endowed privileges. But ours should not be an act of rashness or haste. We should think the matter through and in the ultimate end retain a proper regard for the implications and repercussions that in all probability would arise from our acts. There is no reason why we should not petition for a redress of grievances, but there is every reason why we should not resist the draft in the way it is being done now.

Rocky Shimpo editorial by James Omura. February 28, 1944.

Draft Resisters at Heart Mountain

Frank Seishi Emi

Frank Seishi Emi, a twenty-five-year-old Nisei grocer from Los Angeles, California, was obliged like all adults in WRA camps to fill out the Loyalty Questionnaire in early 1943. Emi's response was that "under the present conditions I am unable to answer these questions." In December, Emi had heard an older camp Nisei, well versed in the U.S. Constitution, proclaim that the government had abridged Nisei rights without due process of law and that, therefore, Nisei should cease pursuing appeasement. Emi responded by forming the Fair Play Committee. The Fair Play Committee maintained that if the government restored their full citizenship rights, Nisei members would gladly comply with selective service requirements. Eventually, sixty-three Heart Mountain Nisei would refuse to take the military preinduction physicals as part of the Army draft, and in early May, a federal grand jury indicted all but one of these resisters. Tried as a group in Wyoming's largest mass trial, the sixty-three men were found guilty on June 26, 1944, and each was sentenced to three years in a federal penitentiary. A month later, Frank Emi and the six other committee leaders were secretly indicted by the same grand jury. On November 2, 1944, Judge Eugene Rice of the Federal District Court in Cheyenne, Wyoming, sentenced all seven leaders of the committee to four years at Leavenworth Federal Penitentiary in Kansas for conspiring to violate the Selective Service Act and for counseling other draft-age Nisei to resist military induction.

One of the few who dared to publicly support the Heart Mountain draft resisters was thirty-one-year-old journalist James Matsumoto Omura. Following the enforcement of Executive Order 9066, Omura had fled from San Francisco to the "free zone" of Denver, Colorado, where he accepted the position of English-language editor for the Rocky Shimpo. *On February 28, 1944, Omura began writing editorials on the Heart Mountain resisters and the reaction to them by those detained in WRA camps (see page 312). Omura's harsh editorials caused the government to pressure the paper to fire him in mid-April 1944. Two months later, he was indicted along with the seven Fair Play Committee leaders. Omura was acquitted, however, under the First Amendment constitutional right of "freedom of the press."*

Emi first publicly shared his story at the Fifth National Conference of the Association for Asian American Studies at Washington State University on March 24, 1988. It was then published in Frontiers of Asian American Studies, *a collection of selected papers and literary works from the conference. This introduction was written with the assistance of Dr. Art Hansen at the California State University, Fullerton.*

*

Today, I hope to dispel the myth that we were all "Quiet Americans"[1]—that, after being stripped of our constitutional rights by our own government, removed from our homes, businesses and jobs, then interned in concentration camps located in God-forsaken areas of the deserts and prairies, we all went quietly and sheep-like into segregated combat units to become cannon fodder to gain acceptance by the Great White Father....

On September 10, 1942, our entire family, my wife, my nine-month-old daughter, parents, two sisters, and brother, all went to Heart Mountain Concentration Camp in northern Wyoming, via the Pomona Assembly Center, where we had been for about four months. We arrived at Heart Mountain in the middle of a violent dust storm. You could not see further than ten or fifteen feet. That first winter was unpleasantly memorable. It

Frank Seishi Emi, right, leader of the Heart Mountain Fair Play Committee, with supporter Kozie Sakai. Heart Mountain, Wyoming. 1944. Photographer unknown.

was the coldest winter in Wyoming history. We were attired in Southern California clothing. None of us had even a topcoat. The barracks did not get an inner wall of celotex until the middle of December. We had our first snowfall in late September. I mention this to give you an idea of the harsh environment into which we were thrust.

My first involvement in the resistance movement, if you will, began with the introduction of the so-called Loyalty Questionnaire.[2] The questionnaire contained thirty questions. Two of the questions, number 27 and number 28 were controversial. Number 27 asked, "Are you willing to serve in the armed forces of the United States wherever ordered?" If you answered "Yes," the implication was that you were volunteering for the Army. Number 28 read, "Will you swear unqualified allegiance to the United States of America and faithfully defend the United States from any and all attacks by foreign or domestic forces—[up to this point, no problem]—and forswear any form of allegiance or obedience to the Japanese Emperor, or any other foreign government, power, or organization?" If a Nisei answered "Yes," he or she was admitting previously sworn allegiance to the emperor. And in the case of an Issei or first generation immigrant, if they answered "Yes," they would become persons without a country. They were prevented from becoming citizens of this country because of racist naturalization laws at [the] time in the United States.

These questionnaires were ill-advised, poorly written, and badly presented to the camps. The more I looked at it, the more disgusted I became. We were treated more like enemy aliens than American citizens. And now this. After studying the questionnaire for some time with my younger brother Art, I finally came up with a response to the questions. To both questions, I was going to answer, "Under the present conditions and circumstances, I am unable to answer these questions." This was my real feeling at the time.

I felt that many would be confused about how to answer these questions. With the help of my brother, we hand printed copies of my answer on sheets of paper and posted them on mess hall doors and other public places throughout the camp, with a notation that these were suggested answers to those two questions. That was my initial activity in the grassroots movement.

About this time, a Nisei pastor made a speech at a gathering urging the people to cooperate with the registration program and to answer in the affirmative to the two questions. After he finished speaking, another gentleman, Kiyoshi Okamoto, got up and spoke. Okamoto, a soil test engineer from Hawaii, was about fifty years old. He talked about the Constitution and the Bill of Rights, and the abridgement of all our rights by the government, without due process. He said that, as American citizens, we should stand up for our rights instead of following a policy of appeasement. The man was well versed in the Constitution. His speech was an inspiration to some of us who had similar feelings. During this period he referred to himself as the "Fair Play Committee of One." After the meeting, several of us got together with Okamoto and had a long talk. This resulted in the formation of the Heart Mountain Fair Play Committee as an organization.

In January, 1944, the Mike Masaoka[3]-JACL inspired draft law was introduced into the concentration camps—the end result of the dismal showing of the volunteer programs at the centers. Needless to say, the draft issue became the most important topic of conversation in the camp. Nobody that I knew applauded that decision to draft interned Nisei. Most adult Nisei commented and complained about the unfairness of it all. Naturally, the young teenagers who were not affected by the draft did not feel strongly about the situation back then, and still do not as adults today.

The Fair Play Committee took up the draft issue. We conducted public meetings to discuss all the ramifications of this program. We initially received permits to hold these meetings. But when the administration got wind of the subject of the gatherings, they refused to give us the permits. Still, we kept holding these meetings. Since the draft was of great concern to the internees, the meetings usually attracted a full house.

Our two main speakers were Mr. Okamoto and Paul Nakadate. The two speakers rather complemented each other. Okamoto was blunt in his speech and sometimes tended to get salty with his vocabulary. Paul, on the other hand, was smooth and polished. Mr. Guntaro Kubota did the Japanese translation for the Issei parents.

The sentiments of the people who attended the meetings were in complete accord with the Fair Play Committee. They agreed with the stand that the Fair Play Committee took on the draft issue—that drafting of Nisei from these concentration camps, without restoration of their civil rights and rectification of the tremendous economic losses suffered by them, was not only morally wrong, but legally questionable.

The Fair Play Committee's policies were set by a steering committee composed of the original members and anyone else who was interested in helping the organization. The meetings were quite lively, especially when we were composing the contents of the speeches and the bulletins. Much of the material was taken from Mr. Okamoto's speech. The first two bulletins were informational. The third bulletin would be a little different.

Some of us wanted the Fair Play Committee to take a more positive stand on the draft issue. As an organization committed to fight for civil rights, we felt that we had to challenge the legality of the draft law as applied to the concentration camps. After a heated session of the steering committee, we members who wanted to test the law prevailed.

There were about 400 in attendance at the next public meeting. Of the assembled group, about 200 were paid-up members of the Fair Play Committee. We presented our resolution to the members. It was unanimously endorsed. However, not all the members that endorsed it resisted when their draft notices came. They were fearful of being arrested and going to jail. We did not hold any ill-will toward those Fair Play Committee members who did not resist. That was their option.

With the endorsement of the members, we printed and distributed the third and final bulletin at the next meeting. Based on the contents of this bulletin, the seven most visible leaders of the Fair Play Committee were indicted and arrested by the FBI a short time later. . . .

We were charged with conspiracy to violate the Selective Service Act and with counseling others to resist the draft. This was on July 21, 1944. Indicted with us was Mr. James Omura, English [language] editor of the *Rocky Shimpo,* a Japanese American newspaper based in Denver, Colorado. This we could not understand. We had never met Mr. Omura, and had never talked with him. We sent news items to him, just as we did to the *Denver Post,* the *Billings Gazette,* the *United Press,* the *Pacific Citizen,* and the *Wyoming Eagle.* He was the only editor to print our news releases, and the only person supporting us with editorials. He showed plenty of guts in doing this, but to charge a newsman with conspiracy for publishing news items was outrageous. The government really did a number on Article I of the Bill of Rights. . . .

During the time that the Fair Play Committee was active in the camp, the JACL-WRA[4]-controlled camp newspaper, the *Heart Mountain Sentinel,*[5] was relentlessly attacking the leaders of the Fair Play Committee and James Omura with their vicious editorials. I think they used every derogatory word in *Roget's Thesaurus.*

We tried to get help from the American Civil Liberties Union (ACLU). What we were not aware of was the ACLU-JACL-WRA axis. All we received was a letter from the New York branch of the ACLU discouraging us from pursuing our struggle. Roger Baldwin, then director of the ACLU, in a letter to Kiyoshi Okamoto dated April 6, 1944, said in part,

1. The men who have refused to accept military draft are within their rights, but they of course must take the consequences. They doubtless have a strong moral case, but no legal case at all.
2. Men who counsel others to resist military service are not within their rights and must expect severe treatment, whatever justifications they feel.

We finally retained A. L. Wirin, a noted constitutional attorney for the ACLU, as private counsel. Mr. Wirin advised us that the chance of winning this case at the district court level was pretty slim, and that our best chance was in the appellate court.

Our trial was held on October 23, 1944, in the Federal District Court in Cheyenne, Wyoming. During our trial a surprise witness appeared in court. His name was Jack Nishimoto, a Nisei in his early forties. He lived near me at Heart Mountain. We had been on friendly terms, since I had done some favors for him when I was driving a truck in camp. We were wondering what he was doing in court. Well, we found out soon enough. When Nishimoto took the stand, he began to tell wholesale lies. In his perjured statements, he attributed false statements to me. In fact, his testimony was all directed against me. I just listened in complete amazement. My amazement turned to anger. I could have beaten the guy to a pulp at that time. Not until then

Fair Play Committee trial. Federal District Court, Cheyenne, Wyoming. June 16, 1944. Photographer unknown.

did I realize what "dirty tricks" the prosecution could employ. We never expected the prosecution would resort to such underhanded tactics.

Looking back, the reason the government tried such tactics, I believe, is because when the FBI questioned me a few days prior to being arrested, I did not give them one bit of information regarding my role in the Fair Play Committee. In order to tie me into the conspiracy, they had to have evidence. Jack was to provide that evidence with his perjured testimony.

When the defense took the stand, we gave the prosecution a surprise. We had planned an offensive strategy. We came right out and said we had done everything that we were accused of doing. Moreover, we had done it openly and in public. Furthermore, we declared our belief that the draft law as applied to the concentration camps was not only morally wrong, but unconstitutional as well. The district attorney seemed taken aback by this turn of events.

As a result of this strategy, Jack Nishimoto's perjured testimony was of no consequence. He just made an ass of himself, besides exposing his role as an informer. When the declassified FBI files became available to the public, Jack's role as an informant for the FBI was there in black and white. In a report made by FBI agent Harry W. McMillen, dated April 24, 1944, he quotes from the report of the Heart Mountain community analyst, Asael T. Hansen,[6] to Dillon S. Myer, director of the War Relocation Authority, detailing Jack Nishimoto's informant role. Hansen relates that Nishimoto named the "big shots" of the Fair Play Committee. Hansen further details how Nishimoto purposely got close to me, visited my living quarters, spied on my personal effects, etc. Nishimoto conjured up imaginary conversations and statements, supposedly uttered by me, and reported them to the FBI via the community analyst. If he had been more truthful, it wouldn't have been as disturbing.

Just as Mr. Wirin had indicated, we lost our case. Judge Eugene Rice sentenced the seven of us to four years at Leavenworth Federal Penitentiary. James Omura was acquitted. However, the court fight left him in bad financial shape. The JACL continued to harass him. This was a trial which never should have taken place for Jim.

We filed an appeal to the Tenth Circuit Court of Appeals. Mr. Wirin requested bail for us, pending the decision of the Appellate Court. The judge refused, stating, "You men are agitators, the camp will be better off without you." We could see the hand of the WRA-JACL behind this. I say this because, later, one of the draft resisters who had worked in the parole office at the penitentiary had obtained a copy of a memo that Dillon Myer, WRA Director, had sent to the head of the prison board. He requested the prison board not to release on parole any of the Japanese American draft resisters. This is just a sample of the underhanded things that went on, and we believed the JACL was probably right in there.

Finally, after eighteen months when the war with Japan had ended, the Tenth Circuit Court of Appeal, sitting in Denver, rendered their decision. They reversed the convictions of all seven leaders. We had finally won our battle. In giving their opinion, Justice Bratton said, "one with innocent motives, who honestly believe[s] a law is unconstitutional and, therefore not obligatory, may well counsel that the law shall not be obeyed." I believe this was one of only two cases won by the Nisei in the Appellate Courts during that period.

Now, to get back to the young men who received their draft notices. There were sixty-three in the first group that resisted. Their trial began on June 12, 1944, before Judge T. Blake Kennedy in the U.S. District Court, Cheyenne, Wyoming. It was headlined in the local papers as the largest mass trial in the history of Wyoming.

While the resisters were awaiting their trial at the Cheyenne county jail, they were visited by the late Min Yasui and Joe Grant Masaoka.[7] The two tried to persuade the resisters to change their minds and enter the Army. They even tried fright tactics by telling the resisters that if they went to the "Pen," the guards would beat them with two-by-fours. Their arguments did not impress the young men. Not one changed his mind.

The trial of the "63" ended on June 20, 1944. They were found guilty and sentenced to three years. About thirty went to McNeil Island Federal Penitentiary. The rest were sent to Leavenworth.

To give you an idea of how "Justice" works, the following were the penalties that various judges dealt to the Nisei resisters even thought the charges were identical. Judge Louis A. Goodman dismissed the indictments against twenty-seven draft resisters from Tule Lake, saying, "it is shocking to the conscience that an American citizen be confined on the ground of disloyalty and then, while so under duress and restraint, be compelled to serve in the armed forces or be prosecuted for not yielding to such compulsion." In Arizona, the judge fined the Poston draft resisters one cent. No jail term. In other camps, the sentences ranged from two to five years.

We filed an appeal on behalf of the "63." The Appellate Court affirmed their convictions. We then filed an appeal to the U.S. Supreme Court. That court refused to review the case. The resisters each served about twenty-seven months of their three-year sentences. At Dillon Myer's request the prison board had denied them parole.

On Christmas Eve, 1947, President Harry S. Truman granted a Presidential Pardon to all Nisei draft resisters.[8] All political and civil rights were restored. The head of the Amnesty Board, former Associate Justice of the Supreme Court Owen J. Roberts, issued a report in conjunction with President Truman's proclamation. In this report the Board commented on the wartime dilemma of the Japanese Americans who had been convicted of violation of the Selected Service Act. It said, in part, "Although we recognize the urgent necessities of military defense, we fully appreciate the nature of their feelings and their reactions to orders from local Selective Boards."[9]

The records of Nisei draft resisters were cleared, and their fight for a principle was vindicated. The government acknowledged that the resisters had a legitimate reason for their action....

A few words about the Fair Play Committee "7." I have mentioned Kiyoshi Okamoto earlier. In his way, he was a remarkable man. A little bombastic in his speeches, his written works were brilliant. Kiyoshi was chairman of the Fair Play Committee, until his exile to Tule Lake. I never saw him again after returning to Los Angeles. Paul Nakadate, also mentioned earlier, was an excellent speaker. He became chairman after Mr. Okamoto was taken away. Paul was twenty-nine years old, married, and had one child. He was from Los Angeles. He passed away at the age of forty-nine. Sam Horino was a single man, about twenty-nine, and one of the original members of the Fair Play Committee. He still resides in Monterey Park. Minoru Tamesa, also single, about thirty, was from Seattle. Minoru was one of the "63," a guest at Leavenworth at the time of the conspiracy trial. He was brought to Cheyenne and, when sentenced for two years in that trial, served it concurrent with his previous sentence. He passed away in his early fifties. Ben Wakaye was the treasurer of our organization. He was about thirty, also single, and one of the "63." He, too, came back from Leavenworth for the conspiracy proceedings. His two-year sentence also ran concurrent with his previous sentence. Ben passed away a few years after returning to San Francisco. The sixth member was Guntaro Kubota, also mentioned earlier. He was an Issei, married to a Nisei girl, and had two children. He was forty-four years old. He was very proficient in speaking and writing the Japanese language. He was a great help to the Fair Play Committee in making our position understandable to the Issei parents of the members. I can still remember a conversation I had with Guntaro one day, while we were sitting in our cell at Leavenworth. He said, "Emi, I'm really proud to be here with you fellows. If I don't ever do anything else in my life, this will be the proudest thing I ever did because I had a part in your fight for a principle." I will never forget his words. Mr. Kubota passed away at the age of sixty-two.

The final member of the "7" was myself. I was twenty-seven at the time and married with two small children. My duties included corresponding with the attorney, sending news items to the papers, and helping with the composition of the bulletins, among other things. Of the seven members involved in the conspiracy trial, Sam Horino and I are the only ones left.

There were a few other members who were quite active but not very visible. They were not arrested, which was fortunate for us, because they could carry on after we were taken away. My brother carried on the correspondence with the attorney, as well as conducting liaison meetings with the parents of the "63" boys. A couple of other individuals I must mention are Kozie Sakai and George Nozawa. The latter was only eighteen at the time, but was a very dedicated and tireless worker. Kozie Sakai was a little older than us. He was never called for military duty. During the trial of the "63," he obtained a pass to go to Cheyenne, where he covered the trial and sent me handwritten coverage of the proceedings, once and sometimes twice a day.

As I think back, I cannot help but admire the dedication of everyone who took part in our fight for justice during those dark days. Yet the story of the Heart Mountain Fair Play Committee's resistance and the resistance in other camps has been almost totally ignored by most writers....

*

Before the closure of the last internment camp, a total of 315 men were imprisoned for draft-law violations. Each resister served an average of two years in federal prisons before President Harry Truman issued them a blanket postwar pardon. As mentioned, the Fair Play Committee leaders' verdicts and sentencing were overturned on appeal after approximately eighteen months of imprisonment.

ENDNOTES

1. See Bill Hosokawa, *Nisei: The Quiet Americans* (New York: William Morrow & Co., 1969).
2. Leave Clearance Registration Form. See Michi Weglyn, *Years of Infamy* (New York: William Morrow & Co., 1976).
3. Mike Masru Masuoka was the wartime head of the JACL, with JACL president Saburo Kido. Masaoka authored "JACL Bulletin 142: Re: Test Cases," and issued it from San Francisco on April 7th, 1942. In it, Masaoka declares, "The National JACL headquarters is unalterably opposed to test cases to determine the constitutionality of military

regulations at this time." Masaoka goes on to enunciate a JACL policy of pursuing good publicity over good law. He argues that those "self-styled martyrs who are willing to be jailed in order that they might fight for the rights of citizenship...," are in fact, endangering all of Japanese America by creating bad publicity, and arousing the hostility of whites against the Nikkei by characterizing them as opposing the United States Army in wartime.

4. The War Relocation Authority (WRA) was created to administer the ten large concentration camps, so-called "relocation centers," and operated as an agency of the Department of Interior. The first director of the WRA was Milton Eisenhower, who left the WRA within a year. Dillon S. Myer took over and was the WRA's last director. See Eisenhower's autobiography, *The President Is Calling* (New York: Doubleday, 1974); Dillon S. Myer, *Uprooted Americans: The Japanese-Americans and the War Relocation Authority During World War II* (Tucson: University of Arizona Press, 1971); and Richard Drinnon's *Keeper of Concentration Camps: Dillon S. Myer and American Racism* (Berkeley: University of California Press, 1987).
5. The *Heart Mountain Sentinel* was, like all the camp newspapers, only nominally written and edited by the Nikkei internees. The camp papers were run by the so-called "Reports Office." "Reports" was a government euphemism for propaganda and censorship. The Heart Mountain Reports Officer was one Vaughan "Bonnie" Mechau. Hosokawa had relocated into his new job in Des Moines by the time the Fair Play Commitee became active. The *Sentinel* was now edited by Haruo Imura from Alameda, California. Articles attacking the Fair Play Committee were written by assistant editors John Kitasako from Palo Alto and Nobu Kawai from Pasadena, California.
6. Asael T. Hansen was a government anthropologist assigned to Heart Mountain Relocation Center as community analyst with the WRA's Community Analysis Section (CAS). Hansen took over his post at Heart Mountain without having had any previous experience with or knowledge of people of Japanese ancestry. He also arrived just as the government had made the Nisei in camp eligible for the draft and the Fair Play Committee was forming. Hansen's CAS report to Dillon Myer became the FBI report and sedition case against the leaders of the Fair Play Committee, signed by FBI agent Harry W. McMillen, dated April 24th, 1944. Emi denies Nishimoto's assertions of having had multiple conversations where Emi described his intent, method, and occasions of influencing young Nisei not to appear for the preinduction physicals; of having told an arrested resister's mother "The Fair Play Committee would take care of him;" of having told Nishimoto, he, Emi, would ask for repatriations to Japan, if the government did not clarify the Nisei citizenship status.
7. Minoru Yasui violated the Army's curfew order to create a test case. He betrayed his own cause and became head of the Denver office of the JACL. He and Mike Masaoka's brother, Joe Grant Masaoka, visited a total of three of the 63 Heart Mountain draft resisters, and Yasui authored a confidential report of his visit to the FBI. In the report he intimates that he visited with all the resisters. He recommends they be separated and put into solitary confinement to break their spirit. The Yasui report is dated April 28th, 1944, National Archives Record Group 210.
8. Title 3—The President, Proclamation 2762, "Granting Pardon to Certain Persons of Violating the Selective Training and Service Act of 1940 as Amended," *The Federal Register*, vol. 12, no. 250, December 24, 1947.
9. Owen J. Roberts quoted in *Pacific Citizen*, January 8, 1948.

Fresno Assembly Camp, by Henry Sugimoto. Oil on canvas, 13 x 16 in. 1942. (above)
Freedom Day Came, by Henry Sugimoto. Oil on canvas, 21¼ x 25¼ in. c. 1945. (below)

Poetic Reflections of the Tule Lake Internment Camp

Violet de Cristoforo

Whatever the reasons for answering "No" to the loyalty questions, that answer branded people as "disloyal" in the eyes both of the U. S. government and many in the Japanese American community. In mid-July 1943, the WRA announced a segregation plan, choosing Tule Lake for internment of those they termed "disloyals." More than 12,000 people who answered "No" to either question, who refused to answer question number 28, who had applied for expatriation or repatriation to Japan, or who had other unexplained evidence of disloyalty in their files were ordered to pack up and transfer into this maximum-security segregation center. In many cases, if an Issei parent voted to repatriate, the spouse and any American-born children had little choice but to follow. In the fall of 1943, the separation of those destined for Tule Lake began.

Violet de Cristoforo was born as Kazue Yamane, in Ninole, Hawaii. At age eight, she was sent to Hiroshima, Japan for her education, returning to America when she was thirteen to attend high school in Fresno, California. Upon graduation, she married Shigeru Matsuda. In 1942, the Matsudas evacuated to Fresno Assembly Center and were then moved to Jerome, Arkansas. In 1943, her husband refused to sign questions number 27 and 28, leaving the spaces blank, so was sent to the Justice Department camp in Santa Fe, New Mexico. Violet, her brother, mother-in-law, and three children were then deported to Tule Lake segregation camp and expatriated with Shigeru to Japan in March 1946.

De Cristoforo eventually resettled and remarried in the United States. Of the hundreds of haiku she wrote while incarcerated at Tule Lake, only fifteen survived. These were published in the chapbook, Poetic Reflections of the Tule Lake Internment Camp.

*

Many Dandelions Are Stepped On Only One Blooming Properly

Dandelions

The Tule Lake Segregation Center was built on volcanic ashes in the desolate lava beds of northern California, near the Oregon border. During the spring and summer it was very dry and dusty, and in the winter it was a muddy swamp, making it impossible for the internees to walk to the mess hall and to the communal washroom and toilet facilities. This condition made it necessary for the internees to build wooden catwalks connecting the barracks and the facilities serving them.

After the long and harsh winter dandelions sprang up between the wooden planks of the catwalks only to be stepped on by passersby. One day, as if by a miracle, I found just one perfect dandelion among the many which had been crushed—as the downtrodden internees had been trampled under foot by circumstances. As each day was a reminder of the humiliating and oppressive existence we were forced to endure, this one perfectly blooming dandelion was a symbol which inspired and fortified me. The pleasure I derived from this one blossom filled me with determination to endure the harsh conditions of camp life and to overcome all obstacles and difficulties.

Flowers On Tule Reeds And Sandy Flats
Brother Confined Over 200 Days

Brother's Imprisonment

The November 4, 1943 warehouse incident, caused by reports of thefts of food for the internees by War Relocation Authority personnel, resulted in confrontations and disturbances at Tule Lake.

Brother Tokio, an innocent bystander, had been asked to help restore order among the agitators. As he was about to do so, he was arrested by WRA Internal Security personnel and accused of taking part in the disorder. During a night of brutal interrogation he was cruelly beaten and, not only was he denied medical treatment for his injuries, but he was imprisoned in the "Bull Pen" of the camp stockade—a place of maximum punishment for serious offenders.

Following the occurrence Army troops took over control of the camp and martial law was declared at Tule Lake.

Then came spring, the snow melted and the tule reeds sprouted and grew. By July the reeds even had blossoms. Brother Tokio was still confined in the "Bull Pen," after nine months of imprisonment without trial or a hearing. Fall was about to come again and, under those conditions of dark uncertainty and desperation, everything was measured in terms of the growth and death of the tule reeds.

Harsh Summer Ground Being Ill Day After Day

Harsh Summer

After a short spring, the severe summer heat of the high plateau reflected from the black volcanic ash became unbearable, especially to one allergic to the wild grasses, weeds, and to the abundant dust of Tule Lake.

Every day was one of emotional and physical illness, of inner struggle, and of resignation.

A Visitor Brings Me Tranquillity And Happiness
The Summerly Ground Is Flat

Visitor

A priest friend was finally transferred to Tule Lake after being incarcerated in several isolation camps as a result of reports by WRA informers, including some of the so-called community analysts and researchers.

His visit to me brought happiness and tranquillity, but also the realization that the summertime ground was still monotonously flat—that nothing had really changed.

Spider Web Turned Black Confined Three Years

Spider Web

My baby is taking a nap and soon I shall leave for the camp hospital to see my dying mother-in-law, who is still waiting to hear from her only son interned in the Santa Fe camp. Letters to my husband and his letters to me, and to his mother, are censored and news is scanty. What shall I tell her today?

This is the third year the Tule Lake Segregation Center has been in operation and even the spider webs have turned black. What a long confinement it has been in our barren room where even a spider web focuses my attention!

Memorized Shape Of The Mountain
Walk In The Same Direction On Winter Days

Shape of the Mountain

Castle Rock Mountain, the last battle ground of the Modoc Indians, was my inspiration during my Tule Lake days. The Castle Rock area was also the location of the WRA Administration Office, the camp hospital, the military police, and the infamous "Bull Pen" of the stockade.

It was in the "Bull Pen" that my brother Tokio was imprisoned for ten months, without due process of law, in the most severe and degrading conditions, after being falsely accused of inciting the November 4 food riots.

I made numerous visits to this area to appeal to the camp authorities for the release of my brother from the "Bull Pen," to plead that my husband, who was being detained in the Santa Fe camp, be permitted to visit his dying mother, and later, that he be allowed to attend her funeral. All to no avail because the authorities were insensitive and indifferent to our plight and branded me a trouble maker for my pains.

How abandoned I felt! How I longed to have the authorities heed my pleas for justice and humane treatment! How I ached for my relatives caught in the web of man's inhumanity to man! And always my vision and my thoughts were drawn to Castle Rock, comparing our fate to the Modoc Indians' last stand in their Lava Bed Campaign of 1872–73.

An Autumn Day Flowers With Thorns A Lump In My Heart

Autumn Day
Brother Tokio, a U.S. citizen by birth, and many of his companions, are being sent to the Justice Department camp for enemy aliens in Santa Fe, New Mexico.

After much pleading with U.S. government agencies and with the Spanish Consulate, the neutral protective power for enemy aliens, my kindly mother-in-law was finally sent to a hospital in Oregon for radium treatment—escorted by two armed soldiers with rifles and fixed bayonets. On the train one sat beside her and the other on the opposite seat. They stood guard over her when she used the train lavatory, and outside her hospital room. What danger did she pose to U.S. security?

Having been treated so shabbily by the government, was it a crime that she had requested repatriation to Japan so she could die in her native country and be buried by her family?

How do I express my feelings of repugnance, except to talk to flowers? How do I suppress my pride? For whom do I shed my tears?

No Flower in Vase: Poems from Tule Lake

From the beginning of Tule Lake as a segregation center, a strongly militant pro-Japan faction emerged and dominated the community. Those suspected to be inu, or informers who collaborated with WRA administrators, were frequently terrorized at night and beaten. In the summer of 1943, a farm-worker internee was killed, and protests immediately formed over both the cause of the accident and the indifferent reactions of the camp authorities. A work strike was called by the internees. On November 1, 1943, National Director Dillon Myer visited Tule Lake, to be faced with a mass demonstration of nearly 5,000 men, women, and children who charged the government with neglect, incompetence, and corruption. A contingent of troops at full-battalion strength armed with a half dozen tanks was alerted; three days after the protest demonstration, Tule Lake was surrounded by a swarm of Army troops, security patrols, and FBI agents. Throughout the nation, this "Jap protest" received considerable press coverage. After curfew was enforced, the arrests of anti-administration agitators began. Tear gas was used on crowds, schools were closed, and all normal activities ceased. The sudden number of arrests led to the building of a prison stockade where inmates were kept from their families and denied medical attention. The Army takeover of Tule Lake would last for six months.

These haiku were written by various internees who had relocated from largely the Jerome and Rohwer internment camps and formed the Tule Lake Valley Ginsha. Many of their haiku were censored and ultimately lost when detainees were expatriated or repatriated to Japan at the end of the war. All haiku presented here were originally published in May Sky, There Is Always Tomorrow: An Anthology of Japanese American Concentration Camp Kaiko Haiku, *compiled and translated by Violet Kazue Matsuda de Cristoforo.*

*

Rain shower from mountain
quietly soaking
barbed wire fence

Suiko Matsushita

We are hopeful
for something
this Fourth of July

Seioshi Kume

Summer mountain
cross on Castle Rock
pitiful last days of Indians

Misen Morimoto

Cosmos in bloom
as if no war
were taking place

Suiko Matsushita

Poor butterfly fluttering
among the flowers
wind is too strong

Senbo Takeda

Winter night
pale faced man
taps my shoulder

Hyakuissei Okamoto

Flower vase
on shelf
no flower in vase

Sei Sagara

Even the croaking of frogs
comes from outside the barbed wire fence
this is our life

Hakuro Wada

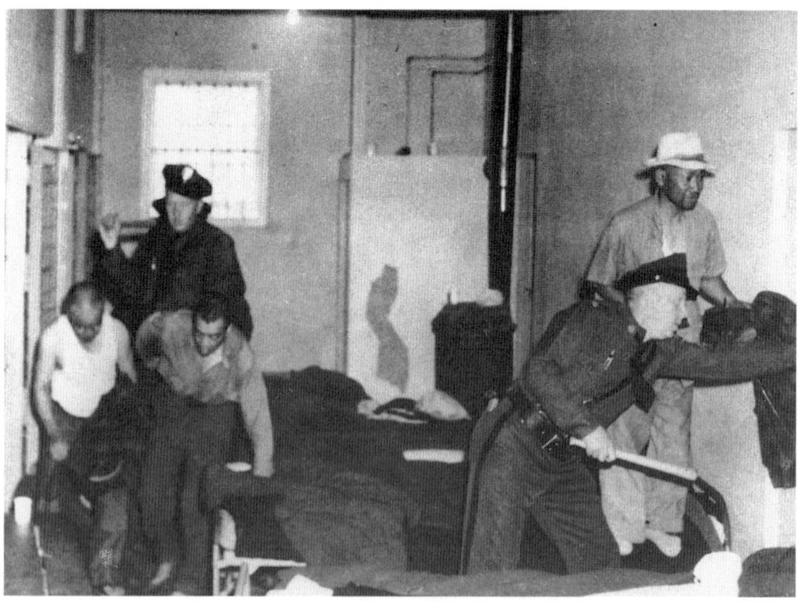

Tule Lake Stockade, Tule Lake, June 1945. Photographer unknown, photograph smuggled out by Wayne Collins. Dissidents were jailed in stockade, some severely beaten.

A Nisei Requests Repatriation

Most revealing of the confusion and anger that surrounded the internees' conflicts brought on by the Loyalty Questionnaire was the decision to repatriate or expatriate to Japan. By the war's end, nearly 8,000 people from Tule Lake, the majority of them Nisei, would renounce their U.S. citizenships and sail for Japan. Procedures for renunciation of one's American citizenship involved submitting a written request to the Justice Department and appearing for a later hearing. After the hearing and a formal renunciation, the Attorney General would grant approval for re- or expatriation. A large number of the people who answered "No/No" tried to cancel their renunciations once they realized the gravity of their decisions, only to be met with government hostility and indifference. Wayne Collins, one of the few attorneys in the U.S. who fought for the rights of the internees, defended those who wished to reverse their decisions, arguing that they had renounced their American citizenship under duress and therefore their cases should be considered null and void. The courts agreed in 1948. In 1950, however, the Ninth Circuit Court of Appeals overturned this ruling, and required that each case be heard individually. The last of these cases was not processed until 1968. The testimony of this anonymous Nisei requesting repatriation is in the WRA files at the UCLA Special Collections and Asian American Reading Room.

*

Well, Doc, I could see by the way you looked at me when I passed you in that truck the other day that you knew I had asked to be expatriated. I said to the other fellow, "Oho, I'll bet he's found out already." I might as well sit down, for I see that we'll have to have this out right now.

In the first place I don't think this is a hasty action. After all, I've been sitting in here for two years thinking. And it isn't just evacuation that is bothering me either. It goes way back farther than that.

I feel that I've made every attempt to identify myself with this country and its people. But every time I've tried I've got another boot in the rear.

Why, when I was a kid I went around with Caucasians almost entirely. I'll admit that most of them were pretty nice to me and treated me like anyone else. But even during the time when I was a kid there were incidents that were hard to take. Let me give you an example. I belonged to a Boy Scout troop. Nearly all the members were Caucasians. I and another fellow were the only Japanese. We lived near Vernon and there was a swimming pool there. One time the whole troop was going there for a swim. When we got there they let everybody else in the pool except this other Japanese and me. They said, "You can't swim here, we don't let Japanese in." Naturally we felt pretty raw but I tried to forget about it and say, "It's just a little thing. No use eating your heart out about it."

I got along well with Caucasians in public school. I got along pretty well in high school. But I noticed that after high school most of my Caucasian friends drifted away. The race wall was up and I couldn't make any headway against it. They talk about mingling with other people. You can't mingle with others if you can't live where they do, if you can't go where they do and if you can't work where they do.

The thing that really woke me up was the work angle. I took in a lot of that stuff about democracy and bettering yourself that they taught me in school. So after I finished high school I enrolled at the Frank Wiggins Trade School. I went in for training in electricity and [to become a] radio technician. You know, I think the Frank Wiggins Trade School is one of the best in the country. Their plan is to have their men working part-time getting practical experience while they are going to school. They have very little trouble placing their men either, for they have all sorts of connections.

So I was working along there doing as well or better than most of the students. Only they got part-time jobs and I didn't get any. I didn't think anything of it for the first six months. After all, I figured that I didn't know much yet and that anyone so inexperienced shouldn't expect too much. But as time went on it just got funny. I knew the head of the place pretty well. He's some kind of a foreigner, a Brazilian, I believe.

He has no race prejudice and did his best to help me. Why, I have sat by his desk while he phoned around trying to find a place that would take me on! He'd call up his former students, fellows who owed a lot to him and with whom he had placed many white students, and they turned him down as soon as they heard I was Japanese. I was there two years and a half and I never got a job. I thought to myself, "What the hell am I doing here? What am I spending my money for if it doesn't get me any farther than this?"

Sure, I could have got a job as a gardener or a houseboy or in a vegetable stall. But I had my fill of that and I wanted work in the line I had trained

Repatriates embarking for Japan. Seattle, Washington, November 24, 1945. Photographer unknown.

myself for. And it isn't only the money and pride. You are held down in your associations and your social life if you can't get a job in your own line. I noticed that as my Caucasian friends of high school days got jobs and began to get somewhere, they drifted away from me. They were on the way somewhere and in their estimation I was just standing still or bound to go backward. The business man and the professional man does not go around with the gardener. You have to belong to the same circle to keep up associations.

So even before the war I was fed up with the way I was treated here. I realized that any white foreigner who came here had a better chance than I had. As soon as he learns the language and a few of the local ways he can't be told from anyone else and no one cares where he came from. But I have a Japanese face that I can't change and as long as I live I'll be discriminated against in this country. Look at the difference in the way they treated the Italians and Germans and what they did to us. You can't tell me that having a Japanese face didn't make a difference.

After all I figure that if it happened once it can happen again. Now they say, "It's all a mistake. We're sorry," and expect us to forget all about it and go off and fight in the Army. But the thing that gets me is that it wasn't any little group or individual that did it, but the United States government. If they had taken the aliens only it would have been one thing. But here I am, a citizen, and they pulled me in too. If your own government is against you and if citizenship doesn't count, what's the use of hanging around, I say.

I know that there are people who say that this country is going to become more democratic and that minority groups are going to be treated better in the future. I can't see much improvement during my life. The Negroes have been in this country for generations, and look how they are treated. And the Japanese will have it particularly tough, for there will be relatives of soldiers killed in the Pacific all over. I don't think that it will be the returning soldiers that will be as bad as the relatives of the ones lost in the Pacific. Maybe things are going to get better in this country for minority groups in a couple of hundred years. But I haven't got that long to wait. Right now I know I could go out and get a job without any trouble because they are in desperate need of trained men. But it will be a different story when soldiers come home and work is slack.

I don't expect an easy time in Japan. I know how tough things are there. I lived there for two years when I was a little boy. You couldn't even bring candy to school. They figured that most couldn't afford it and it would only cause jealousy, and so no one was allowed to bring it. Nothing is plentiful or easy there. I expect a much harder time of it there, at least for the first two years, than I ever had here. But when I get turned down for a job it will be because there isn't a job, and not because I look different from someone else. At least there I'll look like everyone else.

My mother is dead but my father is in Japan. He was on the last boat that left for Japan before the war began. I have two sisters in this country, both married. One wants to go to Japan and one wants to stay here. I'm not sure of what they will do.

Before the war I tried to cancel my Japanese citizenship. I made that request to the Japanese Consul. But I guess the war broke out before the records were sent to Japan. Probably my request was burned. At any rate I'm pretty sure that I'm a dual citizen now. My father let me know in a Red Cross message from Japan. He said, "double status," and that's what he meant. Now, after evacuation, I feel that if I'm going to give up one citizenship, it is going to be the American.

It seems to me that the Nisei are mostly in a fog. They don't know what their citizenship is worth. They don't know what kind of chance they'll have after the war. They don't know what this evacuation is all about. They don't take a stand on anything.

I've been sitting on the fence long enough. I want to know where I stand and I want others to know too. I don't want to be an opportunist waiting to see how it all comes out and then jumping this way or that according to what seems to be my advantage.

I don't think I'd ever forget evacuation. Maybe most of these other fellows can but I'm not built that way. I'm a funny guy. If someone beats me in a fair fight I'll get up and shake hands with him and no hard feelings. But if a gang rushes me and piles on me, even if there are five or six of them, I'll get every one of them, no matter how long it takes to track them down.

It's a funny thing to think about if you're on the receiving end, Doc. Here this government can draft me and send me anywhere to fight. And yet I am not free. I can't go a few miles to Lone Pine to buy myself something. I'm not afraid to die, and I'll fight for any country that treats me right, but I've gone through too much to fall for talk about democracy in this country any more.

V

The cream of the crop—
Nisei soldiers—raised
By wrinkles on the parents' brow

Anonymous

Presidential Statement

Franklin D. Roosevelt

Approximately 33,000 Nisei served in the military during World War II, demonstrating extraordinary heroism in spite of the intense prejudice they faced from the American public. To their humiliation, following Pearl Harbor all Japanese Americans then serving in the armed forces were reclassified as 4C—enemy aliens—and many were discharged. But by early 1943, Nisei volunteers were again accepted and were eventually eligible for the draft. For its size and length of service, the segregated, all-Nisei 100th/442nd Regimental Combat Team would become the most highly decorated unit in the American military service. Lesser known for their contribution to the war due to sworn secrecy were the six thousand Nisei linguists of the Military Intelligence Service (MIS), who would translate and interpret top-secret messages in Japanese for the U.S. Government. In addition, there were Nisei medics and nurses, clerks and broadcasters, and Nisei women who served in the Women's Auxilary Corps. The story of the Japanese Americans who fought in the war is one of rare courage, as they defended democracy when words alone were not enough.

At the end of January 1943, Secretary of War Henry L. Stimson proposed the formation of an all-Nisei military outfit to President Roosevelt, who readily approved. On February 1, 1943, less than a year after signing Executive Order 9066—which authorized the evacuation of American citizens solely on the basis of race and ancestry—the President would write what now seems an ironic statement in support of the Japanese Americans' right to defend their country.

*

The proposal of the War Department to organize a combat team consisting of loyal American citizens of Japanese descent has my full approval. The new combat team will add to the nearly five thousand loyal Americans of Japanese ancestry who are already serving in the armed forces of our country.

This is a natural and logical step toward the reinstitution of the Selective Service procedures which were temporarily disrupted by the evacuation from the West Coast.

No loyal citizen of the United States should be denied the democratic right to exercise the responsibilities of his citizenship, regardless of his ancestry. The principle on which this country was founded and by which it has always been governed is that Americanism is a matter of the mind and heart; Americanism is not, and never was, a matter of race or ancestry. A good American is one who is loyal to this country and to our creed of liberty and democracy. Every loyal American citizen should be given the opportunity to serve this country wherever his skills will make the greatest contribution—whether it be in the ranks of the armed forces, war production, agriculture, government service, or other work essential to the war effort.

I am glad to observe that the War Department, the Navy Department, the War Manpower Commission, the Department of Justice, and the War Relocation Authority are collaborating in a program which will insure the opportunity for all loyal Americans, including Americans of Japanese ancestry, to serve their country at a time when the fullest and wisest use of our manpower is all-important to the war effort.

Very sincerely yours,
[signed]
Franklin D. Roosevelt

FROM *Journey to Washington*

Daniel Inouye

The 100th Infantry Battalion unit of the 442nd Regimental Combat Team, which was composed of Americans of Japanese descent living in Hawaii, began as part of the Hawaii National Guard. War hysteria had resulted in the imprisonment of Japanese Americans on the mainland but not in Hawaii, even though they were two thousand miles closer to Japan. The War Department struggled to come up with a way to handle Japanese Hawaiians. After much discussion, a special segregated battalion was formed and some 10,000 volunteers were accepted. On June 5, 1942, the first unit of 1,432 Japanese Hawaiians (with their Caucasian officers) set sail for Army Camp McCoy, Wisconsin and Camp Shelby, Mississippi. One year later, in September 1943, the 100th Battalion arrived in North Africa, where they were sent on to Italy and immediately into battle. From September to March 1944, the 100th fought their way up the Italian peninsula, suffering heavy casualties: 78 men were killed and 239 wounded in the first month and a half alone. The battalion earned the nickname of the Purple Heart Battalion as almost every soldier in the unit received at least one Purple Heart medal for heroism. On June 15, the 100th was sent into the offensive from the Anzio, Italy, beachhead, where they were joined by the other Nisei unit, the 442nd Regimental Combat Team.

The 100th was a unique formation of soldiers. En route to training, they renamed their outfit the "One Puka Puka," Puka meaning "hole" or "zero" in the Hawaiian language. They spoke a pidgin dialect of Hawaiian, Chinese, Japanese, and English that few non-Islanders could understand, and played ukuleles to keep morale high. More than 90 percent were sons of immigrant parents. Although they never faced the humiliation of the internment camps, they were subject to the same intense pressure to prove themselves as Americans.

United States Senator Daniel K. Inouye was born in Honolulu in 1924 and served three bloody months in the Rome Arno campaign with the U.S. Army's 100th/442nd Regimental Combat Team. During battle, he became a platoon leader and won the Bronze Star and a battlefield commission as Second

Lieutenant. He was awarded the Distinguished Service Cross, and many years later, went on to Washington to represent Hawaii as the first Japanese American member of Congress. Senator Inouye's 1967 autobiography, Journey to Washington, *co-written with Lawrence Elliot, includes vivid accounts of his wartime experiences and his lifelong fight to defend civil liberties.*

*

I passed my college entrance exams and in September 1942, [having] just turned eighteen, I enrolled for a premedical course at the University of Hawaii. For those of us in that wartime class, study as we might, a substantial portion of our thoughts and hopes were directed outside, fixed on that world in conflict, concentrating our fiercest aspirations on the chance that somehow they would allow us into the Army. I was still doing my job at the aid station, but with the emergency in Hawaii past and the grim reports of Japanese victories at Bataan and Corregidor, working at the aid station didn't seem like much of a vital contribution any more.

The War Department had given us some small hope that their harsh preconceptions about Japanese Americans might be changing. A few months earlier, Nisei Guardsmen and early draftees had been organized into the 100th Infantry Battalion, a combat unit not assigned to any regular outfit. Then, little more than a year after the attack on Pearl Harbor, we got the news that did most to unshackle us from stigma and help us really believe that we would be allowed to fight for our country: the War Department announced that it would accept 4,000 Nisei volunteers to form a full-fledged combat team for front-line service without restriction, without constraints. The outfit was to be activated on February 1 and would consist of the 442nd Infantry Regiment, the 522nd Field Artillery Battalion, and 232nd Combat Engineer Company.

President Franklin D. Roosevelt, who personally passed on the plan, had this to say about it: "The proposal of the War Department to organize a combat team [consisting] of loyal American citizens of Japanese descent has my full approval.[...] No loyal citizen of the United States should be denied the democratic right to exercise the responsibilities of his citizenship, regardless of his ancestry....Americanism is a matter of the mind and heart; Americanism is not, and never was, a matter of race or ancestry."

It is hard to express our emotions at this expression of faith by the President. It was as though someone had let us out of some dark place and into the sunlight again. And what chaos in the university auditorium that

January morning when Colonel Clarke, head of the ROTC, called us together and announced that the draft boards were now ready to receive our applications for enlistment! It was as though he'd revealed that gold had just been discovered at the foot of Diamond Head. He later told me that he had a little pep talk all prepared for us, how we now had a chance to do our duty as patriotic Americans, but it was about as necessary as telling those Navy gunners on December 7 to open fire. As soon as he said that we were now eligible to volunteer, that room exploded into a fury of yells and motion. We went bursting out of there and ran—ran!—the three miles to the draft board, stringing back over the streets and sidewalks, jostling for position, like a bunch of marathoners gone berserk. And the scene was repeated all over Oahu and the other islands. Nearly 1,000 Niseis volunteered that first day alone, and maybe because I was in better shape than most of them and ran harder, I was among the first seventy-five.

Everything changed that day and, because there are no fairy-tale endings in real life, not all the changes were for the best. Dozens of boys I knew from the premed courses crowded into the draft board, some of them with only the rest of that last semester to go before graduation. And the long years of war took their toll on every one of us. Some hadn't the heart to go back to school when peace finally came, and some, with families to support, hadn't

Induction ceremony of the 100th Infantry Battalion. Hawaii, c. 1942. Photographer unknown.

the money. Many never came home at all, and among those who did there were those so severely wounded that a career in medicine was out of the question. And so it was that of all those students who had entered the university with such high hopes, and with the hopes and prayers of their parents, not a single one ever became a doctor.

The Army's original plan called for a Nisei outfit of 1,500 from the Islands and 2,500 from the mainland. But the crush of volunteers in Hawaii persuaded them to reverse the proportions. We were given three weeks to wind up our affairs—which most of us would have been happy to do in three days—and there were sentimental and sometimes tearful farewell parties from Koko Head to Kahuku. I suppose mine was fairly typical: the parade of aunts and uncles and cousins, the last whispered words—"Be a good boy; be careful; make us proud!"—and the crumpled $5 or $10 bill pressed into my hand.

And then my bag was packed and my ukulele slung over my shoulder and with my mother and father standing nearby, sad and already a little withdrawn, I elbowed my way into that great swarm of about-to-be GIs on the grounds of the old Washington Intermediate School, just outside the draft board. Girls were draping leis around our necks and the long line of trucks stood waiting to carry us off and in each little family group you could see the mood alternating between piercing sharp anticipation and a kind of melancholy as the men abruptly realized what their mothers and fathers and sweethearts already knew: that this was good-bye and what lay ahead was no boy scout outing....

In 1924, the year I was born, Americans of Japanese ancestry made up a bare five percent sliver of Hawaii's voting population. Less than twenty-three years later, when I was finally discharged from the Army and came home to stay, the Nisei were the largest single voting bloc in the islands, having accounted for three out of every ten ballots cast in the previous year's election. They spurred no social upheaval with their votes then, the usual comfortable Republican majorities were returned to the Territorial legislature, but one could hardly help feeling a certain stir in that postwar spring. There were more Oriental names in the House of Representatives. Good solid Chinese and Japanese families were moving into the better neighborhoods, and the haoles were making room for them without a murmur. Hawaii seemed at a turning point in history, gathering breath as it made ready to push off in directions never before imagined. One could almost feel the ferment of impending change. A quiet revolution was brewing and it was an exciting time to be alive.

The 442nd was very much a part of what was happening. Nor was it only that we had fought valiantly for our country and wanted now to taste the fruits of victory. It was more subtle. For all our Anglo-Saxon first names, we had gone off to war as the sons and grandsons of immigrants, heirs of an alien culture and very much expected—and, I suppose, expecting—to resume our unobtrusive minority status if and when we returned. But the Army had given us a taste of full citizenship, and an appetite for more of the same. We were the "can-do" outfit and we were heady with a sense of ourselves: all those medals and citations proved something, didn't they?

The feeling was infectious. It spread to the old folks, and those were jubilant, heartwarming days for them. The 442nd was toasted and paraded and written about, but our mothers and fathers were the ones who understood, better than any homecoming GI, what we'd brought back with us. They walked tall and proud then, and it was a far cry from the bitter "Speak American!" days.

And if you were young in Hawaii in that pivotal year, if you were ambitious and believed implicitly in the promise of the Declaration of Independence, what did it matter that you had only one arm? You had given it for America and America, at last, was yours.

*

In April 1945, Inouye was leading a platoon of the 2nd Battalion, 442nd Regimental Combat Team when it came under fire from a bunker manned by Italian fascists. As Inouye was taking out a hand grenade, he was hit in the stomach by machine-gun fire. He still managed to throw several grenades into the enemy position and was preparing to throw another when an enemy rifle grenade smashed his right elbow. Twenty-five enemy troops were killed and eight captured in the action. Inouye's right arm had to be amputated as a result of his battle wounds. In May 2000, he was one of nineteen members of the 100th/442nd to receive the Congressional Medal of Honor for his actions during WWII. Only six of the nineteen who were honored were known to be still living.

Action from a Sergeant's Diary

Min Hara

In March of 1941, long before Pearl Harbor, the United States government began recruiting Japanese Americans for military intelligence work. By November, a language school had been established at the Presidio in San Francisco where some sixty men, mostly Nisei and Kibei, were being trained as military linguists. The Military Intelligence Service (MIS) soldiers were attached to 150 units throughout Europe and Asia, serving in every major campaign and in every major battle in the Pacific. They worked at the front and field offices interrogating Japanese prisoners of war and translating captured maps, battle orders, diaries, and other documents. By the end of the war, the MIS Language School, having moved twice from its original location in California, had trained and graduated 6,000 men. Until recently, the achievements of the MIS were a highly guarded, classified military secret.

MIS Staff Sergeant Min Hara's story is from the collection of memoirs, John Aiso and the M.I.S., *published by the Southern California Military Intelligence Service Club, in 1988. When contacted for permission to publish his story, Mr. Hara said that GIs were not allowed to keep diaries, especially during war time. He hastily wrote down his story after the war. Readers will note that the grammar of the piece reflects the haste with which it was written.*

November 20, 1942
Volunteered at Post [Poston?] Relocation Center, Arizona (Colorado Indian Reservation) for U.S. Army Military Intelligence School at Camp Savage, Minnesota. Experienced 135 plus degree heat in the barren desert of Arizona, then a record breaking minus forty-two degree bitter cold winter in the "Land of 10,000 Lakes," Minnesota. Only eight of us enlisted from America's largest concentration camp due to strike action at that time. We went through twenty-six weeks of intensified course while trying to learn to read and write the Japanese language.

Inductees swearing in for the 442nd. Regimental Combat Team. 1943, Manzanar. Photograph by Toyo Miyatake.

July–August 1943

Shipped down to Camp Shelby, Mississippi for accelerated basic training course. We got temporarily attached to 442nd Regimental Combat Team as Company S. Although there is no Company S in the whole U.S. Army, Captain Crowley, the new CO, gave us this designation to indicate SAVAGE. One of the best captains I have met during my four years of service. I hope he lived through the war to see better times.

August 1943

Returned to Fort Snelling, Minnesota temporarily 'till more new barracks were constructed at Camp Savage. Held daily translation practice 'till the day of departure for overseas assignment. Language Teams of ten men each were formed. Our team was headed by a veteran of the Attu-Kiska campaigns, Aleutian Islands, Alaska. Staff Sergeant George T. Hayashida participated in the annihilation of the 2,000 men Attu Garrison. He saw the remains of the base CO Colonel Yamasaki on the battlefield. He interrogated some of the first Radar Technicians (civilians) captured there. His mother or a girlfriend sent him a chocolate cake while he was stationed here, caught up with him at Cape Sansapor, Dutch New Guinea. The cake was hard as a concrete block....

January 1944

Departed with two other teams from the Camp Savage railroad station on a cold winter night for Oakland, California. Scores of GI friends and instructors came to see us off. Got stationed on Angel Island (next to Alcatraz Island) in San Francisco Bay. Made it very inconvenient for us to visit San Francisco on weekends. No place to visit on this bleak island so we volunteered for KP duty since the chow was so delicious.

February 5, 1944

Departed Oakland unescorted for unknown destination on a brand new 10,000-ton "Liberty Ship" named *Ada Rehan.* Zigzagged through the mine fields outside the Golden Gate Bridge. I got seasick when we were still within sight of land, while laying down on the bare deck with no barriers, the huge land swells started to rock our ship, Tom Matsumara came running over admonishing me, "Min, you're going to fall off so I'll tie this rope around your waist." And how I wished that I could so I can swim for shore. We continued zigzagging all the way to the South Pacific. After two days out, we saw an overloaded oil tanker, deck awash, with fighter planes tied down on her deck. But no other ships were to be seen for the next twenty-eight days! To my buddies, this voyage must have been an experience of boredom, but to me, it was thirty-one days of agony. Me an ex-fisherman's son getting seasick 'till we sighted land, the southwestern tip of British New Guinea. As we neared the combat zone in the South Pacific, our Merchant Marine captain asked us to take day and night watches for enemy submarines and aircraft. Not a gripe was heard from any of the twenty-two GI "passengers." The reason for this request was that he was torpedoed two days out of Brisbane, Australia on his previous maiden voyage. As we approached Coral Sea, we suddenly hit a terrible storm which lasted for two whole days. The captain told us that we've been drifting back all during this time in spite of the engine churning full speed ahead. The swells were so big it towered over the superstructure of our ship. The ship rode on some of these swells and the propeller was grinding in free air. Imagine! Our all-metal ship was creaking and bouncing like a ball. A few of the sailors on board had a similar experience while they were up in the Aleutian waters and you can imagine how we felt when they said that their ship cracked in half. Probably this was the only time I did not feel my seasickness. When the calm returned, the night watch was a pleasure being able to see the Southern Cross and millions of other stars due to the clear pollution-free atmosphere. It seemed as though you can see four to five times more stars here than in the Northern Hemisphere. I believe this was the most enjoyable part of our thirty-one day voyage.

March 8, 1944
Arrived in Milne Bay, British New Guinea (now called Papua). We had a submarine scare right before entering this bay, but found it to be a tree trunk floating vertically like a periscope. I saw a black marlin larger than any I have ever seen in any record book of fishing or in a museum, following the garbage we were dumping from the fantail of our ship. Islands off shore looked more beautiful than any Hollywood movie I have ever seen, but found it to be hell after we landed. Slimy mud up to our knees, hot and humid and plenty of mosquitoes. After visiting the base hospital, found out more of our troops were falling victim to malaria and dengue fever than from enemy bullets. Not only out of curiosity, but being typical American souvenir-hungry GIs, we went to see a battleground where the Australian forces had fought off a Japanese landing in the previous year. The wreckages of Japanese wooden landing crafts were jutting out from the sandy beach all over the area, the stench of human dead was still there, as we dug in the sand for souvenirs. I was appalled at the sight of seeing thousands of coconut palm trunks, half a mile deep, two to three miles wide, lopped off at the height of seven to eight feet by naval gun fire. It looked as if a giant scythe went through the whole beachhead.

After taking Atabrine tablets for a month, all the GIs' complexions started to turn yellow. GIs coming down with malaria were usually the ones that avoided taking these bitter pills nor were [they] using their mosquito nettings which were issued to all the troops. They started to put the Atabrine tablets into the bread which made it come out yellow. What a nasty tasting bread! We took all these precautions, but some of us still came down with fever of some sort.

After several weeks of waiting, we finally got attached to the 6th Infantry Division as the 169th Language Detachment, G-2 Section (Intelligence). The troops were mostly from the Midwest and quite a number of Minnesotans. We formed a two-man team and went to each of our three regiments while four men stayed with the division headquarters. The division consisted of 1st Infantry, 20th Infantry, and the 63rd Infantry Regiments and other supporting units. We gave orientation lectures to each and every one of our units on how to identify enemy documents, about the enemy we were going to face, and what our objective will be once we got into combat.

May 1944

We sailed northwesterly several hundred miles to reinforce an independent regiment commanded by Brigadier General Edwin D. Patrick (later to command our 6th Infantry Division) at Maffin Bay, Wakde-Sarmi Sector, Dutch New Guinea (now called Irian). We had a wonderful reunion with couple of Savage grads, T.Sgt. Terry Mizutari and Harry Fukuhara. I still can't forget the delicious lunch Harry gave us in the middle of the jungle, rice with cans of beef, captured, of course. And to this day, I feel bad for our bad manners, leaving all those mess kits for Harry to wash. I interrogated my first of many hundreds of prisoners of war, remnants of the Japanese 10th Air Force from Hollandia, Dutch New Guinea. Most of them were on the verge of starvation since they were all skin and bones. We made them nigiri meshi and told them to go easy since they haven't eaten for over a month, but some just didn't listen. I saw one of them gulp down three rice balls (bigger than our baseball) in a few minutes and I heard he died the following morning. I remember making a bathtub out of a fifty-gallon drum so we could clean up one of the POWs. His physical condition was in such a poor state, from malnutrition and skin infections, washcloth could not be used since his skin peeled off and blood poured out. Fortunately for the prisoner our field hospital received their first supply of penicillin so I believe he survived.

T/4 Sosh Baba and Hiroshi Onishi landed here with the 1st Infantry Regiment prior to our arrival, so we did not see them for several days. I heard that General Patrick's Regiment was almost about to be pushed back into the sea when the 1st Infantry landed. Our division command post moved up to a forward sector a few days later when the Japanese forces started to lob artillery shells so we had to immediately evacuate to a safer ground. Battle of Lone Tree Hill commenced when T/4 Tom Matsumura and T/5 Ted Takano went forward to join the 20th Infantry Regiment. Enemy opposition was so intense, taking prisoners was out of the question. Besides they fought 'till the last man. Tom and Ted were more busy dodging enemy artillery and mortar barrages than getting a chance to interrogate prisoners. They took shelter under an ambulance when the mortar barrages began and they told me that they bounced like Ping-Pong balls. Good thing they had their steel helmets on. T/5 Shiz Kunihiro and I got assigned to the 63rd Infantry Regiment. We moved into the sector adjacent to the 20th Infantry since they advanced a few thousand yards. Heard later from Tom that we dug in exactly where they got clobbered a few days before. We were fortunate in not receiving any more barrages, but the enemy left plenty of Kesshitai so we were constantly on the lookout for sniper fire. Every helmet I picked up and examined had a bullet hole right by the temple. Shiz and I were kept busy interrogating the trickle of prisoners that finally started to come in. Mind you, not voluntarily, they were shell shocked or badly wounded. We worked 'till sunset so Shiz and I were the last to dig our foxholes. I spent the longest night of my life here. Our foxholes were about five yards from the shoreline, water started to seep in from the sea when the tide came up, tropical rain come down in torrents, had to keep our rifle and ammo above water so I held it on top of my helmet all night. We couldn't afford to stick our heads up for fear of a sniper putting a bullet between our eyes. We had to jiggle our helmets on top of our rifle barrels before standing up in the mornings. Took us over a month to overrun Hill 225 for this Battle of Lone Tree Hill. Due to this stiff opposition we hardly took any prisoners. In most cases, the enemy was annihilated or pushed inland while we occupied the shoreline area anywhere from a quarter- to a half-mile deep. Our backs were to the sea so all units had a front line, even our Division Headquarters. We were all recalled to division CP where S.Sgt. George Hayashida headed his team of T/4 Kiyo Fujimara, T/5 George Nakamura, and T/5 Nob Yamashita. We experienced constant harassment from enemy infiltrators and snipers all along the front. One day, three ATIS men showed up from Brisbane, Australia: Sgts. J. Tanikawa (Veteran of WWI), Hugh Tsuneishi, and another fellow (can't remember his name). They were eventually assigned to an outfit on Biak or Noemfor Island. I interrogated a prisoner captured by our paratroopers when they surprised the whole Noemfor garrison sound asleep. Prisoner had a big gash on his stomach so I asked him for an explanation and this was his statement: "We heard of the rapid advance of the American forces along the New Guinea coast so we held a flag-burning ceremony (regimental color) a month before so it would not fall into enemy hands. Our forces were resigned to their fate, to fight to the death. The sounds of gunfire awaken me when I realized that our garrison was under attack. I immediately ran into my pillbox and started to fire my machine gun. However, your forces advanced right in front of my machine gun slot and commenced shooting their flame throwers so I immediately closed my steel door (machine gun slot). The slimy flame came seeping in, our oxygen was being exhausted so I tried committing hara-kiri, but it was so painful, I stopped and decided to come out with my hands up." The prisoner's ears were singed and his stomach wound was superficial. But like many prisoners, he asked, "Am I the first Japanese prisoner?" While accompanying a prisoner back to our "rear lines," we saw all the tanks, half tracks, tank destroyers and other armored vehicles parked on the sandy beachhead which was useless in jungle warfare. The prisoner seeing all this said, "I'm positive we can win every battle if we had just half your equipment." And I said to myself, "I'm sure they can." We were fighting a decimated regiment (223rd Infantry) with a whole division. Must have been a helpless feeling for the Japanese infantrymen to fight a modern warfare with a bolt-action rifle used in the Russo-Japanese War while we carried semiautomatic rifles.... Captured documents started to roll in when we overran some enemy CPs four to five miles up the coast. I was interrogating a prisoner when the documents were unloaded by my feet and swarms of GIs milled around the pile so I asked everyone to move back and give us some space to work. However, one GI didn't move back so I yelled at him, "Get your ass back!" or something to that effect. He said, "OK! OK! " and I looked up to see my Commanding General Charles E. Hurdis smiling at me. The prisoner later asked me who I was yelling at because he noticed the two stars on his lapel. I told him that he was my CG and was he shocked. He said he would have been shot if he spoke like that even to his sergeant.... T/4 Tom Matsumura and myself were to share a pyramidal tent that night, so fortunately for me, we decided to lay our rifles and bayonets in the far corner of the tent. Tropical heat was so unbearable we both slept on canvas cot with only our shorts on. Nature called during the night so I quietly crawled out hoping not to awaken Tom. Suddenly as I was about to crawl into my cot, I felt a body hit me with full force on my back and he started choking me with all his might. I immediately realized that the naked body was Tom's, but he was choking me so hard, I just could not call out. I kept on slapping his thigh 'till he finally released his hold realizing that it was me. "Min, is that you? Min, is that you?" "Tom, Tom, it's me!" We mutually shivered while we chain smoked 'till sunrise. Our first words in the morning were, "Boy! Good thing we left our arms in the far corner." In late August, the 31st Infantry Division landed and took over our whole sector. Then we started on our preparation for our next landing.

September 1944

We sailed for our next beachhead on LSTs. Aerial photography showed no enemy troop concentrations so the few escorting destroyers did not have to bombard the beaches. Our landing at Cape Sansapor, Dutch New Guinea was unopposed. We landed too far south of our objective so we had to walk about two more miles northwesterly. We saw some trees loaded down with black objects so I fired into them, turned out to be giant fruit bats with five-to-six feet wing span. Hundreds flew up, but this was the first and last sight I was to see of these huge bats. Not having any fresh fruits or vegetables for several months, Tom and I immediately went into the jungle in search of it. We ran across plenty of banana and papaya plants, but none of the fruits were large enough to eat. We swam in a water hole right next to the ocean not knowing the dangers of strange water, heard they shot a huge ocean-going crocodile in this water hole the very next day. Later, prisoners told us of seeing their comrades devoured by crocodiles while they were swimming across some river. We picked a spot in a clearing which looked like a former Japanese outpost since they had a small grass hut with a garden alongside of it. We found some lime trees loaded down with fruits and what a treat! Limeade for the next couple of days. The trees were picked clean by the third day, even the one-inch diameter ones were gone. All the GIs that went wading into the jungle that day caught the near-fatal fever. Luckily, Tom and I were spared and we felt no ill effects. The garden was full of egg-plants and konnyaku bulbs left drying all over the ground. Since we were all sick and tired of C rations and dehydrated food, all the GIs were eagerly searching for something fresh. I told a few of our troops to try some of the Japanese "spuds"—konnyaku dama—while I explained to my Nisei team-mates of its bitterness. This bulb is highly acidic so it must have been like biting into a green persimmon, we all had a good laugh when we saw all the GIs make nasty faces after taking a bite. Prisoners from the remnants of the 10th Japanese Air Division, totally destroyed on the ground at Hollandia, Dutch New Guinea started to come in by the hundreds. Taiwan and Korean labor force prisoners came in willingly, but the die-hard Japanese had to be captured with the force of arms. We were kept busy for several weeks, interrogating and processing. The labor forces were being used by the Japanese Army to construct their airfields throughout the Southwest Pacific. A prisoner seeing our landing strip made in a little over two days, using bulldozers, steel landing mats, etc. said, "It would have taken us over half a year since we only had picks and shovels." Due to the life or death situation, cannibalism was practiced by the Japanese troops during their 500-mile trek through the dense jungles. Whenever a large group of prisoners came in, I was able to pick each and every Japanese who practiced cannibalism by just looking at their eyes. Their fierce-looking eyes reminded me of a hungry bengal tiger. Upon interrogation, their only comment was, "It's a matter of survival." I asked several of their combat veterans if it's true that all dying soldiers shouted, "Tenno heika banzai!"—Long live the Emperor!—and their snickering answer was, "maybe one soldier in 10,000." Another interjected, "one in 20,000 is too high!" They said all they ever heard was the word "okasan"—mother—on their dying lips. Most of them being veterans of North China campaigns were apologetic for being captured, but like any human, some didn't give a damn. In fact, they didn't even care if they never got to see their wife and kids. We started to experience nightly air raids by two or three enemy bombers at exactly 8:00 P.M. I always wondered why they never bothered to change their time. Antiaircraft Battery (claiming they were veterans of Guadalcanal, Solomon Islands) came to our assistance with their new radar-controlled guns, but they couldn't knock one plane out of the sky. Meanwhile, our bomber and fighter strips got plastered. Our division CP was hit one night and several of our comrades died in their sleep. George Hayashida, George Nakamura, and I spent two days digging a bomb shelter, laying logs on top, and sand bagging the roof and sides. However, when the bombs came down, I was sleeping right next to the entrance, but I couldn't get my whole body into our shelter since it was jam packed with my nine other teammates. The other seven neglected to dig their own. We counted over 100 shrapnel holes in our roof of our pyramidal tent the next morning. Surprisingly none of us got hit. Especially me with my butt sticking up in the air. All I got for my trouble was "strawberries" all over my legs, hitting the logs as I tried to dive for cover....

Our Issei parents, knowing that they'll never have the chance to become U.S. citizens, constantly dreamt of their homeland. Any Japanese government request or appeal for monetary assistance was gladly met. The appeal during the Manchurian Incident was for cigarette "tinfoil" for construction of parts for their aikokuki. My folks used to make me get up early every weekend to go pick up empty cigarette packs. Then we had to dip them in a wash tub and peel off the foil and roll it up into a ball. Took me over two years to make a ten-pound ball. A dozen years later, their beloved aikokuki is laying their eggs every night over my head. I don't know how my parents would have felt if I was to get killed like this, but I sure felt like kicking myself in the butt.

October 1944

George Hayashida and I flew down to 6th Army Headquarters, then situated at Hollandia, Dutch New Guinea. We were met by seven or eight Japanese Zero fighters and what a scare, but they turned out to be flyboys who fixed it up for their joy ride by painting our insignias upon them. We landed on a former Japanese fighter-bomber strip near Lake Sentani. Mountain piles of Zero fighters and Betty bombers were bulldozed to one end of the airfield. We met a team of first Savage grads attached to our Air Force, crating captured planes to be shipped stateside instead of doing intelligence work. Guess the Air Force didn't know how to make better use of them. We ferried across Humboldt Bay to the 6th Army Headquarters and met several Savage grads who we hadn't seen since we parted at Camp Savage, Minnesota....

Pat Harada and Harry Akune took George Hayashida and me that afternoon to their POW stockade across the bay. Over 600 prisoners were interned here and we've noticed that quite a few were the ones we sent down from the front. Some came forward to thank us for the humane treatment we afforded them when they first came into our lines. The prisoners were feasting on their native dishes since our forces captured their entire food dump intact. Pat took us to see the food dump, cases of canned goods, row after row, stacked five to six feet high. He claimed there was enough food there to feed them for over ten years....

October 1944

Several of us Nisei got the chance to go on a patrol on our Navy's PT boats based at Amsterdam Island. We went deep into enemy-held waters, northwestern tip of New Guinea, but to our disappointment, we did not get to see any action. Maybe we were lucky 'cause we heard one of our PT boats got chased all over the ocean by some Zero fighters the very next day. The other offshore island was called Middleburg where we had our B-24 Liberator bombers. Adjacent to our headquarters area, on the mainland, were mostly B-25 Mitchell Medium bombers, P-38 Lightning fighters and a few P-51 Mustang fighters....During combat, I was never discriminated by our infantrymen or officers due to my ancestry, but of all people, my own language officer. While we were discussing the injustice of our government interning us in a concentration camp, he made this stupid remark, "Min, you should be glad you had this chance to fight for my country." Naturally, I saw RED and told him in no uncertain terms what a white trash of an officer he was and how unfortunate that we had to have a guy like him in command.

December 24, 1944

We spent our Christmas Eve on board a troop transport. I remember the Christmas dinner of turkey, three-inch sliver of FRESH celery, ice cream, and other trimmings. Comments made by the GIs, "They're fattening us for the kill!"...

January 9, 1945

As the dawn light was brightening the sky, I saw my first massive naval bombardment at close range and was amazed to see our warships (battleships, cruisers, destroyers, etc.) move sideways each time they laid down a salvo from all their guns. The whole gulf was full of floating brass shells which reminded me of a timberland cut down with nothing but tree stumps. Landing on Lingayen Gulf, Luzon, Philippines, was accomplished with hardly any opposition. I saw a few Japanese aircraft trying to bomb our ships without any success. Being unable to accomplish their mission, they started to kamikaze on our ships. Due to some snafu by our high command, our fighter air cover did not show up in time. Thousands of antiaircraft fire turned the morning dawn into night by smoke cover. Our overdue fighters arrived, but we had to tell them to get away before some of our ack-acks took care of them. We landed two or three miles west of our assigned beach, ground was pockmarked with holes large enough for a house to fall in from our naval bombardments. We hiked eastward to our assigned area and established our new CP. Within the hour, I interrogated my first prisoner dressed in a civilian white shirt and his khaki pants. The prisoner was wounded with bullet holes clean through his thigh, arm, and shoulder. I was called back to Army Headquarters as a witness for a general court-martial a month later in the trial of this prisoner. The court sentenced him to be hanged as a spy. I interrogated my second prisoner the next day, an Air Force pilot (from Kyoto area) at Santa Barbara, Pangasinan Province. He claimed our ack-ack fire was so intense that he could not get down low enough for an accurate bomb run. I asked him how it looked from the air. "It's just like bucking a fired up steel wall!" Consequently, he tried to crash dive on our ship, but he was shot down in his attempt. None of the Japanese prisoners ever knew we were Japanese Americans, nor did I tell them, but this prisoner said, "I'm positive you're from the Kansai area." My parents came from Wakayama, a part of Kansai. Found very few observant prisoners like this pilot. I spoke to several survivors of the Bataan death march rescued by our 6th Ranger Battalion from the Japanese prison camp at Cabanatuan. They claimed the brutal guards were mostly from Taiwan. They were the Takasagos. Our division tangled with the only Japanese Armored Division on the Luzon Plains. Steel Force—2nd Armored Division, (Tetsu Butai-Dai Ni Shenshya Shidan). I participated in a bayonet charge at Munoz, February 1945; my mission was to try talking a Japanese colonel into surrendering. But to no avail, since they all fought to their death....

T/4 Shiz Kunihiro and I got assigned to the 1st Infantry Regiment situated at San Narciso-San Marcellino Sector, Zambales Province. We stopped by at Bataan Peninsula, walked into the hills and saw a portion of our trenches and found ammo and hand grenades in front of their positions just as they left it when they were told to surrender by Lt. Colonel Jonathan Wainwright in 1942. Later on, I asked a Japanese infantryman who initially

Military Intelligence Serviceman Harry Fukuhara interrogating a Japanese prisoner of war. Aitape, New Guinea, April–May 1944. Photographer unknown.

landed on Bataan why they fought so fanatically. He said, "You might say that now, but you should have seen your forces. They too fought bravely and fanatically when we cut off Bataan in 1941 to 1942." I participated in three reconnaissance patrols. While bringing back a prisoner through a remote village, the Filipino natives started to throw baseball-size rocks at the prisoner sitting alongside me in a Jeep, yelling "Kora dorobo!" I too was in danger of being hit, so I emptied a few rounds over their heads and you should have seen them scatter. The prisoner had tears in his eyes, saying, "I'm quite sure the initial invasion forces must have treated these people terribly." I was more amazed that they spoke in Japanese!

Due to constant interrogations, we found out that the survivors of the Japanese super battleship, *Musashi,* were running loose in the jungles of Zambales Province. My motive in volunteering for these patrols was to capture a high-ranking officer in the Japanese Army or Navy. To this date, I never interrogated an officer beyond the rank of 1st Lieutenant. A prisoner came in one day stating that he saw about fifty Navy personnel all laid up with dysentery in the jungle. Maybe a capture of an admiral might be possible, so our regimental CO gave me the OK to accompany our patrol. It was possible to take a jeep into the jungle, so three of us plus the prisoner headed out ahead of our accompanying troops on the truck. After going inland about five or six miles, we ran into a Japanese patrol, fifteen to twenty of them, armed to their teeth. I didn't have time to call out to them to surrender and they lowered their rifles to engage us in a fire fight. We immediately opened up with a few rounds, and I told my prisoner (hastily, of course), "If you want to get back to Japan alive, don't you leave the jeep." And I then pursued the scattering enemy patrol. To my surprise, the prisoner was calmly sitting in our jeep when I returned from the skirmish. Due to our superior automatic weapons, it saved my life, but this was my closest shave from death. As I was firing ahead at the scattering patrol, I sensed someone behind me, so I hit the ground, rolled over and saw a Japanese soldier about twenty yards away with his rifle aimed right at my back. Saw my whole life flash by in a split second. I emptied three or four rounds into him before he could drive his bolt forward.

First Infantry Headquarters moved to Bacolor, Pampanga Province from San Narciso, Zambales Province. I saw scores of grave markers, victims of the Bataan death march alongside the highway as we came into Bacolor. My most interesting interrogation of the war happened here when seven or eight naval officers from the battleship *Musashi* came in as prisoners. The senior officer, Commander Yoshioka, was carrying the Navy log with him which contained the battle accounts of Pearl Harbor, Midway, etc. MacArthur Headquarters, (now at Manila) sent word asking us to forward the log as soon as possible. I did not get a chance to thoroughly examine it, but what I read was very interesting. Commander Yoshioka was the only Japanese prisoner who asked me for permission to speak. Upon giving him an OK, he said, "I am positive that you are a Nisei." Out of hundreds of POWs that I interrogated, he was the only one who knew we were Nisei. I asked him how he came to that conclusion and he said he read an article about the 442nd RCT fighting in Italy in a newspaper that came from Switzerland through the Red Cross. He figured we (Nisei) might be stationed in Australia, but he was surprised to see us in this combat zone. He had been to our East and West Coasts in one of the *Renshu Kantai* in 1936.

We returned to Division CP in the foothills of the Sierra Madre Range right outside of Marakina (outskirts of Quezon City). The enemy set up a defense position called the Shimbu Line with their usual infantry plus a newly formed rocket battalion. Fighting was so fierce hardly any prisoners came in for us to interrogate. In fact, some companies were offering bounties for bringing in prisoners. During the lull of this battle, we were able to take turns going into Manila for sightseeing. Met scores of ATIS men up from Brisbane, Australia and Hollandia, Dutch New Guinea, who were now stationed at the Manila Race Track. After cracking the enemy forces of the Shimbu Line, our whole 6th Infantry Division moved up to Northern Luzon to participate in the encirclement of General Tomoyuki Yamashita's forces. I was back with the 1st Infantry Regiment up in Nueva Vizcaya Province when I received my order to return to Division CP. Usually we said our good-byes to all our teammates, knowing the ferocity of battle up front, but my replacement, Sgt. George Nakamura, left that day without a word. One hour later, I got a call from 1st Infantry CP saying that George just got killed by a sniper. Our first thought, can't be, because he did not come around to say good-bye to any of us, but once again, to our regret, it was true. War came to an end, but the Japanese Forces under Yamashita's command did not surrender, so S.Sgt. Kiyo Fujimura led a patrol into enemy-held territory to negotiate their unconditional surrender. But, before they could reach any Japanese command post, they ran into a thirty-man Japanese patrol. Kiyo boldly approached them and informed them of the cessation of hostilities while his men watched from a distance. However, due to lack of radio communication with Japan, they were skeptical and unconvinced. So Kiyo returned and told his men that he'll have to bring them over to convince them thoroughly. His patrol would not trust Japanese coming in fully armed, so he went back again, did some fast talking, and got them to come in without their weapons. Kiyo said that he finally convinced them when he threatened to wire Japan and bring one of their Princes. For bringing this mission to a successful conclusion, S.Sgt. Kiyoshi Fujimura was awarded the Silver Star. General Yamashita and his men came in to surrender a few days later to our adjacent unit about 1,000 yards away, but I personally did not see him. I thought surely he would commit hara-kiri.

Our whole division moved out of the Cordillera Mountains to the China Sea coast, San Fernando, La Union Province, and prepared for the occupation of Japan. How we griped upon learning that our 6th Infantry Division was to occupy Tsuruga, Fukui Province, Japan. All our Nisei claimed the Tokaido Line was too far away for convenient travel.

October 10, 1945

Surprise of surprises, next day our order changed to Inchon (Jinsen), Korea. The Korean people did not welcome us GIs with open arms like the

Filipinos, claiming that we came to occupy their land after booting out their former oppressors, the Japanese. Our 169th Language Detachment was disbanded at Chonju, Zenra Hokuda, Korea. Kiyo Fujimura and I re-enlisted for another year in the regular Army to serve in the Army of Occupation, ATIS, GHQ, Tokyo. We visited our parents during our three-month "bonus" furlough offered by MacArthur headquarters to all GIs volunteering for the Army of Occupation. Kiyo went to Iwakuni, Yamaguchi Prefecture, and I went to Tahara, Wakayama Prefecture. We served mostly at ATIS, but we had temporary duty under Lt. Colonel Paul F. Rusch translating the new Japanese Constitution, personal diaries of Prince Fumimaro Konoye, Saionji, General Hideki Tojo, and other "war criminals" of that time. Don't know how Kiyo made out on his accrued time when he got discharged, but I received two days when I got my discharge at Fort Dix, New Jersey. I left the Service with a sour taste in my mouth for their blundering "bureaucracy." Two days of furlough after thirty-five months of overseas duty!

6th Infantry Division
Casualties:
1,174 ....Dead
3,876 ....Wounded
9 ....Missing
Enemy Losses:
23,000+..............Dead
1,700 ....Captured

After Japan surrendered on August 15, 1945, the MIS soldiers were reassigned to civil matters and sent to Japan, contributing significantly to the postwar U.S. Army occupation, interpreting for military government teams, locating and repatriating imprisoned Americans, and interpreting at the war-crimes trials.

One Replacement's Story

Stanley Izumigawa

While the men of the 100th were in combat in Italy, the 442nd Regimental Combat Team began training at Camp Shelby, Mississippi. By June, the 442nd had joined the 100th, who were engaged in heavy fighting near Rome, officially combining the two units. In the autumn of 1944, the units of the 100th/442nd would engage in their bloodiest battle—the rescue of the "Lost Battalion." Trapped deep in the forests of the Vosges Mountains in France, a division of some 300 Texans were caught under German fire, unable to free themselves. For six days, the 100th/442nd fought enemy infantry until it reached the Lost Battalion. By the time the men got back onto safe ground, the dead and wounded of the 100th/442nd numbered 2,000, the team having lost 40 percent of its original strength. The following is Stanley Izumigawa's account of his battlefield experience as a member of the 100th/442nd. Written in 1955, "One Replacement's Story" was published in Collection of Memoirs, Company L 442. Vol. *3 in November 1997.*

From the 442nd to the 100th

The first group of replacements from the 442nd joined the 100th in March 1944 near Benevento, Italy, where the unit was bivouacked after having been pulled off the lines at Cassino. Mitsugu Jio, Kaoru Kajiwara, and I from our squad (lst Platoon, L Company, 442nd Infantry) had volunteered and, still together, were assigned to A Company of the 100th. It was one year from the time we had enlisted, and I was nineteen years old.

We had just completed our basic training in Camp Shelby, Mississippi, and were awaiting maneuvers when the call for volunteers to replace the 100th's casualties overseas came. Why we volunteered I cannot recall, but it was probably a combination of boredom and ignorance.

After some leave time, which allowed us to visit nearby Washington, D.C., we shipped out of Newport News, Virginia, along with several hundred others. The troop ship was alone crossing the Atlantic, and while concerned, we never really worried about a submarine attack. It was ten days before we landed at Casablanca and boarded [forty-by-eight-foot] box cars for the trip across North Africa to the vicinity of the port of Oran....

When we, the first replacement group (there would subsequently be several other replacement groups), finally joined the 100th, those of us assigned to A Company were welcomed in a short talk by its captain, Mitsuyoshi Fukuda. Although I do not recall what he told us, I do recall a conversation that went something like this when we first met some of the 100th's originals.

"How they wen' choose you guys to come as replacements?"

"Oh, we volunteered."

"What? You volunteered? Stupid! How stupid! How dumb can you get? What you think this?"

Not exactly the kind of reception we were expecting; reality was beginning to set in....

The Vosges Mountains (Bruyeres, Biffontaine, Lost Battalion)

Welcome to the war in France. And what a welcome it was. The Vosges Mountains are a series of hills covered with evergreen trees, most eight to twelve inches in diameter. There were trails weaving through most of the forests and roads traversing [some of it].

It was October and beginning to get chilly, and much of the time it rained or drizzled. Much of the time, also, we were uninformed, at least at the rifleman level, of our specific mission and exactly where we were in relation to the rest of the unit and the enemy. Squad leaders guided us as best they could under the circumstances.

The squad leaders were normally sergeants, but because of the high rate of turnover resulting from casualties, squads were often led by PFCs. Similarly, at all levels within the company, those of lower rank temporarily had to take over. Being about the youngest at nineteen and not particularly wanting the responsibility, I was content to let others lead.

When the 100th moved into the thick forest on the first day of action in France, Company A was in reserve, out of harm's way. When we were committed, we moved into position, encountered some artillery fire, pulled back some to get out of it, and started to dig in.

It was late afternoon when artillery again hit our platoon. Shell after shell screamed in, some hitting the trees and bursting above us. I wondered if I should simply move out away from the shelling, but shells were landing all around. It is times like this that one gets religious and prays for safety. To say it is frightening doesn't describe it enough. You have to fight for control

Regimental colors at decoration ceremony, November 12, 1944.
Photographer unknown.

The following quote was found on the back of the above photograph. No citation accompanied the words:

"On seeing only 500 men (out of the usual regimental complement of 4,500), General Dalquist demanded, 'Where are the rest of the men?' With tears streaming down his cheek, Colonel Virgil S. Miller replied, 'Sir, this is all that's left.'"

that you don't panic or shet in your pants. You hug the ground in your hole and try to make yourself a smaller target.

All kinds of thoughts go through your head: "I volunteered for this? No wonder they said it was stupid. I hope the damn shelling stops. We sure picked the wrong place. I hope the next one lands somewhere else. I wish I was somewhere else. I wonder if anybody got it."

The close ones make you cringe and you feel the spray of dirt and debris. You smell the burned powder. "Acrid" is the word usually used to describe it. You don't see the flashes of the explosions because you're head down in your hole or slit trench. And the piercing sound of each shell as it screams in just adds to your terror.

Though it seemed much longer, it was probably just a few minutes. It's over for now, and I'm okay. (Lucky Number 7.)

I looked up and saw Ko Fukuda, the platoon sergeant, at the next hole. He seemed to be helping someone who was hit, so I went over to help him. He says, "I'm hit, too!"

At that, I noticed that he was bleeding from his right shoulder. I put a bandage on his wound as best I could, and all the time he was bandaging the other fellow. There is similar activity all around and the medics are busy. As soon as we can, we clear out to another area.

This was our first day on the line in France, and although I never knew the exact count, about half the platoon was wounded in that barrage, close to twenty men. I didn't know if any were killed. With the replacements we had been getting, we had been almost up to full strength. Such as it was, I hadn't gotten to know any of them. For some of the wounded, it was their first day on the line.

We are walking through the forest, sometimes on trails, sometimes on roads. What's left of a small automobile lies flattened on the road. One or more tanks must have run over it. Much of the time we are just moving, not actually on the attack.

At night sometimes you can see a light here and there in the valley below, maybe even hear voices echoing up, but we don't even think of shooting. For one thing, we don't know how far away the light actually is; there are too many trees in between, anyway. And shooting might only give away our position and draw artillery fire. But we try to relax and get some sleep, taking turns doing guard duty in one- or two-hour shifts. The ground in your slit trench is damp and cold, but you try to get as comfortable as you can, lying down bundled up in your jacket, a blanket, or sleeping bag, rifle nearby.

Every night the supply guys bring up C or K rations and water, ammo for those who need it. Sometimes they even manage to bring up a hot meal and coffee, a real treat. If you need to take a crap, you just dig a hole, squat and do your business, and cover it up. If you're going to smoke, you make real sure the flame is shielded when you light up, and you cup your hands over the cigarette when you draw on it so that the glow does not reveal your position or presence.

After that artillery barrage on the first day, the one that reduced our platoon to half strength, I am one of the remaining "old-timers" and am now one of the squad leaders. As such, I have inherited a Tommy gun, actually a 45-caliber Thompson submachine gun similar to those used by Prohibition-era gangsters in the movies, as my weapon. Some previous user had removed the butt stock or handle, a common practice to make it lighter and easier to carry. The downside was that this also made it more difficult to control and hence much more inaccurate to shoot, as I was to find later.

Between the forested hills there were open fields of various widths. As we came down a hillside, there was a burst of Jerry machine-gun fire to one side.

In this terrain you were always on edge because the forest and undergrowth cut visibility and you never knew when or from where you might get shot at. Even if you are not being shot at directly, machine-gun fire from close by is also terrifying. The sharp crack of small-arms fire is very scary in the confined, forested setting, as the sound is amplified. I sometimes wonder which is worse: facing an artillery barrage or machine-gun fire from directly in front.

Fear is a constant companion. Sometimes you are more frightened than at other times. Strangely, too, sometimes you don't really realize you were scared until later. I suppose as they say in the Army, it depends on the situation and the terrain.

It stood to reason that Jerries would be somewhere near the base of the opposite hill, waiting to cut down anyone venturing into the open space between. The usual strategy, when fired upon by machine guns, was to try and spot where it was coming from and to call in support fire from artilleries, mortars, or tanks, whichever was available.

This time, at least for us, there was no further fire from across, and we crossed the open space and into the woods of the next hill. What was happening with other companies we didn't know. We do know there has been fighting.

We are now walking through the town of Bruyeres. Others in the 442nd have liberated it, and we were just passing through on the way to another forested hill. The street we are on appears deserted. At least we do not see any townspeople anywhere. There is some damage, but it's nothing compared to Anzio.

As we get to the base of a wooded hill about a half mile or so past the town, there is some commotion ahead. Soon I could hear someone crying, crying very loudly, "Mama! Mama!"

We walked up to a foxhole where the crying was coming from and found a Jerry soldier, a young boy whom I guessed was no more than fifteen. Also squatting in the hole, rifle held between his knees, head facing down, and trembling in fright, was an elderly man of about sixty. He was so stiff with fear that it was difficult to pull him out of the hole.

At the top of the hill, one of our guys, bleeding from a head wound but on his feet and walking, was being escorted back. We formed a skirmish line, a couple of yards between men, and started down the hill. Shortly the lieutenant, Richard Hamasaki, on my left, says, "Jerries. You see the Jerries on the trail about thirty yards in front?"

I looked, saw the line of Jerries walking in single file, and nodded.

"Pass the word along! Get ready!"

Spud Munemori was on my right and I turned towards him, "Spud, Jerries, right in front about thirty yards. Pass the word."

He hears me, but, "Where? Where?"

And I pointed. Then I looked back toward the Jerries and saw the last one in line kneeling, rifle shouldered and aimed at me! In a flash the thought goes through my mind, "I'm going to get shot!"

At the same time, instinctively, I dove behind a tree. It was downhill, so as soon as I hit the ground behind the tree, the momentum tilted my helmet forward over my eyes such that momentarily I could not see ahead.

There is no shot. (Lucky Number 8.)

The other guys were still walking ahead, and I thought, "Shet, I can't stay down if the others are up."

So I got up, still half thinking I might get shot, but there was no shooting from them or us. When I hit the ground, the Jerry that had a bead on me must have alerted his buddies and they had all taken off.

What looked like a roadway girdling the hillside appeared a little further down. The lieutenant stopped us there. There was a drainage swale-like depression at the edge of the road where it then dropped off ten feet or so. I dropped into the depression and peered into the woods below. Again about thirty yards below, I spotted a group of five or six Jerries standing just to one side of a foxhole. I don't remember if I told the lieutenant or not. I think I did.

Since I knew my Tommy gun wasn't very accurate, I called Spud, who had a BAR, to join me and pointed out the Jerries to him. They had not seen us. We both lined up our weapons and I aimed, saying, "Shoot when you're ready!"

We both fired at about the same time and kept firing. In no time our quarry was gone. I couldn't tell if we got any of them. I could see white nicks appearing on the trees in front of us as bullets hit them. There were no bodies lying on the ground, and I wondered, "We couldn't have missed them all! I wonder if any fell into the hole."

I was thinking that maybe we should have someone pump a rifle grenade into the hole when the lieutenant said, "Okay, you two damn fools. Come back here before you get shot. We got to move out."

So we never got to know if we had gotten any of them.

As it turned out, that was the only time all through the war that I had a clear shot at Jerries. If I had had a rifle instead of a buttless Tommy gun—oh, well!

I was not one of those to whom things happened, and in retrospect, I'm glad I wasn't. Some guys had many opportunities to kill Jerries, others little or none. When I was on a patrol or when it was our turn to be in front, most of the time nothing happened. Despite the attacks and counterattacks in the various battles, our squad was rarely involved directly in pitched battles with the enemy. . . .

Later, back with the platoon, we moved down from the forest to the edge of the open space ahead. C company had already entered and occupied some of the houses in the very small town of Biffontaine. Part of the platoon moved into a house near the edge of the forest. Our squad was posted about a hundred yards further along a path that curved back into the forest. We were to guard against any counterattack from this direction and started to dig in. Some previous action must have occurred at this particular spot because we recovered a couple of Jerry rifles there. One of the rifles looked quite different. It appeared to be a semiauto, something we were not aware they had.

Just at dusk, mortar shells rustled in on our position. Artillery shells will scream and screech in. Mortar shells come in much more quietly. As we lay in our holes, an antiaircraft gun firing some tracers also opened fire over our position. I stayed down in my slit trench as the tracers lighted up the area in alternating flashes. Mortar shells were still coming in, also, and I wondered if this was the prelude to a counterattack by infantry. When the mortar and cannon fire let up, I heard a cry of, "Medic, medic!"

That was Victor Akimoto in the next hole! I scurried over to him and was getting a bandage ready when a mortar shell landed a few yards away. Even though I wasn't looking in that direction, I saw the flash of the explosion. Dirt and debris hit me, but that was all. I wasn't hurt. (Lucky Number 9.) There was no sign of Jerries approaching, and others came to help me and we got Victor out of there and into the farmhouse. There were no further incidents during the night.

The next morning we watched as a number of wounded, some walking on their own, others, like Victor Akimoto, carried on stretchers by German prisoners of war, set out for the rear. Shortly afterward we heard that in the forest, they had been surrounded and captured by the Germans, except for the last two, who saw what was happening ahead and escaped into the woods. One of these was a medic whom I was to meet up with a few days later.

Sadly, we heard some time later that Victor Akimoto had died in a German hospital. He was a likable kotonk, a real quality guy. Word was that he had been a sergeant in another outfit but had been busted from rank for telling someone off and had joined the 100th.

Back in the farmhouse near Biffontaine, three of us were drinking coffee when a mortar shell hit very close to the doorway. Dave Nagao, who was most in line with the doorway, was wounded through his hand and in his side. As we were trying to help him, he asked if he was going to die. We assured him that he would be all right. The other two of us were unscathed. (Lucky Number 10.)

All through the war, the medics, as the first-aid men were called, did a super job, often moving up and risking getting shot or wounded themselves to help anyone who had been hit. There was a white circle with a red cross painted on their helmets, and they also wore white arm bands with a red cross to identify themselves as noncombatants. They carried no arms, only first aid supplies. They were real heroes!

Days and nights blended one into the other, and it is difficult to remember what we were doing much of the time. We were either in position watching for enemy attack, probing the front a little, or simply moving to the front or to the rear.

Word came down that we were being relieved to get some rest from frontline duty, and we moved back some distance to an area called Belmont.

Oddly, while I remember some names and faces, except for those few, I don't recall my companions much of the time in the Vosges. Even for the short time that I was the squad leader, I only remember the few.

One of those I remember well was Spud Munemori. When the rest was cut short and the battalion was ordered back into the lines tomorrow to go to the aid of a 36th Division battalion that had been cut off and isolated, he came to me and said, "I'm not going back up! I don't care what they do to me, I'm not going back up!"

Somewhat surprised and not really knowing what to say, I let him talk it out.

Very early the next morning, we gathered our stuff in the dark, assembled, and set off. It was so dark that we had one hand on the pack of the man in front to keep the line intact until visibility improved. As if nothing had been me said the night before, Spud was right there in line with the rest of us, much to my relief.

We had moved up the road and into the front and by early evening had dug in for the night. Where we got them I don't recall, but we used small logs to cover our slit trenches to give us added protection from tree bursts, i.e., shells hitting and exploding in the trees.

Mortar shells started landing and we headed for our holes. I was on my hands and knees and was just about to crawl into my partially log-covered slit trench when a shell exploded close behind me and somebody hit me with a sledge hammer, or so I thought. The force of the hit knocked me into the hole face down. I knew I was hit. It was the worst pain that I had ever experienced. I thought my left leg had been blown off at the hip and I yelled out loud, "Oh, no. Damn it! Damn it! God damn it! Damn it! Damn it!"

And I kept on cursing and pounding the ground with my hands in despair. The initial pain had now subsided, but I had to know. With my right leg I felt for my left one, and it was there. There was no feeling in it, but it was there, and I thought, "It's fine, I still have my left leg. It wasn't blown off."

About this time someone came to my aid; I don't know who. The shelling had stopped. They got me out of the hole and cut away the pants leg as I asked, "How bad is it? How bad is it?"

I don't remember what they said, but I concluded I would be all right. And now I recognized Richard Chinen, the medic who escaped capture only a few days earlier, as one of those helping me.

The fellow who would now have to take over as squad leader kept saying something like, "I don't know what to do!"

"Oh, you'll be all right. And can you hold this for me until I get back?"

It was the tiny pistol I had found in Italy, which I still carried. I guess I should have kept it with me because I found out later that he gave it to someone else to hold, and I never saw it again, not that it mattered much.

This was October 28, 1944. I was not there, of course, but two days later the 100th and the 442nd rescued "The Lost Battalion." The 36th Division presented the units with a plaque for this effort and each member received a postcard copy of the plaque.

There was also someone else who was wounded. We were put on stretchers secured over the hood of a jeep and evacuated without incident to a field hospital, then to another.

There were of course other wounded men. When they were ready to work on me, a nurse told me to count backwards from ten and gave me a shot of something. As I started the count, I could see one of the doctors wearing surgical gloves groping with his thumb and forefinger in the thigh wound of a patient on the next table. The wound was bloody and it made a slurping sound as the doctor felt for the bullet or shrapnel that caused the wound. I thought, "That's what they'll be doing with me, I guess." I hadn't counted but a few numbers before the anesthetic sedative put me out.

When I came out of it, the first thing I felt and said was, "I'm hungry."

This before I opened my eyes. An attendant nearby brought me some sliced canned peaches. Delicious!

There was a bandage on the front of my left thigh and some kind of dressing on the original wound. They had X-rayed the wounded area and determined that the best way to remove the piece of shrapnel was to operate from the front, as it had penetrated almost all the way through my thigh. It had entered from the lower part of my ass into the thigh. The doctor who came to check and replace the bandage a few days later said, "You're a fortunate young man. The shrapnel chipped off a small piece of the hip bone but otherwise did not damage anything vital."

He showed me an X-ray film and pointed cut the chipped part of the hip bone. He also gave me the piece of shrapnel, the size of a marble, that they had taken out of my leg.

Yes, I had been wounded, but it was mostly a flesh wound, the kind that heals without complications. (Lucky Number 11.) One or two inches over one way and it would have hit my asshole or taken out my pecker and balls or some vital nerves or bones and left me crippled or handicapped. One of a soldier's worst fears, besides the fear of getting killed, is being hit in the head or face and being disfigured or getting hit in the sex organs and losing his manhood.

Some combat soldiers went through the whole war without ever being wounded and are considered to have been very lucky by the unknowing. But consider this: If they never got wounded, it also means that they went through every battle, that they were on the lines much longer than others, and this can be a very harrowing experience which is extremely stressful and hard on the nerves. For those who are wounded, depending on the severity, it could mean you're out of the war for good or for months or weeks, away from the wear and tear, the stress and strain, the fear and fatigue of being in combat.

For the several months that I was in the hospital and recuperating I was never with any of our guys. I didn't know what was happening in the unit.

The *Stars and Stripes,* the overseas newspaper printed for GIs by the military, carried information about the progress of the war. It also carried Bill Mauldin's cartoons of Willie and Joe, who were revered by the front-line troops.

Whether it was in the hospital or somewhere else, I don't know, but we did once in a while catch Axis Sally, the Nazis' propagandist, on the radio. We did not, however, catch the programs she directed at the 100th/442nd.

While being transported by train along with many other wounded from a field hospital to a convalescent one, we were visited by a strikingly beautiful blonde woman I recognized as Madeleine Carroll, the movie actress, some of whose movies I had seen. Because of the nature of my wound, I was lying on my stomach, and as she passed by she patted me and smiled, "One of those, eh?"

She moved on before I could think to say anything. I knew that she was one of [the first], if not the first, [of] the big stars to give up Hollywood and volunteer to help with the wounded overseas.

At the convalescent hospital I was confined to bed for the first two weeks or so. Nurses on duty periodically helped us with sponge baths. Attendants brought urinals when you needed to take a piss. Remarkably, because of my wound near the asshole, nature temporarily shut down the bodily system such that I had no urge to take a crap for many, many days. I used to worry about how I was going to, but when finally I had to, the wound had sufficiently healed that it was not a problem. Since I was not yet able to get out of bed, a bedpan was brought, a screen provided, it took a while, and I guess I stunk up the place for a while.

When they finally uncovered my wounded leg, I was dismayed to see that it had atrophied to half the thickness of my other leg. I was concerned that it was a permanent condition. There was no pain and I could move by supporting myself on the bed. It wasn't long before I could walk around, and happily, the wounded leg was returning to normal size.

Letter to Father

George Saito

In seven major campaigns, the 100/442nd took 9,486 casualties, or more than 300 percent of its original count. Despite these losses, the 100/442nd received seven Presidential Distinguished Unit Citations and 18,143 individual decorations, including one Congressional Medal of Honor, forty-seven Distinguished Service Crosses, 350 Silver Stars, 810 Bronze Stars, and more than 3,600 Purple Hearts. On July 15, 1946, the men of the 100/442nd were received by President Truman, who praised their bravery and unfailing spirit.

The following letter was written by George Saito, who served overseas with his brother Calvin, while the rest of the family was detained in an internment camp in the States. The letter was written on July 11, 1944 to George's father, Kiichi Saito, four days after his brother was killed in action.

Dear Dad—

I believe the War Dept. has notified you of our loss of Calvin—Dad I am writing you now because I've just learned of his passing—July 7th was the immemorable day—

I can imagine what a shock it was to you, as it was to me, because it happened so soon—on the twelfth day of combat—

A few events and action leading up to the time of his loss as related by a member of his company, are—On the 6th of July his unit was attacking a hill held by the enemy—After a hard fight with even a little hand-to-hand combat, they took the hill—The Jerries, after being shoved off were reforming for a counterattack—In the confusion and disorder of battle, Cal being the radio-man, somehow, got a call through to the artillery to open fire on the enemy—He personally directed and guided the firing on the enemy positions which routed the enemy—His action and doing his job well at this one instance, explained the fellows, saved many of his buddies— Their unit held that hill that night but the next morning the enemy barraged the hill with mortars and he happened to be one of the unlucky ones—His passing was instantaneous—All of the fellows were telling me what a good soldier and radio-man he was and that his loss was keenly felt—

Well dad—now that the inevitable has happened I guess you're wondering about his remains—Right now I can't do much for we're still in battle and I am writing you while at our gun position, but as I understand thing now—they will bury him here in Italy and after the war you can ask the Government to transfer them to an American cemetery in the States. His personal belongings will be shipped to you in time—

Dad—this is not time to be preaching to you but I have something on my chest which I want you to hear—In spite of Cal's supreme sacrifice don't let anyone tell you that he was foolish or made a mistake to volunteer. Of what I've seen in my travels on our mission I am more than convinced that we've done the right thing in spite of what has happened in the past— America is a damn good country and don't let anyone tell you otherwise—

Well dad, the Germans are beginning to throw a few shells our way now so maybe I'd better get down in my hole. If there is anything also that you'd like to know except the place I shall only be too glad to let you know. In time though when we're allowed I'll give you the exact location—

Cheer up dad and do take care of yourself—Regards to all—

Your loving son
George

*

Three months after sending his father this letter, George Saito was tragically killed in battle.

Presentation of a combat honor, December 8, 1945. Photographer unknown.

General Joseph Stillwell presents a Distinguished Service Cross to Mary Masuda. Her brother, Sgt. Kazuo Masuda of the 442nd Infantry, was killed at Cassino in 1944. Army rules prevented the general from pinning the medal directly on the mother, standing behind Mary, who was an enemy alien.

FROM Light One Candle

Solly Ganor

For most of the war, few GIs in Europe knew much about Nazi concentration camps. However, on April 29, 1945, a special unit of the 442nd known as the 552nd Field Artillery Battalion pursued fleeing German soldiers into an area where the Nazis had hidden subcamps of the notorious Dachau concentration camp. Nearly 229,000 Nazi prisoners were processed and held in Dachau, which was the first Nazi concentration camp to be established. When the Nisei came upon a camp, they would knock down the gates and free the death-camp prisoners, horrified and often in tears as they struggled to comprehend what they found there. The inmates were as uncomprehending as their rescuers. According to an article in the November 11, 1991, issue of The New Yorker*—"Reunion" by Peggy Orenstein—one former Dachau inmate recounted:*

> *I saw him and I thought, Oh, now the Japanese are going to kill us. And I didn't care anymore. I said, "Just kill us, get it over with." He tried to convince me that he was an American and wouldn't kill me. I said, "Oh no, you are a Japanese and you're going to kill us." We went back and forth, and finally he landed on his knees, crying, with his hands over his face, and he said, "You are free now. We are American Japanese. You are free."*

After his liberation from the Nazis in 1945, Solly Ganor went to Palestine to join the fight for the independence of Israel. He and his wife moved to California in 1977, and since then have divided their time between the United States and Israel. In 1995, his autobiographical account of the Holocaust was published as a book entitled Light One Candle: A Survivor's Tale from Lithuania to Jerusalem. *It took nearly forty-five years after the war ended for the Nisei participation in the Dachau liberation to become publicly known. Ganor's book is one of few published accounts relating this astonishing story of the Japanese Americans with Nazi concentration camp prisoners.*

*

Kaunas, Lithuania, is a little-known spot on the map for most Americans. It looms large in my memory, however. It is where I spent the greater part of my childhood, and where a large part of the story that follows takes place....

I was eleven years old when Hitler marched into Poland. The weeks and months that followed were fearful ones, as news of atrocities against Polish Jews reached us and refugees began streaming over the border into Lithuania. The Nazis had begun their inexorable march across the face of Europe, and would soon put our old Tsarist forts to hideous use. The next six years would turn out to be far more terrible than even the grimmest pessimists among us could foresee.

In 1939 and 1940 Kaunas became a sort of way station filled with people desperately seeking asylum from the Nazis. They sought help from any country they thought might receive them. Most of them were denied and were turned away by one government after another, including the governments of the United States and Great Britain. The one official who offered the Jews of Kaunas any hope was the representative of a government which shortly became Germany's strongest ally. That man was the Consul of Japan, Chiune Sugihara,[1] who risked his career, his honor, perhaps even his life, to save more than six thousand Jews.

In my memory of those years Sugihara stands out as a single light in a sea of darkness. My family, for various reasons, was not among the fortunate thousands he helped directly, but he remained an inspiration to me throughout the terrible years to come—years spent in the Slabodke ghetto and in the camps of Dachau.

How strange and wonderful it was to recognize Sugihara's ethnic features again five years after I last laid eyes on him, and at the very moment of my liberation. His eyes, and even something of his smile were in the kind face of the GI who brought me back from the brink of death. For it was a Japanese American, or Nisei, who lifted me from a snowbank where German SS guards had left me for dead. The Nisei soldier's name was Clarence Matsumura, and he was with the 522nd FABN—the Field Artillery Battalion of the famous 100th/442nd Combat Team, a regimental-sized unit composed entirely of segregated units of Japanese American troops. These men came both from Hawaii and from the mainland, and many were volunteers. They served on the bloody battlefields of Italy, France, and Germany. The 100th/442nd suffered more casualties and won more medals for its length of service than any other American unit in the war.

The irony is not lost on me that even as Clarence and his kinsmen were fighting and dying for the United States, many of their families were

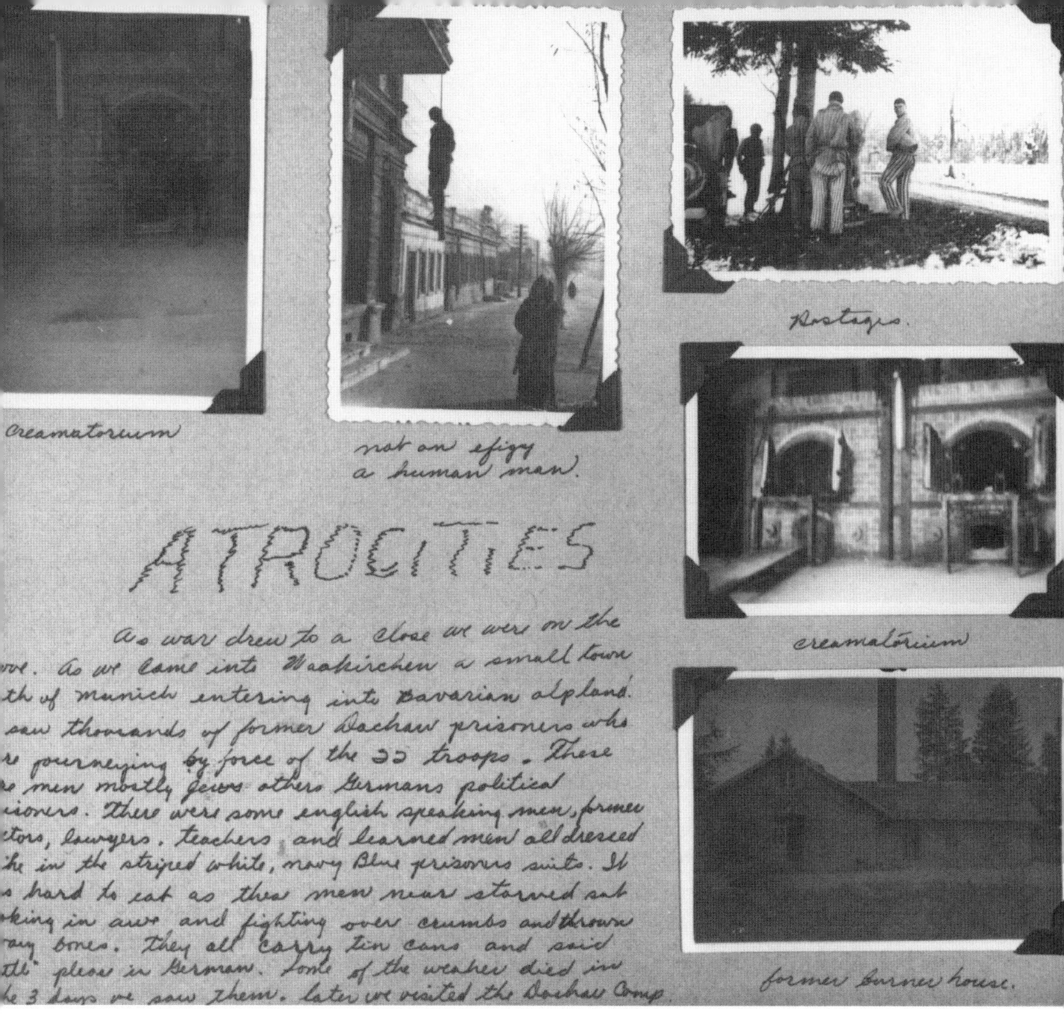

Page from an unknown soldier's scrapbook; 522nd Field Artillery Battalion of the 442nd Regimental Combat Team, c. 1945.

incarcerated in American detention camps. Along with all Americans of Japanese descent living on the West Coast of the U.S. mainland, the families of nearly half of these Nisei troops had been uprooted from their homes and businesses and sent to live in tar-paper barracks in desolate areas. The United States called these detention centers "relocation camps." Concentration camps under another name.

I met Clarence Matsumura on May 2, 1945. Our paths didn't cross again for thirty-six years. During those years I did not speak of my wartime experiences with others, except among those few who survived the ghettos and camps with me. Only they could understand. I found out later that many of our rescuers could not speak of what they saw either. But then, in 1981,

Clarence Matsumura walked into the National Japanese American Historical Society of San Francisco and told his story to Eric Saul, a historian who directed the Presidio Army Museum and later worked with San Francisco's Holocaust Oral History Project. Eric knew of the role that the 522nd Field Artillery Battalion played in the rescue of the infamous Death March from Dachau, but Clarence was the first to come forward and tell his personal story:

> Toward the end of the war, when we'd finally broken the Siegfried Line and the Germans were in retreat, three of my buddies and I pulled into a German village called Wasseralfingen. There was a hill there that was covered with artificial trees. These things looked like they were made of two-by-fours. They had painted 'em green and laid them all out over this hill, which looked like it was man-made, too. Grass was growing on it, but there were no ravines or any natural markings like that. We went around and discovered a tunnel with a great big wire fence across it. There were all kinds of people in there, staring through the fence. We were staring at them, and they were staring back at us, Orientals in U.S. Army uniforms. It took us a few minutes to realize these were not German workers, but prisoners. Polish, Bulgarian, all different nationalities. Inside the tunnel there was a railroad track, with bunk beds all lined up and down one side. Down the other side piles of all kinds of machine parts were laid out. An assembly line ran on the tracks, and it looked like they were putting together 88-millimeter artillery pieces. Antiaircraft pieces, famous for their deadly fire.
>
> These people in the tunnel were afraid to come out at first. We couldn't really talk to them, because nobody seemed to speak English. We more or less figured out what they were doing because we recognized the gun parts. Finally we located a few doctors and lawyers who could speak English, and they explained. The prisoners weren't starving like those we found later, but they were happy to come outside into the air. They had been in that tunnel for so long.
>
> We didn't know anything about slave-labor camps then. We didn't know what the hell was going on.
>
> There were four of us driving around in a weapons transport, mostly on Hitler's autobahns and at highway speeds. Sergeant Mas Fujimoto was driving, and old man Tanaka, acting as observer, was up front, and then there was David Sugimoto, the radio operator, and me. I was there as a repairman. We were acting as forward observers. The Germans were retreating so fast then that our infantry could hardly keep up.

Later on we came to a really peaceful-looking town. It was called Dachau. I had never heard of it before. Right in the middle of town was what looked like a big factory with a high fence all around and two big brick smokestacks in the middle. Before we ever reached it we noticed the odd smell. You just can't describe it, but you never forget it. The smell of decaying human flesh. There were dead corpses all piled up everywhere in there. A lot of them in striped uniforms, many of them naked. This thing is right in the middle of town, and there are dead bodies all over the doggone place. I was very shook up. I kept trying to figure out what the heck is this doggone thing?

We went out into the town, with some men from the battery who could speak German, and started interrogating the townspeople. 'Where are the Soldaten? The guards? Where did they go? Did you know there are all kinds of dead people in there?' Right in the middle of town, and the townspeople claimed that they didn't know anything about any of this. Then someone told us the soldiers had marched a lot of prisoners out of town several days ago. And that a day or two later the last of the soldiers came around and took all the townspeople's animals and bicycles, and just took off.

We took off after them, following the road the townspeople pointed out. Farther along, toward some other villages, we started finding people along the roadside. Almost all of them were wearing black-and-white striped uniforms. I don't know how any of them could stand on their feet. They were nothing but skin and bones. They couldn't speak. Most of them were lying on the ground, many of them unconscious. We were supposed to be chasing down the SS, but these people were starving. They were lying out on the cold ground. We said let's get them into someplace warm, get them some food. We put them into Gasthauses, we put them into barns. We got them inside and got them blankets, gave them water and food, but the rest of our guys kept bringing in more and more people. They kept finding them along the roads. Pretty soon we ran out of places. We went into the villages and got the Germans out of their houses and brought these prisoners in. We put them in their beds, on their sofas, wherever we could make them comfortable. The Germans didn't need the doggone houses. These people needed the houses.

The first thing we got them was water. But the thing was, a lot of them couldn't swallow. They were starving, but only the strong ones could eat or drink, and many of them had lost their teeth from scurvy.

The really weak ones couldn't even swallow water. You could give it to them, but it didn't do any good because it just wouldn't go down.

We contacted our mess crew to find out if there was any way they could make the mush they fed us in the morning. We took powdered eggs and whipped them up with water and then added more water to make them really soupy. But only the strong ones could eat it. Nothing we tried seemed to work on the others.

I remember holding these people up and trying to feed them broth. The word came down that we shouldn't try to feed them solid food because we would only harm them. Give them broth, they said, let them drink if they can, give them mush if they can eat it. We were doing that day and night for several days. We didn't know what else to do. All we could do was clean them up, give them blankets, try to get some broth down them, spoon by spoon. The strange thing was, there were only men there. I don't think I saw any women. But unless you undressed and bathed them you couldn't really tell. They were so emaciated you couldn't tell whether they were men or women.

Did I talk about it with my family, with the other Nisei? No, I didn't talk about it. How could anyone understand who didn't see it? It's not that easy to talk about. It affected all of us. It took us a long time to get over that doggone thing. We couldn't understand why people had to go and do things like that to other human beings. You really can't explain how it is, when you've got all these people, so many of them, and you're trying to help them and they're dying right there in your hands.

Ten years after that interview, in April of 1992, Eric Saul called me in Israel.

April is the most beautiful time of the year in Israel, just before the harsh summer heat invades the country. The orange groves are in bloom, and the sweet delicate bouquet of orange blossoms permeates the countryside. This is the month of Passover, when we celebrate the Israelites' exodus from Egypt some three thousand years ago. It is also the month of Yom Hashoa, the Day of the Holocaust, when the entire country mourns the Jewish victims of the Nazis during World War II. On that day the survivors of the Holocaust remember all their loved ones that perished during the war. For many survivors, the dead include their entire families.

That evening I was sitting on my terrace in Herzelia, listening to the waves wash ashore on the sandy beach below. It always has a calming effect on me. Sometimes I imagine I hear a plaintive note in the constant murmur of the water, as if the sea is reminding me I wasn't true to her. For many years

I was a merchant seaman, plying the oceans of the world, until I left the sea for another woman—my wife Pola.

I'd been restless the whole day. During the war I'd developed a sort of sixth sense warning me of things to come, an instinct for survival that served me well in the camps and again during Israel's War of Independence. It was an uneasy sort of feeling that something was about to happen, and when the telephone rang I didn't want to answer it. It rang several times before I finally picked up the receiver.

"May I speak to Solly Ganor?" It was a pleasant American voice. I hesitated before identifying myself.

"I am here with a group of Japanese American veterans who were among the liberators of Dachau in 1945," the man said. "I was told that you were among the survivors of the Death March from Dachau."

My instincts had been right. This man with the pleasant voice was going to stir up memories I'd kept carefully boxed off from the rest of my life for nearly fifty years.

"Do you recall the name of the place where you were liberated?" he asked. His name was Eric Saul, and he spoke quietly, with sensitivity.

I was silent for a long time, but my heart was thudding in my chest. He waited.

"I was liberated at a small village in Bavaria, called Waakirchen," I finally said.

"Do you remember seeing any Japanese American soldiers when you were liberated?"

Did I remember? Did I remember? How could I ever forget the very first face I saw, at the very moment I emerged from hell? But something within me continued to rebel against this intrusion from the past.

No one who wasn't there, no matter how sensitive or imaginative, could have any inkling of what we went through. Those who were killed in the very beginning were the lucky ones. Those who survived year after year in the ghetto and then in the slave-labor camps around Dachau were ground down to less than nothing. And then in the end, with Hitler's Reich crashing around the Nazis' ears, there was the Death March. That final meaningless, grotesque, inhuman cruelty.

I survived that march, but something inside of me died. Although my body survived intact, my spirit was crippled. In my mind's eye I saw myself as the trunk of a tree that had survived a forest fire. Black and charred beyond recognition, with all my branches gone, I finally managed to sprout new branches in order to live, but the old ones never grew back, and thus I became a different, and somehow lesser, being.

"Yes, I remember the Japanese Americans," I finally said to Mr. Saul. "I remember them well. As a matter of fact, they were the first American soldiers I saw. They were my liberators."

Eric couldn't keep the excitement out of his voice. "After all these years to find you here! It's a miracle! It's a miracle!"

"Yes, it is a miracle," I thought, still wary. I was groping for denials, for excuses not to enter into this dialogue.

Eric sensed my reluctance. "Please," he said. "They have come so far, after so many years. All the way from California and Hawaii. Will you come to meet them?" Eric and Lani Silver, director of San Francisco's Holocaust Oral History Project, had organized this trip for twenty-five liberators and their families. They were being honored by Israel's Knesset.

In the end I relented. How could I not?...

What happened in Jerusalem in the spring of 1992, when I met with Eric Saul, Lani Silver, and the Japanese American veterans, can only be described as a second liberation. As soon as I entered the lobby of their hotel I noticed half a dozen Nisei in their early seventies. In their midst stood a tall young American man in glasses—Eric Saul. He came forward smiling, both arms extended in a gesture of welcome, his whole being radiating kindness. I immediately liked him. He introduced me to the group, who welcomed me warmly. One had been with the 442nd; the rest were veterans of the 522nd Field Artillery. I looked into their faces to see if the particular man who lifted me from the snow so many years ago was among them. I was sure that even after all this time I would know him. But I felt no jolt of recognition.

Soon we were joined by others. Rudy Tokiwa, one of the leaders of the group, was from San Francisco. He was a heavyset man on crutches, a war hero decorated more than once for his valor in combat. I would later discover that the Nisei had been covered with honors.

Another man to whom I took an immediate liking was George Oiye, of Los Altos, California—another decorated veteran. He found a camera on a dead German officer, and he and Susumu Ito, another 522nd veteran, took many gruesome pictures of Dachau and its subcamps when their unit arrived there in April of 1945.

We retired to a corner of the lobby and I began reading an account I'd written, describing where and how I met the men of their battalion. As I spoke one more man joined the group. He stood next to Eric Saul, watching me intently. He was very slim, in his early seventies, with graying hair and glasses. My heart began beating faster. Was it him? Was he my rescuer? So many years had passed—how could I be sure? The group urged me to continue reading. When I got to the part where I was lying half-buried in the snow, more dead than alive, and the four men of the 522nd drove up, I looked up again and met the eyes of the newcomer. They were filled with tears.

I stopped reading; I couldn't go on. I was gripped by such intense feelings that I was unable to speak. I struggled with them, but to no avail. After all the years of trying to suppress the unsuppressable, a tidal wave of emotion erupted inside me, and I started weeping as I had never wept before. There was no stopping me. The boy I had buried deep within me all those years had come out of hiding. It was he who was crying, while my alter ego looked on in astonishment. I couldn't believe this was happening.

During the many years since my liberation I had never cried. I couldn't. A psychiatrist once told me that the trauma of the Holocaust had dried up my tears, that I was like an emotional amputee and would probably never cry again. And there I was, sprouting new emotional branches, or perhaps reviving old ones that weren't really dead, only dormant.

Finally, with the whole group gathered around patting and comforting me, I calmed down. Everyone was surprised at what had happened. Everyone had tears in his eyes.

No one was more surprised than I at all this, and in my embarrassment I tried to explain that this was the first time since my liberation that I had been able to weep. Eric then took my hands in his and smiled at me.

"Don't be embarrassed by your tears. You are among friends here." I looked at the faces around me and saw understanding and compassion in their eyes. I suddenly felt very close to them. We seemed to have bypassed that long process of emotional attachment that usually begins new friendships, and I felt as if I had known these people all my life. I felt tremendously uplifted, as if I had taken some potent drug.

There was a moment of silence, and then suddenly everyone was talking at once, asking questions, recalling where they were at the time of my liberation. They seemed to be affected by my catharsis, as if they had been caught up in my emotional surge. Then Eric pulled me aside and introduced me to the man who had actually unleashed this flood of tears.

"Solly, this is Clarence Matsumura. We think he is the man who saved you."

Clarence, Clarence—that was his name!

We stared at each other, and then he smiled. I knew immediately that it was him. He may have aged, but his smile hadn't changed. We fell into each others arms and it was as if the years simply melted away. I felt weak and he was holding me up, just as he did then, forty-seven years ago, by the side of a road in Bavaria.

Later, as we sat and exchanged memories of that fateful day, he showed me a snapshot of himself as a young soldier. I recognized him immediately! If I had any doubts at all, they evaporated then and there.

As I sat surrounded by my liberators, thoughts and feelings I had suppressed for years surfaced. My new friends had many of their own stories to tell. I was told that one of the men in the 522nd's medical detachment, Ichiro Imamura, had watched a liaison scout shoot the chain off of one of the gates of Dachau. I heard that several men in Charlie Battery—Minabe Hirasaki, Shiro Takeshita, and Raymond Kunemura—had "liberated" a German chicken farm near Waakirchen and made a lot of chicken soup to feed recently liberated prisoners. We talked far into the night, until one of the group reminded us that we were to attend an international press conference that morning. I was to be included. Reluctantly I said good night to my new friends and went to the room they had reserved for me. I was gripped by a tremendous excitement and apprehension.

The idea that I would have to appear before so many people and in front of cameras was terrifying. I remembered the previous year, when I accompanied my friend and fellow survivor Uri Chanoch to speak to a group of young Israeli soldiers about our experiences in Hitler's camps. As soon as I got up to the podium my stomach was tied in a knot and the blood pounded in my ears. I developed a splitting headache and felt quite ill. I vowed I would never again attempt such a thing.

The next day I was completely surprised by my sense of calm. I answered endless questions that morning, and gave long video interviews that afternoon to CNN, ABC, CBS, AP, and God knows how many other reporters. And I actually enjoyed it. It was then that I realized how greatly I had been affected by this second meeting with my liberators. I felt that a new person had emerged, and taken over the reins of my life.

The story of my reunion with Clarence sprouted wings. Few people knew the story of these Nisei and their role in the liberation of the camps, and many press agents and reporters interviewed us during the eight days the group remained in Israel. Since then I have been reunited with Clarence and others from his unit more than once, in Israel, Germany, and the United States. I'm grateful for the time I've been able to spend with them, and especially for the hours I had with Clarence, who passed away in May of 1995, to my enduring sorrow.

Each time I have met with these brave men new memories and recognitions and feelings have surfaced. Each time I have learned more about my rescuers. I often wonder if their experiences in the internment camps, and with American prejudice in general, didn't create in Clarence and his kinsmen some extra spark of understanding and compassion for those they rescued during the spring of 1945. Was there some special bond between the Nisei and the Jews they rescued? I don't know. I do know that my own sense of kinship with the Nisei and the Japanese is strong. This book is dedicated not only to the memory of those loved ones who perished at the hands of the Nazis, but equally, and with enormous gratitude, to Clarence and all the brave men of the 522nd Field Artillery Battalion of the famed 100th/442nd Combat Team, as well as to Chiune Sugihara, whose shining moral example guided me through the darkest years of the Holocaust.

ENDNOTE:

1. Sugihara's proper given name was Chiune, but I knew him as Sempo, a friendly nickname by which he was known in Lithuania.

What Flower Worth the Pain

Going home,
Feeling cheated,
Gripping my daughter's hand,
I tell her we're leaving
Without emotion.

SHIZUE IWATSUKI

Fifty Years

Half a century ago,
we are speaking of another time,
another life.
We are returning to that era of war,
divided loyalties, betrayal,
and incarceration.
Many of us have already gone,
some in fading notoriety,
some with trauma and conflicts
unresolved.

WAKAKO YAMAUCHI

I used to have nightmares, you know. I couldn't sleep. I had to be really exhausted to sleep. Maybe that's why I became a workaholic. I don't know. Like I say, you know, its still there. A certain type of music or a place, you know, you can feel it. You go all the way back forty years, maybe no, maybe yeah, you go back forty years when you're fifteen, sixteen years old, when you're dancing to Glenn Miller's music or something like that, you know, you go back. It just hits you all of a sudden. You never get rid of that. I never can. Maybe that's why I'm always on the go.

Tom Watanabe

Gain

I sought to seed the barren earth
And make wild beauty take
Firm root, but how could I have known
The waiting long would shake

Me inwardly, until I dared
Not say what would be gain
From such untimely planting, or
What flower worth the pain?

Toyo Suyemoto

As I sit out on the balcony by myself and look out over the ocean, images of my past arise as an enveloping mist to fill my mind. Someone said, "When one recalls experiences of the past, they light up in themselves to be like dreams." My dreams, quite definitely, span many changes and different backdrops. Filled with impossible hopes, encountering obstacles to attaining such hopes, then resurrecting such hopes again, the days of my past form a continuum. Now, looking back at earlier days, I feel no regrets. After all this, I feel, it is well that I have had this life.

Seiichi Higashide

Manzanar Relocation Camp, Monument, by Masumi Hayashi.
Panoramic photo collage, 1995.

Afterword

I had just turned fifteen when my family and I left our tiny storefront home on Ventura Boulevard in North Hollywood, rode in our friends' cars to Los Angeles, and boarded a bus along with other families. Our guard was a young soldier who predicted we'd all be returning home in two weeks. It took most of the day to travel the 200 miles or so to reach Manzanar Assembly Center. It looked sparse. Our barracks had yet to have the windows installed. Our new home, a twenty-by-twenty-five-foot cubicle, was bare except for steel cots. We each had a blanket and an empty sack which we later filled with straw to make mattresses. Decades later, I would learn that the barracks were just like those in our prisoner of war camps that housed German, Italian, and Japanese POWs.

I graduated from Manzanar High School in June 1944. Life in camp had been hard on inmate morale. I vowed never to return to school. I received permission to leave a week after graduation to find my way in "free America."

Although I had spent more than two years in Manzanar—not the predicted two weeks—I had no idea of the big picture: of the why and how of what had happened. Even after fifty-six years, the history of the camps is far from understood. We still don't know what hit us.

Unlike the "breaking news" you see on television, writing history takes time. It takes even more time when our government is the wrongdoer. Governments, especially one that is as proud of its democratic traditions as America, do not like to admit to wrongdoing.

I hated being Japanese in wartime America. The use of the J-word was blatant. We were "Japs" all over the place—in newspaper headlines, political speeches, radio comedy routines, popular songs ("You're a Sap, Mr. Jap"). We were "sneaky," "treacherous," even "lecherous." Political cartoons characterized the "Japs" as monkeys and as men who lusted after white women. I must say, it was awfully hard for me to think of my parents as being subhuman, to say nothing of sex-starved.

Despite all these corrosive and ultimately tiresome distortions of us as the "yellow peril" to white America, a more insidious betrayal of our Constitution's guarantees and protections was underway, a betrayal that threatened the very democratic freedoms and rights that we believed our enemies in Germany, Italy, and Japan were threatening.

President Franklin Roosevelt's "date which will live in infamy" was soon followed by another: February 19, 1942, the day he signed Executive Order Number 9066. This is the date that Japanese Americans memorialize each year as their Day of Remembrance. The order gave the secretary of war and designated military commanders the power to exclude and detain "any or all persons" who turned out to be of Japanese ancestry. As the fortunes of war determined, the first designated commander was the particularly flawed Lt. Gen. John L. DeWitt. He commanded the Western Defense Command, covering the eight westernmost states. E. O. 9066 used the device of "military areas" to which exclusion and detention orders were applied. We think of such areas as being strictly military—a naval yard or a military aircraft factory. Yet, like the phrase "any or all persons," "military areas" became an omen of what was to come when DeWitt defined the areas as a broad, roughly 100-mile-wide swath of territory along the entire Pacific Coast plus southern Arizona. Later, the entire state of California became such an "area"—a massive abuse of language and power.

The fear that fueled the J-word seemed to take flesh as official policy. At first, DeWitt issued a curfew order that restricted Japanese Americans to

Gravesite memorial at Klamath Falls, Oregon. Tule Lake Pilgrimage, 1980. Photographer unknown.

their homes from dusk to dawn and to traveling less than five miles from home. In the weeks that followed, DeWitt ordered the exclusion and detention of all 115,000 persons of Japanese ancestry from the West Coast and southern Arizona. Approximately 5,000 "voluntarily" left the exclusion zone and escaped internment; the remaining 110,000 entered the camps. (In issuing his orders, we later discovered, DeWitt vastly exceeded the recommendation of the military's own intelligence advisors. The Office of Naval Intelligence had been assigned the task of assessing the threat posed by Japanese communities before Pearl Harbor and had recommended an orderly roundup of 3,500 identified suspects of Japanese ancestry. And DeWitt went even further: for about a year, he did not allow Japanese American soldiers in uniform to be unescorted while in the exclusion zone.

At about the time the program of exclusion and detention began, a civilian agency, the War Relocation Authority (WRA), was established to give the appearance of civilian control. The WRA, a mask for military authority, contrived euphemisms. We were being "evacuated" or "relocated," not "excluded" or "detained." We were called "evacuees" or "relocatees," not "prisoners" or "internees." Our camps were called "relocation centers," not "internment camps." President Franklin Roosevelt, however, was far more candid in two of his press conferences when he called them "concentration camps."

Trying hard to be good Americans who spoke proper English, we quickly adopted the official words. Even today, many former internees continue to speak of "the evacuation" and "relocation camps." But the euphemisms did not improve camp life.

I was to learn many years later that the life of prisoners of war was better than ours, with respect to food especially, but also with respect to rights. Their treatment was controlled through international treaties to which a POW could appeal; we had no means of appeal at all. Even the great writ of habeas corpus, embedded in the first article of the Constitution of the United States, defined as "Thou shalt have the body in court so that the lawfulness of restraint may be determined," had been ignored. The Constitution allows, under extreme circumstances, for the writ to be suspended but never to be ignored.

Still, all was not lost. There were a few brave souls who challenged the general's and the government's edicts by violating them, thereby entering the courts. Minoru Yasui challenged the curfew order. Gordon Hirabayashi challenged both the curfew and exclusion orders. Fred Korematsu challenged the exclusion order. These challenges went all the way into the Supreme Court and forced the government to take extraordinary, secret measures at deception before the Court to ensure a ruling upholding the mass exclusion and detention of Japanese Americans as constitutionally tenable. (These secrets were eventually revealed. Even the government could not anticipate the Freedom of Information Act that, in 1966, enabled access to once confidential documents such as these.)

Then, in 1944, when military conscription was reinstated for Japanese Americans, 315 young men refused induction for various reasons. An organized and articulate resistance occurred in the camp at Heart Mountain, Wyoming: eighty-five young men insisted that their freedom and constitutional rights be restored to them and to their families as a necessary condition for their military service. They refused induction, were arrested, tried, and convicted for violating the draft.

These challenges were crucial in defining the history of the internment. They demonstrated the importance of a basic requirement of democracy: that resistance by individuals to constitutional violations by our government is a responsibility of citizenship and is in the best tradition of democracy itself. The protesters said that the camps, the mass exclusion, and detention of Japanese Americans tore the fabric of our democracy and that such tears needed repair.

Almost three decades later, in 1970, Edison Uno made a proposal to the Japanese American Citizens League (JACL) for the League to seek redress for these wartime violations of Japanese America's constitutional rights. The proposal slowly evolved into a movement. As is common with such civil rights movements, the leaders included those who remembered the pain of particularly abusive treatment. As a high school senior in the Minidoka, Idaho camp, Henry Miyatake had written an essay challenging the constitutionality of the camps and was denied his diploma for refusing to change the essay's topic. Aiko Yoshinaga became a mother in the Manzanar, California camp and had to resort to "after-hours acquisitions" of the canned milk needed to feed her infant daughter. Harry Ueno, a man with a wife and three children, also at Manzanar, was jailed with fifteen other "troublemakers" and shipped to and confined for about a year at a remote, high security camp, all without charges, hearing, or trial. They and their stories were at the movement's heart.

In 1979 and the early 1980s, several related though autonomous initiatives emerged. In 1979, the San Francisco-based JACL—the major lobbying voice for Japanese America—supported a congressional bill for the establishment of the Commission on Wartime Relocation and Internment of Civilians, a fact-finding body which was to determine whether a wrong had been committed in the mass evacuation and internment. At the same

Testimonies of camp losses at the Los Angeles hearing of the Commission on Wartime Relocation and Internment of Civilians, 1981. Photograph by Roy Nakano.

time, some who were impatient for results and doubtful of the commission approach, formed the National Council for Japanese American Redress (NCJAR), based in Chicago and Seattle, and supported the first redress bill, which was introduced by Representative Mike Lowry of Washington state. The bill was intended, not so much to succeed, as to register an alternative voice to that of the JACL. Once the commission was enacted into law in 1980, the NCJAR turned its attention away from Congress and towards the courts. The commission held public hearings in several cities with major populations of Japanese Americans, and produced its report in early 1983. At about this time, three legal teams working pro bono filed coram nobis petitions in U.S. district courts in Portland, Seattle, and San Francisco on behalf of Minoru Yasui, Gordon Hirabayashi, and Fred Korematsu, respectively, whose early protests had challenged the wartime actions. A coram nobis petition seeks to have an earlier court conviction—for which the sentence has already been served—reopened in court and examined on the basis of new evidence, for the purpose of vacating the conviction and expunging the record. Also, at this time, the NCJAR filed the class-action lawsuit of *William Hohri, et al., v. United States* in the district court of the District of Columbia. This lawsuit, the costs of which were paid by the NCJAR, sought compensatory damages based upon twenty-two causes of action.

Supporting the commission's inquiries, and the simultaneous court actions, was an important, productive research effort going on in the National Archives—one of history making as well as history writing—conducted by Aiko Herzig-Yoshinaga and Jack Herzig and their network of friends and associates. The coram nobis petitions and the lawsuit brought about an intensified effort of research for evidence and legal precedents. In effect, the legal actions were a battle of new research versus the legions of attorneys in the U.S. Department of Justice.

The combined efforts of the commission's inquiries, the lawsuits, and the fact-finding research had results. The commission's national public hearings served to educate America about the camps and to galvanize Japanese American support for redress. The commission also produced a fresh, vastly improved official account of the wartime history in its report, *Personal Justice Denied.* Most significantly, the commission's 1983 recommendations led to the legislation for the redress enacted in 1988.

The three coram nobis cases succeeded not only in vacating the wartime convictions; they eroded the unfortunate precedents established in the wartime courts.

Once the Hohri lawsuit was filed, the government's main defenses were procedural efforts to keep the lawsuit from going to trial. While some of these were overcome at the district court level, statute of limitations and sovereign immunity required appeals and, ultimately, review by the U.S. Supreme Court. When the lawsuit died in October 1988, the results were mixed and unsatisfactory. Nevertheless, the lawsuit defined and documented the injuries of our wartime internment and provided a more appropriate measure of repair at $220,000 per individual, a significant amount which helped prod lawmakers into action during congressional debates regarding redress.

On August 10, 1988, redress was enacted into law as the Civil Liberties Act of 1988, from which checks for $20,000 and a presidential letter of apology flowed to each surviving person who suffered internment- or exclusion-related injustices. Though the payment was nominal and the apology tepid, the act of redress was well received.

As a young Japanese America, we had abandoned our homes and most of our belongings, taking only what we could carry, and were transported to the camps. It was a dark time, filled with hostile images, a time of desperation and a clouded future. Once released into "free America," we started new lives in unfamiliar communities and schools with whatever housing or jobs we could find.

As we grew and developed in mind and spirit, we remembered the camps and read the books about them that began, ever so slowly, to appear. A few of us found kindred spirits in the civil rights movement and began to wonder about our own affirmation of freedom and citizenship. We uncovered the hidden history of our wartime trauma, the why and how of the camps. We learned there was something we could do about it. So, taking our time, we raised the banner—and the money—and went to Congress and into the courts to revisit and repair our injuries. We realized we could carry much more. And we did.

William Hohri
April 2000

Appendix A:

Historical Documents

Request for a Declaration of War

Yesterday, December 7, 1941—a date which will live in infamy—the United States of America was suddenly and deliberately attacked by naval and air forces of the Empire of Japan.

The United States was at peace with that nation, and, at the solicitation of Japan, was still in conversation with its government and its emperor looking toward the maintenance of peace in the Pacific. Indeed, one hour after Japanese air squadrons had commenced bombing in Oahu, the Japanese ambassador to the United States and his colleague delivered to the secretary of state a formal reply to a recent American message. While this reply stated that it seemed useless to continue the existing diplomatic negotiations, it contained no threat or hint of war or armed attack.

It will be recorded that the distance of Hawaii from Japan makes it obvious that the attack was deliberately planned many days or even weeks ago. During the intervening time the Japanese government has deliberately sought to deceive the United States by false statements and expressions of hope for continued peace.

The attack yesterday on the Hawaiian Islands has caused severe damage to American naval and military forces. Very many American lives have been lost. In addition, American ships have been reported torpedoed on the high seas between San Francisco and Honolulu.

Yesterday the Japanese government also launched an attack against Malaya.

Last night Japanese forces attacked Hong Kong.

Last night Japanese forces attacked Guam.

Last night Japanese forces attacked the Philippine Islands.

Last night the Japanese attacked Wake Island.

This morning the Japanese attacked Midway Island.

Japan has, therefore, undertaken a surprise offensive extending throughout the Pacific area. The facts of yesterday speak for themselves. The people of the United States have already formed their opinions and well understand the implications to the very life and safety of our nation.

As commander in chief of the Army and Navy I have directed that all measures be taken for our defense.

Always will we remember the character of the onslaught against us. No matter how long it may take us to overcome this premeditated invasion, the American people, in their righteous might, will win through to absolute victory. I believe I interpret the will of the Congress and of the people when I assert that we will not only defend ourselves to the uttermost but will make very certain that this form of treachery shall never endanger us again.

Hostilities exist. There is no blinking at the fact that our people, our territory, and our interests are in grave danger.

With confidence in our armed forces—with the unbounded determination of our people—we will gain the inevitable triumph—so help us God.

I ask that the Congress declare that since the unprovoked and dastardly attack by Japan on Sunday, December 7, a state of war has existed between the United States and the Japanese Empire.

President Franklin D. Roosevelt

Executive Order No. 9066

Authorizing the Secretary of War to Prescribe Military Areas

Whereas the successful prosecution of the war requires every possible protection against espionage and against sabotage to national-defense material, national-defense premises, and national-defense utilities as defined in section four, Act of April 20, 1918, 40 Stat. 533, as amended by the act of November 30, 1940, 54 Stat. 1220, and the Act of August 21, 1941, 55 Stat. 655 (U. S. C., Title 50, Sec. 104):

Now, therefore, by virtue of the authority vested in me as President of the United States, and Commander in Chief of the Army and Navy, I hereby authorize and direct the secretary of war, and the military commanders whom he may from time to time designate, whenever he or any designated commander deems such actions necessary or desirable, to prescribe military areas in such places and of such extent as he or the appropriate military commanders may determine, from which any or all persons may be excluded, and with such respect to which, the right of any person to enter, remain in, or leave shall be subject to whatever restrictions the secretary of war or the appropriate military commander may impose in his discretion. The secretary of war is hereby authorized to provide for residents of any such area who are excluded therefrom, such transportation, food, shelter, and other accommodations as may be necessary, in the judgement of the secretary of war or the said military commander, and until other arrangements are made, to accomplish the purpose of this order. The designation of military areas in any region or locality shall supersede designations of prohibited and restricted areas by the attorney general under the proclamations of December 7 and 8, 1941, and shall supersede the responsibility and authority of the attorney general under the said proclamations in respect of such prohibited and restricted areas.

I hereby further authorize and direct the secretary of war and the said military commanders to take such other steps as he or the appropriate military commander may deem advisable to enforce compliance with the restrictions applicable to each military area hereinabove authorized to be designated, including the use of federal troops and other federal agencies, with authority to accept assistance of state and local agencies.

I hereby further authorize and direct all executive departments, independent establishments, and other federal agencies, to assist the secretary of war or the said military commanders in carrying out this executive order, including the furnishing of medical aid, hospitalization, food, clothing, transportation, use of land, shelter, and other supplies, equipment, utilities, facilities, and services.

This order shall not be construed as modifying or limiting in any way the authority heretofore granted under Executive Order No. 8972, dated December 12, 1941, nor shall it be construed as limiting or modifying the duty and responsibility of the Federal Bureau of Investigation, with respect to the investigation of alleged acts of sabotage or the duty and responsibility of the attorney general and the Department of Justice under the proclamations of December 7 and 8, 1941, prescribing regulations for the conduct and control of alien enemies, except as such duty and responsibility is superseded by the designation of military areas hereunder.

Franklin D. Roosevelt
February 19, 1942

California Anti-Alien Land Law
(Adopted by Initiative, November 2, 1920)

The people of the State of California do enact as follows:

Section 1. All aliens eligible to citizenship under the laws of the United States may acquire, possess, enjoy, transmit, and inherit real property, or any interest therein, in this state; in the same manner and to the same extent as citizens of the United States, except as otherwise provided by the laws of this state.

Section 2. All aliens other than those mentioned in section one of this act may acquire, possess, enjoy, and transfer real property, or any interest therein, in this state, in the manner and to the extent and for the purpose prescribed by any treaty now existing between the government of the United States and the nation or country of which such alien is a citizen or subject, and not otherwise.

Section 3. Any company, association, or corporation organized under the laws of this or any other state or nation, of which a majority of the members are aliens other than those specified in section one of this act, or in which a majority of the issued capital stock is owned by such aliens, may acquire, possess, enjoy, and convey real property, or any interest therein, in this state, in the manner and to the extent and for the purposes prescribed by any treaty now existing between the government of the United States and the nation or country of which such members or stockholders are citizens or subjects, and not otherwise. Hereafter all aliens other than those specified in section one hereof may become members of or acquire shares of stock in any company, association, or corporation that is or may be authorized to acquire, possess, enjoy, or convey agricultural land, in the manner and to the extent and for the purposes prescribed by any treaty now existing between the government of the United States and the nation or country of which such alien is a citizen or subject, and not otherwise.

Section 4. Hereafter no alien mentioned in section two hereof and no company, association, or corporation mentioned in section three hereof, may be appointed guardian of that portion of the estate of a minor which consists of property which such alien or such company, association, or corporation is inhibited from acquiring, possessing, enjoying, or transferring by reason of the provisions of this act. The public administrator of the proper county, or any other competent person or corporation, may be appointed guardian of the estate of a minor citizen whose parents are ineligible to appointment under the provisions of this section.

On such notice to the guardian as the court may require, the superior court may remove the guardian of such an estate whenever it appears to the satisfaction of the court:

(a) That the guardian has failed to file the report required by the provisions of section five hereof;

(b) That the property of the ward has not been or is not being administered with due regard to the primary interest of the ward; or

(c) That facts exist which would make the guardian ineligible to appointment in the first instance; or

(d) That facts establishing any other legal ground for removal exist.

Section 5.

(a) The term "trustee" as used in this section means any person, company, association, or corporation that as guardian, trustee, attorney-in-fact, or agent, or in any other capacity has the title, custody, or control of property, or some interest therein, belonging to an alien mentioned in section two hereof, or to the minor child of such an alien, if the property is of such a character that such alien is inhibited from acquiring, possessing, enjoying, or transferring it.

(b) Annually on or before the 31st day of January every such trustee must file in the office of the secretary of state of California and in the office of the county clerk of each county in which any of the property is situated, a verified written report showing:

(1) The property, real or personal, held by him for or on behalf of such an alien or minor;

(2) A statement showing the date when each item of such property came into his possession or control;

(3) An itemized account of all expenditures, investments, rents, issues, and profits in respect to the administration and control of such property with particular reference to holdings of corporate stock and leases, cropping

contracts and other agreements in respect to land and the handling or sale of products thereof.

(c) Any person, company, association, or corporation that violates any provision of this section is guilty of a misdemeanor and shall be punished by a fine not exceeding $1,000 or by imprisonment in the county jail not exceeding one year, or by both such fine and imprisonment.

(d) The provisions of this section are cumulative and are not intended to change the jurisdiction or the rules of practice of courts of justice.

Section 6. Whenever it appears to the court in any probate proceeding that by reason of the provisions of this act any heir or devisee can not take real property in this state or membership or shares of stock in a company, association, or corporation which, but for said provisions, said heir or devisee would take as such, the court, instead of ordering a distribution of such property to such heir or devisee, shall order a sale of said property to be made in the manner provided by law for probate sales of property and the proceeds of such sale shall be distributed to such heir or devisee in lieu of such property.

Section 7. Any real property hereafter acquired in fee in violation of the provisions of this act by any alien mentioned in section two of this act, or by any company, association, or corporation mentioned in section three of this act, shall escheat to, and become and remain the property of, the State of California. The attorney general or district attorney of the proper county shall institute proceedings to have the escheat of such real property adjudged and enforced in the manner provided by section 474 of the Political Code and title eight, part three of the Code of Civil Procedure. Upon the entry of final judgment in such proceedings, the title to such real property shall pass to the State of California. The provisions of this section and of sections two and three of this act shall not apply to any real property hereafter acquired in the enforcement or in satisfaction of any lien now existing upon, or interest in such property, so long as such real property so acquired shall remain the property of the alien, company, association, or corporation acquiring the same in such manner. No alien, company, association, or corporation mentioned in section two or section three hereof shall hold for a longer period than two years the possession of any agricultural land acquired in the enforcement of or in satisfaction of a mortgage or other lien hereafter made or acquired in good faith to secure a debt.

Section 8. Any leasehold or other interest in real property less than the fee, hereafter acquired in violation of the provisions of this act by any alien mentioned in section two of this act, or by any company, association, or corporation mentioned in section three of this act, shall escheat to the State of California. The attorney general or district attorney of the proper county shall institute proceedings to have such escheat adjudged and enforced as provided in section seven of this act. In such proceedings the court shall determine and adjudge the value of such leasehold or other interest in such real property, and enter judgment for the state for the amount thereof together with costs. Thereupon the court shall order a sale of the real property covered by such leasehold, or other interest, in the manner provided by section 1271 of the Code of Civil Procedure. Out of the proceeds arising from such sale, the amount of the judgment rendered for the state shall be deposited with and distributed by the court in accordance with the interest of the parties therein. Any share of stock or the interest of any member in a company, association, or corporation hereafter acquired in violation of the provisions of section three of this act shall escheat to the State of California. Such escheat shall be adjudged and enforced in the same manner as provided in this section for the escheat of a leasehold or other interest in real property less than the fee.

Section 9. Every transfer of real property, or of an interest therein, though colorable in form, shall be void as to the state and the interest thereby conveyed or sought to be conveyed shall escheat to the state if the property interest involved is of such a character that an alien mentioned in section two hereof is inhibited from acquiring, possessing, enjoying, or transferring it, and if the conveyance is made with intent to prevent, evade, or avoid escheat as provided for herein.

A prima facie presumption that the conveyance is made with such intent shall arise upon proof of any of the following groups of facts:

(a) The taking of the property in the name of a person other than the persons mentioned in section two hereof if the consideration is paid or agreed or understood to be paid by an alien mentioned in section two hereof;

(b) The taking of the property in the name of a company, association, or corporation, if the memberships or shares of stock therein held by aliens mentioned in section two hereof, together with the memberships or shares of stock held by others but paid for or agreed or understood to be paid for by such aliens, would amount to a majority of the membership or the issued capital stock of such company, association, or corporation;

(c) The execution of a mortgage in favor of an alien mentioned in section two hereof if said mortgagee is given possession, control, or management of the property.

The enumeration in this section of certain presumptions shall not be so construed as to preclude other presumptions or inferences that reasonably may be made as to the existence of intent to prevent, evade, or avoid escheat as provided for herein.

Section 10. If two or more persons conspire to effect a transfer of real property, or of an interest therein, in violation of the provisions hereof, they are punishable by imprisonment in the county jail or state penitentiary not exceeding two years, or by a fine not exceeding $5,000, or both.

Section 11. Nothing in this act shall be construed as a limitation upon the power of the state to enact laws with respect to the acquisition, holding, or disposal by aliens of real property in this state.

Section 12. All acts and parts of acts inconsistent or in conflict with the provisions hereof are hereby repealed; provided, that

(a) This act shall not affect pending actions or proceedings, but the same may be prosecuted and defended with the same effect as if this act had not been adopted;

(b) No cause of action arising under any law of this state shall be affected by reason of the adoption of this act whether an action or proceeding has been instituted thereon at the time of the taking effect of this act or not and actions may be brought upon such causes in the same manner, under the same terms and conditions, and with the same effect as if this act had not been adopted;

(c) This act in so far as it does not add to, take from, or alter an existing law, shall be construed as a continuation thereof.

Section 13. The legislature may amend this act in furtherance of its purpose and to facilitate its operation.

Section 14. If any section, subsection, sentence, clause, or phrase of this act is for any reason held to be unconstitutional, such decision shall not affect the validity of the remaining portions of this act. The people hereby declare that they would have passed this act, and each section, subsection, sentence, clause, and phrase thereof, irrespective of the fact that any one or more other sections, subsections, sentences, clauses, or phrases be declared unconstitutional.

Japanese American Claims Act

Chapter 814, 80th Congress, 2nd Session, July 2, 1948

AN ACT

To authorize the attorney general to adjudicate certain claims resulting from evacuation of certain persons of Japanese ancestry under military orders.

Be it enacted by the Senate and House of Representatives of the United States of America in Congress assembled, that the attorney general shall have jurisdiction to determine according to law any claim by a person of Japanese ancestry against the United States arising on or after December 7, 1941, when such claim is not compensated for by insurance or otherwise, for damage to or loss of real or personal property (including without limitation as to amount damage to or loss of personal property bailed to or in the custody of the government or any agent thereof), that is a reasonable and natural consequence of the evacuation or exclusion of such person by the appropriate military commander from a military area in Arizona, California, Oregon, or Washington, or from the Territory of Alaska, or the Territory of Hawaii, under authority of Executive Order Numbered 9066, dated February 19, 1942 (3 CFR, Cum. Supp., 1092), section sixty-seven of the Act of April 30, 1900 (48 U. S. C. 532), or Executive Order Numbered 9489, dated October 18, 1944 (3 CFR, 1944 Supp., 45). As used herein "evacuation" shall include voluntary departure from a military area prior to but in anticipation of an order of exclusion therefrom.

Limitations; Claims Not To Be Considered

Section 2.

(a) The attorney general shall receive claims for a period of eighteen months from the date of enactment of this act. All claims not presented within that time shall be forever barred.

(b) The attorney general shall not consider any claim

(1) by or on behalf of any person who after December 7, 1941, was voluntarily or involuntarily deported from the United States to Japan or by and on behalf of any alien who on December 7, 1941, was not actually residing in the United States;

(2) for damage or loss arising out of action taken by any federal agency pursuant to sections 4067, 4068, 4069, and 4070 (relating to alien enemies) of the Revised Statutes, as amended (50 U. S. C. 21–24), or pursuant to the Trading with the Enemy Act, as amended (50 U. S. C. App., and Supp., 1–31, 616);

(3) for damage or loss to any property, or interest therein, vested in the United States pursuant to said Trading with the Enemy Act, as amended;

(4) for damage or loss on account of death or personal injury, personal inconvenience, physical hardship, or mental suffering; and

(5) for loss of anticipated profits or loss of anticipated earnings.

Hearings; Evidence; Records

Section 3.

(a) The attorney general shall give reasonable notice to the interested parties and an opportunity for them to be heard and to present evidence before making a final determination upon any claim.

(b) For the purpose of any hearing or investigation authorized under this act, the provisions of sections nine and ten (relating to examination of documentary evidence, attendance of witnesses, and production of books, papers, and documents) of the Federal Trade Commission Act of September 26, 1914, as amended (15 U. S. C. 49, 50), are hereby made applicable to the jurisdiction, powers, and duties of the attorney general. Subpoenas may be served personally, by registered mail, by telegraph, or by leaving a copy thereof at the residence or principal place of business of the person required to be served. A verified return by the individual so serving the same, setting forth the manner of service, shall be proof of service. The United States marshals or their deputies shall serve such process in their respective districts.

(c) A written record shall be kept of all hearings and proceedings under this act and shall be open to public inspection.

Adjudications; Payment of Awards; Effect of Adjudications

Section 4.

(a) The attorney general shall adjudicate all claims filed under this act by award or order of dismissal, as the case may be, upon written findings of fact and reasons for the decision. A copy of each such adjudication shall be mailed to the claimant or his attorney.

(b) The attorney general may make payment of any award not exceeding $2,500 in amount out of such funds as may be made available for or this purpose by Congress.

(c) On the first day of each regular session of Congress the attorney general shall transmit to Congress a full and complete statement of all adjudications rendered under this act during the previous year, stating the name and address of each claimant, the amount claimed, the amount awarded, the amount paid, and a brief synopsis of the facts in the case and the reasons for each adjudication. All awards not paid under subsection (b) hereof shall be paid in like manner as are final judgments of the Court of Claims.

d) The payment of an award shall be final and conclusive for all purposes, not withstanding any other provision of law to the contrary, and shall be a full discharge of the United States and all of its officers, agents, servants, and employees with respect to all claims arising out of the same subject matter. An order of dismissal against a claimant, unless set aside by the attorney general, shall thereafter bar any further claim against the United States or any officer, agent, servant, or employee thereof arising out of the same subject matter.

Attorneys' Fees

Section 5. The attorney general, in rendering an award in favor of any claimant, may as a part of the award determine and allow reasonable attorneys' fees, which shall not exceed 10 per centum of the amount allowed, to be paid out of, but not in addition to, the amount of such award.

Any attorney who charges, demands, receives, or collects for services rendered in connection with such claim any amount in excess of that allowed under this section, if recovery be had, shall be guilty of a misdemeanor, and shall upon conviction thereof be subject to a fine of not more than $2,000, or imprisonment for not more than one year, or both.

Administration

Section 6. For the purposes of this act the attorney general may

(a) appoint a clerk and such attorneys, examiners, interpreters, appraisers, and other employees as may be necessary;

(b) call upon any federal department or agency for any information or records necessary;

(c) secure the cooperation of state and local agencies, governmental or otherwise, and reimburse such agencies for services rendered;

(d) utilize such voluntary and uncompensated services as may from time to time be needed and available;
(e) assist needy claimants in the preparation and filing of claims;
(f) make such investigations as may be necessary;
(g) make expenditures for witness fees and mileage and for other administrative expenses;
(h) prescribe such rules and regulations, perform such acts not inconsistent with law, and delegate such authority as he may deem proper in carrying out the provisions of this act.

Appropriations

Section 7. There are hereby authorized to be appropriated for the purposes of this act such sums as Congress may from time to time determine to be necessary.

Approved July 2, 1948

Fair Play Committee Bulletin

"One for all—all for one."
"No person shall be [...] deprived of life, liberty, or property, without due process of law, nor [shall] private property be taken for public use without just compensation." [Amendment] V, Bill of Rights.

"Neither slavery nor involuntary servitude, except as [a] punishment for crime whereof the party shall have been duly convicted, shall exist within the United States or any place subject to their jurisdiction." [Amendment] XIII, Bill of Rights.

We, the Nisei have been complacent and too inarticulate to the unconstitutional acts that we were subjected to. If ever there was a time or cause for decisive action, IT IS NOW!

We, the members of the FPC are not afraid to risk our lives for our country. We would gladly sacrifice our lives to protect and uphold the principles and ideals of our country as set forth in the Constitution and the Bill of Rights, for on its inviolability depends the freedom, liberty, justice, and protection of all people, including Japanese Americans and all other minority groups. But have we been given such freedom, such liberty, such justice, such protection? No!! Without any hearings, without due process of law as guaranteed by the Constitution and Bill of Rights, without any charges filed against us, without any evidence of wrongdoing on our part, 110,000 innocent people were kicked out of their homes, literally uprooted from where they have lived for the greater part of their lives, and herded like dangerous criminals into concentration camps with barbed-wire fences and military police guarding it, AND THEN, WITHOUT RECTIFICATION OF THE INJUSTICES COMMITTED AGAINST US NOR WITHOUT RESTORATION OF OUR RIGHTS AS GUARANTEED BY THE CONSTITUTION,

WE ARE ORDERED TO JOIN THE ARMY THRU DISCRIMINATORY PROCEDURES INTO A SEGREGATED COMBAT UNIT! Is that the American way? NO! The FPC believes that unless such actions are opposed Now, and steps taken to remedy such injustices and discriminations IMMEDIATELY, the future of all minorities and the future of this democratic nation is in danger.

Thus, the members of the FPC unanimously decided at their last open meeting that until we are restored all our rights, all discriminatory features of the Selective Service abolished, and measures are taken to remedy the past injustices thru judicial pronouncement or congressional act, we feel that the present program of drafting us from this concentration camp is unjust, unconstitutional, and against all principles of civilized usage, therefore, WE MEMBERS OF THE FAIR PLAY COMMITTEE HEREBY REFUSE TO GO TO THE PHYSICAL EXAMINATION OR TO THE INDUCTION IF OR WHEN WE ARE CALLED IN ORDER TO CONTEST THE ISSUE.

We are not being disloyal. We are not evading the draft. We are all loyal Americans fighting for JUSTICE AND DEMOCRACY RIGHT HERE AT HOME. So, restore our rights as such, rectify the injustices of evacuation, of the concentration, of the detention, and of the pauperization as such. In short, treat us in accordance with the principles of the Constitution.

If what we are voicing is wrong, if what we ask is disloyal, if what we think is unpatriotic, then Abraham Lincoln, one of our greatest American presidents, was also guilty of such, for he said, "If, by the mere force of numbers, a majority should deprive a minority of any Constitutional right, it might in a moral point of view justify a revolution."

Among the one thousand–odd members of the Fair Play Committee, there are Nisei men over the draft age and Nisei girls who are not directly affected by the present Selective Service program, but who believe in the ideals and principles of our county, therefore are helping the FPC in our fight against injustice and discriminations.

We hope that all persons whose ideals and interests are with us will do all they can to help us. We may have to engage in court actions, but as such actions require large sums of money, we do need financial support and when the time comes, we hope that you will back us up to the limit. ATTENTION MEMBERS! FAIR PLAY COMMITTEE MEETING, SUNDAY, MARCH 5, 2:00 p.m. BLOCK 6-30 MESS., PARENTS, BROTHERS, SISTERS, AND FRIENDS INVITED.

An American Promise

By the President of the United States of America

A Proclamation

In this Bicentennial Year, we are commemorating the anniversary dates of many of the great events in American history. An honest reckoning, however, must include a recognition of our national mistakes as well as our national achievements. Learning from our mistakes is not pleasant, but as a great philosopher once admonished, we must do so if we want to avoid repeating them.

February 19th is the anniversary of a sad day in American history. It was on that date in 1942, in the midst of the response to the hostilities that began on December 7, 1941, that Executive Order No. 9066 was issued, subsequently enforced by the criminal penalties of a statute enacted March 21, 1942, resulting in the uprooting of loyal Americans. Over 100,000 persons of Japanese ancestry were removed from their homes, detained in special camps, and eventually relocated.

The tremendous effort by the War Relocation Authority and concerned Americans for the welfare of these Japanese Americans may add perspective to that story, but it does not erase the setback to fundamental American principles. Fortunately, the Japanese American community in Hawaii was spared the indignities suffered by those on our mainland.

We now know what we should have known then—not only was that evacuation wrong, but Japanese Americans were and are loyal Americans. On the battlefield and at home, Japanese Americans—names like Hamada, Mitsumori, Marimoto, Noguchi, Yamasaki, Kido, Munemori and Miyamura—have been and continue to be written in our history for the sacrifices and the contributions they have made to the well-being and security of this, our common Nation.

The Executive Order that was issued on February 19, 1942, was for the sole purpose of prosecuting the war with the Axis Powers, and ceased to be effective with the end of those hostilities. Because there was no formal statement of its termination, however, there is concern among many Japanese Americans that there may yet be some life in that obsolete document. I think it appropriate, in this our Bicentennial Year, to remove all doubt on that matter, and to make clear our commitment in the future.

NOW, THEREFORE, I, GERALD R. FORD, President of the United States of America, do hereby proclaim that all the authority conferred by Executive Order No. 9066 terminated upon the issuance of Proclamation No. 2714, which formally proclaimed the cessation of the hostilities of World War II on December 31, 1946.

I call upon the American people to affirm with me this American Promise—that we have learned from the tragedy of that long-ago experience forever to treasure liberty and justice for each individual American, and resolve that this kind of action shall never again be repeated.

IN WITNESS WHEREOF, I have hereunto set my hand this 19th day of February in the year of our Lord 1976, and of the Independence of the United States of America the 200th.

[signed]
Gerald R. Ford

THE WHITE HOUSE
WASHINGTON

A monetary sum and words alone cannot restore lost years or erase painful memories; neither can they fully convey our Nation's resolve to rectify injustice and to uphold the rights of individuals. We can never fully right the wrongs of the past. But we can take a clear stand for justice and recognize that serious injustices were done to Japanese Americans during World War II.

In enacting a law calling for restitution and offering a sincere apology, your fellow Americans have, in a very real sense, renewed their traditional commitment to the ideals of freedom, equality, and justice. You and your family have our best wishes for the future.

Sincerely,

GEORGE BUSH
PRESIDENT OF THE UNITED STATES

OCTOBER 1990

Appendix B:

Chronology

1941

December 7 Pearl Harbor is attacked by the Japanese. Presidential Proclamation No. 2525 gives blanket authority to attorney general for a sweep of suspects.

December 8 Treasury Department seizes all banks and businesses owned by people of Japanese descent.

December 9 Many Japanese-language schools are closed.

December 11 FBI warns against possession of cameras or guns by suspected "enemy" aliens.

December 27 Attorney general orders all suspected "enemy" aliens in West to surrender shortwave radios and cameras.

December 30 California revokes liquor licenses held by noncitizen Japanese.

1942

January 1 Attorney general freezes travel by all suspected "enemy" aliens; orders surrender of weapons.

January 14 President Roosevelt orders re-registration of suspected "enemy" aliens in West.

January 27 Los Angeles city and county discharges all people of Japanese descent on civil service lists.

January 29 U.S. Attorney General Francis Biddle issues the first of a series of orders establishing limited strategic areas along the Pacific Coast and requiring the removal of all suspected "enemy" aliens from these areas.

January 31 Attorney general establishes fifty-nine additional prohibited zones in California, to be cleared by February 15.

February 4 Attorney general establishes curfew zones in California, to become effective February 4.

February 14 Lt. Gen. J. DeWitt, Commanding General of the Western Defense Command, sends a memorandum to Secretary of War Henry L. Stimson recommending the removal of "Japanese and other subversive persons" from the West Coast area.

February 19 President Roosevelt signs Executive Order No. 9066, authorizing the Secretary of War, or any military commander designated by the secretary to establish "military areas" from which "any or all persons may be excluded."

February 20 Secretary of War Stimson designates Lt. Gen. DeWitt as military commander empowered to carry out an evacuation within his command under the terms of the Executive Order No. 9066.

March 2 Lt. Gen. DeWitt issues Proclamation No. I, designating the western half of the three Pacific Coast states and the southern third of Arizona as military areas and stipulating that all persons of Japanese descent will eventually be removed.

March 7 Army acquires Owens Valley site in California for Manzanar temporary detention center.

March 11 Lt. Gen. DeWitt establishes the Wartime Civil Control Administration (WCCA), with Col. Karl R. Bendetsen as director to carry out the internment plan.

March 16 WCCA establishes military areas in Idaho, Montana, Utah and Nevada, and designates 934 prohibited zones to be cleared.

March 18 President Roosevelt signs Executive Order No. 9102, creating the War Relocation Authority (WRA) to assist persons evacuated by the military under Executive Order No. 9066. Milton S. Eisenhower is named director.

March 20 WCCA acquires Santa Anita in California as a temporary detention center.

March 21 President Roosevelt signs Public Law 503 (77th Congress), making it a federal offense to violate any order issued by a designated military commander acting under authority of Executive Order No. 9066.

March 22 First large contingent of Japanese and Japanese Americans is moved from Los Angeles to the Manzanar temporary detention center.

March 23 Lt. Gen. DeWitt issues Civilian Exclusion Order No. 1, ordering the evacuation of all people of Japanese descent from Bainbridge Island in Puget Sound and their removal by March 30 to the temporary detention center in Puyallup, near Seattle.

March 24 Curfew for all aliens and people of Japanese descent is proclaimed for Military Area 1 and other strategic areas in West, effective March 27. WCCA acquires sites for temporary detention centers in California at Merced, Tulare, Marysville, and Fresno.

March 27 Lt. Gen. DeWitt issues Proclamation No. 4, effective March 29, forbidding further voluntary migration of Japanese and Japanese Americans from the West Coast military areas.

April 3 First compulsory incarceration of Los Angeles internees in Santa Anita temporary detention center.

April 28 Seattle internees are sent to temporary detention center at Puyallup, called "Camp Harmony."

April 28 One hundred and thirty-two Alaskan internees are sent to Puyallup temporary detention center; later they are transfered to Minidoka internment camp.

May 8 The first contingent of internees arrives at Poston, the Colorado River internment camp near Parker, Arizona.

May 19 Western Defense Command issues Civilian Restriction Order No. 1, establishing all temporary detention centers in the eight far western states as military areas and forbidding residents to leave these areas without the expressed approval of the command.

May 27 The first contingent of internees arrives at the Tule Lake internment camp in Northern California. This group includes internees from Puyallup and Portland temporary detention centers.

June 1 The Manzanar temporary detention center is transferred from WCCA to WRA jurisdiction and is converted to Manzanar internment camp.

June 1–4 Internees arrive directly from rural Oregon and Washington to Tule Lake internment camp.

June 2 Lt. Gen. DeWitt issues Public Proclamation No. 6, forbidding further voluntary migration of people of Japanese descent from the eastern half of California and simultaneously announces that all such people will eventually be removed directly to internment camps.

June 17 President Roosevelt appoints Dillon S. Myer to succeed Milton S. Eisenhower as Director of WRA.

July 13 Mitsuye Endo petitions for a writ of habeas corpus, stating that she was a loyal and law-abiding U. S. citizen, that no charge had been made against her, that she was being unlawfully detained, and she was confined in an internment camp under armed guard and held there against her will.

July 20 Gila River internment camp near Phoenix, Arizona, receives its first internees from Turlock temporary detention center.

August 7 Western Defense Commander announces completion of removal of more than 110,000 Japanese Americans from their homes.

August 10 Minidoka internment camp near Twin Falls, Idaho, receives its first contingent of internees from the Puyallup temporary detention center.

August 12 Heart Mountain internment camp near Cody, Wyoming, receives its first group of internees from the Pomona temporary detention center.

August 15 Farm laborers strike at Tule Lake internment camp.

August 27 The Granada internment camp near Lamar, Colorado, is opened with the arrival of a group from Merced temporary detention center.

September 11 The Topaz internment camp near Delta, Utah, receives its first group from Tanforan temporary detention center.

September 18 The Rohwer internment camp near McGehee, Arkansas, receives its first group of internees from the Stockton and Santa Anita temporary detention centers.

October 6 The Jerome internment camp near Dermott, Arkansas—the last of the ten internment camps to open—receives a group of internees from the Fresno temporary detention center.

November 3 The transfer of internees from temporary detention centers is completed with the arrival of the last group at Jerome internment camp from Fresno temporary detention center.

1943

January 4 WRA field offices are established in Chicago, Salt Lake City, Cleveland, Minneapolis, Des Moines, New York City, Denver, Kansas City, and Boston.

January 23 Secretary of War Stimson announces plans to form an all-Japanese American combat team to be made up of volunteers from both the mainland and Hawaii.

February 8 Registration, via the Loyalty Questionnaire, of all persons over 17 years of age for Army recruitment, segregation, or relocation begins at most internment camps.

April 23 Eleanor Roosevelt spends a day at the Gila River internment camp.

June 21 *Hirabayashi v. United States* and *Yasui v. United States*: the Supreme Court rules that a curfew may be imposed against one group of Americans citizens based solely on ancestry and that Congress, in enacting Public law 77-503, authorized the implementation of Executive Order No. 9066 and provided criminal penalties for violation of orders of the Military Commander.

1944

February 16 President Roosevelt signs Executive Order No. 9423, transferring WRA to the Department of the Interior.

May The all-Japanese American 442nd Regimental Combat Team is sent to the Italian front, joining the 100th Infantry Battalion in June.

June 6 D Day: Allied forces begin the invasion of France.

June 30 Jerome internment camp is closed. Remaining personnel are transferred to Granada, Poston, and Rohwer internment camps.

December 17 The War Department announces the revocation (effective on January 2, 1945) of the West Coast mass exclusion orders which had been in effect against people of Japanese descent since the spring of 1942.

December 18 The WRA announces that all internment camps will be closed before the end of 1945 and that the entire WRA program will be liquidated on June 30, 1946.

December 18 *Korematsu v. United States:* the Supreme Court rules that one group of citizens may be singled out and expelled from their homes and imprisoned for several years without trial, based solely on their ancestry.

December 18 In ex parte Endo, the Supreme Court rules that WRA has no authority to detain a "concededly loyal" American citizen.

1945

April 29 442nd all-Japanese American regiment frees prisoners at Dachau Concentration Camp.

May 8 V-E Day: Germany surrenders.

August 15 V-J Day: Following the U.S. bombing of Hiroshima and Nagasaki, Japan surrenders, ending World War II.

September Western Defense Command issues Public Proclamation No. 24, revoking all individual exclusion orders and all further military restrictions against persons of Japanese descent.

Oct 15–Dec 15 All WRA internment camps are closed, except Tule Lake.

1946

March 20 Tule Lake internment camp is closed.

June 30 War Relocation Authority program officially terminates.

October 30 Crystal City internment camp, operated by the Justice Department, releases last Japanese American internees, ending the Japanese American Internment Program.

1948

July 2 Japanese American Claims Act is passed, giving internees until January 3, 1950, to file claims against the government for damages to or loss of real or personal property as a consequence of the evacuation. Total of $31 million is paid by the government for property lost by internees, equaling less than 10¢ per dollar lost.

1976

February 19 President Gerald Ford formally rescinds Executive Order No. 9066.

1983

June 23 *Personal Justice Denied,* the report of the Commission on Wartime Relocation and Internment of Civilians (CWRIC), concludes that exclusion, expulsion, and incarceration were not justified by military necessity, and that the decisions to do so were based on race prejudice, war hysteria, and a failure of political leadership.

October 4 In response to a petition for a writ of error coram nobis by Fred Korematsu, the Federal District Court of San Francisco reverses his 1942 conviction and rules that the internment was not justified.

1989

November 2 President George Bush signs Public Law 101-162, guaranteeing funds for reparation payments to the WW II internment survivors beginning in October 1990. For the Japanese American community, it marks a victorious end to a long struggle for justice. For the nation, the President's signature reaffirms the country's commitment to equal justice under the law.

Adapted from the Civil Liberties Public Education Fund website.

Appendix C:

Assembly Centers and Internment Camps

▲ Assembly Centers
● War Department Internment Camps (Relocation Centers)
■ Justice Department Internment Camps

Assembly Centers

Fresno, California (May 6–October 30, 1942; 178 days.) 5,100 evacuees from central San Joaquin Valley (CA).

Manzanar, California (As Assembly Center March 21–May 31, 1942; 72 days.) 9,600 evacuees from Bainbridge Island (WA); Los Angeles county; Sacramento and Amador areas (CA).

Marysville, California (May 8–June 29, 1942; 72 days.) 2,400 evacuees from Colusa, Yuba, Placerville, and Sacramento areas (CA).

Merced, California (May 6–Sept. 15, 1942; 133 days.) 4,500 evacuees from north San Francisco Bay Area and north San Joaquin Valley (CA).

Mayer, Arizona (May 7–June 2, 1942; 27 days.) 250 evacuees from Arizona.

Pinedale, California (May 7–July 23, 1942; 78 days.) 4,800 evacuees from Pierce, King, and Kitsap counties (WA); Hood River county (OR); San Francisco, Fresno, and Sacramento (CA).

Pomona, California (May 7–August 24, 1942; 110 days.) 5,400 evacuees from Los Angeles, San Francisco, and Santa Clara counties (CA).

Portland, Oregon (May 2–Sept. 10, 1942; 132 days.) 3,700 evacuees from Multnomah and western Oregon counties and central Washington counties.

Puyallup, Washington (April 28–Sept. 12, 1942; 137 days.) 7,400 evacuees from Seattle, Tacoma, and Alaska areas.

Salinas, California (April 27–July 4, 1942; 69 days.) 3,600 evacuees from Monterey, Santa Cruz, and San Benito counties (CA).

Santa Anita, California (March 27–October 27, 1942; 215 days.) 18,000 evacuees from Los Angeles, San Diego, and Santa Clara counties (CA).

Stockton, California (May 10–Oct. 17, 1942; 161 days.) 4,300 evacuees from San Joaquin county (CA).

Tanforan, California (April 28–Oct. 13, 1942; 169 days.) 7,800 evacuees from San Francisco Bay Area (CA).

Tulare, California (April 20–Sept. 4, 1942; 138 days.) 5, 000 evacuees from Ventura, Santa Barbara, San Luis Obispo, Los Angeles, Sacramento counties (CA).

Turlock, California (April 30–August 12, 1942; 105 days.) 3,600 evacuees from Solano, Alameda, Los Angeles, and Sacramento counties (CA).

Walerga / Sacramento, California (May 6–June 26, 1942; 52 days.) 4,700 evacuees from San Joaquin and Sacramento counties (CA).

Internment Camps (Relocation Centers)

Central Utah (Topaz), Utah

Abraham, Millard County; 140 miles southwest of Salt Lake City
First internees: 215 from Tanforan and Santa Anita Assembly Centers (CA)
Maximum population at one time: 8,130; total: 11,212
Internees from: California

Operation: from September 11, 1942 to October 31, 1945

Colorado River (Poston), Arizona

Colorado River Indian Reservation, Yuma County; 12 miles south of Parker
First internees: 250 from Mayer Assembly Center (AZ)
Maximum population at one time: 17,814, September 1942; total: 19,534
Internees from: Assembly Centers in Salinas, Santa Anita, and Pinedale (CA); Mayer, (AZ)
Operation: from May 8, 1942 to November 28, 1945

Gila River (Rivers), Arizona

Gila River Indian Reservation, Sacaton, Pinal County; 50 miles south of Phoenix
First internees: 520 from Turlock Assembly Center (CA)
Maximum population at one time: 13,348, November 1942; total: 16,655
Internees from: Fresno, Santa Anita, Stockton, Tulare, and Turlock (CA).
Operation: from July 20, 1942 to November 10, 1945

Granada (Amache), Colorado

Granada, Prowers County; 140 miles east of Pueblo
First internees: 212 from Merced Assembly Center (CA)
Maximum population at one time: 7,318, October 1942; total: 10,295
Internees from: Merced and Santa Anita Assembly Centers (CA)
Operation: from August 27, 1942 to October 15, 1945

Heart Mountain, Wyoming

Vocation, Park County; 13 miles northeast of Cody
First internees: 290 from Pomona Assembly Center (CA)
Maximum population at one time: 10,767; total: 14,025
Internees from: California, Oregon, and Washington
Operation: from August 12, 1942 to November 10, 1945

Jerome (Denson), Arkansas

Jerome, Chicot and Drew Counties; 30 miles southwest of Arkansas City
First internees: 202 from Fresno Assembly Center (CA)
Maximum population at one time: 8,497, November 1942; total: 10,241
Internees from: California
Operation: from October 6, 1942 to June 30, 1944. (Last camp to open, first to close.)

Manzanar, California

Manzanar, Inyo County; 5 miles south of Independence
First internees: (as Assembly Center) from Bainbridge Island (WA)
Maximum population at one time: 10,046, September 1942; total: 11,062
Internees from: California and Washington
Operation: from March 22, 1942 (as Assembly Center) to November 21, 1945

Minidoka (Hunt), Idaho

Gooding, Jerome County; 25 miles northeast of Twin Falls
First internees: 210 from Puyallup Assembly Center (WA)
Maximum population at one time: 7,318; total: 10,295

Internees from: Oregon and Washington.

Operation: from August 10, 1942 to October 28, 1945

Rohwer, Arkansas

Rohwer, Desha County; ½ mile north of Rohwer

First internees: 250 from Santa Anita and Stockton Assembly Centers (CA)

Maximum population at one time: 8,475, November 1942; total: 11,928

Internees from: California

Operation: from September 18, 1942 to November 30, 1945

Tule Lake (Newell), California

Newell, Modoc County; 35 miles southeast of Klamath Falls, Oregon

First internees: 447 from Portland (OR) and Puyallup (WA) Assembly Centers

Maximum population at one time: 18,789, September 1942; total: 29,490

Internees from: Assembly Centers in Mayer (AZ); Manzanar, Marysville, Pinedale, Pomona, Salinas and Walerga/Sacramento, (CA); Portland (OR); Puyallup (WA)

Operation: from May 27, 1942 to March 20, 1946. (Last to close.)

Justice Department Internment Camps

Bismarck, North Dakota
Crystal City, Texas
Missoula, Montana
Santa Fe, New Mexico

Other Camps (not on map)

Assembly Inn, Montreat, North Carolina
Fort Lincoln, North Dakota
Fort Livingston, Alexandria, Louisiana
Fort Meade, Maryland
Fort Richardson, Alaska
Fort Sill, Oklahoma
Leupp, Arizona
Moab, Utah
Sand Island, Hawaii
Seagoville, Texas
Stringtown, Oklahoma
Tulahoma, Tennessee

Glossary

Japanese Terms

-kun Mr.; used after surname, with young men only
-san Mr., Mrs., Miss; used after surname
abunai dangerous
aikokuki airplane
arigato thank you
arigato gozaimasu thank you very much
bara-bara boom boom
benshi a person who reads dialogue aloud during silent movies, as in a play
butoku-kai martial arts association
cha tea
chambara slang for samurai film; literally: "clang boom," from the sound effects during the fight scenes
chigire gumo stray clouds
dogo sukui a comic dance about a man fishing for loaches; literally: loach rescue
furoshiki wrapping cloth for carrying parcels
geta a wooden sandal with elevated platforms
go a popular Japanese board game of military strategy
hakujin white person, Caucasian
haole white person, Caucasian (Hawaiian)
hara-kiri suicide by disembowelment
inu informer, spy; literally: dog
Issei first generation of Japanese who immigrated to the United States
itsuka someday, one of these days
judo a Japanese martial art
kaiko haiku a free-style form of Japanese poetry that originated in 1915
kami god, gods
kamikaze a suicide action by certain Japanese World War II pilots in which they would fly their planes, which were often laden with explosives, into Allied targets; literally: divine wind
kendo a Japanese martial art similar to fencing; literally: way of the sword
kesshitai suicide troops; literally: never give up
keto derogatory term for white person, Caucasian; literally: hairy breed
Kibei Japanese Americans born in the United States and educated in Japan
kita makura pillows laid out to face north
konnyaku a starchy, edible root vegetable
Kora dorobo! Hey! You crook!
kotonk mainland Japanese American; literally: the empty sound of one's head when a coconut falls on it

kubimaki a heavy neck cloth, scarf
Meiji the period of reign of Emperor Mutsuhito of Japan, 1868–1912
mochi pounded rice cake
nagare no tabi a metaphor for having no control over one's destiny; literally: a stream's journey
nigiri meshi a meal consisting of rice balls
Nikkei person of Japanese ancestry; a Japanese American
ninja secret agent; a spy who practices the ancient Japanese art of subterfuge
Nippon Japan
Nisei second generation Japanese Americans, born in the United States
o-bento portable box lunch
okasan mother
o-koto Japanese thirteen-string instrument
Rafu Shimpo Los Angeles Japanese daily newspaper
Renshu Kantai a training ship cruise
Rocky Shimpo Rocky Mountain [Rocky] Japanese daily newspaper
samurai warrior aristocracy of Bushido Japan
Sansei third generation Japanese Americans
shikata ga nai a common phrase meaning "it cannot be helped"
sumi ink
Takasagos Taiwan aborigines
Tatsuta-maru the name of a ship
Tenno heika banzai! Long live the Emperor!
Tokado Line the name of a railway line in Japan
tonedo pimples, acne
Wah shoi! Heave ho!
Yonsei fourth generation Japanese Americans

World War II Military Terms and Slang

5th Army unit of the U.S. Army that took part in the Italian campaign in WWII
ack-ack antiaircraft guns or their fire; originally a term used by British signalers
BAR Browning automatic rifle
Betty bomber the Allied code name for the Mitsubishi G4M-type seven-place twin-engine long-range bomber developed for the Japanese Naval Air Force and first flown in 1939
blister a bulge built into a warship to protect the vessel against torpedoes and mines
botas water bags
C rations standard U.S. military field rations that include canned goods and some luxury items such as chocolate and cigarettes
CG Commanding General
CO Commanding Officer

court-martial military courts of law convened to try military personnel

ex parte a legal action taken, conducted, or applied for to benefit one party only; literally: on one side only

fifth column a literal translation from the Spanish, "quinta columna," first used by General Emilio Mola in October 1936 during the Spanish Civil War. Referring to the four columns of troops advancing against Madrid, the "fifth column" was said to be secret supporters of the enemy, engaged in espionage and sabotage. The term came to mean any secret sympathizer with the enemy

flyboy an aviator

G-2 the intelligence division of the U.S. War Department General Staff

Gasthaus German for "guest house"

Gestapo German secret police

Jerry slang for a German. Adopted by the Americans from the British slang for chamberpot, which the German helmets resembled

K rations emergency U.S. military field rations that were lightweight and could be easily carried

LG a U.S. Navy guided-missile cruiser

lista negra Spanish for "black list"

LST landing ship tank

PT a U.S. Navy motor torpedo boat

RTC Regimental Combat Team

S.Sgt Staff Sergeant

snafu slang used by U.S. military personnel in World War II; an acronym from the phrase "situation normal all fucked up"

Soldaten German for "soldiers"

T.Sgt. Technical Sergeant

T/4 Technician Fourth Grade

T/5 Technician Fifth Grade

Tommy gun a Thompson submachine gun

writ of coram nobis a legal action with the purpose of correcting an error in a previous judgement. Its function is to bring before the same court—rather than a different or higher court—that rendered the judgment, matters of fact, which, if they had been known at the time, would have resulted in a different judgment. Literally: "our court."

writ of habeas corpus a right granted by the U.S. Constitution that guarantees to persons being imprisoned that they can be brought before a judge who will determine if the detention is lawful. This right can be suspended during times of war. Literally: Latin for "you have the body."

Zero fighters the Mitsubishi Zero-sen fighter, a single-engine, single-seat fighter-interceptor and fighter-bomber developed for the Japanese Naval Air Force and first flown in 1939. Also called *Zeke.*

Permissions

Text Permissions

Angelou, Maya. *I Know Why the Caged Bird Sings.* © 1969 by Maya Angelou. Reprinted by permission of Random House, Inc.

Anonymous. *A Nisei Requests Repatriation.* WRA files, UCLA Special Collections and Asian American Reading Room.

Anonymous. "Beyond the Fence." In *Denson Magnet,* 1944.

Anonymous. A *WRA Center Lexicon of Japanese American Terms.* WRA files, UCLA Special Collections and Asian American Reading Room.

Breed, Eleanor. "War Comes to the Church Door: Diary of a Church Secretary in Berkeley, California, April 20 to May1, 1942." In *Files Relating to the Evacuation of Japanese and Japanese Americans: Berkeley, Calif., 1942–1975* (BANC MSS 83/36 c).

de Cristoforo, Violet K. From *Poetic Reflections of the Tule Lake Internment Camp, 1944.* © 1987 by Violet Matsuda de Cristoforo.

Dellums, Ronald. Excerpt from the *Congressional Record*-House. Thursday, September 17, 1987. 100th Congress, 1st Session, 133 *Congressional Record* H 7555.

Emi, Frank Seishi. "Resistance at the Heart Mountain Concentration Camp and the Fair Play Committee." In *Frontiers of Asian American Studies.* Pullman: Washington State University Press, 1989.

Ganor, Solly. *Light One Candle: A Survivor's Tale from Lithuania to Jerusalem.* Reprinted with permission from "Light One Candle" by Solly Ganor, published by Kodansha America Inc. © 1998.

Hara, Min. "A True M.I.S. Action from a Sergeant's Diary." In *John Aiso and the M.I.S.: Japanese-American Soldiers in the Military Intelligence Service, World War II.* Edited by Tad Ichinokuchi. Los Angeles: M.I.S. Club of Southern California, 1988.

Hatashita, Isohei. "Isohei Hatashita letters." Gift of George Matsutsuyu and Emiko Hatashita Matsutsuyu. Japanese American National Museum (94.98.8).

Hayami, Stanley. "Diary." Gift from the Estate of Frank Naoichi and Asano Hayami, parents of Stanley Kunio Hayami. Japanese American National Museum (95.226.1).

Higashide, Seiichi. *Adios to Tears.* Seattle: University of Washington Press, 2000. Reprinted by permission of the University of Washington Press.

Houston, Jeanne Wakatsuki and James D. Houston. "A Common Master Plan." In *Farewell to Manzanar.* © 1973 by James D. Houston. Reprinted by permission of Houghton Mifflin Co. All rights reserved.

Iijima, Ben. "The Day We Left," from the diary of Ben Iijima. In The Japanese-American Evacuation and Resettlement Records, 1930–1974. (BANC MSS 67/14 c, Section 3, b 12.10). Reprinted by permission of Tomi Iijima.

Inouye, Daniel K. with Lawrence Elliot. Reprinted with permission of Simon & Schuster from *Journey to Washington.* ©1967 by Prentice-Hall, Inc.; renewed 1995 by Senator Daniel K. Inouye.

Izumigawa, Stanley. "One Replacement's Story." In *Collections of Memoirs, Company L 442,* Vol. 3. Edited by Genro Kashiwa. Honolulu: 1997.

Kashiwagi, Hiroshi. *The Betrayed.* © 1993 by Hiroshi Kashiwagi.

Kazato, Toyo. *Chigire gumo.* Tokyo: Nihon Bun Geisha, 1965. English version, *Stray Clouds,* translated by Ernie Kazato and Helen Hasegawa.

Kiyota, Minoru. *Beyond Loyalty: The Story of a Kibei.* Honolulu: University of Hawaii Press, 1997.

Miyamoto, Kazuo. *Hawaii: End of the Rainbow.* Tokyo and Boston: Charles E. Tuttle Co., Inc., 1972.

Mori, Toshio. "One Happy Family." In *Trek,* June 1943. Reprinted by permission of Steven Mori.

Musick, Clay H. "Seaman First Class Clay H. Musick, USS *Arizona.*" In *Remembering Pearl Harbor: Eyewitness Accounts by U.S. Military Men and Women.* Edited by Robert S. LaForte and Ronald E. Marcello. © 1991 by Scholarly Resources Inc. Reprinted by permission of Scholarly Resources Inc.

Okada, John. *No-No Boy.* Seattle: University of Washington Press, 1979. Reprinted by permission of the University of Washington Press.

Okubo, Miné. *Citizen 13660.* Seattle: University of Washington Press, 1994. Originally printed by Columbia University Press, 1946. © by Mine Okubo.

Ota, Lillian. "Campus Report." In *Trek,* February 1943.

Ota, Mabel. In *And Justice for All: An Oral History of the Japanese American Detention Camps.* Edited by John Tateishi. New York: Random House, 1984.

People's World. "Counterfeit Patriotism" (January 9, 1942); "On Treatment of Aliens" (February 2, 1942); "Hysteria Is Going to Help the Axis" (February 23, 1942). Editorials reprinted by permission of the San Francisco State University Labor Archives.

Pinza, Ezio. *Ezio Pinza: Autobiography.* New York: Rinehart and Company, Inc., 1958. Copyright by Doris L. Pinza, Harold H. Stern, William H. Leak, and Joseph Gimma. Reprinted by permission of Doris L. Pinza.

Rafu Shimpo. "All-out Victory" (December 10, 1941); "Give Us a Chance" (December 20, 1941); "There's Work to Do for Every Loyal Nisei" (February 15, 1942). Editorials reprinted by permission of the *Rafu Shimpo.*

Roosevelt, Eleanor. "A Challenge to American Sportsmanship." From *Collier's,* October 16, 1943.

Roosevelt, Franklin D. "Presidential Statement" February 1, 1943. US. Government archives.

The *Sacramento Bee*. "President Warns Against Persecution of Aliens" (January 5, 1942); "Army Is Given Free Hand to Curb Aliens, Citizens" (February 23, 1942).

Saito, George. "Letter, July 11, 1944." Gift of Mary S. Tominaga, Japanese American National Museum (94.49.42).

The *San Francisco Chronicle*. "Japanazis or Japaryans" (January 7, 1942); "Alien Hysteria Mostly Imaginary" (February 6, 1942); "These Decisions Were After the War (February 9, 1942); "Facts Force America to Stop Pussyfooting" (February 21, 1942); "Not Civil Liberties but Military Necessity" (March 7, 1942). Editorials reprinted by permission of The *San Francisco Chronicle.*

Schraubi, Globarius. "Yule Greetings, Friends!" *Trek,* December 1942.

Sekerak, Eleanor Gerard. "A Teacher at Topaz." In *Japanese Americans: From Relocation to Redress.* Edited by Roger Daniels, Sandra C. Taylor, and Harry H. L. Kitano. Seattle: University of Washington Press, 1991. Reprinted by permission of the University of Washington Press.

Simpson, Peter. "Recollections of Heart Mountain." In *Remembering Heart Mountain: Essays on Japanese American Internment in Wyoming.* Edited by Mike Mackey. Powell, Wyo.: Western History Publications, 1998.

Takei, George. "Chill Wind of Tule Lake." In *To The Stars: The Autobiography of George Takei.* © 1994 by George Takei. Reprinted by permission of Pocket Books, a Division of Simon & Schuster.

Uchida, Yoshiko. "Tanforan: A Horse Stall for Four." In *Desert Exile: The Uprooting of a Japanese American Family.* Seattle: University of Washington Press, 1982. Reprinted by permission of The Bancroft Library, University of California, Berkeley.

Uno, Kay. In *A Fence Away from Freedom.* Edited by Ellen Levine, © 1995 by Ellen Levine. Used by permission of G. P. Putnam's Sons, a division of Penguin Putnam, Inc.

Wong, Nellie. "Can't Tell." Originally published in *Dreams in Harrison Railroad Park* (1977), *Letters to America* (1995), *Unsettling America* (1994), and *The Open Boat: Poems from Asian America* (1993). Reprinted by permission of Nellie Wong.

Yamamoto, Hisaye. "The Legend of Miss Sasagawara." In *Seventeen Syllables and Other Stories.* © 1988 by Hisaye Yamamoto DeSoto. Reprinted by permission of Rutgers University Press.

Yoneda, Elaine Black. "Testimony to the CWRIC." Los Angeles, Calif.: 1981.

The following were sources for some of the brief excerpts:

de Cristoforo, Violet Kazue Matsuda, ed. *May Sky, There is Always Tomorrow: An Anthology of Japanese American Concentration Camp Kaiko Haiku.* Los Angeles: Sun & Moon Press, 1997. Excerpts from the following poets: Yotenchi Agari (pp. 65, 179); Tojo Fujita (p. 120); Tokuji Hirai (p. 120); Soichi Kanow (p. 179); Seioshi Kume (p. 331); Honjyoshi Kunimori (p. 120); Ryokuin Matsui (p. 111); Suiko Matsushita (p. 331); Misen Morimoto (p 331). Yajin Nakao (p. 120); Sho Nakashima (p. 178); Hyakuissei Okamoto (p. 331); Shiho Okamoto (pp. 178, 179); Konan Ouchida (p. 120); Neiji Ozawa (p. 151); Sei Sagara (p. 332); Senbinshi Takaoka (p. 120); Senbo Takeda (p. 331); Hakuro Wada (p. 332).

Florin Japanese American Citizen's League. [Oral history project]. Reprinted by permission from the Florin JACL. Excerpts from the Marion Kanemoto and Jerry Enomoto oral histories (p.58) and Reiko Nagumo papers (Name, p.).

Hashizume, Sato. Excerpt from "The Food." (p. 109). Reprinted by permission of Sato Hashizume.

Iwatsuki, Shizue. "Untitled." (p. 67). In *Touching the Stones: Tracing One Hundred Years of Japanese American History.* Portland, Oreg.: Oregon Nikkei Endowment, 1994. Reprinted by permission of Lawson Inada.

Kanazawa, Tooru. (p. 59). Reprinted by permission of Tooru Kanazawa.

Levine, Ellen, ed. *A Fence Away from Freedom.* © 1995 by Ellen Levine. Reprinted by permission of G. P. Putnam's Sons, a division of Penguin Putnam Inc. Excerpts from the following oral histories: Ernest Uno (p. 70); Yosh Kuromiya (p. 116).

Myer, Dillon. (p. 265). In *Uprooted Americans: The Japanese Americans and the War Relocation Authority During World War II.* Tucson: University of Arizona Press, 1971.

Ozaki, Muin. "Untitled." (p. 261). In *Poets Behind Barbed Wire.* Edited and translated by Jiro and Kay Nakano. Honolulu: Bamboo Ridge Press, 1983.

Sakamoto, George. (p. 286). Oral history excerpt. Reprinted with permission from the Seabrook Educational and Cultural Center, Inc.

Sanchez, Gilbert, of the Frente de los Pueblos Unidos. (p. 58). Excerpted from his testimony to the Commission on Wartime Relocation and Internment of Civilians. Los Angeles, 1981.

Suyemoto, Toyo. "Gain." (p. 389). Originally published in *Trek* magazine, December, 1942. Reprinted by permission of Toyo Suyemoto.

Takei, Sojin. "Arrest." (p. 1). In *Poets Behind Barbed Wire.* Edited and translated by Jiro and Kay Nakano. Honolulu: Bamboo Ridge Press, 1983.

Tateishi, John, ed. *And Justice for All: An Oral History of the Japanese American Detention Camps.* New York: Random House, 1984. Excerpts from the following oral histories: Fred Fujikawa (p. 63); Emi Somekawa (p. 60); Yuri Tateishi (p. 62); Tom Watanabe (p. 388–389).

T.D. (p. 276). In *Denson Magnet,* 1944

Tsukamoto, Mary. (p. 6). In *We the People: A Story of Internment in America.* San Jose, Calif.: Laguna Publishers, 1987.

Yamauchi, Wakako. "Fifty Years," (p. 388). Excerpt from "Poston, Arizona: A Personal Memory." Originally published in essay form in *The View from Within: Japanese American Art from the Internment Camps 1942–1945.* Edited by Russell Leong. Los Angeles: the Japanese American National Museu, the UCLA Wight Art Gallery, and the UCLA Asian American Studies Center, 1992.

Graphic Permissions

The editor and publisher wish to acknowledge the help and assistance of the museums and private collections from which the images in this book were borrowed.

Courtesy of Frank Abe and www.resisters.com: Page 318.

Courtesy of the Bancroft Library: Page xvii (#1967.014: GC-219); Page 6 (HA-251); Page 47 (GB-424); Page 60 (GA-35); Page 62 (GC-261); Page 64 (GC-514); Page 65 (GA-642); Page 84 (BE-277); Page 110 (CB-114); Page 112 (BE-600); Page 113 (AE-773); Page 114 (BE-167); Page 116 (AE-546); Page 115 (DA-589); Page 118 (DA-623); Page 130 (DA-633); Page 137 (AD-601); Page 222 (BE-591); Page 240 (AD-587); Page 247 (CB-14); Page 263 (AB-469); Page 276 (AD-708); Page 282 (BI-122); Page 301 (BE-162).

Courtesy of the California Historical Society: Pages 8–9, published by the Wartime Civil Control Administration; California Historical Society, North Baker Research Library Manuscript Collection (FN-32053 and FN-32054); Page 10, published by the Wartime Civil Control Administration/U.S. Department of Agriculture; California Historical Society, North Baker Research Library Manuscript Collection (FN-32035).

Courtesy of the Center for Creative Photography, University of Arizona: Page 149, © 1998 Center for Creative Photography, The University of Arizona Foundation.

Courtesy of Frank Seishi Emi: Page 314.

Courtesy of Masumi Hayashi: Page 391.

Courtesy of Fumi Inada: Page 284–285.

Courtesy of the Japanese American National Museum: Page 83, gift of George Matsutsuyu and Emiko Hatashita Matsutsuyu (94.98.8); Page 103, gift of Ibuki Hibi Lee (99.63.2); Page 134, gift of Ibuki Hibi Lee (96.601.37); Pages 138–141, gift from the Estate of Frank Naoichi and Asano Hayami, parents of Stanley Kunio Hayami (95.226.1); Page 160 (94.195.13); Page 165 (94.195.15); Page 184, gift of Hisae Uno (2000.15.3); Page 187, gift of June Hoshida Honma, Sandra Hoshida, and Carole Hoshida Kanada (97.106.1Q); Page 280, gift of the Gihachi and Tsugio Yamashita Family, courtesy of Archie

Miyatake (94.166.180; Page 305, collection of Hisae Uno, courtesy of Patricia Takanashi (25.1992.2); Page 324, gift of Madeleine Sugimoto and Naomi Tagawa (92.97.67 and 92.97.73).

Courtesy of Jack Matsuoka: Page 225.

Courtesy of June Mukai McKivor, ed.: Page 117, from *Kenjiro Nomura: An Artist's View of the Japanese American Internment.* Seattle: Wing Luke Asian Museum, 1991.

Courtesy of Archie Miyatake: Page 349, National Archives photo.

Courtesy of the National Archives: Page 17 (44-PA-1475); Page 30 (44-PA-2155).

Courtesy of the National Japanese American Historical Society: Page 63, Acme Photos photo; Page 58, San Francisco Public Library photo; Page 70, National Archives photo; Page 109, Japanese American Citizens League photo; Page 111, Library of Congress photo; Page 122, National Archive photo; Page 147, Harry Iwafuchi photo; Page 176, National Archives photo; Page 179, Japanese American Research Project photo; Page 218, from the Kanji Nishijima collection; Page 233, Library of Congress photo; Page 289, San Mateo JACL photos; Page 332, Wayne M. Collins photo; Page 335, National Archives photo; Page 345, Hawaii State Archives photo; Page 359, U.S. Army Signal Corps photo; Page 365, U.S. Army Signal Corps photo, National Archives; Page 379, 442, Collections.

Courtesy of the Chiura Obata Family: Page 40; Pages 48–49; Page 57; Page 298.

Courtesy of Mine Okubo: Pages 88–96; Page 230.

Courtesy of Gregg Omura: Page 312.

Courtesy of Princeton University Library: Page 21, United Service to China Archives, Public Policy Papers.

Courtesy of The *San Francisco Chronicle:* Page 192. Reprinted by permission.

Courtesy of the Seabrook Educational and Cultural Center: Page 286.

Courtesy of Madeline Sugimoto: Pages 256–259, from the Kings Art Center loan collection.

Courtesy of the Thomas Takeuchi family: Page 114, from *The Minidoka Interlude.* Originally published in 1944, reprinted in 1989.

Courtesy of Time-Life, Inc.: Page 52.

Courtesy of the Tule Lake Committee: Page 394.

Courtesy of Visual Communications: Page 59; Page 397.

Suggested Reading List

Assembly Center Newspapers

Arbogram, Marysville Assembly Center, Marysville, California
Camp Harmony News Letter, Puyallup Assembly Center, Puyallup, Washington
El Joaquin, Stockton Assembly Center, Stockton, California
Evacuazette, Portland Assembly Center, Portland, Oregon
Grapevine, Fresno Assembly Center, Fresno, California
Mercedian, Merced Assembly Center, Merced, California
Pacemaker, Santa Anita Assembly Center, Arcadia, California
Pinedale Logger, Pinedale Assembly Center, near Fresno, California
Pomona Center News, Pomona Assembly Center, Pomona, California
T A C, Turlock Assembly Center, Turlock, California
Tanforan Totalizer, Tanforan Assembly Center, San Bruno, California
Tulare News, Tulare Assembly Center, Tulare, California
Village Crier, Salinas Assembly Center, Salinas, California
Walerga Wasp, Walerga/Sacramento Assembly Center, Sacramento, California

Internment Camp Newspapers

Denson Tribune, Jerome Internment Camp, Denson, Arkansas; 1942–44
Gila News Courier, Gila River Internment Camp, Rivers, Arizona; 1942–45
Granada Pioneer, Granada Internment Camp, Amache, Colorado; 1942–45
Heart Mountain Sentinel; Heart Mountain Internment Camp, Heart Mountain, Wyoming; 1942–45
Manzanar Free Press, Manzanar Internment Camp, Inyo County, California; 1942–45
Minidoka Irrigator, Minidoka Internment Camp, Hunt, Idaho; 1942–1945
Poston Chronicle, Poston Internment Camp, Poston, Arizona; 1942–45
Rohwer Outpost, Rohwer Internment Camp, Rohwer, Arkansas; 1942–45
Topaz Times, Topaz Internment Camp, Topaz, Utah; 1942–45
Tulean Dispatch, Tule Lake Internment Camp, Newell, California; 1942–43

Internment Camp Studies

Axford, Roger W. *Too Long Silent: Japanese Americans Speak Out.* New York: Media Publishing and Marketing, Inc., 1986.

Bosworth, Allan R. *America's Concentration Camps.* Introduction by Roger Baldwin. New York: W. W. Norton & Company, Inc., 1967.

Chang, Thelma. *"I Can Never Forget": Men of the 100th/442nd.* Honolulu: Sigi Productions, Inc., 1991.

Chuman, Frank F. *The Bamboo People: The Law and Japanese Americans.* Del Mar, Calif.: Publisher's Inc., 1976.

Commission on Wartime Relocation and Internment of Civilians. *Personal Justice Denied: Report of the Commission on Wartime Relocation and Internment of Civilians,* 2 vols. Washington, D.C.: Government Printing Office, 1982; Seattle: University of Washington Press, 1997.

Corbett, P. Scott. *Quiet Passages: The Exchange of Civilians between the United States and Japan During the Second World War.* Kent, Ohio: Kent State University Press, 1987.

Crost, Lynn. *Honor by Fire: Japanese Americans at War in Europe and the Pacific.* Novato, Calif.: Presidio Press, 1994.

Daniels, Roger. *Concentration Camps, North America: Japanese in the United States and Canada During World War II.* Malabar, Fla.: Robert E. Krieger Publishing Co., 1981.

———, Sandra C. Taylor, and Harry H. L. Kitano. *Japanese Americans: From Relocation to Redress.* Salt Lake City: University of Utah Press, 1986; Rev. ed. Seattle: University of Washington Press, 1991.

———. *Prisoners Without Trial: Japanese Americans in World War II.* New York: Hill and Wang, 1993.

———, comp. and ed. *American Concentration Camps: A Documentary History of the Relocation and Incarceration of Japanese Americans, 1942–1945,* 9 vols. New York: Garland Publishing, 1989. vol 1: July 1940–December 31, 1941; vol. 2: January 1, 1942–February 19, 1942; vol. 3: February 20, 1942–March 31, 1942: vol. 4: April 1942; vol. 5: May 1942; vol. 6: June 1942–December 1942; vol. 7: 1943; vol. 8: 1944 and 1945, Japanese of Hawaii; vol. 9: Raising Japanese American Troops, June 1942–November 1945.

de Cristoforo, Violet Kazue Matsuda. *Poetic Reflections of the Tule Lake Internment Camp, 1944.* Santa Clara, Calif.: Privately printed, 1988.

de Cristoforo, Violet Kazue Matsuda, compiler, translator. *May Sky, There is Always Tomorrow: An Anthology of Japanese American Concentration Camp Kaiko Haiku.* Los Angeles: Sun & Moon Press, 1997.

Dower, John W. *War Without Mercy: Race and Power in the Pacific War.* New York: Pantheon Books, 1986.

Drinnon, Richard. *Keeper of Concentration Camps: Dillon S. Myer and American Racism.* Berkeley: University of California Press, 1987.

Embrey, Sue. *The Lost Years 1942–1946.* Los Angeles: Midnight Press, 1971.

Fox, Stephen R. *The Unknown Internment: An Oral History of the Relocation of Italian Americans During World War II.* Boston: Twayne Publishers, 1990.

Fujimura, Bunya. *Though I Be Crushed: The Wartime Experiences of a Buddhist Priest.* Los Angeles: Nembutsu Press, 1985.

Fukuda, Rev. Yoshiaki. *My Six Years of Internment: An Issei's Struggle for Justice.* Commentary by Stanford M. Lyman. San Francisco: Konko Church of San Francisco, 1990. Originally published in Japanese in 1957.

Ganor, Solly. *Light One Candle: A Survivor's Tale from Lithuania to Jerusalem.* New York: Kodansha America, Inc., 1998.

Gardiner, C. Harvey. *Pawns in a Triangle of Hate: The Peruvian Japanese and the United States.* Seattle: University of Washington Press, 1981.

Garfinkel, Claire. *The Evacuation Diary of Hatsuye Egami.* Pasadena: Intentional Productions, 1995.

Girdner, Audrie and Anne Loftis. *The Great Betrayal: The Evacuation of the Japanese-Americans During World War II.* Toronto: Macmillan, 1969.

Grodzins, Morton. *Americans Betrayed: Politics and the Japanese Evacuation.* Chicago: University of Chicago Press, 1949, 1974. Based on a 1945 doctoral dissertation, "Political Aspects of the Japanese Evacuation," University of California, Berkeley.

Hansen, Arthur A. and Betty E. Mitson, ed. *Voices Long Silent: An Oral Inquiry into the Japanese American Evacuation.* Fullerton: Oral History Program, California State University, Fullerton, 1974.

Harrington, Joseph D. *Yankee Samurai: The Secret Role of Nisei in America's Pacific Victory.* Detroit: Pettigrew Enterprises, Inc., 1979.

Hawaii Nikkei History Editorial Board Staff. *Japanese Eyes, American Heart: Personal Reflections of Hawaii's World War II Nisei Soldiers.* Honolulu: University of Hawaii Press, 1998.

Higashide, Seiichi. *Adios to Tears.* Seattle: University of Washington Press, 2000.

Hirano, K. *Enemy Alien.* Translated by George Hirano and Yuri Kageyama. San Francisco: Japantown Art and Media Workshop, 1984.

Hohri, William. *Repairing America.* Pullman: Washington State University Press, 1988.

Houston, Jeanne Wakatsuki and James D. Houston. *Farewell to Manzanar.* Boston: Houghton Mifflin Co., 1973.

Ichihashi, Yamato. *Morning Glory, Evening Shadow: Yamato Ichihashi and His Internment Writings, 1942–1945.* Edited with an Essay by Gordon H. Chang. Palo Alto, Calif.: Stanford University Press, 1999.

Ichinokuchi, Tad, ed. *John Aiso and the M.I.S.: Japanese-American Soldiers in the Military Intelligence Service, World War II.* Los Angeles: Military Intelligence Service Club of Southern California, 1988.

Ichioka, Yuji. ed. *Views from Within: The Japanese American Evacuation and Resettlement Study.* Los Angeles: UCLA Asian American Studies Center, 1989.

Inouye, Daniel K. with Lawrence Elliot. *Journey to Washington.* Englewood Cliffs, N.Y.: Prentice-Hall, 1967.

Irons, Peter, *Justice at War: The Story of the Japanese American Internment Cases.* New York: Oxford University Press, 1983.

Kaneshiro, Takeo, comp. *Internees: War Relocation Center Memoirs and Diaries.* New York: Vantage Press, 1976.

Kikuchi, Charles. *The Kikuchi Diary: Chronicle from an American Concentration Camp.* Edited with and Introduction by John Modell. Urbana: University of Illinois Press, 1973.

Kitagawa Daisuke. *Issei and Nisei: The Internment Years.* New York: Seabury Press, 1967.

Kiyota, Minoru. *Beyond Loyalty: The Story of a Kibei.* Translated by Linda Klepinger Keenan. Honolulu: University of Hawaii Press, 1999.

LaForte, Robert S. and Ronald E. Marcello, eds. *Remembering Pearl Harbor: Eyewitness Accounts by U.S. Military Men and Women.* Wilmington, Del.: Scholarly Resources, Inc., 1991.

Levine, Ellen, ed. *A Fence Away from Freedom.* New York: G. T. Putnam and Sons, 1995.

Mackey, Mike, ed. *Remembering Heart Mountain: Essays on Japanese American Internment in Wyoming.* Powell, Wyo.: Western History Publications, 1998.

Manzanar Committee. *Reflections in Three Self-Guided Tours of Manzanar.* Los Angeles: Manzanar Committee, 1999.

Masumoto, David Mas. *Country Voices: The Oral History of a Japanese American Family Farm Community.* Del Rey, Calif.: Inaka/Countryside Publications, 1987.

Matsuda, Kazue (see de Cristoforo, Violet Kazue Matsuda).

McWilliams, Carey. *Prejudice, Japanese Americans: Symbol of Racial Intolerance.* Boston: Little, Brown and Company, 1944.

Mirikitani, Janice, et al., eds. *Ayumi: A Japanese American Anthology.* San Francisco: Japanese American Anthology Committee, 1980.

Miyakawa, Edward. *Tule Lake.* Waldport, Oreg.: House by the Sea Publishing Co., 1979.

Miyamoto, Kazuo. *Hawaii End of the Rainbow.* Tokyo and Boston: Charles E. Tuttle, 1964, 1972.

Mori, Toshio. *Yokohama, California.* Introduction by William Saroyan. Caldwell, Idaho: Caxton, 1949; Introduction by Lawson Fusao Inada. Seattle: University of Washington Press, 1985.

Myer, Dillon S. *Uprooted Americans: The Japanese Americans and the War Relocation Authority During World War II.* Tucson: University of Arizona Press, 1971.

Nakano, Jiro and Kay Nakano, eds. and trans. *Poets Behind Barbed Wire.* Honolulu: Bamboo Ridge Press, 1983.

Nicholson, Herbert V. and Margaret Wilke. *Comfort All Who Mourn: The Life Story of Herbert and Madeline Nicholson.* Fresno, Calif.: Bookmates International, Inc., 1982.

Okada, John. *No-No Boy.* Rutland, Vt.: Charles E. Tuttle, 1957; San Francisco: Combined Asian American Resources Project, Inc., 1976; Seattle: University of Washington Press, 1979.

Okihiro, Gary Y. *Storied Lives; Japanese American Students and World War II.* Afterword by Leslie A. Ito. Seattle: University of Washington Press, 1999.

Sarasohn, Eileen Sunada. *The Issei, Portrait of a Pioneer: An Oral History.* Palo Alto, Calif.: Pacific Books, 1983.

Shibutani, Tamotsu. *The Derelicts of Company K: A Sociological Study of Demoralization.* Berkeley: University of California Press, 1978.

Shirota, Jon. H. *Pineapple White.* Los Angeles: Ohara Publications, 1972.

Sone, Monica. *Nisei Daughter.* Boston: Little, Brown and Co., 1953. Introduction by S. Frank Miyamoto. Seattle: University of Washington Press, 1979.

Spicer, Edward H., Asael T. Hansen, Katharine Luomala, and Marvin K. Opler. *Impounded People: Japanese Americans in the Relocation Centers.* Washington D.C.: U.S. Department of Interior, U.S. Government Printing Office, 1946; Tucson: University of Arizona Press, 1969.

Stegner, Wallace. *One Nation.* Boston: Houghton Mifflin, 1945.

Suzuki, Lester E. *Ministry in the Assembly and Relocation Camps of World War II.* Berkeley: Yardbird Publishing Co., Inc., 1979.

Tajiri, Vincent, ed. *Through Innocent Eyes: Writings and Art from the Japanese American Internment by Poston I Schoolchildren.* Los Angeles: Keiro Services Press and the Generation Fund, 1990. Originally compiled in 1943 as *Out of the Desert,* edited by Ray Ranchi and Paul Takeda.

Takei, George. *To the Stars: The Autobiography of George Takei.* New York: Simon & Schuster, 1994.

Tanaka, Chester. *Go for Broke: A Pictorial History of the Japanese American 100th Infantry Battalion and the 442nd Regimental Combat Team.* San Francisco: Go For Broke, Inc., 1982.

Tateishi, John, ed. *And Justice for All: An Oral History of the Japanese American Detention Camps.* New York: Random House 1984.

tenBroek, Jacobus, Edward N. Barnhart, and Floyd Matson. *Prejudice, War, and the Constitution.* Berkeley: University of California Press, 1954, 1975.

Tsukamoto, Mary and Elizabeth Pinkerton. *We the People: A Story of Internment in America.* San Jose: Laguna Publishers, 1987.

Tule Lake Committee. *Second Kinenhi: Reflections on Tule Lake.* San Francisco: Tule Lake Committee, 2000.

Uchida, Yoshiko. *Desert Exile: The Uprooting of a Japanese American Family.* Seattle: University of Washington Press, 1982.

———. *Journey to Topaz.* New York: Charles Scribner's Sons, 1971.

Weglyn, Michi. *Years of Infamy: The Untold Story of America's Concentration Camps.* New York: William Morrow & Co., 1976.

Yamamoto, Hisaye. *Seventeen Syllables and Other Stories.* Piscataway, N.J.: Rutgers University Press,1988.

Yamauchi, Wakako. *Songs My Mother Taught Me: Stories, Plays & Memoir.* New York: Feminist Press, 1994.

Yoneda, Karl. *Ganbatte: The Sixty-Year Struggle of a Kibei Worker.* Los Angeles, Calif.: Asian American Studies Center, UCLA, 1983.

Internment Art and Photography

Adams, Ansel Easton. *Born Free and Equal: Photographs of the Loyal Japanese-Americans of Manzanar Relocation Center, Inyo County, California.* New York: U.S. Camera, 1944.

——— and Toyo Miyatake. *Two Views of Manzanar: An Exhibition of Photographs.* Los Angeles: UCLA Wight Art Gallery, 1978.

Armor, John and Peter Wright. *Manzanar.* Commentary by John Hersey. New York: Times Books, 1988.

Conrat, Maisie and Richard Conrat. *Executive Order 9066: The Internment of 110,000 Japanese Americans.* Cambridge: Massachusetts Institute of Technology Press, 1972.

Eaton, Allen Hendershott. *Beauty Behind Barbed Wire: The Arts of the Japanese in Our War Relocation Camps.* New York: Harper and Row, 1952.

Gensensway, Deborah and Mindy Roseman. *Beyond Words: Images from America's Concentration Camps.* Ithaca, NY: Cornell University Press, 1987.

Hill, Kimi Kodani, ed. *Topaz Moon: Chiura Obata's Art of the Internment.* Berkeley: Heyday Books, 2000.

Inouye, Mamoru, ed. *The Heart Mountain Story: Photographs by Hansel Mieth and Otto Hagel of the World War II Internment of Japanese Americans.* Los Gatos, Calif.: Mamoru Inouye, 1997.

Ishigo, Estelle Peck. *Lone Heart Mountain.* Los Angeles: Anderson, Ritchie & Simon, 1972.

Leong, Russell, ed. *The View from Within: Japanese American Art from the Internment Camps, 1942–1945.* Los Angeles: Japanese American National Museum, UCLA Wight Art Gallery, UCLA Asian American Studies Center, 1992.

Matsuoka, Jack. *Camp II, Block 211.* San Francisco: Japan Publications Inc., 1974.

McKivor, June Mukai, ed. *Kenjiro Nomura: An Artist's View of the Japanese American Internment.* Seattle: Wing Luke Asian Museum, 1991.

Okihiro, Gary Y. *Whispered Silences: Japanese Americans and World War II.* Joan Myers, Photographer. Seattle: University of Washington Press, 1996.

Okubo, Miné. *Citizen 13660.* Seattle: University of Washington Press, 1994.

Tunnell, Michael O. and George W. Chilcoat. *The Children of Topaz: The Story of a Japanese-American Internment Camp Based on a Classroom Diary.* New York: Holiday House, 1996.

About the Editors

LAWSON FUSAO INADA is regarded by many as the poet laureate of Japanese America. His collection, *Before the War : poems as they happened* (1971) was the first volume of poetry by an Asian American to be published by a major publishing house. He is co-editor of *Aiiieeeee!* (1983) and *The Big Aiiieeeee!* (1991) and author of *Legends from Camp* (1992) and *Drawing the Line* (1997). Inada is a multiple recipient of NEA Poetry Fellowships and has read his works at the White House. He has been Professor of English at Southern Oregon State College since 1966.

PATRICIA WAKIDA is a Yonsei whose parents were interned as children in the Jerome and Gila River camps. She is a graduate of Mills College, where she concentrated on English literature and Asian Studies. Her honors work focused on the Japanese literature that emerged in the wake of the atomic bomb. Her essays, fiction, and poetry have appeared in *International Quarterly,* The *San Francisco Bay Guardian, Kyoto Journal,* and *Rafu Shimpo.* She is currently special projects coordinator at Heyday Books.

WILLIAM HOHRI is a Nisei born in San Francisco in 1927. He was interned at the Manzanar camp during his high school years and graduated from the University of Chicago after the war. Hohri was the chairperson of the National Council for Japanese American Redress (NCJAR) and was the lead named plaintiff in the NCJAR's class action suit, "William Hohri, et al. v. U.S.A." He is the author of *Repairing America : An Account of the Movement for Japanese-American Redress* (1988) and a columnist for the *Rafu Shimpo* newspaper.

---

i

Fuzzy and Johnson were friends. They were young men with careers, families, and the means to enjoy Sunday outings. So on this day, they set out to hike and fished the rugged region of the Kings River Canyon while their wives and kids—Fuzzy had a son, Johnson a daughter—stayed at a canyon campground.

It was a fine day for a picnic, but Fuzzy's wife worried about her sick mother in town. She wanted to make a call, but there was no phone around. "I know where there's a telephone—follow me!" said the little girl, and she led the group on a winding path through the forest to a clearing where, sure enough, stood a phone booth.

ii

The woman who used the phone recounts the incident with amazement: "Geraldine was just a toddler, but she was so confident! I don't know how she knew where to go, but we sure followed her! And it was so good to hear Mama's voice."

That small story was to loom large in memory, for shortly after the outing, both families were imprisoned in the county fairgrounds. My mother made the call. I was the other child, Fuzzy's son.

iii

I've served as editor of this collection, which is to say I've helped gather, select, and arrange the included materials. However, this book is the result of an extensive process and an actual project conducted and coordinated by project director, Patricia Wakida.

Patricia was responsible for the research, for making all the necessary contacts, for overseeing the production schedule, and for bringing all the materials, including the artwork and photographs, to the table for editing and formatting to happen. Without Patricia, there wouldn't be a book.

She has truly led the way, demonstrating remarkable vision, the gift of intuition, and a powerful sense of direction. She also happens to be Geraldine's daughter, Johnson's granddaughter.

iv

It certainly struck me as auspicious being introduced to Patricia on the premises of Heyday Books in Berkeley, California, for as the descendants of Fuzzy and Johnson, both gone, we were about to embark on a journey into the canyon of history. Who knew what lay ahead?

In essence, we were to be the follow-up crew to what had been implemented and experienced by thousands upon thousands of people. And despite all the subsequent research and materials produced about the internment, an air of mystery continues to shroud the experience.

v

From the outside, the camps may have appeared as neat and orderly as any prison or military installation, but on the inside there were conflicts, degrees of disorder and difficulty, and the entire range of human emotions that varied, not only from person to person, but from day to day.

The very creation of the camps created chaos and confusion, and arbitrary impositions by the government served to further that confusion. For, during the period of confinement, some internees were transported out of the camps to work on American farms and in American cities, to attend American colleges and to serve sentences in American prisons; some were sent to other camps and some even shipped to Japan. Moreover, the American military sent internee-soldiers to serve in the South Pacific, Australia, Asia, and throughout Europe. How to encapsulate all that history in a single volume?

vi

As voices arose in the canyon of history—soft voices, loud voices, young voices, old voices—and as the voices continued to resound, reverberate, resonate, the walls of the canyon began to gradually dissolve, revealing the grand landscape of the human condition, and the wide sky of wisdom and compassion. We had arrived at the heart of the matter.

vii

The river flows.

Lawson Fusao Inada
May 2000